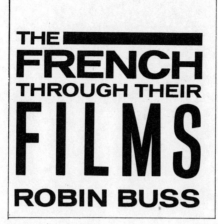

THE FRENCH THROUGH THEIR FILMS

ROBIN BUSS

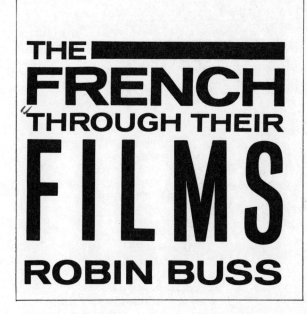

THE FRENCH THROUGH THEIR FILMS

ROBIN BUSS

UNGAR • NEW YORK

1988
Ungar Publishing Co
370 Lexington Avenue
New York
NY 10017

Printed in Great Britain by
Anchor Brendon Ltd
Tiptree, Essex

Library of Congress Cataloging-in-Publication Data

Buss, Robin.
  The French through their films.

  Includes index.
  1. Motion pictures—France—History. 2. Motion
pictures—Social aspects—France. 3. France—Social
life and customs—20th century. 4. France—
Civilization—1901–   . 5. National characteristics,
French. I. Title.
PN1993.5.F7B83 1988   791.43′75′0944   87-35701
ISBN 0-8044-2089-0

Contents

Acknowledgements

I should like to thank the many people who have helped me in various ways during the writing of this book, in particular Michael Church, for his encouragement from the start of the project; Timothy Auger, my editor at Batsford; and Madeline Saunders for her help with compiling the reference material. I should also like to thank the staff at the British Film Institute Stills Library for supplying photographs.

Acknowledgement for permission to reproduce stills is given in the captions to the illustrations. Every effort has been made to trace copyright holders and to obtain permission from them to reproduce stills from the films.

Preface

'It is not with impunity' Marcel Carné writes in his memoirs, 'that young Frenchmen are taught, from the age of four or even earlier, to applaud the spectacle of Mr Punch giving the policeman a good hiding.' And he goes on to describe the hilarity that greeted Cécile Sorel's reply when she was summoned before one of the committees of enquiry set up after the Second World War to investigate collaboration with the German occupier: 'Gentlemen, if you did not want me to receive them in my home, you should not have let them into the country!'

Dislike of authority and a ready wit that appears (but, perhaps, only appears) to make light of serious matters, are characteristics that we think of as 'typically French'; the French themselves prize them just as the British prize their own peculiar sense of humour and fair play. But Carné is wrong if he implies that disrespect for authority should be attributed directly to the influence of spectacles, entertainments and literature. After all, Punch and Judy, *Guignol*, *Hanswurst und seine Frau* are also to be found in the Italian *teatrino di burattini* as *Pulcinèlla*, in the Spanish *títeres* as *Polichinela*, and no doubt elsewhere under names more various than the type of entertainment they provide. If *Le Guignol* were peculiarly French, one might have the basis for a piece of crude sociological theory. It would still have to contend with the fact that the forces of law and order are themselves staffed by Frenchmen and, as far as I know, the *Gendarmerie Nationale*, the *Garde Républicaine* and those other elements that make up the allegedly despised representatives of authority do not face any major problems of recruitment. French people who had applauded Punch and laughed at Cécile Sorel's reply to her accusers also made up that committee of enquiry. They were French, the men and women who in those postwar purges executed many thousands of their fellow-citizens (the precise number can never be fixed). The chuckles that acknowledged Sorel's witticism had the same accent as the jeers that greeted the shaven heads of those others accused of consorting with the occupier as they were paraded through the streets of Paris or Lyons.

It is not with impunity, as Carné might have remarked, that one sets out to define the 'Frenchness' of the 50 million or so individuals who can lay claim to that quality. A book that proposes to study, on the one hand, the French and, on the other, their films, suggests an equation to one element of which it is

7

impossible to assign any precise value. There are difficulties, too, with 'their films', given the substantial contribution of foreigners to the industry and the number of co-productions; but one can argue a way out of that dilemma. The temptation is to simplify the first part of the problem, either by recourse to sociological and statistical data which may give the appearance of scientific backing to a definition of the society at a particular moment, or by starting with what General de Gaulle called 'a particular idea of France' (when he wrote, with his usual grandiloquence, in a celebrated passage in his war memoirs: '*je me suis toujours fait une certaine idée de la France*').

Statistics and other similar evidence can serve their purpose, and I shall use them from time to time, without wishing to suggest that they can describe more than some of the boundaries of what it means to be French. As for de Gaulle, even though the Constitution of the Fifth Republic which embodied some aspects of his 'particular idea of France' was accepted by 79 per cent of those who bothered to vote in September 1958, one is still left with one-fifth of this electorate who were opposed to it and, as later events were to show, a number who had apparently misunderstood precisely what he intended. Electoral approval declined, to 62 per cent in 1962 (of 77 per cent of the total electorate), to 55 per cent in 1965, to 46 per cent in 1969. It is no exaggeration to say that this decline represented in part the declining popularity of 'a particular idea of France'.

There has never, in any case, been *one* France; only, at various times, ideologies like de Gaulle's that would seek to impose unity on the diverse elements that make up the society and on the collection of individuals that is 'the French people'. Hearing Cécile Sorel's ironic reply to the commission of enquiry, a French man or woman might say that it was unlikely to come from a woman who had spent all her life in, say, Concarneau or Roscoff, while at the same time suggesting that there was an element of 'peasant slyness' in its false naivety. The women who have had to suffer the ravages of two wars between France and Germany in this century and the young peasants who have fought in them might have reason to question the 'gentlemen' in Paris who let 'them' into the country. Those living in a society and sharing its history, individual though they may be in their outlook, also necessarily share some attitudes towards the world and towards the society to which they belong.

This book is about those attitudes as they are expressed in the collection of works that make up French Cinema, each of them the product of the efforts of many individuals and designed to fulfil various needs of their producers and their audiences. I have not tried to write a history of French Cinema: there are already several of those. From time to time, especially in the first two chapters, I have found it convenient to adopt a broadly chronological approach, but I feel that such an approach can be, in many ways, misleading. We divide history into decades (the twenties, the thirties), implying fits and starts where there is, in fact, continuity. To speak of one generation and the next may make sense in a family, but not in a whole society where there is constant renewal and confrontation between the outlook and experiences of individuals born at different times. There are men and women still alive who have known the whole of cinema history, from the early silents to the latest Godard, and the society represented in films is a composite of ideas and attitudes belonging to individuals of many generations.

Film is the most powerful medium we have for investigating societies. Unlike literature or painting, which appeal to only one of our senses, a sound film conveys impressions on several levels at the same time. Moreover, because the camera is unselective, some of what it shows escapes the control of the person directing it and, because it is a mechanical means of representation, its images carry a minimum of interpretation. For this reason, a film made on location in Paris in 1908 has the value of an historical document: there is no better source for a knowledge of the physical appearance of the city and its inhabitants at that moment.

To understand how those people thought and felt, we turn to written sources. But as cinema developed as a narrative medium, and still more with the coming of sound, films were also able to bear witness to this, while retaining the ability to convey the actual appearance of things. Looking at a film, we have the nearest equivalent to real experience and a film about France may indeed tell us more about the country and its people than a visit, because it takes us inside the society in a way not available to tourists.

Still, we need to be cautious. The picture cinema gives of a society at a particular moment is necessarily incomplete. There is the hand of the censor, which has always fallen more heavily on cinema than on any other art form, precisely because cinema carries this conviction of realism, and because it is a popular entertainment. In virtually every country, at different times, censors and critics have worried about the image of their country that films might give to foreigners, and their fears are not entirely unjustified. The Italian woman who exclaimed despairingly: 'That's France!' after seeing *Quai des Brumes* at the Venice Biennale in 1938 confirmed such fears and should be a warning to us. There is more to the French than their films.

For one thing, each film exists in a particular cultural context and reflects preconceptions about art, characters, and so on. In addition, it is the product of an entertainment industry, made by people who belong to a particular social class or group whose work will reflect the outlook of that class, conditioning their answers to the questions 'what story shall we tell?' and 'how shall we tell it?' The preconceptions of film-makers and the expectations of audiences help to decide these things and to create stereotyped characters and situations. And, considering that the films themselves are part of the reality, that they help to condition the views of their audiences, nothing could be more problematical than to perceive the truth about that doubtful entity, the French, through the often deceptively clear mirror of their films.

What we can do is to study the actual image of France and French people in the French cinema and place it in some kind of social and cultural context. In trying to do so, in what follows, I have had to take into account chiefly what might be called 'quality' films. Many more 'popular' films have not survived from earlier periods (it is estimated, for example, that 70 per cent of the output of the French cinema industry between 1929 and 1939 is wholly or partially lost), and much of the 'popular' cinema is not available to an English-speaking audience, since it is never shown even in specialized film theatres. Since my purpose in looking at representations of French society in the cinema is to make film-going more enjoyable and films more 'readable', I see little point in discussing a mass of work that few people are likely to see. On the other hand, while I have stayed broadly within the canon of the 'quality' cinema and the product of France's better-known directors, I have tried to avoid aesthetic judgements on the films, leaving those to critics and historians; and I may, for example, devote some space to examining a film like *Ascenseur pour l'échafaud* [134]* which no one would count among Louis Malle's 'best' films. I hope that my reasons for analysing any particular film will be clear and I apologise for what may appear to be inexplicable omissions, eccentricities or partialities.

François Truffaut's celebrated article in *Cahiers du Cinéma* in 1954 ('Une Certaine tendance du cinéma français') was based on 'a particular idea' of French cinema: literary adaptations, giving priority to the scriptwriter and making the director merely 'the gentleman who adds the pictures'; so it is a surprise to find *The Times* writing in 1946, in a review of Maurice Cam's *Métropolitain* (made in 1938), that 'this film is *typically French* in that it tells its story in pictures. Sound, dialogue and, of course, sub-titles are there, but as embellishments . . .' – *typically French*: the emphasis is mine. The contradiction between these two 'particular ideas' of French cinema should serve as a reminder of the inconstant and changing nature of this cultural phenomenon.

Different interpretations of the character of French cinema itself are not irrelevant to the subject of this book, so its first chapter is an attempt to assess the place of film culture in France. Film has the peculiar ability to show and, simultaneously, to interpret what it shows, to represent a scene and to give an 'angle' on it. French cinemagoers, as well as foreigners, acquire some of their notions about the society in which they live through the cinema and French film-makers have learned to see it partly in films made by others, so that cinema representations of particular characters or locations take on a certain authority which influences subsequent perceptions of these same types or places. What Truffaut and the other writers in *Cahiers du cinéma* attacked in the 'quality cinema' of the postwar period was what they saw as that cinema's pursuit of certain themes because they were 'cinematic' and not because they corresponded to a continuing social reality, as if the art which a society produces were not itself part of its reality. No one doubts that the very fact of the nineteenth-century English novel's reticence about sexual relationships has something to tell us about Victorian society and Victorian attitudes, so

* Numbers in square brackets refer to the films listed in the reference section.

when French films of the 1950s depict gangsters or historical figures rather than dealing with social topics like abortion or political ones like the Algerian war, this too is not irrelevant to the understanding of attitudes at that time. And individual experience confirms that what may be 'untrue' in a sociological sense, can be 'true' in a personal one: that a film from the 1950s or 1960s, which might have seemed to its contemporaries deplorable, appearing scrupulously to avoid tackling some pressing social or political concern, is reviewed 20 years later and revealed as somehow containing the very 'essence' of its period. It is this fascinating and changing relationship of films to the society they represent and the society that produced them, that accounts for the popularity of old movies in the television age.

1 Film culture in France

Cinema was the product of science, industry and art, in that order. Auguste and Louis Lumière's invention, according to *Le Monde illustré* in 1896, could 'reproduce life and movement', transforming still portraits into a living record of loved ones: 'death will no longer be absolute', claimed a writer in *La Poste* after the demonstration on 28 December 1895 at the Grand Café in Paris – though for Louis Lumière the more prosaic aim was to sell cameras and the first films were probably designed not for exhibition as works of art, but for demonstration purposes to attract amateur purchasers of the machine. They soon became an attraction in their own right.

During the 20 years following the exhibition at the Grand Café, France dominated world production both of completed films and of film stock. Louis Lumière was the first to exploit the new medium as an industrial enterprise, sending out teams of operators to make and project films. His lead was followed by Georges Méliès and by Charles Pathé whose company, Pathé Frères, established itself as the giant of the industry up to the First World War. By 1907 it had offices in some 15 cities, including London, New York, Moscow, Berlin, Milan, Calcutta and Singapore; seven years later, the number had increased to 41 and Pathé enjoyed a virtual monopoly in many small countries. In a partially successful attempt to restrict their operations in the USA, Edison brought an action in 1904 against Pathé and Méliès, but it was the war in Europe, and the shortsightedness of the French government, that finally allowed the United States to establish its hegemony in the industry.

The hundreds of films made by the Lumières, Pathé and Méliès consisted of short documentaries, fantasies (showing the medium's ability to create visual illusions), melodramatic sketches and animated tableaux, like *L'Histoire d'un crime* (1901) which Ferdinand Zecca directed as head of production at Pathé. There was no inevitability about the application of the Lumières' invention to these genres: they were the use made of it in a particular society in which cinema was at first an extension of journalistic reportage and of the music hall. Despite early recognition of its potential as a scientific tool and as a method of 'living portraiture', cinema did not acquire the prestige of a science and, unlike still photography, was not immediately associated with painting. Instead, it took its place in the culture as a fairground attraction, on the level of the 'popular' culture of the music hall and the *fête foraine*.

The early Lumière 'documentaries' have acquired historical value as a record of contemporary events and scenes. They show children at play, washerwomen, Parisian street scenes, peasants ploughing with oxen. Cameramen travelled to bring back exotic films from Tunis, Cairo or Algiers and newsworthy events like the inauguration of President McKinley, the Universal Exhibition of 1900, the Carnival in Nice and Buffalo Bill's circus. Even these films, made by operators who simply cranked the camera in front of whatever they wished to record, are not neutral: the camera showed what the operator decided to film and its presence affected the subject. Passers-by in a New York street can be seen giggling at the contraption and a French peasant making hay is so distracted by it that he walks forward, staring fixedly towards the lens and waving his rake inches above the ground.

The invention also began to influence its operators' view of the world. One Lumière cameraman, Albert Promio, crossing the Grand Canal by boat, found himself visualizing the scene on film. A moving platform overcame the limitations of the early camera on its fixed tripod and, copying Promio's example, film-makers began to take travelling shots from boats, trains, trams, fire-engines, the New York El train and the lift in the Eiffel Tower, aware that the audience could be stirred by what happened behind the camera, as well as by what went on in front of it.

Méliès filmed the coronation of Edward VII in his Montreuil studio, before the event, using the form of service as a guide. On the day, the service in Westminster Abbey had to be shortened because the King was unwell and Edward, who was favourably impressed by Méliès's work, ragged him on the camera's startling ability to record even those parts of the ceremony that had not taken place! On the other hand, one should not be too quick to assume, because audiences would pay to see such reconstructions of events, that they believed in the actuality of what the camera portrayed. On the contrary, Méliès was a conjuror whose cinema was an extension of this form of magical entertainment and his audiences may have had a sophisticated awareness of different levels of cinema reality. Tricks with the camera were common, in Méliès's films and in comedies like *Onésime horloger* (1912), in which the central character speeds up time in order to obtain an inheritance. More important than the audience's ability to distinguish between direct representation of reality, and trickery, is the fact that cinema, as a medium of information, was marginal: an audience would expect to be amused, not to have its perceptions of society and events formed by what it saw on the screen. Consequently, these early audiences' reliance on it as a representation of different levels of reality, was almost certainly less than our own.

Promio called his travelling shots 'panoramas', recalling a popular nineteenth-century vogue for panoramic displays mentioned in Balzac's *Père Goriot*. The attraction of this kind of display derives from three sources: the appeal of the unknown (Tunis, Venice, etc., to Parisians who had never visited these places); seeing the known from a new angle (when I lived in London near the Post Office Tower during the 1960s, when the observation platform was open to the public, I used to take visitors there and invariably we turned the telescope on my kitchen window); and the products of the imagination made real (bird's-eye views, tableaux of the Battle of Waterloo 'authenticated' by historical research, etc.).

Using the novelty of the camera, cinema exploited these three types of appeal to the taste for the exotic, the everyday and the imagined. There were 'genre' scenes (Lumière's 'feeding baby'), gags, mimes, Biblical tableaux and conjuring tricks. Comedy, using the slapstick forms of music hall, dates from *L'Arroseur arrosé* (in which the gardener is sprayed with his own hose) and the Lumières went on to do sketches involving a trick played on a concierge and a fight between two women (in which the 'actresses' are visibly laughing at their own antics) as well as brief historical scenes (Joan of Arc, the Duc de Guise, a battle). Méliès's plots included several on fantasy voyages or drunken nightmares, allowing him to evoke fantastic beasts and journeys to 'impossible' places (the Moon, the pole). Zecca, at Pathé, made moral fables and melodramas. The themes of the Pathé and Méliès comedies of 1905–6 have been analysed and leading subjects were absent-minded professors, Whites turned into Blacks, mishaps to photographers, the disastrous effects of alcohol (a large category) and accidents involving unpleasant smells and lavatories.

Like the views over the European quarters of Algiers or the 'picturesque' representations of the Casbah in the early Lumière documentaries, the comic themes of these films may give clues to attitudes in the early part of the century. But their interpretation demands caution, understanding and common sense. One should remember two things, above all: that, while the cinema was able to perform technical tricks (showing a man being automatically dressed up in a woman's clothes, for example), the themes and characters it used came directly from theatre and music hall; and secondly, that cinema was marginal as a form of entertainment, its audience was limited and its makers had little sense of social responsibility. What early comedy reveals, in its stock characters, are the stereotypes of popular imagination: the drunk, the concierge, the naughty boy, the cuckold, the bill-sticker, the maid, the cook, the baker, the beggar, the Auvergnat, the lovers, the virago, the cripple; surrounded by their props, from glue-pots and rolling pins to smelly shoes and lavatory brushes. Settings were 'downstairs' rather than 'upstairs', the apartment house rather than the *château*, the barracks of the *soldat de deuxième classe*, not the officers' mess.

* * * * *

However, within a decade the pioneers had realized the potential of cinema as an accessory to the 'superior' culture enshrined in literature, theatre and the schoolroom; and the economic advantage to be gained from extending its appeal to different classes at home and in an international market where France was dominant. They began to depict religious scenes as well as

15

pornographic ones, historic events and a 'better class' of comedy. The comedies of Max Linder, André Deed ('Boireau' or 'Foolshead'), Charles Prince ('Rigadin', 'Whiffles', 'Moritz', according to whether the films were shown in France, Britain or Germany), Léonce Perret and others have begun to move into a lower-middle-class environment where, if the central comic character is not necessarily a bourgeois, his girl-friend's father probably is. 'Boireau' in particular was constantly committing social gaffes. By the early dramas of Louis Feuillade the environment of the country house is taken almost for granted as a 'neutral' setting, in *L'Oubliette* (1912), for example, or *L'Erreur tragique* (1913). *Le Coeur et l'argent* (1912) depicts the tragic consequences when an inn-keeper's daughter is persuaded to further her mother's ambitions by renouncing the man she loves and marrying an older man of superior class.

These Feuillade films starred René Navarre and Suzanne Grandais: the first was to make his name as Fantômas, while Grandais, who died in 1920 at the age of 27, had already by the time of her death established an image as a simple Parisian *midinette*, a lower-middle-class working girl around whom, in René Jeanne's words, 'hovered an atmosphere of a busy workshop . . . (and) peaceful apartment with a canary and a pot of geraniums'.

In Navarre and Grandais, French cinema had found two of its earliest non-comic 'stars'. The founding in 1908 of the Société Le Film d'Art, by André Calmettes and the Comédie Française actor Le Bargy, as well as creating the term 'art film', gave the medium a new aspiration. Partly controlled by Pathé, the company used well-known players from the theatre and its films mark the first serious attempts to depict character. Le Bargy himself appeared in *L'Assassinat du Duc de Guise* (1908), while Réjane (*Madame Sans-Gêne*) and Sarah Bernhardt (*La Reine Elisabeth*, *La Dame aux camélias*) gave prestige to later productions. The cinema was acquiring respectability, though some might say not necessarily to its advantage.

* * * * *

A respectful attitude to material and cast did not encourage experimentation with the camera or with narrative and reverence for literature and theatrical tradition were at times to weigh heavily on a medium which had to wait a long time before acquiring a status comparable with that of other arts. Many of the best actors and actresses in French cinema, if they did not belong exclusively to film, came to it from music hall, cabaret or the café-concert, rather than from the conventional stage. Max Linder, France's first international star, may have begun as an actor on the boulevards, but he was only 22 when he made his first film in 1905. Musidora, Noël-Noël, Maurice Chevalier, Jean Gabin, Arletty, Michel Simon, Fernandel, Paul Meurisse, Albert Préjean, Bourvil, Yves Montand, Simone Signoret and Jacques Tati started as singers or performers on the popular stage. Raimu's career began in the *caf'conc'* before Pagnol chose him to play Marius. Pierre Brasseur and Serge Reggiani had hardly made their stage débuts when they started work in films.

In contrast, the classical theatre has provided few stars: Madeleine Renaud, Jean-Louis Barrault, Françoise Rosay, Jules Berry, Charles Vanel, Charles Dullin, Fernand Ledoux, Marcel Levesque and, of course, Louis Jouvet whose celebrated clashes with Michel Simon (they once set out to get each other drunk during the filming of *Drôle de drame* – both succeeded and both played magnificently) seem like the collision of two worlds, Jouvet's quick wits, irony and distinction with Simon's coarse vitality: Voltaire and Rabelais, perhaps. As for Gérard Philipe, one of the few actors who, like Jouvet, could move easily between cinema and theatre, his stage and screen careers began almost simultaneously.

It was not so much that stage actors despised cinema (though, up to the Second World War, many did) as that film-makers, when they started to explore the potential of their medium, realized that it demanded a different style of acting from the stage. The great theatre director André Antoine, when he started to make films, chose to work chiefly with non-professionals, choosing an actor who had 'the right mug for the part'. Carl Theodor Dreyer used the same criterion, picking Eugène Silvain as Cauchon in *La Passion de Jeanne d'Arc* [13] not because he was a well-known actor, but because, as *doyen* of the Théâtre Français he had the 'authority' for the role; and casting as the English soldier Warwick a Russian café proprietor with the appropriate personality and physique. During the 1920s, several foreign actors, especially Russian émigrés, found work in France until their careers were cut short by the coming of sound.

But it was not only a question of that. Other directors (e.g. Bresson), like Antoine and Dreyer, have preferred to work with amateurs in accordance with a particular interpretation of cinema art and the distinction they see between its demands and those of the stage. Henri Troyat's novel *Grandeur nature* (1936), precisely because it is not written by a film-maker and because it attributes a relatively low cultural status to cinema, gives important clues to the way in which these questions might be perceived at a crucial moment in cinema history. The chief character in the novel is a middle-aged theatre actor who takes the opportunity to launch his 12-year-old son as a movie star: there are parallels with the career of a child star like Julien Duvivier's protégé, Robert Lynen. Manipulated by an unscrupulous director, the boy is an overnight success, then returns to obscurity.

Troyat makes a crucial distinction between the hard work and technique needed by stage actors, with the unforced, 'natural' technique of the screen, to show the screen actor as a fabrication of the director, cinema science and the cinema industry. Backstage, the theatre too may be sordid and the life of its employees precarious, but they find compensation in moments of contact with their audience and in work that calls for real artistry (Troyat makes his central character's father a mime artist, suggesting a decline from acting which gives total control over the material and a high level of artistic skill in a non-realist art, to the realism of the screen which demands no skills beyond those within the reach of an untrained 12-year-old). The implied conclusion is that the cinema is not concerned with art, but with hype and manipulation. Admittedly, its reputation had not been enhanced, at the time when he wrote the novel, by the collapses of Gaumont and of Pathé-Nathan, the latter a notorious fraud case which ended in Bernard Nathan's imprisonment.

On the other hand, as the industry became able to offer celebrity and money, an increasing number of actors and (especially, perhaps) actresses made their débuts in cinema and survived the fate of the matinée idol to establish solid reputations: Micheline Presle, Michèle Morgan, Danielle Darrieux, Gaston Modot, Martine Carol, Jean Marais, Daniel Gélin, Brigitte Bardot. By Bardot's time, even a fine actor most of whose work was done for the theatre (say, Georges Wilson) sacrificed much of his national and all international celebrity. As far as actors are concerned, *La Poste* could have been right in 1895 when it claimed that, thanks to cinema, death was no longer absolute.

* * * * *

Until some time around the 1950s, even in the country that pioneered cinema, dominated the industry in its early years, established the first film societies and specialist periodicals and invented the 'art film', the cultural status of cinema was not entirely resolved. Despite those early appearances by Sarah Bernhardt, silent cinema found its literary counterpart less in the 'high' art of classical theatre and 'serious' fiction, than in literature where events and action predominated: the *roman-feuilleton* (especially the serial novels of Eugène Süe whose *Mystères de Paris* were adapted in 1912 by Georges Denola) or the detective novel (Victorien Jasset's Nick Carter series of 1908–12). Thence developed of an original narrative form in Louis Feuillade's original screenplays for his series *Fantômas* [117], *Les Vampires* and *Judex*, in 1913–17.

By the 1920s, intellectuals like Louis Aragon were expressing admiration for the populist appeal of this cinema and for films 'with neither philosophy nor poetry' (a condescending recommendation that was not calculated to enhance the status of cinema in a culture where poetry and philosophy were considered the highest goals of art). What seems surprising now is that silent film was considered primarily a narrative medium, rather than being related from the start to the visual arts. Partly, this may have been because photography, as an art form, was associated with the academic or *pompier* realism most despised by the avant-garde, so it was not until the 1920s, thanks to the example of Russian, German and Swedish film-makers, that French artists began to experiment with film and to heed the Dadaist appeal for 'subjectless' cinema. It was not therefore until after the First World War, with what Sadoul calls the 'Impressionist school' (Louis Delluc, Marcel L'Herbier, Jean Epstein, Germaine Dulac, René Clair) that directors set out to explore the wider visual possibilities of the camera, and painters like Fernand Léger (*Le Ballet mécanique*, 1924) saw its potential as an extension of Dada, Cubism or Surrealism. Meanwhile, there was Abel Gance.

Gance was not an artist like Léger, Picabia or Man Ray. His ambition had been to make his name as a poet, writing verse plays and epics, and in spirit he was a product of the Romanticism of the 1820s. But he also turned to acting, on stage and on film, and to writing screenplays for Gaumont and Pathé. In 1912, he directed his first films for Le Film Français and in the same year wrote an article in *Ciné-Journal* (9 March 1912) proclaiming that cinema was 'a sixth art' and arguing that it was 'more than just a facile source of entertainment and, in fact, the synthesis of all previous art forms' (see Norman King's *Abel Gance*, BFI, 1984). Between 1915 and 1918, he was working for Le Film d'Art as a director and in 1920 formed his own company to produce *La Roue* (with support from Pathé who distributed the film in 1923).

Gance's relationship to the Romantics and the nature of his ambition are important for an understanding of his work. The Romantics had carried forward a process, already evident in the eighteenth century, through which the concept of poetry was extended beyond the realm of literature and the Poet elevated to the status of supreme creative artist. Gance shared with Cocteau this Romantic belief in his ability to find and make 'poetry' in everything he touched and both men believed in the 'poetic' quality of the cinematic image: much the same outlook is to be found in the theoretical writings of the Russian director Andrei Tarkovsky. With Gance (unlike Cocteau) this faith in poetry was combined with a populist approach that exalted the melodramatic genres of cinema, and Gance's combination of high artistic ambition and faith in these early narrative forms of cinema was revolutionary.

La Roue [84] is the story of a railway worker, Sisif, who becomes the rival of his own son and of another man for the love of an orphan girl. Exaggerated, over-acted, it ran for eight hours in its original version and for seven-and-a-half hours even in the version finally released by Pathé. But Gance's defects are also his qualities. His 'populist Romanticism' saw Sisif (Sisyphus) as a mythical hero, ennobled by work and by his love for the railway and its machines, standing at the head of a line of working-class heroes in French cinema; while Gance's belief in film as art encouraged him to experiment with techniques of montage to give the work extraordinary visual and rhythmic appeal. This technical experimentation, inspired perhaps by Gance's meeting with D. W. Griffith in 1921, was to be taken still further in his most famous work, *Napoléon* [12].

Though Gance was concerned with using such technical devices to tell a story, making form and content, as in an epic poem, indissoluble, his experiments with form led others to foresee the possibility of freeing film from its literary and narrative associations. René Clair dismissed the 'curious plot' of *La Roue* as irrelevant: 'If only this man ... was willing to create a pure documentary! If only he would renounce literature and have confidence in cinema!'; and he was joined by other 'Impressionist' directors: Dulac claimed that Gance was 'above all a poet', defining cinema as dramatic, 'but a drama conceived in a completely new way, completely divorced from the rules that govern theatre and literature', while Epstein stressed the view that 'poetry is not to be found only in verse'.

When Dulac wrote of 'the *rules* that govern theatre and literature', she was speaking as part of a cultural tradition that had been much concerned with debate on formal constraints and the definition of genres; and where the status of cinema as an art had to be decided partly by situating it in relation to other forms, and deciding whether it was essentially narrative (the novel), dramatic (the theatre) or visual (painting). The 'Impressionist' conclusion, that cinema was one of the visual arts – a form of 'visual poetry' – was theoretically consistent. But it overlooked the fact, recognized by Gance, that film had developed as a popular, narrative medium and that it was a narrative that it appealed to the public, who went to the cinema to be entertained. They enjoyed the narrative genres of Hollywood cinema, not the 'visual poetry' of the 'Impressionists'.

Simone Weil's journal of her experiences as a factory-worker in the mid-1930s records meeting a fitter who told her that the talkies had killed cinema which was, in essence, a perfect extension of photography. This nostalgia for the 'pure cinema' of the 'Impressionists' survived the coming of sound by many years: I remember being given it as an essay topic at school in the 1950s. But sound only confirmed what the industry had long appreciated: that the market was primarily for narrative films. The celebrated debate in the 1930s between René Clair and Marcel Pagnol was, in this sense, futile. Clair defended the thesis of cinema as primarily a visual medium; Pagnol argued that it was not truly an art in its own right, but a means to preserve great dramatic performances. In fact, both men were probably driven, in debate, to defend extreme positions and certainly ones which they did not hold to in practice. The films of Clair are narrative and those of Pagnol more than just records of his plays.

However, Pagnol's relegation of cinema to the subordinate role of preserved theatre was a threat to its claim as an independent art form and there was another more serious challenge to its status before the intellectual élite of the country could give it general acceptance as anything more than (in Marcel Duhamel's words) 'an entertainment for helots'. As an industrial product involving the work of writers, producers, technicians and actors, cinema failed to meet a major requirement of art in Western culture: that it should be the product of a single creator. This is the dilemma that had to be resolved in the 1950s by the writers who developed the theory of a *cinéma d'auteurs*: taking the most obviously commercial and industrial cinema of all, that of Hollywood, they argued that the central creative vision could be located in the director who thus became an artist in the same way as the author of a play or the composer of a symphony.

Gance had already come to the same conclusion: there was only one creator of *his* work. His shooting scripts (though not always strictly followed) prescribe every shot, angle, edit and even the reaction to be cajoled out of the spectator.

His directing style was frankly dictatorial (or, perhaps, 'Napoleonic'); in an appeal to the actors and technicians working with him on *Napoléon* in 1924, he proclaimed that the film would 'allow us to enter once and for all into the temple of the Arts through the great doorway of History. An inexpressible anguish grips me at the thought that my willpower, and even the sacrifice of my life, will be to no avail if you do not, each and every one of you, give me your undivided loyalty at every moment.' He demanded 'absolute dedication' from everyone involved in the production and the renunciation of 'all petty personal considerations'. No doubt about the *auteur* here.

The problem of the creator virtually disappeared, in any case, with Structuralism, which was more interested in the analysis of cinematic genres, and in the political climate after 1968 when collective work was seen as inevitable or preferable to the product of an isolated individual. When Marxist writers like Pierre Macherey were elaborating a theory of 'literary production' that treated the lonely writer as part of the productive chain of industrial society, the matter of whether film was the product of a single creator, or of many, came to seem meaningless. The generally accepted view was that expressed in a school textbook on contemporary French literature, published in 1970, which argued that 'cineasts' (a neutral word capable of referring to scriptwriters and directors) aimed not so much to 'rival literature as to express, by different means but with the same depth and perhaps greater intensity, what the writer expresses', adding that 'this has often been called *cinéma d'auteur'* (*La Littérature en France de 1945 à 1968*, published by Bordas).

* * * * *

The theoretical debates of the 1920s were academic in more than one sense. France had lost its hegemony in production and in sales of films and film stock during the First World War. The successful campaign of American producers to take over has been described by Kristin Thompson (1985). Where the output of new films in France stood at around 25,000–30,000 metres one year before the outbreak of war, it fell to less than 10,000 by 1916 and in December of that year only one-third of the films shown in France were home-produced, 27.8 per cent coming from the USA and 25.4 per cent from Italy.

American films filled the gap left by the decline in French production, due to the demands of the war effort, and they were more entertaining and better-made than the home product. The Americans had started to develop narrative techniques that were to become almost universally accepted conventions. Even when American imports fell during the 1920s, French producers were unable to respond and the result was an increase in imports from elsewhere, particularly Germany. The French and German film industries entered on a long period of collaboration that was to last through the 1930s, regardless of the difference in the political systems of the two countries.

To protect the industry against American competition, the French government, like others, adopted a quota system, adjusted in 1931 to take account of the introduction of sound. The rules restricted foreign films in original version to only 10 cinemas (raised to 20 after 1933) and demanded that dubbed versions should be made in Paris. Dubbing was only one solution to the language problem; another was the production of several versions of a film, shot from a script translated into perhaps 15 languages and using native actors.

During the 1930s, the press alternatively mourned the death of the French film industry and announced the birth of a 'national school' of cinema. There was justification for both views. The industry was not healthy, especially after the Gaumont and Pathé-Nathan disasters, but it maintained a steady flow of films: 1178 were distributed in the period 1930–39, as well as 156 French-language versions made abroad, which compares well with Sadoul's estimate (1962) of around 850 films in the decade before 1930 and 920 in the 10 years following the Liberation (including a large number of co-productions). The films of the 1930s were of high quality and most critics would argue that they made a distinctive contribution to world cinema (justifying the notion of a French 'school').

An industry with high capital costs requires a strong home market and French cinema attendance has always lagged behind that in Britain or the United States. Sound cinema increased audiences which stabilized in the 1930s at around 250 million admissions a year in around 4100 cinemas. The economic crisis brought a decline in box office receipts, but as the decade continued there was a rise in living standards and in leisure time. The deteriorating international situation may have brought an increased demand for distractions and the Second World War certainly did: admissions rose, reaching 402 million by 1945 and peaking in 1947 at 424 million. However, this should be compared with attendances in Britain where a slightly larger population achieved a peak in 1945 of 1585 million admissions, equivalent to around 30 visits per person per year, in contrast to the French average of around 10. Certainly there were reasons for this different use of leisure time in the two countries in social custom and habits (restaurants and cafés offered an alternative in France), climate, population distribution and availability.

Television did not make the same impact in France during the 1950s as in Britain or the USA, but cinema admissions fell despite this, to reach 355 million in 1960. From then on, as General de Gaulle realized, la télé had become a major source of information and entertainment: only a million sets in 1959, three times that number in 1963. Cinema admissions continued to decline, but less fast than in Britain and when, in 1969, they reached rough parity with Britain at 184 million, the decline was halted. In the 1980s, admissions were still running at between 180 and 190 million, equivalent to 3.5 visits per person per year. Broadly speaking, this was lower than the USA, considerably lower than the USSR, and higher than Britain (1.5 visits), Japan (1.3), Belgium, West Germany or Austria. This means that, in their cinema-going habits, the French were similar to the Italians, the Swiss and the Danes, but I doubt if it allows one to draw any far-reaching conclusions about the national character.

The industry was in fact healthier than the figures might suggest: some 230 feature-length films being produced every year (more than any country except India, Japan and the USA). This was partly because of government support, through direct grants and through a quota system imposed on television under which 50 per cent of televised films had to be French. The quality of French television, closely controlled by the government until the late 1970s, was generally admitted to be poor, while cinema, from the period of the New Wave onwards, had high intellectual prestige. Perhaps the battles over the cinema's status as art had not been entirely a matter of disinterested theory. On the other hand, the less elevating aspect of the high rate of admissions was that a good deal could be accounted for by the relaxation of censorship which allowed a flood of pornographic films in special cinemas. There was not one audience, but several, sometimes overlapping groups of cinema-goers: fans of porno movies, intellectuals looking for art films, children and adolescents attracted by the special effects of *Star Wars* and its successors or imitators.

* * * * *

The experience of cinema-going varied according to locality and so according to class. Bernard Barbey, critic of the *Revue hebdomadaire*, ventured outside the Parisian first-run theatres in 1935 to visit a country cinema and found conditions very different from what he was used to: the range of films was limited and programmes did not include the usual 'shorts' before the main feature. 'Is there a documentary? I like documentaries', says a character in Nelly Kaplan's *La Fiancée du pirate* [158], before the start of a show given by a travelling projectionist who has set up the projector on the bar of a village café (there isn't).

The industry soon discovered the profits to be made by giving a film an exclusive run at an expensive theatre before putting it on general release. This meant that, even in Paris, say during the 1950s and 1960s, there were four distinct outlets for films: on the one hand, the first-run cinemas around the Champs-Elysées and the Boulevard des Capucines showed French and foreign films (the latter sub-titled, not dubbed) *en exclusivité*, compensating for high prices with plush seats, carpets and, sometimes, an artificially scented atmosphere. There was no smoking and the usherette expected a reasonable tip to put in her little bag (after all, it was almost certainly her wage).

At the other end of the scale were the local *cinémas de quartier* where the seats felt more like public transport than the lounge of an expensive hotel. Here, foreign films were invariably dubbed, John Wayne and James Stewart having apparently had voice training from Charles Dullin, and standards of exhibition (for example, focusing) were less reliable. You might end up in the back row with a couple not concerned by the doing of John Wayne or James Stewart, or in the front rows with some rowdy *blousons noirs*. The commercials

23

were by Jean Mineur Publicité and in the interval the audience was encouraged to enjoy an *esquimau Gervais* or a packet of caramels.

These cinemas dealt in more or less the same modern films and were distinguished mainly by their standards of comfort. The *cinémas d'art et d'essai*, meanwhile, showed a mixture of old films, cinema classics, independents and some intellectually more demanding works. Their repertoire, even so, was broader than that of most London 'art houses' in the late 1950s: French critical opinion had been quicker to recognize the talent of Hollywood directors who tended to be dismissed by Anglo-Saxon critics as mere entertainers. *To Be or Not to Be*, *Hellzapoppin* and Westerns were perennial favourites, beside Ealing comedies like *Kind Hearts and Coronets* (*Noblesse Oblige* in France). These art cinemas were very small, centred on the Latin Quarter around the Rue Champollion or the Rue de la Huchette, catering for a student audience and one that took cinema seriously, without necessarily liking 'serious' films. Finally, there were cinema clubs, like the Ciné-Club at the Cité Universitaire which was open to residents and students and showed, twice a week for practically nothing, an astonishing range of films from everywhere in the world.

There was also the Cinémathèque, an unclassifiable institution, giving three shows a day of different films on its screens at the Rue d'Ulm and the Palais de Chaillot. It was open to everyone and very cheap: there were seasons of particular directors and other organized events, but the place was no model of efficiency and the best thing was often to take pot luck, pay a couple of francs and see whatever happened to be on offer. Once when I did this, a fat, flamboyant man, with his coat draped over his shoulders, walked to the front of the hall to introduce the film. I am sorry to say that I found him rather irritating. It was Henri Langlois.

Langlois had founded the Cinémathèque in 1936 with Georges Franju and two years later helped to set up an international body, the Fédération Internationale des Archives de Film. Eccentric, enthusiastic, he played a major role in French cinema history by encouraging preservation. But he was an individualist who resented interference. The archive grew well beyond his control and when he died it was found to be in an appalling state, with many films piled up unprotected or stored in the wrong boxes, and many wholly or partially damaged. It was said that Langlois's most publicized legacy was a huge task of restoration and cataloguing.

Despite this, the Cinémathèque was his monument and it played a crucial role in film education, especially for the young directors who were to make the so-called New Wave. In the brief period between 1958 and 1962, nearly 200 new film directors made first films, aided by the willingness of investors to give money to virtual unknowns and by the development of light, hand-held cameras. Technical polish was not, in any case, as important as the spontaneity and immediacy that their British counterparts were finding in work for television. Neither television nor the established procedures of the cinema studio were attractive to them: most never served the recognized apprenticeship as assistants. Against the background of a culture that tended towards academism, good taste and conformity, the cinema appeared as iconoclastic and far more open in access to both film-makers and audiences than most other means of artistic expression.

* * * * *

The director may be the 'author' of the film, and most directors would claim 'authorship' of their works, but no one is more acutely aware of the limits to their 'authority' than directors themselves. Carné, in the book of memoirs which he called *La Vie à belles dents*, devotes several pages to the problems he had dealing with his producer Grégor Rabinovitch during the making of *Quai des brumes* [2], pages which might sound racist if they did not reflect the usual grumpiness of directors at such constraints; he also speaks of actors 'I could work with', actors 'of whom I was sure' or who could 'be relied upon'. He tells us that the subject of *Les Portes de la nuit* [37] was one that he, personally, did not want to make and that he was 'unenthusiastic' about working with the two stars. He describes his problems with the censor (especially over a film that he tried to make about the juvenile detention centre on Belle-Île), his admiration for the set designer Alexandre Trauner, his break with the scriptwriter Jacques Prévert and, inevitably, the problem of raising financial support. Much the same can be read in the writings of any film director. Where other artists may speak of struggles to realize their vision against the constraints imposed by the material or by financial hardship, film 'authors' inevitably grumble about the restricting effects of having to work with producers and designers, scriptwriters and actors and against audience expectations, routine critical hostility and moronic censorship.

As well as these external constraints, the cinema 'artist' tailors his vision according to his own preconceptions about genre, setting, plot and so on, before finally coming up against the central requirement of translating it into the 'language' of film. The image on a cinema screen is not the 'real' world, but acts as a signifier of it. Within the context of the cultures and ideologies through which we ascribe meanings to the 'real' world, screen images have connotations which are expressed in the codes of 'cinema language'.

The cinema is especially privileged in its ability to exploit the connotative implications of its signifiers, because it combines the iconographic features of a visual medium with the narrative features of a literary one. Gabin's cloth cap and Jules Berry's hat, tie and checked overcoat in *Le Jour se lève* [90] mark one out as a workman, the other as a bourgeois, meanings which are reinforced by the fact that a contemporary audience would hardly expect Gabin to play a middle-class crook, or Berry an honest working-man. The connotations of such iconographic clues may vary according to audience and period.

As I mentioned earlier, Dreyer chose a Russian, Alexandre Mihalesco, to play Warwick in *La Passion de Jeanne d'Arc* [13] because he felt the man had the right 'look' for the part of an English captain. He dressed him in a peculiar uniform: flat helmet, dark jacket, Sam Browne belt, jodhpurs and boots, with a chain around his neck. The opening credits of the film, showing a hand turning the pages of the manuscript record of Joan's trial, emphasize Dreyer's wish to convince his audience of the authenticity of its representation of those distant events. In 1927, then, an English medieval army officer looked like that. Today, the flat helmet makes Warwick look like nothing so much as a Second World War fire warden.

La Passion de Jeanne d'Arc is not a still icon, but a continuous narrative and the final credits are preceded by a message recalling the enduring love of the French people for St Joan. Taking these credits in isolation from the film, we might assume that Dreyer had set out to give the conventional interpretation of Joan as a symbol of French resistance to foreign domination. This is the primary meaning of the story of Joan of Arc for a French audience and, less than 10 years after the end of a war in which France had driven off a foreign invader, that is how an audience would expect to interpret the film. What Dreyer does is to assert his own reading of the events, in spite of his final caption.

Having emphasized the veracity of its account by the first reference to the contemporary manuscript, Dreyer's film confines itself purely to the confrontation between Joan and her judges, leaving aside altogether the historical context of the Hundred Years' War. Warwick, the English officer, and Cauchon, the French bishop, stand side-by-side as allies against Joan, not as enemies. The concentration on Joan's persecution and suffering voids the film of any wider, nationalistic content and the contrast between Joan's simplicity and Cauchon's learning amounts to a class distinction that culminates in the final scenes of popular revolt, brutally suppressed, following Joan's execution. The cumulative effect is to shift the emphasis in the final caption from the *French* people's love of Joan as a nationalist symbol, to the French *people's* love of Joan, as a symbol of resistance to the oppression of the State (Warwick) and the Church (Cauchon).

Dreyer's film belongs to a particular genre: historical narrative based on reconstruction of real events (as opposed to period films that use a historical setting for fictional narratives), and it shows how a film conveys its meanings through visual and narrative means. But the representation of real events and the reading of history are not the only way in which a film can speak to its audience about questions of politics and religion, peasants and priests, nationalism and class. The writers of *Cahiers du cinéma* in the 1950s already perceived that a strength of cinema, especially of American cinema, was its ability to construct 'parables', using the conventions of genres like the thriller, the gangster movie, science fiction and so on, to translate into fictional narrative some profound concerns of society at a particular time. In general, the writers of *Cahiers* found French cinema lacking in such myths and parables, too little concerned with contemporary social issues and too much with 'quality' adaptations of literary works from the past. With the advantage of hindsight, however, we may disagree and in the next chapter, bearing in mind the many constraints that make cinema inevitably a distorting mirror of reality, I shall try to survey the myths and parables in which film-makers have encoded the underlying concerns of French society at different moments in the history of the twentieth century. *La Passion de Jeanne d'Arc* (a French film, though it was made by a Danish director), with its subversion of a nationalist story to convey a message of popular revolt and individual resistance to the oppression of the State, seems a good place to start.

I. DIRECTORS AT WORK

1. Méliès studio

2. René Clair filming   (NATIONAL FILM ARCHIVE)

3. Lelouch filming   (NATIONAL FILM ARCHIVE)

II. HISTORY AND WAR

4. Renoir: *La Marseillaise*   (CONTEMPORARY FILMS)

5. *La Grande illusion*   (CONTEMPORARY FILMS)

6. *Les Enfants du paradis* (NATIONAL FILM ARCHIVE)

7. *L'Espoir* (NATIONAL FILM ARCHIVE)

8. *Fort Saganne*   (ALBINA/LES FILMS A2)

9. *Le Temps détruit*   (INA)

10. *La Passion de Jeanne d'Arc*   (CONTEMPORARY FILMS)

11. *Casque D'Or*   (NATIONAL FILM ARCHIVE)

12. *Journal d'un curé de campagne*   (NATIONAL FILM ARCHIVE)

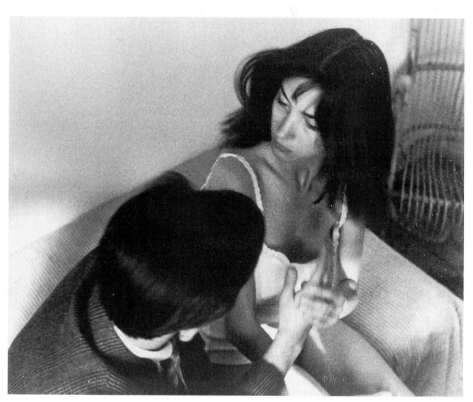

13. *Je vous salue, Marie*   (THE OTHER CINEMA)

14. *A nous la liberté* (SECA/MARCEAU COCINOR)

15. *La Belle équipe* (NATIONAL FILM ARCHIVE)

16. *Le Crime de Monsieur Lange*   (DOMINIQUE H. DES FONTAINES)

17. *La Bête humaine* (NATIONAL FILM ARCHIVE)

18. *Le Salaire de la peur* (MARCEAU COCINOR/CIC/VERA)

19. *La règle du jeu*   (CONTEMPORARY FILMS)

20. *Le Jour se lève* (VAUBAN PRODUCTIONS)

21. *Les Vacances de Monsieur Hulot* (NATIONAL FILM ARCHIVE)

22. *Occupe-toi d'Amélie* (NATIONAL FILM ARCHIVE)

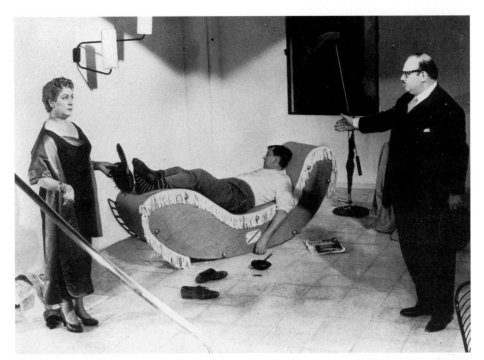

23. *Mon Oncle*   (NATIONAL FILM ARCHIVE)

24. *Hypothèse du tableau volé*   (BFI/INA)

2 The mood of the times

The struggle for individual rights against the normalizing pressures of institutions might be seen as one of the enduring themes of history, reaching a peculiarly acute stage in the twentieth century. At first glance, the French cinema has been consistently on the side of the individual, rather than the institutions, which is much to its credit. But this sweeping conclusion needs to be modified in several respects.

Firstly, it should not lead to any hasty assumptions about the French character or the national passion for individual freedom. A persistent struggle against normalizing institutions implies the persistence of these institutions. Secondly, while the leading characters in a film may be perceived as individuals and appeal for our sympathy in their struggles to achieve happiness and fulfilment, the cinema is a notorious creator of stereotypes and a host of secondary characters, some merely glimpsed in the background of the story, may combine to make cinema one of the most powerful media for reinforcing conservative values. Thirdly, film-makers belong to a particular social group; directors may have their origins in different classes, be they children of cabinet-makers (like Carné) or great artists (like Renoir), but their outlook will be conditioned to some extent by the industry for which they work. And, fourthly, their products will be conditioned by preconceptions about art, fidelity to literary sources and other constraints.

Love and sexual relationships have been the central theme of Western literature since the Middle Ages and remain the central theme of most films. To treat this theme in a mythical and universal manner, literature and cinema tend to seek a 'neutral' social setting which will vary from time to time. For medieval audiences, this was the castle of courtly romance, for Racine's plays it may be the Roman imperial court or Theseus's palace. The setting is a transparency through which the audience can identify with the actors. The emperors, kings and queens in Racine are not shown at work as rulers: like the oilmen in *Dallas*, they devote most of their time to private matters.

The bourgeois drawing-room in the Boireau comedies or the *château* in the early dramas of Feuillade, as I mentioned earlier, provides an equally 'transparent' setting. We take for granted the servants who hover in the background when they are required by the plot. And, though the cinema's contrary appetite for variations in background or local colour means that it is not possible to be dogmatic, one can none the less distinguish at different times the environments that came close to being 'transparent' or 'neutral' backgrounds for a particular period. The term 'drawing-room comedy', for example, is not insignificant and the French *comédie mondaine* which implies a particular social world, more or less corresponds. The films of Yves Mirande (*Baccara*, 1935; *A Nous deux, Madame la Vie*, 1937; *Le Chasseur de chez Maxim's*, 1939) evoke a wealthy class from the previous decade in their night-clubs and 'modern-style' salons, and only marginally to satirize it.

Another sub-genre of the 1920s and 1930s, with a similar 'transparent' location, was the Russian film, a love story of the Steppes involving beautiful aristocratic women and handsome officers in pre-revolutionary times. Between 1934 and 1938, Raymond Chirat has counted no less than 36 films on such Russian-imperial themes, inspired partly by the group of White Russian émigrés who were a significant feature of the cinema industry from the 1920s. Despite the military uniforms, there is little military action: ballrooms and drawing-rooms provide the settings; love, duels and occasionally espionage, the plots; and balalaikas and falling snow the mood. They have titles like *Nuits de feu, La Tragédie impériale, Les Nuits moscovites, Troika sur la piste blanche, Les Nuits blanches de Saint-Pétersbourg*, which promise extremes of passion and changing fortunes against the high contrast of black nights and white landscapes. When actors like Ivan Mosjoukine failed to make the transition to talking pictures because of their (genuine) Russian accents, directors turned to Gaby Morlay, Victor Francen or Harry Baur, removing the product still further from reality and deeper into myth.

Of course, there is in one sense nothing 'neutral' about this nostalgia for the Tsarist world, a mere 20 years after the Russian Revolution, at a time of violent confrontation between Communism and Fascism in Europe. But it would be ridiculous to think of these films as 'anti-Communist propaganda' in any real sense. They were not directed against Communism in France or towards the restoration of the Russian imperial régime. The attraction of the pre-revolutionary aristocracy, for the makers of such films, was precisely that it was a lost class and its romantic appeal, giving it such power as fantasy, lay in its unattainability, its separation from current concerns, its potential as myth. The same was true, to some extent, of the salons and night-clubs of the *comédie mondaine*, designed to appeal to the fantasies of the poor rather than to the actual experience of the rich.

In the period after World War II, especially, the underworld could supply a conventional setting for films that were less about crime and punishment, than about loyalty, solidarity and friendship. But the *milieu* is more conventional than 'transparent', and more overtly political because of the social nature of crime. The society that has defined a character as a criminal or a gangster is inevitably present in a film about him. Frequently such films can be seen as a form of political allegory: the emphasis on friendship and loyalty in the 1950s gangster movies, like *Touchez pas au grisbi* [131] or *Du rififi chez les hommes* [133], being a hang-over from the betrayals of the Occupation, and the 1960s and 1970s detective or gangster movie suggesting more or less openly that the 'alternative' society of criminals is much like the world of big business or politics (and, more importantly, vice versa), or that there is a 'police underworld' no more moral than the criminal one.

The very high proportion of literary adaptations in French cinema, especially up to the directors of the New Wave, was another way of achieving a kind of 'transparency', the contemporary or historical environment associated with a particular novelist serving as a screen through which the audience could become involved in the emotions of the main characters. This is by no means a necessary consequence of literary adaptation: Aurenche and Bost's adaptation of Emile Zola in René Clément's *Gervaise* [96] directs attention specifically to the problems of the working class and, before accusing directors of adopting the 'safe' solution of literary adaptation, one should remember that several chose to update the text, to make it more relevant, risking criticism for tampering with it. The most 'neutral' films are set in what Jeancolas (1979) calls '*le contemporain vague*', a period recognized by the audience as 'the present' but distinguished by no particular contemporary features. As Jeancolas also remarks, this 'vague contemporary' is found much less in films made after 1970 when period is often indicated by reference to precise events or by such hints as copies of newspapers or political posters, or intrusive clues (the intercutting of newsreel footage) which oblige the audience to locate the action precisely.

Increasingly, from the time of Vadim's *Et Dieu créa la femme* [153], made in 1956, the 'transparent' background is that of a particular class, leisured and comfortably well-off. The characters are not so rich that one asks where their money comes from, but rich enough to have the leisure to indulge in affairs with each other. Their possession of leisure may be emphasized by a holiday context, as in some of Eric Rohmer's Moral Tales or Comedies and Proverbs [e.g. 82]. If they have any profession, it is both glamorous and socially marginal, like the racing driver of *Un Homme et une femme* [78] or the 'big business' in which the characters of Losey's *La Truite* [81] are supposedly involved. These characters are seldom, if ever, seen at work, which is merely the means of play, or in relation to members of other classes who make brief appearances to service the needs of the central characters, as servants, shopkeepers and so on. The luxurious, modern-style furnishing of the thirties *comédie mondaine* gives way to a less obtrusive form of good taste in the sixties, and the motor car ceases to be a symbol of wealth and becomes an inevitable possession: driven in prewar films by a chauffeur and used to ferry its contents ostentatiously from apartment to night-club and back, it now takes to the open road, the means of their freedom and a testimony to it. Even films which set out to criticize this lifestyle often take it largely for granted and provide it with no real social context.

Paris or the countryside, when they are not particularized in some way, can serve as 'transparent' urban or rural settings (which I discuss in Chapter 3); age, too, may be an element of 'transparency'. Jules Berry, as the impoverished and not entirely trustworthy bachelor André Leclerc in *Baccara* (1935), gives his age as 44 (Berry was in fact 46, so he is perhaps illustrating the character's untrustworthiness). Marcelle Chantal who plays opposite him as Elsa, must be in her thirties, even in the film's terms. There is nothing unusual, in thirties romantic comedy, in centring interest on members of these age-groups, especially when they have a sexual relationship that might be considered unacceptable in younger heroes and, especially, heroines (the relationships described in *Le Blé en herbe* [168] were shocking in 1954). The 'transparent' age was to be considerably reduced by the 1960s, its lowering being helped by the fact that, with changing economic and social circumstances, it was more plausible for adolescents and young adults, particularly as students at school or university, to have the leisure to enjoy romantic relationships without the need to define their social status. These 'transparent' contexts give the least interrupted view of love, sex and the emotions related to them, but the precise conditions which are most likely to allow audiences to forget work, money and other everyday concerns and indulge these more interesting fantasies, vary from time to time.

* * * * *

The Lumière and Méliès comedies of the first decade of the century, through a genre inherited from the music hall and popular theatre, enshrine a society of clear distinctions in class and status. They seem peculiarly appropriate, in retrospect, to *la belle époque*, in its supposed insouciance as well as its stability.

Despite the Belgian film *Maudite soit la guerre*, made by Alfred Machin in 1913 and released just before the outbreak of war, the image of military life in the cinema is predominantly that of the Pathé short of 1905 in which an unfortunate captain is mistakenly doused by his men with a bucket of water intended for a drunkard who is disturbing the barracks ... The Army, even outside comedy, is shown as a masculine world of disciplined high spirits and comradeship, and the occasional representation of military action, in Lumière sketches like *Défense d'un drapeau* (c. 1900), emphasizes heroism and triumph, completely outside any context of actual war.

The French authorities were slow to recognize the potential of cinema in wartime for information, encouragement and entertainment. A proposal to set up an official camera unit at the start was turned down by Marshal Joffre, so the first great engagement of the war (the Battle of the Marne in September 1914, when the French turned back the German advance on Paris) went unrecorded. A film unit was subsequently formed and newsreel footage produced. Not surprisingly, as a corollary to this, the war provided an excuse for creating a system of censorship, involving several levels, from the Ministry of the Interior and the Prefecture of Police, to the local authorities, who were able to prevent even the showing of films passed for exhibition elsewhere.

General censorship was applied to newsreels: when Marshal Pétain was shown wincing as he tasted the troops' wine, this evidence of fastidiousness, on the part of a war leader with a reputation for the 'popular touch', was banned.

As for encouragement, there was a succession of patriotic films, bearing the most eloquent titles in the history of cinema: *Alsace, Mère française, Coeur de française, Chantecoq* (the national cockerel being honoured), *Les Poilus de la revanche* ('poilus' was the civilian name for the soldiers, the revenge, presumably, was for the defeat of 1870), *La Voix de la patrie, Vendémiaire* (the victories of the revolutionary army against the Prussians could be recalled and isolated from the events of the Revolution itself). But it was as escapist entertainment that cinema came into its own, with an influx of American serials like *The Perils of Pauline* supplying the demand created by the drop in French production. Louis Feuillade, whose series *Fantômas* dates from 1913–14, was already working in the genre and, returning to Gaumont in 1915, began the 12 episodes of *Les Vampires*, followed by *Judex* (1916) and *La Nouvelle mission de Judex* (1917).

The plots developed like soap opera as they were being filmed and actors who arrived late on set or received their call-up papers were liable to be cut from the script at the last moment. This improvisation, and the occasional illogicality that resulted, thus reflected some of the insanity of the time. When the world goes mad, one must improvise. In the trenches another serial dragged on, apparently unending. The soldier on leave could be sure that a new villain would replace the Chief Vampire and that Musidora, as the evil Irma Vep (anag.), would be lurking in the shadows; returning to the front, he found the same mud, the same trenches and the same implacable enemy as before.

Apart from the Surrealists, who appreciated his imaginative improvisation, Feuillade did not appeal to postwar audiences and was only re-discovered, thanks partly to Henri Langlois, in the 1940s and 1950s. André Bazin remembered seeing his films at the Cinémathèque where characteristic uncertainties in projection enhanced the impromptu nature of Feuillade's method. During the war itself there were those who, with unintended irony, called for the banning of representations of violence and crime. As the conflict ended, attention was concentrated more on rationalization. Abel Gance, in the first version of *J'Accuse* (lost, except for a mutilated reconstruction), proclaimed that the war had been justified by the new society that would emerge from it. The final scene of the film showed the dead rising to demand this reparation for their sacrifice, and they did rise, haunting society for the next 20 years.

* * * * *

The statistics tell some of the story: 1,400,000 killed, one in 25 of the population, mainly young men; three million wounded; countless numbers bearing the psychological scars of fighting or bereavement. The landscape of northern France was devastated and the economy shattered by the war debt and the disruption of industry.

33

Industry, for its part, recovered rapidly and the surge of industrial growth drove a wedge between this 'modern' sector, and the 'traditional' sector of agriculture. Depression followed and films like *A Nous la liberté* [85] suggest conditions that made for the rapid rise or fall of industrial enterprises and suspicion of the new rich, as well as fears of the subjection of humans to machines in 'factory-prisons'; in contrast, there was to be growing nostalgia for the values of rural life. The peasant classes had made the greatest sacrifice of men in the war and their 'backwardness' was accentuated by the high average age of those who remained, pointing the contrast between 'country' (old men and women living a timeless existence on the land) and 'town' (dynamic, industrial and moving through *les années folles* – the Jazz Age).

The Russian Revolution, as well as supplying émigrés for the cinema industry, suggested one version of the future, the United States another. The Communist Party (PCF) was founded at the Congress of Tours in 1920, when the pro-Bolsheviks split away from the Socialist Party. The working class had come back from the front expecting conditions to improve (one part of the legacy of Gance's rising dead), but it was still relatively weak. Its new militancy, however, was threatening to the middle class which retreated into conservatism as a defence against Bolshevism, on one side, and the Bohemianism of Jazz Age Paris on the other.

Films dealt directly with these political preoccupations of the ruling class. In René Le Sompteur's *La Croisade* (1920), a war hero returns to find his region devastated and sets about rebuilding his father's factory on the basis of co-operation between management and workers: 'we must hope,' wrote the *Courrier cinématographique*, 'that all will end well as it does in the film, with a victory for common sense, and with a clear and beneficial union between Capital and Labour'. A similar message informed the 12 episodes of Le Prince's *L'Empereur des pauvres* (1921), a family saga adapted from the novels of Félicien Champsaur. There are corresponding appeals for a return to the land and to stable prewar values: Théo Bergerat's *La Terre commande*, Max de Rieux's *La Grande amie* and Jean Choux's *La Terre qui meurt*.

The theme of urban corruption, explicit or implicit in such films, became linked with that of financial corruption as the economic crisis worsened. Marcel L'Herbier's *L'Argent* [72], updating Zola's novel about the Stock Exchange, introduces a theme which was to take on sinister overtones as it became linked with the image of the 'cosmopolitan' financier: one critic accused L'Herbier's film of not being realistic because it failed to introduce these 'Armenians, Jews and Levantines'. *Baccara* (1935), to take just one example of a film that did, involves the disappearance of a foreign financier who has been speculating against the franc, and the trial of his mistress (also a foreigner) for complicity in his crime. In the event, she is acquitted, partly because she has entered a marriage of convenience with André Leclerc (Jules Berry), to keep her French nationality, and partly because André, despite his dissolute character, is a war hero.

34

The veterans were a continuing legacy of the war. The memorials and cemeteries that are a feature of every town and village in the country were constant reminders and the focus of local ceremonies. André Leclerc is modest about his medals, but most veterans wore them with aggressive pride. The Associations d'Anciens Combattants, and other related or 'patriotic' organizations, often saw themselves as guardians of the national conscience, liable to censor works which they considered insulting to the dead and to the country for which they had fought, through pressure on the mayors and *préfets* responsible for banning films at a local level. Buñuel's *L'Age d'or* was banned in 1930 after protests from the Ligue des Patriotes and an anti-semitic group, the Ligue Antijuive. A *conseiller municipal*, Le Provost de Launay, wrote an open letter to the *préfet de police* expressing disgust at the showing of the film 'a stone's throw from the monument to the Unknown Soldier' and *Le Figaro* (7 Dec 30) described the film as besmirching 'fatherland, family and religion' and, returning to the subject three days later, accused it of 'Bolshevism'.

Films using war veterans were liable to special difficulties. Raymond Bernard's *Le Croix de bois* (1932), filmed on the Great War battlefields, resorted to them, particularly when the Army refused its co-operation for certain scenes: 'you don't expect my regiment to march past a ham actor disguised as a general!', Bernard was told by one colonel, who also refused outright to let them be filmed covered in mud, instead of in their best dress uniforms. Eventually Bernard called on veterans who were happy to oblige. But the second version of Gance's *J'Accuse* [33] attracted criticism (see my note).

The veterans brought home two contradictory outlooks: a shared military experience, and a hatred of war. In peacetime, there were different ways in which these could be reconciled. One was in the comedies of military life so popular in the 1930s, stressing the positive aspects of service: comradeship and good-humour, while doing without the unpleasantness of fighting. The genre had in fact existed in theatre for many years before the war, often with musical accompaniment, and transferred easily to sound cinema, where music was an important element (during the first sound decade, film shows frequently included live performances by singers which preceded the film). Jeancolas (1983) has counted at least 20 of these military comedies or melodramas between 1932 and 1935 and they continued to be made, with actors like Bach and Fernandel specializing in them: *Le Champion du régiment, Le Coq du régiment, La Caserne en folie, La Mariée du régiment, La Garnaison amoureuse, La Margoton du bataillon, La Fille du régiment* and, the best-known, *Les Gaîtés de l'escadron*. They could be compared with the British military comedies of the 1950s, like *Private's Progress* and the first 'Carry On' film, *Carry on Sergeant*, though I can think of no French equivalents after the Second World War.

Another solution was to relocate the events in time or place by setting them in historical or colonial contexts. René Le Somptier's *Les Fils du soleil* (1924), Renoir's *Le Bled* (1929), Duvivier's *La Bandera* (1935) and Poirier's *L'Appel du silence* (1936) use stories of the Rif war, the conquest of Algiers, the Spanish Foreign Legion (with a dedication to Franco) and the life of Charles de Foucauld (officer and Catholic missionary killed in the Sahara in 1916). Fernandel met Robert le Vigan in *Un de la légion* (Christian-Jacque, 1936), to provide a mixture of colonialist epic and military vaudeville. The latter predominated. It was beyond the powers of Le Vigan to upstage Fernandel.

Both the musical comedies and the colonialist dramas exalted some, but not all, military virtues. In Maurice Gleize's *Légion d'honneur* (1938), a wounded lieutenant convalescing in the Camargue falls in love with the wife of his best friend, but decides to sacrifice happiness to return to the desert (a sort of secular Charles de Foucauld). Male comradeship is the value that unites the musical comedies to the romantic melodramas and behind both is an ethic of honour, patriotism and self-denial (accepting sacrifices with good humour or a sense of duty). The qualities of order and discipline and the efficient weaponry that make an effective fighting force are less prominently displayed.

Of course, the colonialist films have a disturbing lack of awareness of the less desirable side to France's 'civilizing mission' in Africa. After some 50 years, the genre has been revived, with clear critical intentions. The thesis of Bertrand Tavernier's *Coup de torchon* [51] is that, like the men around the pool table in the film, the colonialist either considers 'natives' as lower than animals, or goes crazy and, perhaps, like the police chief, becomes a mass-murderer. Alain Corneau's *Fort Saganne* [52] casts Gérard Depardieu as a legionary who is at the same time a typically individualist hero, becoming aware of the limitations of military values. With a feminist heroine and a climax that takes its hero to the horrors of the Great War, Corneau's film is an evident attempt to combine later perceptions with the excitement of the thirties epics. Its comparative failure perhaps shows, as Francis Veber remarked to me, that 'you can't make a left-wing colonialist film'.

Neither the political Right nor the Left wanted war, though their interpretations of the deteriorating international situation and the threats to peace were as divergent as their ideas of *la nation* and what constituted it. Newsreels took up where the military comedies and melodramas left off, showing the defensive preparations of the army and, more generally, exalting its achievements and traditions. Léon Poirier's *Verdun, vision d'histoire* (1928), remade in a sound version as *Verdun, souvenirs d'histoire* [29], advocated the government policy of rapprochement with Germany, while Marcel L'Herbier's *Entente cordiale*, which the director later described as 'something of a history lesson', giving 'not only an anecdotal, but also a diplomatic understanding', celebrated the alliance with Britain in 1939. In the same year, Jean de Loubignac made a documentary drama answering the question *Sommes-nous défendus?* (in the affirmative, naturally) and *Double crime sur la ligne Maginot* (1937), adapted by Félix Gandéra from a spy novel by Pierre Nord, was an opportunity to display France's famous eastern defensive system, as reconstructed in the studio.

Against these arguments (that the country was prepared, well-protected and secure in its alliances), there were more directly pacifist statements: Léo Joannon's *Alerte en Méditerranée* (1938) allegorized the spirit of Munich in a story about French, British and German captains co-operating against smugglers. The fact that Léonide Moguy's *Le Déserteur* (1939) had to be retitled *Je t'attendrai*, shows the sensitivity of the government at this moment and helps to appreciate the context of *Quai des brumes* [2], where Carné never explains the circumstances of Gabin's desertion from the army.

Of Renoir's film *La Grande illusion* [34], Prédal (1972) says that it 'faithfully reflects the state of public opinion in 1937' and, unjustly, dismisses the view that it shows class divisions as more important than national ones, also accusing it of 'disguised antisemitism' in its portrait of the Jew Rosenthal, because he is shown to be richer than the French prisoners and 'fighting only to protect his fortune'. Given the circumstances of the time when the film was made, and the film's argument (the need for solidarity between the representatives of modern French society, Maréchal and Rosenthal, as opposed to the outmoded aristocratic values of de Boeldieu and Rauffenstein), his reading is unfair to Renoir.

* * * * *

The films of the thirties offer warnings and reassurances, avenues of escape and the prospect of dead ends. They are less preoccupied with the personal concerns of happiness and misery, than with the public ones of cynicism and hope. Whether they depict human beings in an industrial environment as the prisoners of industry (*A nous la liberté*) or in a Utopian rural one (*Regain*), they show little faith in contemporary, organized society and even those films which accept it as an inescapable premise generally consider its institutions to be corrupt and propose as another inescapable premise that fulfilment can be achieved only through love, in the constitution of the ideal couple.

There was a moment, around the time of the Popular Front in 1936, when hope predominated over cynicism. The government of Léon Blum only survived a year (though, in name, the front lasted until 1938), during which it fulfilled some hopes with the Matignon agreements, ensuring trade union rights, paid holidays, security against unfair dismissal and the 40-hour week; and disappointed others, particularly in its failure to give military help to the Spanish Republicans. But the Popular Front mood extended beyond and went deeper than Blum's government. In May 1936, after the elections, there were strikes and factory occupations involving more than a million workers: Georges Monca's *Choc en retour* (1937) presages these in a right-wing comedy where the boss (played by Michel Simon) instigates the strike. Julien Duvivier's *La Belle équipe* [87] tells how a group of workers spend the money from a win on the lottery to start a restaurant outside Paris as a co-operative enterprise. Duvivier brings in several themes of the time: unemployment, foreign refugees, financial swindles, workers' co-operatives; and the film, which shows the original group of five friends reduced to two (Jean Gabin and Charles

Vanel), both in love with the same woman, was made with two contrasting endings. In one, the dispute ends in murder; in the other, they decide to bury their differences and give up the woman for the sake of their joint enterprise and their friendship.

La Belle équipe illustrates the attractions and the limitations of the 'populist' film, the sentimental theme and the melodramatic elements partly blunting the political message. But the very fact that so many of these films introduced working-class heroes and heroines was remarkable in European cinema at the time; and the mood of the Popular Front made it possible for film-makers to treat political themes in a new way, even when the context was romance. Some directors, like Jean Renoir and Jean-Paul Dreyfus (Le Chanois) were politically active, using their work to support the Front and the PCF.

Renoir's La Marseillaise [15] and Le Crime de Monsieur Lange [88] are probably the best distinctly 'popular front' films: the first tells the story of the Revolution through the ordinary people of Marseilles, flocking to Paris to support the revolutionaries; the second is about a writer of Westerns whose books are produced by a small printing works run by Batala (Jules Berry). When Batala disappears to avoid his creditors, and is presumed dead, his nephew agrees that the workers should run the firm as a co-operative. It is a huge success, but Batala returns (disguised as a priest!) and threatens to resume control, so the inoffensive Monsieur Lange (René Lefèvre) kills him. Lange flees with his girlfriend, is stopped at the Belgian frontier and tells his story to a group of workers in a café: the main action is shown in flashback. They discuss whether to hand him over to the police, and decide to let him escape.

Though there is an anticlerical joke in having Batala dress up as a priest, the PCF line was one of conciliation of different factions in the Front; the priest in Dreyfus' Le Temps des cerises (1937) says: 'one must also believe in a paradise on earth'. Le Temps des cerises, funded by the PCF, contrasts the fate of two Frenchmen born in 1895, one in a château, the other in a working-class family, and it ends with an impassioned plea for retirement pensions for old people – the kind of issue on which the Communists could expect wide popular support. This film, and La Vie est à nous (1936), directed by Renoir with the help of Dreyfus and Jacques Becker, show the PCF making intelligent use of the cinema in support of its election campaigns.

When André Malraux made L'Espoir (1939, finished in 1945), using men who were actually fighting in the Spanish Republican cause, hope had in fact gone. France was at the mercy of obscure forces and impulses beyond easy understanding. Ordinary people longed for happiness, peace, reasonable working conditions and the occasional breath of country air: Jean Boyer's Prends la route (1936) had used the excuse of the first paid holidays for industrial workers to show a couple of popular singers touring the country. But these reasonable expectations were to be denied. No wonder some believed that the world was at the mercy of pathological sadists and liars. No wonder it sometimes felt like being trapped in a room from which there was no escape. No wonder *Le Jour se lève* [90] has been seen as such a powerful metaphor for its time.

* * * * *

The period of the German occupation and the Vichy government has almost certainly received more attention from film historians than any other in French cinema history. Partly this is because of the almost prurient delight some take in reopening the sores. For left-wing writers, it is agreeable to remind the Right of past misdemeanours – the complicity of the French police, for example, in the deportation of Jews. Jeancolas (1983) and Prédal (1972) remind us that anti-semitism was already present in 1930s French society.

Others have felt an ambiguous attraction to the period: the novels of Patrick Modiano, for example, use for literary ends the themes of disloyalty and sexual and political corruption which carry over from the financial and social scandals of the 1930s; his script for Louis Malle's *Lacombe Lucien* [49] is bathed in this atmosphere and, if the period of the Occupation can be seen as a continuation of the struggles of the 1930s, so the various reinterpretations of the Occupation and the Resistance, from *La Bataille du rail* [35] onwards, are the extension of its political conflicts up to the present.

In 1939, a number of films, including *La Règle du jeu* [58] were banned as 'depressing, morbid [and] immoral' and, with the Occupation, censorship of films became exceptionally strict. From 1940 onwards, there were regulations demanding that cinema proprietors should exhibit notices on the screen, announcing measures against anyone demonstrating with laughter or catcalls during the newsreel and threatening cinemas with closure if such incidents took place. Lights were partly to be left on as a further discouragement.

Goebbels strongly believed in the power of cinema and especially fiction films (direct propaganda tending to become counter-productive), but he did not wish, either, to have French audiences attending high-quality films which might give an exalted idea of French culture; so he proposed that the French market be provided mainly with cheap entertainment. 'It is not our job to supply Frenchmen with good films,' he wrote. For this reason he described as an 'incredible lack of political sense' the decision of Alfred Greven, director of Continental Films in Paris, to allow Christian-Jacque to make *La Symphonie fantastique* (1942), which gave far too flattering a picture of Berlioz's achievement.

As far as the industry itself was concerned, the close prewar collaboration between France and Germany in this field meant that there was little difficulty for the Germans in taking it over.

Marcel Carné, for example, had already worked for the German firm UFA on *Quai des brumes* [2] when they obliged him to accept a producer, Grégor Rabinovitch, who was a Jewish refugee from the Nazis: 'business is business',

Carné remarks of this surprising choice which was to cause him numerous problems during the shooting of the film. Returning to Paris in 1940 ('the Parisians seemed to be completely unaware of the presence of the occupier'), he was called to see Greven, whom he found 'shifty, authoritarian and determined to take full advantage of a power acquired for him by others', and insisted on complete freedom in the choice of subjects and that any film he undertook should be shot in France. Eventually, according to Carné's account, this was reluctantly conceded and Greven invited him to his home, in the Rue Beaujon, where he kept open house to guests from the world of cinema and theatre every Thursday.

'I went there, just once . . .' If the Carné memoirs take on a defensive note at this time, and if he quotes with delight Cécile Sorel's reply to the postwar committee investigating her relations with the Germans, it is because, like many others, he was also investigated in the postwar purges. To work at all under German occupation meant compromises, so the tone is defensive. The many gradations of compromise involved can be measured by comparing Carné's fairly relaxed account of his wartime activities with the newsreel interview in which Maurice Chevalier tries to make light of his singing tour in Germany, his habitual *insouciance* sounding decidedly false. Sacha Guitry, in *Quatre ans d'occupation* (1947), writes of his association with the Germans in terms of 'the professional obligations of a man of my kind', 'the natural curiosity of the writer' and, incredibly, his publisher's insistent demands for a further instalment of his memoirs. Ernst Jünger, from the other side, describes Guitry welcoming him to his home and presenting him with autographed letters by Debussy and Octave Mirbeau. Deceptions and self deceptions were inevitable in the circumstances of the time.

One category of films made under the Occupation is easy to define: these are the films of overt, anti-semitic, anti-Communist or pro-Nazi propaganda, relatively small in number, including documentaries made by the Fascist militia, Marcel Déat's RNP or the Légion des Volontaires Français which were given a restricted showing at party meetings. There were also French versions or compilations from German films, like *Le Péril juif* and *Face au bolchevisme*, which got wider exhibition.

As well as these overtly Nazi films, there were others which in varying degrees may be interpreted as supporting the 'National Revolution', the official doctrine of Vichy France. Identification of these is to a great extent a matter of interpretation, since they were mainly feature films, not direct propaganda. The attribution of guilt by association is common among later writers on the period: films like Pagnol's *La Fille du puisetier* (1940) which contains a scene showing the family listening to Marshal Pétain's broadcast of June 17 and praised by *Le Film* in 1941 ('a great film . . . reconciliation in love for the country'), are obvious targets and have led to a revised assessment of Pagnol's pre-war work in the light of the 'National Revolution' appeal for a return to the land and the exaltation of traditional peasant values.

There is certainly a high level of continuity between the films made before the war and those made during the Occupation. Hollywood was out of bounds, but there was an increased demand for the kind of escapist entertainment it had provided, so the period was good for the industry. But an analysis by Jean-Pierre Bertin-Maghit of 140 films made between 1940 and 1944, seeking evidence of Vichy propaganda, yields rather dubious results. It is hardly convincing evidence of the population policies of the Vichy government, for example, that most films deal with young couples (70 per cent aged between 20 and 30) and have a happy ending which implies that they married and had lots of children: these are typical features of the kind of Hollywood films French audiences enjoyed. As for the observation that many of the films involve middle-class characters, often belonging to the liberal professions (especially artists and writers), it is one that could be made of most periods in French cinema: the middle classes and the liberal professions are 'transparent' elements, like the couple who live happily ever after.

The same is true of most other themes which Bertin-Maghit identifies: a contrast between sincere and insincere love related to the purity of women and the need for struggle to achieve happiness; appeals for social integration and an end to class conflicts; the city depicted as a place of perdition and the country as one of salvation. These themes are picked up from prewar literature or cinema, and offered for acceptance or reinterpretation in the light of circumstances.

Indeed, this continuity is the essence of Vichy. The 'National Revolution', despite its name, was not presented as a violent upheaval, but as return to the traditional values of *travail, famille, patrie*, a slogan that could be equally well adopted by Stalinist Russia, supporters of the American way of life and a host of others. *Premier de cordée* [107] was certainly not made as propaganda for Pétain, and others (*Le Mistral*, 1942; *Patricia*, 1942) may not have been either: to say they were, suggests looking for scapegoats. As for films made before the war, it is playing Vichy's game to attribute Pétainist meanings to them, demonstrating the very continuity that the collaborationist government set out to assert. In any case, the slogan *travail, famille, patrie* needs to be interpreted in a very loose way before one can apply it to *Regain* [103], a rural anarchist film, with a message of 'neither God nor master' which would have stuck hard in the throats of the authoritarian Vichy Catholics.

Most of all, the desire for national survival and recovery to which Pétain appealed, was a legitimate one in 1940 (though it became less so as resistance was organized and as Vichy began to demonstrate the extent of its subservience to the Nazis). There may have been a number of naive people who continued to work in the cinema industry, but there were few Fascists.

Interestingly, if one compares *Les Visiteurs du soir* [17] with the earlier Carné-Prévert collaborations, there is a change: the message of the final image of this medieval romance, with the lovers turned to stone, is one of hope. Their hearts continue to beat. Carné's story is precisely dated ('May, 1485'), but its central theme of the triumph of love and faith, despite the pact with the devil, was capable of a particular interpretation in the light of circumstances. 'What is signed, is signed!' Gilles is told by Dominique, played by Arletty in a medieval version of the sophisticated and cynical women of her prewar films; and the devil (Jules Berry, again in a characteristic role) warns the lovers: 'you may forget your chains ... but I am still here'. These fatalistic pronouncements should, on the model of *Quai des brumes* or *Le Jour se lève*, prepare us for a tragic ending, but here faith triumphs over cynicism and the audience is left with a paradoxical message of optimism.

* * * * *

Around 1960, I was talking to a friend in his room at the Cité Universitaire, and he showed me a group photograph of himself and his classmates from the final year at his *lycée* in Limoges. He pointed to one of the faces: 'He's dead ... so is he.' Like Michel, about four of the young men on the photograph were students whose military service had been deferred; the rest, most of them, were in Algeria.

Writers on the history of French cinema tend to express surprise, and sometimes disgust or contempt, at the virtual absence from films of the colonial wars that divided the country and were directly responsible for the collapse of the Fourth Republic in 1958. While the country was experiencing these traumatic upheavals, the cinema could do nothing better than stare at some previously undiscovered fragment of Brigitte Bardot. To take such a view is to overlook two facts. The first, frequently cited by film directors themselves, is that the censor and producers simply blocked films proposing to deal with sensitive political issues, Indo-China and Algeria coming top of the list, or with those social topics like abortion which are sometimes also mentioned in the indictment against the cinema of the 1950s. Even books on the Algerian war were banned; literature has always enjoyed greater immunity from censorship than film because it appeals to a more select audience and because it is consequently less easily seen as 'an inspiration to crime, propagating immorality, dangerous even to the faith ... endangering the health of the soul', as Louis Salibert wrote in 1921. The case of *Les Nouveaux messieurs* [54] is exemplary: a play allowed for exhibition was banned on film; and the banning of Stanley Kubrick's *Paths of Glory* (1957), describing an execution of men from a battalion in the French Army during World War I that had refused to advance, demonstrates the extreme sensitivity of the censor to criticism of the military. Any film about Algeria that could have been made in these circumstances would have described the glorious achievement of the Legion or the *paras*, as the few films about Indo-China did; and that was not likely to please the critics any more than the cinema's battle to be allowed to reveal another inch of Bardot.

If anything, it was society that was at fault, not the cinema. And the second fact, sometimes overlooked by Anglo-Saxon critics, is society's need to recover from its wounds. The divisions caused by the political confrontations and economic disasters of the 1930s had been reconciled in Britain and the United States in the external alliances and national unities of World War II. British cinema of the war years is a potent expression of this theme: 'we was all one'. In France, the Occupation had greatly deepened the wound and there was a need to propose a myth around the fiction of a 'nation' united in resistance, through such films as *La Bataille du Rail* [35] (with only a few, excluded from this concept of the 'nation', collaborating with the enemy). It was not until the 1970s that the other side of the story could safely be examined. But, in the circumstances of the Cold War and the colonial wars, France was no easy country to govern, even without the added irritant of a politically engaged cinema.

The cinema that the French got, in fact, was the one most likely to heal their wounds and reconcile them to each other. The films of the late 1940s and the 1950s, described in *Cahiers du cinéma* under the disparaging label *cinéma de qualité*, were precisely that: a 'quality' product, of the sort that the French have always prided themselves on making well, like good clothes, good cooking or good wines. The directors, actors, scriptwriters and technicians were masters of their crafts, and, in relying largely on adaptations of novels, they emphasized the strength and continuity of the country's literary achievement.

Contemporary issues were certainly not absent from the films of this period, even outside the work of André Cayatte. Raymond Borde found plenty of relevance in such unlikely places as *Ali Baba et les 40 voleurs* [39] or *Papa, Maman, la bonne et moi* [152], where, apart from the comments quoted in my note on the film, he praises the non-racist portrait of a North African.

If critics were beginning to discover that a film could carry a hidden message about its politics behind the grotesque spectacle of Fernandel singing 'Je suis Ali, Ali Baba', so they were beginning to realize, too, that such meanings could be more powerfully conveyed when expressed in this kind of 'code'. By the end of the 1950s, some were detecting, beyond the conventions of a routine suspense thriller like Louis Malle's *Ascenseur pour l'échafaud* [134], a whole host of messages about France in 1958 (see my note to the film).

The thriller and the gangster film were treated at the time as mere bread-and-butter productions (hence Sadoul's regret that Malle, as a novice director, should be saddled with *Ascenseur pour l'échafaud* just to satisfy his producer's idea of a 'commercial' subject). In fact, such genre films are exceptionally instructive and revealing in relation to society at a given moment. The genre itself is like the framework of a traditional tale, which the storyteller can confidently adapt to fulfil or deny expectations and to suggest different levels of meaning. So a genre film is quite capable of dealing with the same basic material as any other type of narrative: the patient performance of a difficult task is much the same in *Du rififi chez les hommes* [133] as in *Un Condamné à mort s'est échappé* [42]. And, while thrillers, gangster movies and so on are made with a particular purpose (usually to do with pleasing audiences and making money), there is no harm in suggesting that some may owe their appeal to their aptness for their time. *Le Jour se lève* [90] and *Quai des brumes* [2] belong peculiarly to the late 1930s, as *Le Salaire de la peur* [95] belongs to the mid-1950s, with its despairing picture of men trying to escape from exile in a mythical South American town which has the atmosphere of a colonial backwater.

* * * * *

The cinema of the New Wave was the product of a society enjoying considerable material prosperity and at last emerging from its colonial entanglements. General de Gaulle, like Gabin in *Le Cave se rebiffe* [140], had been called out of retirement for 'one last job' and, in the shadow of his autocratic presidency and his 'particular idea of France', the middle classes began to enjoy the benefits of their prosperity, safe, after 1962, from the fear that their children would die on a hillside in the Aurès or a backstreet in Algiers.

The country's growing affluence and self-confidence were evident, and helped to disguise the poverty of some sections of the population. The cinema experienced an extraordinary burst of activity and some films (*Les 400 coups* [169], *Le Beau Serge* [111]) examined the realities and problems of life in Paris or the provinces in a fresh way: comparing *Les 400 coups* to other films of the period, I can think of nothing better than the old cliché that it 'spoke a new language'. Seeing it again recently, I was astonished at Truffaut's ability to capture the details of life in the Paris streets, the school, the small apartment, that were the everyday experience of the less well-off and their children at the time. It stands, for me, beside a quite different film, Chris Marker's documentary *Le Joli mai* [61], as a document for understanding the hidden face of France in the early years of the Fifth Republic.

However, the 'new language' was more often used to record the most visible faces of the country, if only because these happened also to be the most photogenic. The political ambiguities of the New Wave were summarized in the work of Jean-Luc Godard: the censor banned *Le Petit soldat* when it was made in 1960, and on its release three years later, left-wing critics were disappointed to find that the director had not made up his mind which side to support. Most of the new lightweight cameras, often in the hands of film-makers happy to admit that they were not sure how the things worked, were pointed at the new apartment blocks, the stylish interiors and, above all, the Citroëns DS and ID that symbolized the lifestyle of the new class. By the time of *Un Homme et une femme* [78], it seemed that the 'new language' might be contained in a pocket phrase book. Lelouch had something to say about fast cars, lovers on the beach, soft-focus lenses and windscreen wipers, and he said it over and over.

Despite attempts by rival gangs to persuade him to go back to retirement, the Boss clearly had no intention of doing so and there was a pervasive sense of frustration among my friends in the Union Nationale des Etudiants de France. In Strasbourg, the student union was taken over in 1967 by an anarchist group which promptly abolished it and published a pamphlet, *De la misère en milieu étudiant*, denouncing the 'opium of the intellectuals' and the misleading differentiation of equally inane products (Godard and Lelouch were given as examples). Advising students that if they had to read books, they should steal them, and unkindly describing the student class as 'the most faithful customer of theatres and cine-clubs and the most avid consumer of [art's] deep-frozen corpse, cellophane-wrapped in supermarkets for the housewives of over-production', it ended with a call for workers' councils and the outbreak of 'the revolutionary festival': '*play* is the ultimate rationality of this festival, and the only rules it can obey are life without boredom and enjoyment without let or hindrance'.

* * * * *

A year later, the authors nearly had their wish. 'Society is a carnivorous flower,' the walls of Paris announced in May 1968. 'Art is dead, don't consume its corpse.' Godard, described on the same walls as *le plus con des suisses prochinois*, began the process of self-criticism that was to occupy his films during the next 10 years.

The 'events' of 1968 themselves were television 'events' and, although Paris was certainly an exciting place to be in May and June of that year, the country was not slow to realize that revolution had passed it by. De Gaulle survived, to be succeeded in an orderly fashion by Georges Pompidou, then by Valéry Giscard d'Estaing. History, a character in a novel of the seventies remarked, seemed to be happening elsewhere.

The 'events' had not achieved what their instigators wanted, but they had not been entirely fruitless. Flanked by a powerful reactionary Right and a host of *groupuscules* on the Left, the Socialists and Communists concentrated their minds and united behind a joint manifesto, recalling the days of the Popular Front (a point made in Chris Marker's 1977 documentary *Le Fond de l'air est rouge*). There were benefits for education, the feminist movement, the ecologists. Most of all, there was a sense of *contestation*, a feeling of hostility to the establishment and anger at the awfulness of the world and the mess that had been made of it. Jeancolas (1974) underlines the conformity of the cinema under Pompidou, pointing out, for example, the 1930s archetypes which recur in films like Pierre Richard's *Je sais rien, mais je dirai tout* (1973) and the limits which the opposition appeared to accept; but noting that there was a much greater willingness to locate films in a real present, rather than the 'vague contemporary' of earlier times. But he observes, too, what is excluded from this: leftists and peasants, minorities and immigrants, and the *marginaux* of every description. By the end of the decade, there was a growing body of films dealing with the fringes of French society or offering a radical critique of society.

45

It would be wrong to exaggerate, however. There was also the matter of distribution and audience. The vast majority of people still went to the cinema for an entertaining night out, not for a hard look at social or political problems, and flocked to see Louis de Funès [183], rather than the latest Claude Faraldo [8]. By the mid-1980s, the cinema had certainly gained in scope. Film-makers dealt broadly with a range of social issues [163], attacked received ideas and dogmas [70], absorbed the lessons of contemporary sociology and historiography [27], examined the lives of the working-class, of women [161], of the family [162], of farmers [109] from a convincing and original point of view, and made works that defied classification in their effort to convey a variety of experiences [9].

In the main, the films of the 1980s, despite the economic depression, expressed the outlook of a prosperous, confident society. The *rétro* fashions of the early seventies had vanished and there was little of the dreamy nostalgia which seemed to afflict the British cinema revival of the same period (in *Chariots of Fire*, *A Private Function*, *The Weather in the Streets*, and a host of others, as if to be truly 'British' meant to live at some earlier time). But combining popular appeal, technical quality and social analysis usually meant working within a tested narrative genre; and, as it had been 30 years before, the most prominent genre in the 1980s was still the crime story or police thriller which could be adapted for formal experiments [10, 148], social analysis [116], political allegory [149], to show an alternative society [126] or to support the existing one (Maurice Pialat's *Police*, 1985). The cinema of the eighties certainly gave a rounded portrait of a country which might, or might not, be an accurate representation: it depended, as it always had, on which of its many social and geographical communities constituted your particular idea of France.

3 Geographies

'*J'ai deux amours: mon pays et Paris*', Joséphine Baker sang in what was to become her theme-tune, referring to her origins in the United States and to her adoptive home. But for a French man or woman, *mon pays* can have a variety of meanings, according to context. For François, in Claude Chabrol's film *Le Beau Serge* [111], *mon pays* could mean France, if he was speaking to a foreigner. In conversation with a Parisian, it might refer to the region of *le Limousin* or, less probably, to the *département* of Creuse, one of the three that make up that historical region. But for François (and still more for Serge, the provincial who has not taken the road to Paris), it is the little village of Sardent which would be most immediately and most intimately evoked by the word, and a French man or woman who sang of two loves, *mon pays et Paris*, would convey a quite different message from Joséphine Baker's: affection for Paris, as the capital city, a shared possession of all French people; and loyalty to some provincial homeland, *mon village, mon pays, mon petit bled*. There were many, and not only foreigners like Baker, who considered Paris as a second home.

There has always been movement from the countryside to the capital, but in France, where the proportion of the population employed in agriculture stood at over 40 per cent in 1910 and remained at over 35 per cent in 1945, the change from a largely rural to a decisively urban society came late in comparison with other industrialized European countries. It took place, in fact, within the period of cinema history and one would expect this fundamental social change to be reflected in cinema.

It is, but obliquely. The drift towards the town almost inevitably involves the younger, the more ambitious or the better-educated part of the population and it is these new urban-dwellers (François rather than Serge in Chabrol's film) whose lives find a reflection in cinema. Film, for reasons of production and of distribution, is an urban industry. The Provençal studios founded by Marcel Pagnol in the 1930s are an exception: the vast majority of French films have been produced in the Parisian suburbs from where they can call on the designers, technicians and actors who also, in the majority, make their base in the capital.

This does not entirely explain the use of Paris as a setting. In films made before the late 1950s, important exterior shots were not filmed on location, but on lavishly constructed sets. Marcel Carné got Alexandre Trauner to simulate

47

the district around the Canal Saint-Martin outside the studios at Billancourt for *Hôtel du Nord* [120] and to build a replica of the Barbès métro station at Joinville for *Les Portes de la nuit* [37]: both were within a few miles of the actual sites. It was not convenience of location work that determined the choice of Paris as a setting for films in this period, but another form of 'transparency'. The décors for the two Carné films just mentioned are celebrated because they reproduce precise Parisian locations, but most 'Parisian' films cannot be identified with one particular quarter of the city. The action takes place mainly in 'typical' streets, with cafés, shops, perhaps a market, perhaps some street furniture like a news-stand or the *colonnes Morris* which carry advertisements for theatres and concerts; or in a 'typical' six- or seven-storey apartment block, around a central courtyard. This apartment block, in *Sous les toits de Paris* [118], provides a microcosm of society; its stairway, in *Les Portes de la nuit* [37], *La Belle équipe* [87] and *Le Jour se lève* [90], its courtyard in *Le Crime de Monsieur Lange* [88], serve as meeting-places for the characters or concentrate the drama; its age and eccentricities are exploited in *Mon oncle* [76] as a source of visual humour and a symbol of a traditional way of life. The Paris of these films is perceived less as a city different from other cities, than as a universal urban environment where workers, bourgeois, aristocrats, shop-keepers, writers, criminals and kind uncles live, but not peasants or provincials. This almost invisible version of Paris is the natural setting for the diverse characters that most interest French cinema.

* * * * *

Between this 'normal' human habitation and a place where human life is absent (for example, up a mountain in the Alps), there is a range of inhabited locations. These are the countryside and the provinces, where one or two cities (Marseilles, Lyon, Bordeaux) acquire a distinctive character. In the main, however, they exist primarily as generalized 'provincial' settings and the countryside is defined by the absence of features that characterize the town. In short, the norm (against which an increasing number of films made since the late 1950s appear, however, as deviations), defines Paris as the place where people live when they are not to be considered primarily as 'characters', 'provincials' or 'countryfolk'.

Not that Paris, and the ordinary life it represents, is necessarily depicted as an ideal. The theme of escape pervades French cinema. In *Le Crime de Monsieur Lange* [88], where the Parisian story is encapsulated in flashback between the scenes on the border, we understand that Lange and Valentine are fleeing not towards a better place, but towards a future time when social justice, not capitalist law, will govern France. But this optimism is rare. A host of films from the 1930s onwards centre on the idea of escape to an unattainable paradise: the remembered tropical islands which bring together the lovers in *Les Portes de la nuit* [37] or the 'elsewhere' towards which Gabin struggles in *Pépé-le-Moko* [32], *Quai des brumes* [2] or *Au-delà des grilles* (1949), only to die

48

within sight of the ship that will take him there. The image is reversed in *Le Salaire de la peur* [95] where the 'tropical paradise' turns out to be a kind of Devil's Island and the characters yearn for escape to Paris. But in all these cases, the hopes of 'ordinary' people for a better life are given a location in which they might, were it not for fate or the wickedness of others, be realized.

The tropical island or the unspecified place, outside the reach of the camera, where Gabin can restart his life, are by definition unattainable. The countryside of France, however, can give a tantalizing glimpse of what might be. The lovers in *Casque d'Or* [130], Becker's tale of the underworld and demi-monde at the turn of the century, have to leave Paris: in self-defence, Manda (Serge Reggiani) has committed murder and he is wanted by the police. After meeting Casque d'Or (Simone Signoret) by the river, he goes with her to a farm near Joinville where they can hide out in safety.

The next morning, Casque d'Or wakes alone; but she is reassured by the sight of Manda's bundle on the chair. In the courtyard, Madame Eugène is doing her washing. A change of scene reminds us that the police investigation continues, but the lovers meet, walk through the woods and, returning to the town square, hear music from the church. It could be a funeral, Manda suggests. But it is a wedding. 'Do you love me?' Casque d'Or asks him as they go inside.

They leave the church, its bell now tolling ominously, and meet Félix who tells them that Manda's friend Raymond has been arrested for the murder. That night, Manda ponders whether to return to Paris and give himself up. The next morning, Casque d'Or wakes to see that his bundle has disappeared. Their idyll is over.

The Joinville episode is all the more isolated by its parallels and contrasts with respect to the rest of Becker's film. The simple happiness and wisdom represented by Madame Eugène (an idealized figure of a countrywoman at peace with herself and the world) or the bride and groom in the church, are placed firmly beyond the reach of Manda and Casque d'Or, both in location and in time. Regardless of the period in which the film is set, they signify a past way of life and in this, as in many other films, the church, facing a village square, is made the focus of traditional values, but values which no longer apply to the 'ordinary' urban environment. Indeed, the church porch, with worshippers coming and going from mass, serves as a gateway to this now alien way of life. The lovers in *Casque d'Or*, aspiring to its promise of peace and respectability, hovered just inside; Mouchette [113], rejected by the village community, passes in front of it; François, in *Le Beau Serge* [111], sits on the church steps, talking to the priest who reminds him of his lost vocation; and in *Biquefarre* [109], a character remarks on the emptiness of the church square which, in the days of *Farrebique* [108], 36 years earlier, was a crowded meeting-place after mass. The camera, in these and other films, studies the coming and going of people through the church porch (usually old women in black) from the point of view, literally and metaphorically, of an 'outsider'. There is even an attenuated version of the same idea in *Sans toit ni loi* [163] when Mona is left sitting in the car while Madame Landier goes to attend a conference of agronomists.

'You said we'd go and pick lilacs at Easter,' Françoise (Jacqueline Laurent) tells François (Jean Gabin): the countryside as a paradise for urban workers can be evoked, in this case [90], by a greenhouse, but a car horn interrupts the conversation and brings them back to reality. In *La Grande illusion* [34], the German farm is a refuge not from city life, but from war and the class, national and racial distinctions that lead to it. '*Her* German, I can understand,' Gabin tells Dalio, as he starts to fall in love with the widow in whose house they are hiding. The unchanging work of the farm and the continuity of the natural environment across the artificial boundaries erected by men (the two prisoners cannot be sure precisely when they have reached the Swiss border), suggest an uncorrupted, prelapsarian world which in *La Faute de l'Abbé Mouret* [66] is a literal paradise, a walled garden untouched by guilt and sin.

This myth of the Fall of Man and of expulsion from paradise may be given very divergent meanings within the same formal structures: hence the confusion between the Vichy nationalist ideal of a return to the soil, expressed in some films made during World War II, which was an essentially reactionary yearning for a particular idea of 'peasant' France; and some prewar films, like those which Marcel Pagnol made from stories by Jean Giono, proposing a form of rural anarchism, *ni Dieu, ni maître*, with totally different implications. Both, admittedly, start from a premise of the corruption of city life inspired partly by the experience of France's industrial revolution and, more immediately, by the political and financial scandals of the interwar years. But they proceed to very different conclusions. In *Angèle* [100] and *Regain* [103], a girl is rescued from urban degradation to start life anew in the Provençal hills: the title of the second film means literally 'aftermath', the grass that grows in a meadow after the first mowing; but more commonly 'revival', 'renewal' or 'recovery'. As Gedemus, Fernandel is a comic figure, a knife-grinder who believes in 'progress', and he serves to bring together the couple of Panturle (Gabriel Gabrio) and Arsule (Orane Demazis) who will ultimately revive the life of the abandoned village of Aubignane.

In *Regain*, it is this couple, with their rejection of all social restraints, who are the 'real' characters: the closer the other participants get to the city and to society, the more 'unreal' they become and the uniformed characters (the station master, the gendarmes, the *garde champêtre*, the seed merchant) are mere puppets, alienated from the natural life of hard work and the open air. 'On the whole, dress for obedience is not dress for work,' Panturle remarks.

Rebuilding the church in Aubignane never enters Panturle's scheme of things: *Regain* belongs to a current in French provincial and peasant life largely neglected in literature and cinema, and only recently given its proper weight by historians. While in certain regions (e.g. Brittany) the peasantry has been Catholic and conservative, there are others which have a long tradition of revolt, ignored by the Right because it did not conform to an image of Catholic

France, and by the Left because it deviated from the Marxist assessment of the peasantry as a potentially unrevolutionary class, Marx himself being as dismissive of 'the idiocy of rural life' as he was of religion, 'the opium of the people'.

* * * * *

As Maréchale tends the 'German' cows in *La Grande illusion* [34], he is led inevitably to think of his grandfather's cows in France, and for Pagnol, too, the 'rural paradise' belongs as much to the past of childhood and grandparents as to the better world of the future. The reverse of the 'rural paradise' is the 'rural slum' depicted in such films as *Goupi-Mains-Rouges* [105] and *La Fiancée du pirate* [158], where country life is backward, repressive and hidebound by tradition. In short, the countryside is much like childhood, combining the contradictions of innocence and freedom from social constraints with the repressive control exercised by parents and grandparents. And, given the 20th-century migration from country to town, it is at least plausible that for many people the countryside should have some of these associations with childhood and the past.

Take the example of Pagnol whose father's weekend cottage in the hills (as he recounts in his fictionalized autobiographies) provided the family with a refuge from the confinement of Marseilles. Pagnol senior was a primary-school teacher, one of the *instituteurs* created in the 1880s by Jules Ferry with the introduction of universal primary education who went into rural communities as missionaries for republican and lay values. In the town, the conflict between State and Church over education could be ignored, but in a small country parish, the *curé* and the *instituteur* often confronted each other across the same market square.

Who gained the upper hand depended largely on location. In the West, the Catholic and Royalist counter-revolution of the Vendée in the 1790s remained a vital memory into the present century. In the southern *départements* of Hérault, Tarn, Vaucluse and Bouches-du-Rhône, the Restoration 'White Terror' left a strong republican tradition which survived and is still reflected in electoral terms. Further distinctions can be made between small peasant proprietors, who would vote according to conscience, and tenants of large landowners, who often voted with their landlords. The rural ideal in the films of Pagnol is not so much one of a simple return to nature, as of the liberation of rural society from town, Church and large landowners, viewed in the light of the strict republican morality of Pagnol's father and the happy memories of hunting and wandering across the Provençal hills.

Pagnol was in touch with one strand in the complex ideological geography of rural France, and was able to express it because of his love of the countryside, his family background and his acquaintance with the work of Giono who turned to a rural, anarchist ideal as a result of his experiences in World War I. But, like Pagnol's Marseilles film studio, this identification of and with a particular region is a rarity and the increasing urbanization of the country meant that fewer and fewer film-makers (with the exception of Chabrol and Rouquier, discussed below) would have such direct associations with regional and country life.

The introduction of paid holidays by the Popular Front government of 1936, as well as offering the urban worker the means to realize his dream of lilac-picking, gradually brought the countryside back into the cinema in a new role. In the postwar period, *Les Vacances de Monsieur Hulot* [110] and *Le Blé en herbe* [168] virtually abolish the specific features of Brittany; the location becomes an anonymous middle-class seaside resort. Much the same had happened to the Mediterranean coast some 20 years earlier in such films as *Pension Mimosas* [102], though the clientele is naturally richer; and it was to happen 20 years later, again to Brittany, in *Pauline à la plage* [82], except that here the characters live in second homes: they are no more part of the region, or more interested in it than Monsieur Hulot; they just own more of it. Already, by the 1950s, Antoine Doinel's longing to see the sea [169] marks him out as an underprivileged child. The privileged majority saw provincial France in August and as tourists.

* * * * *

You do not have the feeling that the prewar Pagnol-Giono films are addressed primarily to an audience of town-dwellers and this is something else that differentiates them from most of the films of Vichy. *La Terre qui renaît*, *Jardin sans fleurs* and *Croisade de l'air* (all made in 1942) define themselves by their subject-matter as films reacting against rural depopulation and small families, or in favour of Pétain's policy of giving city children a country holiday. The restriction of wartime cinemas to one feature film per programme encouraged the making of documentary 'shorts', and these, too, tend to depict rural craftsmen, implying an audience not familiar with their techniques and products. A company called 'Artisans d'Art du Cinéma' made 24 documentaries, mainly on such topics, between 1940 and 1942: the title of one, *Petits artisans, grands artistes* (1942), sums up their message. But the best-known of this type are the documentaries of Georges Rouquier, *Le Tonnelier* (1942) on the work of the cooper, *Le Charron* (1943) on the cartwright. Like other 'artisanal' documentaries and like his full-length works *Farrebique* [108] and *Biquefarre* [109], they celebrate the continuity of peasant life, but, paradoxically, assume an audience which needs the film-maker's mediation to understand it.

In fact, *Biquefarre*, filmed in 1982 as a return to the family depicted in *Farrebique*, no longer makes any assumptions. Its thesis is that, faced with competition inside the EEC, peasants have no alternative but to become *agriculteurs*, or proletarians of the land, and it suggests that they are unable or unwilling to renounce the traditions of individualism that prevent this transformation. Only after a bitter struggle does the central character manage to buy the plot of land that will keep his farm as a viable unit and the film deals convincingly with this perennial problem of *remembrement*, placing the audience in a position where it can understand and sympathize with the farmer's attachment to the soil and his alleged 'greed' and 'acquisitiveness'.

Though the film ends on a note of guarded optimism, the impression it leaves is painfully depressing. Rouquier, whose work seemed reactionary in the context of 1940s Vichy, turns out to have a progressive concern for the environment, in the light of the ecological movement of the 1970s. The fertilizer that we see destroying the wildlife at the edge of the field, poisons the farmer himself when a sack of it breaks open. Piglets drop dead and cows have become machines for the production of milk.

Farrebique and *Biquefarre* were precisely located in the villages of Goutrens and Rignac in the Aveyron, and between the two films Chabrol's *Le Beau Serge* [111] went to the director's own village of Sardent to write an ambiguous morality about the young man who has escaped and the one who stayed behind. With more than a hint of Hitchcockian guilt, it reverses its original thesis of François, the success, and Serge, the alcoholic failure; and, more than for this contrivance, the film is memorable as one of the first to reverse also the established formula, making Sardent the tangible location in which 'real people' live, and Paris the illusion.

Ultimately, however, in this as well as in his later films, Chabrol turns out to have a town-dweller's view of provincial society, exploiting the secrets behind the surface of village or small-town life in his thrillers just as, say, Agatha Christie used English village settings for the same purpose. However precisely they are located (*Poulet au vinaigre* [116], for example, acknowledges the participation of the inhabitants of a particular village in south-east France), most audiences perceive such films as taking place in a generalized 'provincial' environment. And the increased use from the 1960s onwards of colour film-stock has introduced a new variant on the idealized rural setting. Jeancolas (1979) praises *La Veuve Couderc* [115] for its attention to the Burgundian landscape, but it is doubtful whether the film brings its audience any closer to the reality of the place. A church, with sunlight and shadow revealing the different tones of the surface, suggests beauty unchanged since the Middle Ages, only to recall the images in medieval illuminated manuscripts, the paintings of Courbet or the Impressionists. Human figures become passers-by, hardly distinguished by accidents of dress from their ancestors 500 years earlier and the traditional women in black make their way to church or to market. As with Chabrol's references to Hitchcock, art intervenes even in these later perceptions of rural life.

* * * * *

Two films may sum up aspects of the representation of the countryside in French cinema: Louis Malle's *Lacombe Lucien* [49] and Bertrand Tavernier's *Un*

Dimanche à la campagne (1984). The first of these subverts the proposition that rural life is either paradise or slum, by depicting it in terms of both stereotypes.

The film is set in and around Toulouse during World War II. When we first see Lucien he is in his parents' farmyard, killing a chicken, and the archetype of the brutal, ignorant peasant boy. This image seems to be confirmed when, after the local *instituteur* has rejected his overtures to the Resistance, he joins the Fascist *milices*. In the tawdry society of these collaborators, he discovers a sense of power and self-importance, apparently as indifferent to the interrogations going on in the basement as he was to the spectacle of the headless chicken running about the yard.

His 'work' brings Lucien into contact with M. Horn, a cultured Jew who lives with his mother and his daughter in an apartment that expresses the refinement of the *haute bourgeoisie*: Lucien fingers the art objects that symbolize this culture as if they had arrived from an alien civilization.

The transformation starts when Lucien falls in love with M. Horn's daughter. Her race means nothing to him, his Fascism going no deeper than his commitment to the Resistance. His ignorance becomes simplicity, his simplicity innocence, and as the war ends the two lovers escape to the mountains to enjoy one of those brief rural idylls which are a cinema cliché. The story of the Fall is thus reversed and Lucien absolved ('innocented', in Franglais) before a brief title on the screen tells us that he was arrested, tried and executed as a collaborator. Faced with this compound of two modes, reversing the usual story, audiences and critics found the film ambiguous and were unsure about its political message.

As for *Un Dimanche à la campagne*, one can just imagine a particular type of spectator emerging from the cinema: 'the colour! A painting by Monet!' 'The interiors: pure Vermeer!' Tavernier's film makes continuous reference to painting through its use of colour and photography, and concerns in fact a painter, now an old man, entertaining his son, daughter and grandchildren at his country home. It is the period before World War I, the son is a conventional family man, the daughter a modern young woman preoccupied with a tormented love affair. The old man just wants to preserve harmony for what he realizes may be one of their last Sundays together.

Tavernier gives us all the elements a Parisian audience would associate with the countryside: interpreted primarily through the perceptions of painters, it means peace, childhood, nostalgia, family and the past. Above all, perhaps, it means food. After all, France is a major agricultural producer and all those market vegetables, meats, wines and cheeses start way beyond Les Halles ('how can you govern a country which has over 300 cheeses?' De Gaulle is supposed to have asked). Appropriately, the characters in Tavernier's film never seem to stop eating. The housekeeper, Mercedes, usually appears up to her elbows in flour or at the chopping board. The old man's appetite may be flagging, but he does not forget to invite the others for lunch, dinner or a snack. Indeed, the only crisis in an understated film comes when the daughter

54

threatens to drive back to Paris early, to see her lover, which might spoil the dinner *en famille*. The table around which they eventually eat symbolizes their re-found unity.

A tarragon omelette, in Renoir's *Une Partie de campagne* (1936) is a work of art. An ability to appreciate a potato salad, properly made, in *La Règle du jeu* [58], is more important than the right family background. For Renoir, both as a director and as a character in his films, attitudes to food can indicate anything or everything. Early in *La Règle du jeu*, when Octave (Renoir) refuses breakfast, it is a sign of distress. Bit by bit, the misunderstandings that have disturbed him are resolved and he begins to accept what eventually grows into a substantial breakfast, decidedly more English than continental in menu terms.

Though food continues to occupy a central place in social life, Renoir's gargantuan enjoyment came, with time, to look like over-indulgence. Ferreri's *La Grande bouffe* (1973) took criticism of Western appetites to sickening extremes, but reaction had set in some time earlier. Office workers used to have a two-hour lunch break, this being the minimum necessary to progress through hors-d'oeuvre, main course, salad, cheese, fruit and wine that, until the arrival of *le fast-food*, was considered essential to sustain life between a light breakfast and a heavy dinner. Women would traditionally devote much of the day to family meals, planning, shopping and cooking. The further one got from the fast-moving and 'artificial' centre of urban life, the older one was (young people were able to manage with the tin plates of student restaurants, though they still got five courses on them), the greater the part food would play in one's life, both as a preoccupation and a time-consumer. To the Parisian, the provinces have always offered the supreme attraction of regional cuisine, from the Provençal magnificence of the Oustaù de Baumanière in Les Baux to the solid Alsatian *chou croute* or the Breton pancake, peasant food elevated to a regional delicacy. Exotic cuisines may be sampled in Paris, as can regional specialities, but they are better enjoyed *sur place*.

Clearly, the pressures of modern life conflicted with the total gastronomy of Renoir (food as the measure of all things), and by the 1960s reaction had started to set in. The 'modernity' of the characters in Lelouch's *Un Homme et une femme* [78] lies partly in their preference for fast cars over slow dinners. When Jean-Louis, Anne and her two children meet in a restaurant, the table carries nothing more enticing than a vase of flowers, some hors-d'oeuvres and a salad: a presage of *la nouvelle cuisine*, perhaps, but hardly a feast. They toy with some shrimps, which the children refuse, and there is a discussion about tomatoes. Before we know where we are, Jean-Louis has lit a cigarette and the waiter is clearing the table. As Tati observed in *Mon Oncle* [76], the postwar bourgeoisie was starting to show an American concern with health and hygiene, and is more likely to be seen picking at appetizers or mixing drinks, than sitting down to enjoy a sumptuous dinner.

Sharing food still remains important, however. Sleeping together may be just another episode in the sex war, but eating together signifies harmony. Father and son trying to get by in the kitchen of *Les 400 coups* [169], in the absence of the mother, the 'natural' provider, who is gallivanting around; father and daughter dining in a restaurant in Alain Cavalier's *Un Etrange voyage* (1981), to denote their reconciliation; the 'children' in *Les Enfants terribles* [167] teasing the guests in the restaurant at the seaside hotel or discovering the erotic possibilities of crayfish; the marriage feast in *Gervaise* [96]; the members of the co-operative around the table in *Le Crime de Monsieur Lange* [88]; the bourgeois dinner in *Subway* [126]; these, and innumerable other examples, indicate some of the many meanings food can acquire, its obtrusive presence in the films of Renoir and its virtual absence from those of, say, Bresson and Godard, suggesting polarities of sensuality and austerity, physicality and intellectuality.

* * * * *

The countryside of *Un Dimanche à la campagne* might be pleasant to look at, a provider of good things and somewhere to pass the weekend, but only an old man, too tired to paint, would want to live there. The life of a provincial town did not even have those advantages in Henri Decoin's *Les Inconnus dans la maison* (1942), in Clouzot's *Le Corbeau* [106] and *Les Diaboliques* [132], in Chabrol's *Le Boucher* [114] and *Poulet au vinaigre* [116] and in a host of other thrillers with provincial town settings, down to the Franco-British co-production *Les Louves* (1985), directed by Peter Duffell and set in wartime Lyons. Inquisitive and sometimes murderous old women seem to be the principal inhabitants of these places. Though it is true that with time they have become more specific as to location, Tavernier's *L'Horloger de Saint Paul* (1974) or Chabrol's *Les Fantômes du chapelier* (1982) not only recall those Vichy films about rural crafts with the watchmaker and hatter in their titles, they also find provincial town life interesting chiefly because it seems a good setting for murder. Some Frenchmen may have objected to the implications of the German title given to *Le Corbeau* [106] – 'A Small French Town' – as if what the film showed was true of all such, but French directors have not shown themselves particularly averse to perpetuating the myth.

This is why a few films, including Pagnol's Marseilles trilogy [99] and Jacques Demy's musical *Les Parapluies de Cherbourg* [112], that celebrate the lives of 'real people' in the provinces, are so refreshing. Pagnol loved the Provençal hills as he loved the free, generous and affectionate peasant boy who was his companion (in his autobiographical *Le Château de ma mère*, published in 1957), but they were separated by background and education: Lili, he tells us, left his village for the first and last time to die in Flanders. But Pagnol understands Marseilles society from the inside and while César and the others in his bar in the old port belong to a convention of picturesque regional 'characters', Fanny, with her illegitimate baby, Marius, with his yearning to escape to that 'elsewhere' the dream of which he shares with so many other figures in French cinema, and, ultimately, César, too, as an affectionate grandfather and loyal friend, are universal characters exhibiting universal emotions.

Les Parapluies de Cherbourg may be very different in idiom (all the dialogues are sung on a kind of recitative), but it is remarkably similar in plot. Again, the young girl, pregnant, abandoned by her lover, has to choose single parenthood or a safe marriage to a man she does not love. The film celebrates Cherbourg, as Pagnol celebrated Marseilles, as a real place and since, in Demy's film, the young man goes off to do his national service in Algeria, we are reminded all the more forcefully that these events are not happening in the closed environment of some province, comprehensible only to those who live there, but in a part of France that has shared the country's recent history.

* * * * *

The quaintness of the provinces was precisely what attracted Jacques Tati and, after the country postman of *Jour de fête* (1948), he discovered in Monsieur Hulot [110] the ideal vehicle for his comedy: ungainly, oddly acrobatic, contending with an environment not built for someone of his size or shape, he provides a walking observation post on the foibles of mankind.

The counterpart of the 'rural slum' is the progressive, modern city; that of the 'rural paradise' is an urban environment which is dangerous, dirty and industrialized. When Hulot returned from his holidays, he found Paris threatened and in *Mon Oncle* [76], *Playtime* [125] and *Trafic* (1970), he denounced the threat with increasing bitterness. The films are beautifully made and very funny, full of visual gags that are as out-of-tune with the tradition of French comedy since the arrival of sound, as Hulot is out-of-tune with 'progress'. In *Mon Oncle*, made in 1958, photography and soundtrack point the contrasts between Hulot's old quarter of Paris, housing a perfectly integrated society (almost a fragment of provincial city tucked away in a corner of Paris), and the modern suburb inhabited by his brother-in-law Arpel, an industrialist whose mechanized contemporary home is a monument to pretentiousness, discomfort and soulless lack of taste. Between them, father and uncle struggle for the soul of Hulot's young nephew. They are also struggling for the soul of France.

What Tati stood for in *Mon Oncle* was not the antique in itself. Like any city that has been inhabited continuously since medieval times, Paris retains vestiges of different periods, from the Roman Arènes de Lutèce, through its medieval cathedral, Tour Saint-Jacques, Musée de Cluny and so on, up to the Centre Beaubourg and beyond. What is special about Paris, however, is the city that emerged from the massive restructuring by Haussmann in the 1850s. This Paris was a space which its inhabitants felt was created to their size. It was large enough to contain everything necessary for human happiness (even, if your delusions should get the better of your common sense, the railway stations and later air terminal through which you could escape to some 'elsewhere'); yet it was possible to walk the length of it from the Place de la Nation to the Place de l'Etoile and the breadth of it, after a day or two of rest, from the Sacré-Coeur to the Parc Montsouris. Its 20 *arrondissements*, spiralling out from the centre, were bounded by the exterior boulevards, more or less following the line of the old fortifications. You would not be able to walk these, because of distance and boredom, the dullness of the scenery prefiguring what Parisians supposed was the dullness of the suburbs beyond.

Within these easily-defined spaces, was a public city remarkable for its variety. A tourist coach would take you to the outstanding monuments, recorded in early films by the Lumière cameramen and others or featured in René Clair's fantasy *Paris qui dort* [175] and numerous other films: Notre-Dame, the Louvre, the Conciergerie, the Panthéon, etc., and those post-Haussmann monuments like the Eiffel Tower and the Sacré-Coeur. Each had its accumulation of history. Then there were the different quarters, associated with different pursuits or occupations: les Halles, the Latin Quarter, Montmartre, Montparnasse, the elegant districts, the great shopping streets, the popular areas. Sacha Guitry even made a film recounting the history of France, in a highly romanticized form, through the story of one avenue, the Champs-Elysées [16].

This public city, then, seemed as varied as its inhabitants; but, to those inhabitants, the most striking feature of Paris was its homogeneity. Hunting for somewhere to live, perhaps a cheap maid's room on the top floor of an apartment building, you would emerge from an unknown métro station into streets that were immediately familiar, with the same cafés, little local restaurants and shops, and 19th-century apartment blocks from the top floor of which you would look out through your window onto a familiar pattern of leaded roof-tops. Only as you began to explore this new quarter more thoroughly would you discover its individual charms, the *passages*, the courtyards, steps, squares and parks that made it different from any other.

It is this homogeneity, which allows it to be at once unfamiliar and yet undeniably Paris, that makes it such an attractive location for cinema. It combines the particular and the universal, and never more clearly than in the typical Parisian apartment block. The first French talking picture of real quality, Clair's *Sous les toits de Paris* [118] discovered a city of lovers, *apaches*, workers, concierges, clerks, bourgeois and eccentrics, brought together in these buildings, with their gradations of wealth and status from lower to upper floors, their courtyards and their stairways. The courtyard in *Le Crime de Monsieur Lange* [88], the stairway in *Le Jour se lève* [90], the two together in *La Belle équipe* [87], natural theatres in which a small community can react to a win on the lottery and a blind man stumble across a corpse, provided writers and directors with the opportunity for marvellous inventions. The stairway sees its inhabitants resolving their conflicts as they adjust to the postwar world [37], but can also observe the loneliness of a boy going down to empty the rubbish [169].

These intermediate locations, linking the private space of the apartment to the public ones of cafés, shops, *bistrots*, markets, bars, *brasseries*, workshops and cabarets, may do something to explain the popular bias of French cinema in contrast to that of Britain or the USA. In Britain, for example, the rows of back-to-back cottages provided no overlap between private interior and public meeting-place. Henry Cornelius's *Passport to Pimlico* (1949) and Charles Crichton's *Hue and Cry* (1947) make use of the bomb-sites created by Adolf Hitler's plans for redesigning London, but the playgrounds offered to London children by the Luftwaffe had no history and a brief future. The British pub was, until recently, a largely male preserve and the weather is usually no encouragement to lounge around on the street (*Passport to Pimlico* adopted the pretext of an exceptionally hot summer). A film like Maurice Cam's *Métro-politain* (1938), in which a worker travelling to a building-site by the overground métro thinks he witnesses a murder, could transfer easily to a London setting, using the overground sections of the tube, to be re-made as Herbert Mason's *A Window in London* (1939); but there were no British equivalents to most of the popular or working-class locations around which the majority of French films of this type revolved.

* * * * *

When Jacques Becker made *Casque d'Or* [130] in 1952, though the story was set in the 1890s, he was able to show a Paris that had changed little in the intervening years. He takes pleasure, in fact, in superficial differences: costumes, the riverside *bal musette*, the workman's *bistrot*, Serge Reggiani stepping off the back of a horse-drawn omnibus (in 1952, it would have been the rear platform of a motor bus). Behind these, the fabric of the city is unchanged. Two years later, he used similar themes of underworld loyalties and betrayals in a contemporary context, in *Touchez pas au grisbi* [131], and the two films, thanks to the continuity of the setting, come together as part of a timeless Parisian myth, instead of being divided by half a century of history.

Because of the survival of this fabric from the mid-19th to the mid-20th century, history tends to be perceived as a continuity, rather than as a fracture between past and present. Paris could be 'seen by' Emile Zola either updated, as in Marcel L'Herbier's 1928 version of *L'Argent* [72], or left in the original period, as in René Clément's *Gervaise* [96], without losing authenticity or relevance. The urban environment of Zola's Paris was easy for film-makers to recapture and for audiences to accept. Zola's novels were, in fact, popular with film-makers from the early years of the century: *L'Assomoir*, as well as Clément's adaptation, was made in 1909, *Nana* by Jean Renoir in 1926, *Thérèse Raquin* by Jacques Feyder in 1928 and by Carné in 1953, *La Bête humaine* by Renoir in 1938, and so on. The depiction of the seamier side of Parisian life was also part of his appeal. An adaptation from Eugène Süe's *Mystères de Paris* in the first years of the century and the use of urban locations in the Feuillade serials [117] also imply that just beyond the broad boulevards and elegant residential quarters, within the same space bounded by the exterior boulevards, lies a dangerous underworld where criminals, prostitutes, police and masked avengers lead a parallel existence. This marginal Paris, dramatized to thrill respectable cinema-goers, has remained part of the Parisian myth, from Georges Denola's *Mystères de Paris* of 1912 to Luc Besson's *Subway* [126], a box-office success of 1985.

Subway, like *Métropolitain*, is a celebration of the métro, but of a system that bears little resemblance to the art nouveau railway that endured, virtually unchanged, into the 1960s. In that decade, pressures of transport and population profoundly altered the face of the city. It bowed to the motor car and motorways were constructed around and through the centre of the city. De Gaulle's arts minister, André Malraux, initiated a programme for washing clean the façades of the great monuments. Touching-up was accompanied by rebuilding, first in the huge complex at La Défense, then the Tour Montparnasse and a host of other glass and concrete erections. The market at Les Halles was removed to Rungis, outside the city, and replaced by the Forum, an underground complex of shops and cafés, and by the most blatant legacy of the Pompidou era, the Centre Beaubourg, all paint and pipes, precisely evoking the former President's taste for contemporary abstract art in the sixties international style. The building and the performance area in front of it have proved a success, but the street theatre outside and exhibition areas, libraries and other preserves of high culture inside marked a break with the traditional high and low cultures of Paris. Outside and in, the performers were younger and more international, like the Hollywood-influenced young directors who had made the New Wave in cinema 15 years earlier.

Standing on the Montagne Sainte-Geneviève in 1835, Balzac's hero Rastignac looked out over the rooftops of the city towards the Place Vendôme and the Invalides, to launch his challenge to Parisian society: 'A nous deux maintenant!' From the same spot, 125 years later, he would have seen much the same prospect, with the addition of the Eiffel Tower to the left and, away in Montmartre, the Sacré-Coeur. Another two decades, and he would hardly have recognized the view as Paris. In the vast housing estates of the new suburbs like Sarcelles, he might have doubted he was still on planet Earth. But if the old Paris had appealed to film-makers because of its continuities with the past, so the new one appealed to a new generation because of its ruptures and its international associations. The New Wave directors who wrote for *Cahiers du cinéma* preferred the modernity of American films to the 'quality cinema' of France and their own country was beginning to offer them comparable locations.

Louis Malle's *Ascenseur pour l'échafaud* [134] had already made use of them. Its central character is an ex-paratrooper whose plans for murder involve climbing up the outside of an office block with a rope. This cool modern character is contrasted to the young crook who tries to emulate him but only manages to commit the incompetent murder of a German tourist: unlike

25. *A nous la liberté* (SECA/MARCEAU COCINOR)

26. *Touchez pas au grisbi* (NATIONAL FILM ARCHIVE)

27. *Ascenseur pour l'échafaud*
(NOUVELLES EDITIONS DE FILMS)

28. *La Chinoise* (GLENBUCK FILMS)

29. *Themroc* (THE OTHER CINEMA)

30. *Police* (ARTIFICIAL EYE)

VIII. THE COUNTRY

31. *Regain*   (ARTIFICIAL EYE)

32. *Casque D'Or*   (NATIONAL FILM ARCHIVE)

33. *Lacombe Lucien*
(NOUVELLES EDITIONS DE FILMS)

34. *Sans toit ni loi* (ELECTRIC PICTURES)

IX. THE LAW

35. *Les 400 coups*   (NATIONAL FILM ARCHIVE)

36. *Bande à part*   (NATIONAL FILM ARCHIVE)

37. *Détective*   (ARTIFICIAL EYE)

38. *Subway* (ARTIFICIAL EYE)

39. *Poulet au Vinaigre* (MK2)

X. YOUNG PEOPLE

40. *Les 400 coups*   (NATIONAL FILM ARCHIVE)

41. *Mon Oncle*   (NATIONAL FILM ARCHIVE)

42. *Les Tricheurs*   (SILVA)

43. *Le Salaire de la peur*   (MARCEAU COCINOR/CIC/VERA)

44. *Le Blé en herbe*   (NATIONAL FILM ARCHIVE)

45. *Le Blé en herbe* (NATIONAL FILM ARCHIVE)

46. *Du rififi chez les hommes*
(NATIONAL FILM ARCHIVE)

47. *Poulet au vinaigre*   (MK2)

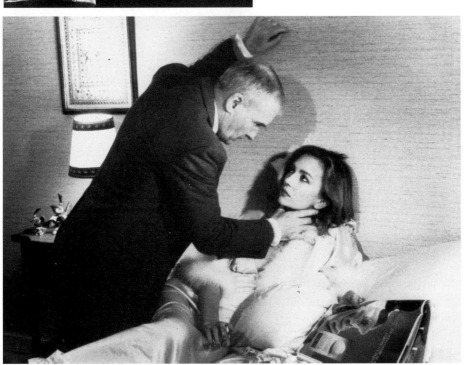

48. *Jules et Jim*   (GALA)

49. *Fort Saganne* (ALBINA/LES FILMS A2)

50. *Subway* (ARTIFICIAL EYE)

51. *Je vous salue, Marie* (THE OTHER CINEMA)

Ronet, he still belongs to the backstreet world of the *chambre de bonne* and the corner florists'. He cannot handle the pressures of fast living. But the old world gets its revenge: Ronet is trapped in a lift when the night-watchman (a former NCO who, to Ronet's annoyance, still calls him *'mon capitaine'*) cuts off the electricity. Colonial entanglements and unreliable lifts (to find one in Paris you only had to look for the words *en panne* or *en dérangement*) were among the frustrations encountered by the smart young technocrats trying to steer France into the fast lane.

Technocracy won out in the end. Gaullist hostility to US economic, social and linguistic influence, in an age of mass communications, was impossible to combine with a drive towards modernization. The take-over by General Electric of the French computer firm, Les Machines Bull, in 1964 had a symbolic as well as economic significance. Even before that, the battle was lost: just as the rediscovery of Hollywood led the New Wave in cinema, so American literary influences led the New Novel: in the 1950s, university students who opted for a degree course in English found that one-quarter was devoted to American literature, so they emerged knowing more about Faulkner and Dos Passos than most of their counterparts in British universities. The chief character in *Subway* is called Fred, the police, nicknamed Batman and Robin, swear in English and the inspector drinks J & B whisky. The Brahms concert at the end of the film is interrupted by reggae.

The thriller moves out of the reassuring comradeship of the Parisian backstreets and into the anonymous, international locations of the contract killer [145], or the confusing styles, multiple references and breathless pursuits of Godard [138, 142, 143]. When it returns to Paris, the old sense of homogeneity has gone. Instead, it discovers disturbing parallel police forces [144] and in quarters like Belleville, exploits the 'foreignness' of the immigrant population [149], for stories of prostitution and drug-dealing, that, in films like Maurice Pialat's *Police* (1985), veer towards racism. The thrill of the Becker and Dassin films of the 1950s was the thrill of being told that the man beside you in a corner bar might be a gangster, even though the bar and the man looked just like a hundred others in Paris. The North African drug-pushers and pimps in *Police* are defined by their difference from the Frenchman beside you at the bar, as well as by their criminality, and they inhabit what the film also defines as a 'foreign' enclave within the city. Wherever you chose to stand, in the Paris of the 1980s, in front of the Centre Beaubourg, in Belleville, in Montparnasse, on the Place de l'Etoile/Général de Gaulle, or watching the traffic on the Quai d'Orsay, you would be struck by the discontinuities with the largely 19th-century city so often celebrated during the first six decades of French cinema.

4 Histories

During the Cultural Revolution in China, a visiting French journalist is supposed to have asked an official what he considered to be the significance of the French Revolution for China. The Chinese Communist thought for a while, then gave his opinion: 'It is too early to say.' Perhaps it is also too late: great historical events tend to become progressively devoid of meaning as time goes on. If you go to Orléans in May and listen to the revolutionary anthem played at the celebrations to honour Joan of Arc, you witness the meeting of two universally recognized symbols from French history. What they mean depends very much on your point of view.

The cross of Lorraine, Joan's province, was adopted by General de Gaulle in 1940, but Saint Joan was also brandished by Vichy as a symbol of a contrary version of national survival. Rouget de Lisle's 'Chant de guerre pour l'armée du Rhin', the 'Marseillaise' as the Parisians called it, has been mouthed by right- and left-wing presidents, each imbuing it with whatever meaning he chose. A country that in the past 200 years has experienced several changes of political régime (five republics, two royal houses, two empires, one commune and Vichy) has an acute need for some national symbols so devoid of meaning that different factions can salute them with a clear conscience.

The first film devoted to Joan of Arc was made by Georges Hatot as early as 1898. The story was well-known from the account in Michelet's *Histoire de France* and from popularization in numerous nineteenth-century schoolbooks, so it made excellent material for silent film. The publication of the records of Joan's trial, and her canonization in 1920, emphasized a rather different figure from the military leader. It is not surprising that Bresson [19] should make a sound film concentrated solely on the trial, but that Dreyer should do so [13], despite the limitations imposed by silent cinema, shows a strong commitment to Saint Joan, rather than Joan the warrior. In the court, the military and their values are all on the other side. There are no battles in the film, and no royal pageantry. The angry crowd scenes at the end make Joan's defiance of authority potentially a call to revolution.

While Dreyer was asserting the rights of this individual against the state, Abel Gance followed a very different course in his version of Bonaparte [12]. In the most celebrated French film of the silent era, the aspirations of the Revolution find progressive expression in the personal ambitions of Napoleon.

The mob is assembled, realized and eventually controlled through its representative, the visionary genius of history. It all reads like the opening of Lucan's *Pharsalia* where the poet, addressing the emperor, proclaims that the disasters and suffering of the Roman Civil War have been worthwhile since they culminated in Nero's glorious reign. The difference is that Lucan was writing in a spirit of irony; Gance is serious.

People of different political persuasions can celebrate Bastille Day and salute the figure of Joan of Arc, without worrying that these national symbols cover divergent meanings: Catholic Joan is incompatible with 'protestant' Joan, the bourgeois revolution with the proletarian one. Wajda's *Danton* [26] analysed the confrontation between the last two through the personalities of Danton and Robespierre, but was perhaps more concerned with answering the question: 'what is the significance of the French Revolution for Poland?' In this respect, historical films are not at all 'safe', though they were one of the few genres encouraged under the Occupation. They speak about the past, but they speak *for* the present, because they speak in the present, though on three different modes of present time. There is the present of the period depicted on the screen, which may be any moment in the past; there is the present of the time when the film was made, which alters perceptions of the past; and there are the successive present moments at which the film is seen by its audiences. An audience in 1986 will be more aware, perhaps, of Gance's Romanticism, but less of the way in which his Napoleon can be 'read' as a type of Mussolini. And if they did see him as Mussolini, it would be Mussolini as the ally of Hitler, a very different plate of pasta from the dictator of 1927.

Nonetheless, the distance of historical events from immediate social and political concerns gives a perspective which allows one to contemplate both with detachment. A shared national past, even one involving civil war, revolution and a struggle between rival concepts of the nation, remains above all a *shared* past; and this perhaps explains why an opinion poll taken in the decade following World War II put historical films top of the list with French audiences.

The further away it is, the more the past can serve to unite. The Middle Ages have been especially popular as a setting for films, in different modes from fantasy [17, 24] to assertive realism [21]. The significance of the Revolution itself may still be a matter of debate, but a national history divided by it into old and new régimes offers an additional bonus: the French royal court can be enjoyed with none of the nationalistic overtones of Herbert Wilcox's *Victoria the Great* (1937). So Bertrand Tavernier's *Que la fête commence...* (1975), set in the Regency of Philippe d'Orléans between 1715 and 1723, indulges in the court tittle-tattle that makes Saint-Simon's memoirs of this period so delightful to read and gives a sympathetic picture of the Regent as a man of relatively advanced views, but does not in any way subscribe to the ideology of his régime. In fact, the conclusion is that the political order he represents is doomed.

64

The nearer one gets to the present, however, the more dangerous certain historical subjects become. There are several major films about the revolutionary period and the Napoleonic epic, and literary sources from the nineteenth-century novel have provided the basis for numerous historical adaptations, as well as the detailed social background for original plots. There is one large gap. The 1970s saw the centenary of the Paris Commune of 1871, three years after it had been specifically evoked by the student movements of 1968. But there have been no major features made in France on the period, only a total of some 10 films, for cinema and television, mainly documentaries and shorts of less than 30 minutes running time (though Jean Grémillon did make plans for a feature-length film that was never produced). In Soviet cinema, on the other hand, there are several films on the Commune, including the massive silent epic *The New Babylon* (1929). The reason why this episode has been virtually ignored in France, despite a good literary source in the novels of Jules Vallès, could be that the Commune has acquired a fairly unambiguous political meaning for both Right and Left. It is an historical subject, but by no means a 'safe' one.

The 1970s saw instead some historical films, for television as well as cinema, which gave a sensitive analysis of politics under the Ancien Régime. Superficially, *Que la fête commence ...*, the television drama series about Mazarin, and others, may have resembled the bedroom history of *Caroline chérie* or *Remontons les Champs-Elysées* [16], but in fact they were concerned with a relationship between personalities and politics which, under the régime of President Giscard d'Estaing, remote and yet personalized by initiatives such as the President's breakfasts with 'ordinary' French families, suggested a degree of cynicism with the process of decision-making. They also demonstrate the continuing strength of the *cinéma de qualité*: excellent scripts, lavish sets, a strong cast. The genre does not usually inspire great originality in technique or interpretation, but it is often a framework for thoughtful and entertaining cinema.

Tavernier demonstrates another feature of cinema history: unlike historical writing, both fact and fiction, film cannot be limited to purely political events, however much it may seem to confine itself to the court. The tragedies of Racine unfolded in a court setting that belonged to classical mythology or biblical story, but found an immediate response in the court of Louis XIV for which they were performed. The cinema is required to be specific, in a way that Racine was not, about details of appearance, costume and furnishings. If it ventures outdoors, it must illustrate features of the landscape and buildings, show crowds and their occupations and, in general, pay attention to the surface texture of everyday life. The realization of historical scenes and dramas was one of the first concerns of cinema and it is perhaps no accident that the medium has developed in parallel with a shift of emphasis in historical writing from high politics to low life. It is hardly possible for a film totally to ignore the lives of ordinary people, and director, scriptwriter and art director will need

65

answers to a host of questions that even the historical novelist can overlook. An historian can write that the treaty was signed, the film-maker must show that the signatories did not use ball-point pens.

Historiography has been one of the major achievements in French writing over the past two decades, involving historical studies that combine meticulous study of contemporary documents with sweeping revisions of the matter of history. These historians, who have grown up in an age of sociology, structuralism and also of the cinema, include writers like Jean Delay, a doctor and psychologist, who has set out in *Avant Mémoire* to study his maternal ancestors from the sixteenth century to illustrate, among other things, the extent of class mobility in a Parisian family from that time. The project which these historians have undertaken finds a direct reflection in cinema. It includes: disinterring local histories to reverse the centralizing tendency of orthodox political history [23], reinterpreting conventional views of the past through structuralist, Marxist or other insights [21, 24], and giving a historical dimension to aspects of human behaviour, such as sexuality and sexual attitudes, previously considered outside the domain of history, through the application of sociological and anthropological methods of investigation to historical periods [27]. Over the past 80 years, film has provided a growing archive of increasing value for both political and social history, and is making a direct contribution to the study of the past; but it may also have played a less obvious part in the way that we interpret historical events.

* * * * *

In a sense, every film is a piece of history. The same reasons (mainly commerce, censorship and convention) that have discouraged film-makers from tackling certain historical subjects, have discouraged them still more from looking at the contemporary political process and documentaries about this are rarer than features, the relaxation of censorship coinciding with television's affirmation of its supremacy in the field (though see [67]). But a fragment of the history of class relationships, for example, can be seen in every film set in the present, however closely it approximates to Jeancolas's idea of the 'vague contemporary'. And, in particular, the way of life and the behaviour of the bourgeoisie have been subjects, often for attack, sometimes taken for granted as 'transparent'.

The majority of French people appear bourgeois to an outsider, but do not consider themselves as such. They prefer to say that they belong to the working-class, or to the *classes moyennes*, the terms 'bourgeois' and 'bourgeoisie' having acquired derogatory connotations, largely because of their use in literature. Usually, the bourgeois is the other, of superior or inferior class depending on the status of the speaker, and especially the representative of conventional society for the artist: 'I call anyone who thinks in a vulgar way *bourgeois*,' Flaubert wrote. The exception is *la cuisine bourgeoise*, good plain cooking which may even be preferable to any other, including *la haute cuisine*;

but feminists would probably consider that when a Frenchman calls his wife *la bourgeoise*, the derogatory implication is still intended.

In film, at least, the outward signs of dress and behaviour that indicate a member of the *bourgeoisie* are seldom meant to flatter. The rural petty bourgeoisie is contrasted with the hard-working peasantry in *Regain* [103] and represented by the seed merchant Monsieur Astruc with his three-piece suit, watch and panama hat. We learn the guilty secrets of the provincial bourgeoisie in *Le Corbeau* [106], *Thérèse Desqueyroux* [77] and *Poulet au vinaigre* [116] – the last being perhaps a sample of *cuisine bourgeoise*. And the Parisian new and upper bourgeoisie has been treated with every degree of contempt from the gentle humour of *Mon Oncle* [76] to the savage ironies of Buñuel [79].

This conventional middle class is often seen as so close to its nineteenth-century ancestor that literary sources depicting the bourgeoisie of the last century are frequently updated, suggesting this continuity (see [71], [72]); the same technique to emphasize class continuity was later used on literature depicting the working class (see [89], [96]). In both cases, this implies a society in which the forces of social control have been consistently monopolized by one group against the other. The link is not one that the ruling class itself likes to underline. When it represents itself, it depicts its behaviour as normal or 'transparent', and its films prefer to show the army through the conventions of the military comedies of the 1930s and the police as Maigret, providing the solution to a mystery for the benefit of the audience, or Louis de Funès, the comic gendarme [183], no more credible than the officer of military farce. The real face of the conservative 'silent majority', and its strength, could be seen at the rallies in support of De Gaulle in 1968, and it was quite unlike its cinema image.

The dominant conservative class is by no means wholly Catholic: there is a strong tradition of scepticism in conservative France which is both regional and historical in origin. But the Catholic Church is, with the army, the police and the ubiquitous state bureaucracy, a force of social control. Léon Poirier's biography of the Catholic soldier Charles de Foucauld, *L'Appel du silence* (1936), illustrated the alliance, but the majority of film directors, Amédée Ayfre remarked in his book *Dieu au cinéma* (1953), seemed to lack any religious conviction. This was partly to do with the Church's narrow view at that time of what constituted a 'religious film'. Film-makers like Delannoy were clearly concerned with social and spiritual themes (see his adaptations of *La Symphonie pastorale* [59] or Henri Queffélec's *Dieu a besoin des hommes* (1950)). But the Church, especially after the experience of the worker-priest movement (see [61]) which had tried to perpetuate the rapprochement between Catholics and Communists or Socialists from the years of the resistance, was wary of any association of religious and social themes. 'In [Dassin's] *Celui qui doit mourir*, all rich people are uniformly bad and all poor people uniformly good,' *La Croix* wrote in 1957, criticizing what, on a literal reading of the New Testament, might be considered an essentially Christian stereotype.

Church and State may sometimes be at odds (as they were over the issue of Catholic schools in 1984 when the Socialist government was forced to abandon plans to merge the two systems). But governments come and go, while the establishment, to which the Catholic establishment belongs, endures.

The Catholic bourgeois is probably more bourgeois than Catholic, and the Catholic intellectual closer to the intelligentsia than to the Church. The intellectual tradition is free-thinking and anti-clerical to an extraordinary degree, in comparison with Britain or the USA. The Church is sensitive to direct attacks on its institutions or its doctrines, as it showed in reactions to *Suzanne Simonin* [63] and *Je vous salue, Marie* [70]. In face of more general anti-clericalism, it is learning the virtue of dignified silence. When you consider the stereotypes of churchmen in British cinema and compare it with the ferocity of Franju ([66], [77]), or the jolly feminist send-up of Catholic and bourgeois conformism in *La Fiancée du pirate* [158], you sense the power of an institution that inspires such hostility.

Catholic intellectuals, sandwiched between their beliefs and the free-thinking tradition of their class, tend towards Jansenism and the austere, individualistic spirituality of Bresson [60], finding nothing more distasteful than the association of religious orthodoxy and political conservatism. For real hatred of the bourgeoisie, you have to read the novels of Georges Bernanos (see [113]) and François Mauriac (see [77]), two Catholic writers who considered hypocritical, devout, right-thinking bourgeois as criminal; atheists were merely unenlightened. After all, Mauriac's preferred adaptation of *Thérèse Desqueyroux* [77] was made by a notorious non-believer. Mauriac collaborated on the script, knowing that his name would help Franju with the censor and the Catholic Office.

* * * * *

The ordinary people of the middle and working classes, among whom the majority of the French would put themselves, were faced during the 1920s and 1930s with three major crises over which they felt they had little or no control. The first was a steadily deteriorating international situation, threatening a repetition of the Great War which had devastated the country. The second was rapid industrialization which appeared to regiment workers, subjecting them to the power of machines and explicitly, in René Clair's *A nous la liberté* [85] compared to imprisonment. The third was the economic crisis, attributed to financial corruption and speculation and, as contemporary reviews of Marcel L'Herbier's *L'Argent* [72] illustrate, considered to be different in type as well as in scale from previous crises.

One line of escape from all these problems is simply to drop out of conventional society, after taking a close look at what it has to offer, like René Clair's heroes or Boudu in Renoir's film *Boudu sauvé des eaux* [73]. The central character in Agnès Varda's *Sans toit ni loi* [163] tries to follow the same route some 50 years later, but the director implies that it is now closed. The figure of the tramp has always been a utopian one and, in fact, the picture that Renoir gives of the real lives of migrant Italian workers in *Toni* [101] is no more rosy than the one Varda gives of North African migrants in her film. Those who really exist on the fringes of society and whose national origin or poverty exclude them from full participation in it, are not to be envied.

The society that Emile and Louis reject at the end of *A nous la liberté* is not only one which reduces ordinary workers to the status of machines, but one where the political system actually encourages corruption. In *Avec le sourire* (1936), Maurice Chevalier plays an unprincipled 'hero' in a world where venality, not honesty, is rewarded, while Feyder's *Les Nouveaux messieurs* [54] and Pagnol's *Topaze* [57] suggest that the worker or lower-middle-class schoolteacher who tries to participate through the system is bound eventually to be corrupted by it. 'There is nothing dishonourable about wanting to be a member of parliament,' a character remarks in *Eusèbe député* (1938), while André Berthomieu's film tends to imply precisely the opposite: Michel Simon plays a simple-minded clerk, elected because of a mistake on the ballot paper and too innocent to realize that Jules Berry is using him to obtain government money for developing the spa waters in 'Sanzeau-les-Bains' as cover for a profitable speculation. Eventually, Simon is happy to be allowed to resign his post and return to his desk, leaving politics to the politicians.

The politicians are a class on their own. At election time, naturally, 'all candidates are for the people, it's more convenient', as one of them remarks in *Eusèbe député*, so, for the time being, they pretend also to be of the working class: 'take off your monocle ... we're sons of the people!' This cynicism about the political process suggests both disillusionment with society as it is, and disbelief in the ability of ordinary people to change it. The strength of the class system in the 1930s is underlined by Albert Valentin's film *L'Entraîneuse*, in which a night club hostess falls in love with the son of a bourgeois. Recognized by the young man's father, who tells her 'you don't mix towels and dishcloths', she returns to her job. The father, a customer of the club, suggests that in compensation for breaking off her engagement to his son, he will set her up as his own mistress.

Even the films of the Popular Front era which may appear to propose a radical critique of the system, often end in only partial solutions. *La Belle équipe* [87] and *Le Crime de Monsieur Lange* [88] find that narrative conventions oblige them to personalize the issues to the point where their message becomes ambiguous: Duvivier's film certainly touches on most of the issues of the time, from co-operative enterprise to political refugees, but ends with a dispute over a woman. Renoir also pleads strongly in favour of co-operatives and worker management, but makes Batala cynical in his personal as well as his business dealings, thus weakening the film's attack on a class that makes a distinction between personal and business morals.

Similarly, the Communist Party's *Le Temps des cerises* (1937), made to support the PCF campaign in the 1937 local elections, starts by contrasting the fate of two children from different backgrounds and contains some memorable scenes, notably the one where an old peasant confronts the local *châtelain* responsible for his wife's dismissal from her job. But it resolves itself into a relatively uncontentious plea for old-age pensions, a reform behind which people of different political ideologies could unite, at a time when the generation most depleted by the Great War was having to support an earlier one, now forming a very visible class of elderly people. In Julien Duvivier's *La Fin du jour* (1939), the inmates of a private home for retired actors, inspired by a trouble-maker (Michel Simon), start to demand their right to participation in running the home (an evident reference to the demands made by workers during the Popular Front period). The director, however, has to tell them that the management has run out of money and, unless a donation is made, the home will close and their 'little family' be dispersed to state-run asylums. 'You don't like private charity,' he announces. 'See how you like public charity, then.' In the end, of course, the 'family' is saved at the last moment and Simon humiliated, the implication being that people of the same 'social layer' (a term which the politician Léon Gambetta preferred to 'class') are happiest together: towels and dishcloths don't mix.

What is remarkable about French cinema of the 1930s is its willingness to study the 'dishcloths' and the sympathetic picture it gives of them. Few British or American films of the time, if one excludes gangsters from the ranks of the working class, treat workers as real people, 'heroes', capable of emotions and aspirations with which the audience is expected to identify. Still fewer see them against the background of their work. The factory in *A nous la liberté* [85], like the one in its successor, Chaplin's *Modern Times* (1936), is a caricature. But the railway of *La Roue* [84] is real enough, if romanticized, and the entire working environment depicted in *La Bête humaine* [89] is a carefully-observed portrayal of the conditions in which railmen worked at the time when the film was made. Gabin, in *Le Jour se lève* [90], is a paint-sprayer who knows something about health and safety at work, and in *Remorques* [91], a tug-boat captain whose personal and working life are seen as activities involving a single character, not as completely distinct. Surprising, too, in comparison with British cinema of the period, is the fact that he has both a wife and a mistress, a luxury seldom allowed in Britain to any outside the upper-middle classes.

When, at the turn of the century, Jules Renard asked Lucien Guitry what work by Victor Hugo he should read to the ordinary people of Chaumont, he was told *Ruy Blas*, because 'peasants are more interested in duchesses than in themselves'. Sacha Guitry, in his films, seems to have followed his father's advice and directors who wanted to make films about the lives of working people were liable to encounter the prejudices of producers who felt that they were 'bad box-office'. Films like *Le Jour se lève* and *Remorques* were made in the face of a prejudice that said audiences wanted to see either the doings of duchesses or those of prostitutes. The censorship that forbade the use of 'bad language' in films, also inhibited realistic portrayal of working-class life. The salon remains the conventional setting for a majority of films, but this may not be entirely the fault of film-makers and if the picture given of French society by its cinema during the 1930s appears incomplete, one should perhaps consider the films being made in other countries and be grateful that the image we are given, despite some stereotypes, often has the power to evoke a credible picture of contemporary life.

* * * * *

Even while asserting this presence of working people in French films during the 1930s, one has to recognize that it gives only a glimpse of working-class culture, and that a romanticized one. An analysis by Véronique and Pierre Sefani (*Cahiers de la cinémathèque*, 23–24, 1977) gave the professions of leading and secondary characters in 47 films made between 1930 and 1939. The Sefanis set out primarily to study female characters, but included males for purposes of comparison. Scientists (13 per cent) and criminals (12 per cent) came top among male leads, followed by artists and industrialists or financiers, then the army/police, politicians, lawyers and journalists. Workers (8 per cent) and tradespeople (6 per cent) came bottom of the list of those with jobs.

Work is the most obvious link between the individual and society, one point above all where the personal history of each among us joins the schoolbook history of Saint Joan, the rulers of the Ancien Régime, the revolutionaries of 1789 and the class struggles of the last century. How we identify with these depends largely on our social position, which decides how we perceive the society and how it perceives us. The postwar films of misbehaviour among young people (e.g. [170]) featured students and the children of the rich bourgeoisie who, because they had no work, could be considered part of a social problem, not a political one. The films of factory occupations after 1968 (e.g. [68]) were something quite different. As Claude Faraldo illustrates in *Bof!* (1971) and *Themroc* [8], the most fundamental rejection of society is to walk out of your job.

It is not an option open to most women in the films of the 1930s. The Sefanis discovered that, in their sample, nearly half (43 per cent) of the female leads had no profession (and a further 14 per cent were students or intellectuals). The remaining categories were represented, in this order, by: artists, tradespeople, prostitutes, spies/thieves, domestic servants (the largest group among secondary characters, after those with no job), workers or shop assistants and charitable workers.

Of course, neither of these sets of figures for male and female workers has any obvious relationship to the real distribution of employment at the time. The jobs given to men (and still more, as I suggest later, those given to women) perform a narrative function, putting the characters somewhere between the people next door and the princes and princesses of fairy stories: a 'typology of employment' among the characters in Hans Andersen and the brothers

71

Grimm would produce far more surprising results. Those in scientific, intellectual and artistic professions are freer to become universal characters, like the ones Eric Rohmer uses in his Moral Tales, and Comedies and Proverbs [82], and to criticize film-makers for wanting to achieve this universality ignores the need for the industry to maximize its audience and denies the right to artistic freedom, which seems a trifle unjust. Taking the official statistics in one hand and your 'typology' of cinema characters in the other, is entertaining rather than informative, because film has more subtle ways of depicting society and social attitudes.

Whole areas of popular culture are certainly omitted from prewar cinema partly because, as 'entertainment' in their own right, sport, music, etc., did not need to be transferred to another medium, any more than later films have felt obliged to depict characters spending much of their leisure time watching television (though Jean Boyer's *Prends la route* in 1936 showed two popular singers cycling around the country, combining popular music with a major sporting and leisure activity). More important than the gaps left by the non-representation of such and such a job or activity, is the impression that, once defined in a particular social role, few characters show any signs of mobility. Those from any section of society may want to get away, they may yearn for the country, or for another country, but it is not often that they succeed in moving upwards or sideways. Dishcloths or towels at the start of the film, they are still hanging on the same peg at the end. Fifty years later, much greater mobility, both social and geographical, is not only possible but often taken for granted. The worker's son in Claude Sautet's *Un Mauvais fils* (1980) comes home after serving a jail sentence in America for pushing drugs. He learns that the economic crisis has made it far more difficult for young people to find jobs than when he left France, but manages to get work loading lorries with some North Africans. One of them tells him that the work is so hard that few Frenchmen can stick it, the implication being that these immigrant workers alone are trapped at the bottom of the pile. Bruno moves on to an antiquarian bookshop and finally gets the job he has always wanted, working with his hands, as a cabinet-maker. On the way, he has acquired a middle-class girlfriend and almost a substitute father in the scholarly, homosexual bookseller who is determined to help him and Catherine to kick their heroin habit.

Bruno's job-hunting is incidental to the main narrative of the film, which concerns his relationship with his father, and so all the more persuasive as an indication of mobility. Even more striking when one compares recent films with those made before 1960, is the obliteration of distinctions between the material culture of the different classes. Of course, there are still great differences between the homes of peasants and those of aristocrats: the peasant boy in Louis Malle's *Lacombe Lucien* [49], as I mentioned in the last chapter, is fascinated by the elegant furnishings in Monsieur Horn's apartment, and the young criminal in the same director's *Ascenseur pour l'échafaud* [134] covets the sports car that he steals, knowing he will never be able to afford one like it. Leaving aside certain extreme cases, however, one is struck by the convergence of taste and means among people of different classes. In the 1930s, it was easy to show social distinctions: art directors put Gabin in a single room with a wardrobe, a cupboard and a bed, pinned some photographs of men with bicycles on the walls, and arrived at the 'typical' unmarried worker's room; the upper middle class lived in 'contemporary' surroundings, with much more space, carpets, glass, objets d'art, cocktail cabinets and so on. Distinctions of taste, style and housing, dress and leisure activities which persist in reality, despite levelling influences, have become less obtrusive on the screen.

* * * * *

In Jean Vigo's *A propos de Nice* [55] and Eli Lothar's *Aubervilliers* [92], there is documentary evidence of the contrast between rich and poor in the 1920s and the 1940s. From time to time we are reminded that the Italian immigrant workers in *Toni* [101] are the predecessors of the inhabitants of the shanty-towns in Nanterre whose living conditions shocked the students living on the nearby university campus in 1968. Some films, like Mehdi Charef's *Le Thé au harem d'Archimède* (1985), make serious attempts to investigate the culture of minorities, but the mainstream cinema is content to exploit its picturesque qualities. When, in Bob Swaim's *La Balance* [149] or Maurice Pialat's *Police* (1985), this means equating it with the drug-dealing, pimping sub-culture of the 'dangerous quarters' of Paris, the result is disturbing. The image of the Arab is no longer that of the noble desert prince who rides again in the final scenes of *Fort Saganne* [52], still less that of the pleasant neighbour who is an incidental character in *Papa, Maman, la bonne et moi* [152], but more alien and considerably more sinister.

Cultured and civilized though it may be, France has not always shown itself especially enlightened in its treatment of social problems. The racism of the 1980s, directed mainly against North Africans, is only superficially different from the anti-semitism of the 1930s. The public execution at the end of *Casque d'Or* [130] reminds us of a practice that continued into the 1930s (and beyond, if you include the executions of collaborators in the postwar purges). The death penalty itself was not finally abolished until the early 1980s, making France one of the last European countries to take this step, though there had been a long campaign in which films by André Cayatte [see 129] and Claude Lelouch [146] played a part with gruesome accounts of the way in which 'the widow' carried out her task.

Criminals, according to the cinema, are not much unlike the rest of us and their society a part of ours. During the war, resistance was a 'criminal' activity and the gangsters of *Touchez pas au grisbi* [131] possess the same qualities of loyalty and courage as *résistants*. What they want, ultimately, is for the war to end so that they can retire to enjoy a peaceful old age. When their counterparts in *Du Rififi chez les hommes* [133] pause to reflect on their ambitions, they turn out to be no more greedy or violent than the rest of us. The Italian Cesare wants the money for his sisters' dowry, Tony le Stépanois hopes to regain his health and his girlfriend Mado and the third member of the gang is concerned chiefly with ensuring a reasonable life for his family. Though they live in an enclosed world of night-clubs, cafés, apartments, empty houses and deserted banks, mixing only with those of their own 'social layer', this lack of contact with ordinary society only serves to emphasize that, far from being dangerous to us, they are eager to break out of the trap and join the audience on the other side of the screen.

The postwar economic recovery brought obvious benefits, but the need to bring together the elements of a society divided by the occupation may have helped to discourage reform of its institutions. The offices of 1930s bureaucrats, and the petty officials themselves, have hardly changed 20 years later. The school yard and the classroom in *Remontons les Champs-Elysées* [16] could be the same that Truffaut uses for *Les 400 coups* [169], with the difference that Guitry is complacent and Truffaut is angry. Women obtained the vote in 1944 and equal pay two years later, but they are still often treated as little more than bargaining counters between the men in the gangster films of the 1950s. This may or may not be true of the behaviour of criminals, but it is bad news if you consider these films as metaphors for politics or business.

As well as employment, the Sefanis also examined the relationships of female to male characters in their analysis of some films from the 1930s. The largest categories were young girls or fiancées, and wives or mothers. About 15 per cent were prostitutes or demi-mondaines, followed by mistresses. There was one Lesbian relationship and a small number of servants or governesses among leading characters, but these, like mothers-in-law and other female relatives apart from mothers or wives, were much more common in secondary roles. Only as actresses or singers could women in these films really hope to escape from dependence on the male characters. Indeed, the relative frequency of prostitutes as central characters suggests that they become more than just a portrait of a single social group, merging with wives and girlfriends to suggest the dependency of most women in a society where men control political and economic power. Older women, in the roles habitually played by Arletty and Françoise Rosay, often have considerable independence of mind and means, but even they seldom take an active part in the development of the plot. The passivity of the younger women is still more striking. When not actually bought and sold, like Orane Demazis in *Regain* [103], they wait, like Jacqueline Laurent [90] and Michèle Morgan [2], for Jean Gabin to liberate them from the dominance of repulsive, but apparently irresistible lovers; what happens to them at the end of these films, after Gabin has met his inevitable fate, seems irrelevant. The only way out of an intolerable marriage is probably murder, the solution adopted by the wives in *Le Dernier tournant* [128], *La Vérité sur Bébé Donge* [151] and several others. If Gabin himself turns out to be a sadistic sex-fiend [89], the outlook is bleak indeed.

Naturally, these films betray some male anxieties about the 'unreliability' of women, who may easily be seduced by the charms of that evident rogue, Jules Berry, or harbour secret thoughts of doing away with the master who, though he looks like a harmless imbecile with a bald patch and a pot belly, enjoyed considerable powers over his wife even after the changes to the Code Civil in 1938. The Women's Liberation Movement of the 1970s has accomplished a great deal, including a change in attitudes, but there is still evidence of masculine insecurity about women's behaviour. In the thrillers of the 1980s, the women pass from lover to lover, as often as not from the criminals to the police. The difference between them and the girlfriends of 30 years earlier, is that they are no longer the subject of bargaining. Charlotte Rampling in *On ne meurt que deux fois* (1985) and Sophie Marceau in *Police* (1985), hop into bed with their respective policemen for just one reason: they happen to feel like it. The genre, and the film-makers, are faintly disturbed by them.

Earlier independent women were often, for the sake of credibility, given professions in show-business or acting, as the analysis of 1930s films by the Sefanis demonstrates. This served, too, as a convenient excuse for bringing music-hall stars into film roles: Edmond Gréville built *Princesse Tam-Tam* (1935) around Joséphine Baker; Christian-Jacque put Baker's rival, Mistinguette, into *Rigolboche* (1936), neither being remarkable films, except perhaps for the implausibility of their plots. In the second, Mistinguette makes her way in life despite a fatherless child and a charge of manslaughter pursuing her from the colonies. What is worth noting is that the fictional show-business career that provides the vehicle for these stars had in real life given them fame and independence. Demazis, Morgan and others might be asked to play passive characters, but Baker and Mistinguette were not actresses – their films prove that, if nothing else – and it is harder to imagine them taking subordinate roles. Older film stars were not only given strong characters because of a stereotype of the forceful experienced woman, but also because they had established reputations. The screen image of an actress or actor is carried over from one film to the next, accumulating meanings and, while films create stars, stars in their turn create films.

In prewar cinema, this took time. But when the young starlets of Marc Allégret's *Futures vedettes* (1955) put on their dancing shoes, they heralded the arrival of a new version of screen woman, young, yet not innocent, independent without either social position or prostitution, who seems to owe her relative freedom from men to a pervasive curiosity about male society that invites her to explore it and to exploit its weaknesses. The year before Allégret's film, Françoise Sagan had published *Bonjour tristesse*: at 19, she could write authoritatively about adolescent girls. And the year after appearing as one of those *Futures vedettes*, Brigitte Bardot achieved the promised stardom in *Et Dieu créa la femme* [153]. The old dichotomies were resolved: young women did not have to be either innocent or prostitutes, and independent women did not have to be middle-aged. There was a possibility that some of these women might, as they grew up, refuse to swallow the story that they did not need political power, since they already exercised power in the home.

* * * * *

The public face of Catholic conservatism worn by the régime instituted by De Gaulle in 1958 and typified in Madame de Gaulle ('Tante Yvonne'), applied one set of values to private morals and another to politics. De Gaulle may have been right to give independence to Algeria, but the army brought him to power on the understanding that he was a supporter of *l'Algérie française*; Max and Tony le Stéphanois would have known how to respond to this apparent betrayal of trust and the gangsters of the OAS saw themselves less as terrorists, more as characters in the movies. De Gaulle responded by setting up the undercover, parallel police whose ends justified adopting the same means as the people they were fighting: the identity of police and criminals in many thrillers since the 1960s comes directly from the reputation acquired by these *barbouzes*. The OAS was certainly evil, like any organization prepared to use indiscriminate violence for political ends, but the purpose of their opponents was more the maintenance of state power than a moral or democratic crusade. In fact, De Gaulle's determination to weaken the parties of Right and Left, and to create and hold a strong, 'non-ideological' Centre established its own morality of power and efficiency, with an undoubted appeal for the technocrats of the new France. They were happy to operate under the umbrella of a well-oiled government machine, not a creaking parliament, welcoming the Franco-German rapprochement (see Raymond Borde's comment on the German businessman in [134]), putting prosperity and energetic action before ideology. Their values are reflected, more than criticized, in Godard's *Le Petit soldat* [45], and show as much in the lack of motivation of the characters in his early thrillers [138, 142, 143] as in the sugary romances of Lelouch [78] or that director's hymn to the brotherhood of man [25].

However, as Godard demonstrated, the technological revolution contained the seeds of its own destruction, not only in its environmental effects [64], but in the bewildering growth of communications which meant that French society was bombarded with simultaneous messages from outside and in. In *Lumière d'été* [75] or *Le Point du jour* [94], Grémillon and Daquin found conventional forms adequate to contain their stories of working-class life and industrial conflict. Godard, for *Tout va bien* [68], starts with a kind of Brechtian political drama about a strike in a textile factory, but by the end we are listening to a lengthy (and, frankly, boring) debate about sexual politics between Jane Fonda and Yves Montand. Self-criticism and criticism of the culture that the middle-class prized as its most valued possession, was not something to be indulged in from time to time, but a permanent state of mind. The events of 1968 could not be confined more than momentarily to the educational system: they involved everything, from the *bidonvilles* at Nanterre, to the Third World, the Vietnam war and the Thoughts of Mao Zedong [6].

Since 1968, it has been impossible to consider French society without at the same time taking into account the international patchwork of *Sans soleil* [9]. It is not so much a feeling that history may be happening elsewhere, as the realization that it is happening everywhere. They were right after all, those films of the 1930s: it is an illusion to think that we can escape from our history if we cannot get to the gang-plank of the ship that is waiting to take us away.

This is the place, as Wordsworth remarked in the context of the French Revolution, in which we find our happiness, or not at all. The word hangs on that episode of French and universal history (often seen from this side of the Channel as merely a bloody episode) like a charm. Happiness is a new idea in Europe, announced Saint-Just before Dr Guillotin's 'widow' claimed him, while the Marquis de Sade, whose concept of happiness was rather special, invited his compatriots to 'one more effort' if they wished to become true republicans. His recipe was as personal as Saint-Just's was political, insisting that republican liberties start, not with a reform of political institutions, but with incest, inviting the children of the Revolution to add a literal interpretation of fraternity to the liberty and equality they had acquired. The policy is still usually considered extreme. In the dull days of the 1970s, however, when political action seemed condemned to disappointment and economic recovery was giving way to recession, it was not only feminists who decided that it was time to look again at the most basic of social institutions, and to suggest that structural reform might start inside the family.

5 Families

'I perspire with anxiety,' Eugène-Marie's mother says in Roger Vailland's *Un Jeune homme seul*, 'whenever his father forces me to let him go to the cinema, because I know full well that bad thoughts are born in crowds and in darkness.' And in 1954, three years after Vailland's novel was published, the *Revue international du cinéma* noted that one-quarter of films on 'love or sentimental themes' had been given unfavourable moral ratings by the Catholic Office du Cinéma.

The films of the 1950s look harmless today, but at the time the anxieties of Eugène-Marie's mother and the Catholic Office were ordinary enough. The cinema frequently encourages 'bad thoughts'. Going there is like going to school: the child is taken outside the family and discovers fantasies beyond parental control.

It is no accident that a large proportion of French films have as their central characters a couple without family ties. Orphans and widows are not unknown in a country which has experienced both world wars and, still more recently, colonial ones. But the orphans and widows, prostitutes, mistresses enslaved by sadistic animal-trainers, or unhappy wives married to war profiteers, with whom the heroes of French cinema up to the 1950s fall in love, have a social status which serves another function: that of freeing them from the imprisonment of family and class. 'There's one person who bothers me ... If I had known he was your father ...', Gabin tells Jacqueline Laurent in *Le Jour se lève* [90]; but Jules Berry isn't her father and, that misunderstanding sorted out, the director is not interested in supplying the missing relative. *Déclassées* by their liberation from the family, these women are free to fall in love with men who, as often as not, enjoy a similar lack of immediate relatives. Past attachments may haunt the widow of *Un Homme et une femme* [78], but only, we suspect, for the length of the film.

It is not easy to make love with mother looking over one's shoulder, unless she is the mother in *Le Souffle au coeur* [172]: in that case, it is hard to know what she might do. The absence of relatives for these heroines (and often for the heroes as well), helps to universalize their situation, or their predicament, but at the same time illustrates the strength of the institution from which they have been released. The bourgeois parents of *Le Blé en herbe* [168] may not be too concerned if their son stays out all night, but bourgeois audiences in 1954

79

were shocked by his seduction of the girl next door. On the other hand, the desire to escape may imply the search for a happy ending which will unite the lovers in a new family to replace the one they have lost (or, apparently in some cases, never had in the first place), so there is some ambiguity in the desire for freedom. The institution is by no means ideal, but we are led to believe that the ideal couple might reform it. The alternatives tried in the more liberal climate of the 1960s and 1970s do not get to the heart of a problem that lies, as Maurice Pialat understands [162], in parents and children being able to redefine their relationship as time goes on.

For young children, the problems are minimal within the traditional family, and only occur when the normal pattern is disturbed: young orphans [164] are entirely to be pitied. Childhood, outside school, is a state of poetry and fantasy: the grown-up 'children' of *Les Enfants terribles* [167], encumbered only by Gérard's benevolent uncle, possess the genius that allows the child of Albert Lamorisse's *Le Ballon rouge* (1956) to transform a drab urban environment. Not that Montmartre was ever that drab, and dozens of French children have played across the screen through its squares and up its stairways, innocently observing its more seedy inhabitants. This child-like vision accuses us, in *Les Jeux interdits* [38], but consoles us, in *Les 400 coups* [169], for present and remembered miseries.

In the teasing games of children we can envy the first rebellion against the prison house that has now firmly closed around us: they play, without malice, in *Mon Oncle* [76] as in *L'Argent de poche* [173], and assert their independence from the class-ridden historical world of their parents. But already in *Un Dimanche à la campagne*, the boys tossing their caps in front of the church and the little girl obediently tending her doll, remind us that there is no avoiding its stereotypes.

Most of all, there is no escape from the inevitability of school. The entrance to the Maison des Examens in Paris, featured in numerous films, symbolizes the fear of failure as well as the promise of success in a meritocratic society. 'Passe ton bac d'abord': the title of Maurice Pialat's film (1979) sums up that long interval between the unknowing freedom of infancy and the enjoyment of adult privileges. French schools built during the past 20 or 30 years are open prisons which disguise their function behind pleasant modern exteriors, sometimes made still more attractive by a government policy which allocated subsidies to modern artists for work on public buildings. Their inmates, wearing no uniform, discovering the compensations of mixing with fellow-sufferers of their own age, seem to make the best of a bad job. Older school buildings are more honest: those rain-swept courtyards, with the corrugated roof of the *préau* offering little shelter and a row of unhygienic lavatories making their special contribution to the atmosphere, lack only the figure of the *surveillant*, the officer responsible for school discipline, to complete the image of a nineteenth-century jail. In the classroom and outside it, they certainly expressed respect for intellectual discipline.

Even Jean-Louis Trintignant, playing a would-be drug-smuggler invented in the course of the film *Trans-Europ-Express* [5], is obliged by the gang for which he works to pass a series of exams and, like a schoolboy, hides his bondage magazine inside a copy of *L'Express*. The train may liberate him from the narrative conventions of the traditional novel and permit him, like Alain Delon and Nathalie Baye who meet on the train in *Notre histoire* [83], to be invented as he goes along, but it is not that easy to get away from one's early schooling.

* * * * *

In extreme cases, Franju says [136], the middle-class family will see delinquency as madness and have the offender put away. In France, as in other countries, the older generation after the war was obsessed with the behaviour and misbehaviour of young people, whether from a working-class background [171] or from the wealthy middle class [170]. The second of these, Carné's *Les Tricheurs*, was an attempt to get inside the skins of the students and *fils de papa* who migrated in the evening from their homes in the 16th *arrondissement* to the cellar clubs of Saint-Germain-des-Prés. They were a new version of Jazz Age youth, lower down the social scale, higher on the scale of car ownership and allegedly more cynical about life and more likely to sleep around. Critics of the film, which was not the success Carné had hoped, found it less daring than it pretended to be, but this relative respectability was shared by the young people it depicted. The family provided a safety net for most of these rebels, as it would continue to do. One of them, no doubt, became the mother in Francis Veber's *Les Compères* (1983) who, when her own son drops out and joins a gang of hippies to be with the girl he loves, and her conventional husband will make little effort to find him, enlists the help of two former lovers (Pierre Richard and Gérard Depardieu) by convincing each of them that the boy is really his son. By the 1980s, the events and characters from the tragedies of 25 years earlier were repeating themselves as farce.

That a respectable middle-class mother, in Veber's film, should have had two lovers at the very moment when she was supposed to be conceiving a child with her husband, is good comic material, like the Rabelaisian infidelities of the baker's wife [104]. The figure of the cuckold has been a farcical one since the Middle Ages and a society long tolerant of men's sexual irregularities, has gradually extended this tolerance more generally, with the vote and equal pay, to women. The behaviour of the girls in *Les Tricheurs* is 'punished'; but fate in Carné's films was never on the side of the deserters and outsiders. And Mic and Clo, daringly modern in 1958, did nothing exceptional by the standards of Cholé in the last of Eric Rohmer's Moral Tales, *L'Amour l'après-midi* (1972) or his later Comedies and Proverbs [82]. The title of this second series refers back to the plays of Musset: their bitter-sweet treatment of the entanglements of love, in which the satisfaction of sexual desire is a necessary episode, but not a central obsession, also reflect the priorities of nineteenth-century Romantic literature.

A more liberal moral climate meant a more ready acceptance that young women might give up their virginity before marriage, but there was no lack of warnings of the emotional risks to these Paulines [82], and occasionally, as in Claude Goretta's *La Dentellière* [98], of the danger of crossing social boundaries to mix dishcloths and towels. Dissatisfaction with the restrictions of conventional marriage also led to the proposal of radical alternatives in films like Coline Serreau's comedy *Pourquoi pas?* (1977) where the three central characters live together in harmony and their example starts to become infectious. Why not? There was nothing very new about this: *La Règle du jeu* [58] had been about the failure of an 'open' marriage. Truffaut's *Jules et Jim* [44] and *La Peau douce* [157] examined the pains and possibilities of the eternal triangle. The anarchic central character in Claude Faraldo's *Bof!* (1971), a close relative of Themroc [8], begins by rejecting his boring job delivering wine and is soon sharing his wife with his widowed father. Having accepted this, the revelation that the father was responsible for his own widowhood (the mother was an invalid, obviously bored with life) is dismissed after a few moments' reflection. In Faraldo's radical revision of social conventions, the baby is first drowned in the bath-water to make sure that everything goes.

In the more austere 1980s, most of the alternatives enthusiastically welcomed ten years earlier were starting to look tarnished. Mona [163] does not find happiness even among the hippies and drop-outs she encounters in her wanderings around southern France: the North African worker rejects her because of pressure from his peers, the hippie farmers demand even harder work from her than she would have to give in a conventional job and the others she meets belong to a violent sub-group of drug-takers and thieves. None of them can offer her the absolute freedom that she seeks. During her brief life, she is envied by those caught in the trap of orthodox society, but ultimately she is to be pitied. Agnès Varda's film joins a long line asserting that the dream of escape is an illusion, to be indulged only in the cinema.

* * * * *

Between this life *Sans toit ni loi* [163] and *Le Destin de Juliette* [161], trapped in a forced marriage with an alcoholic husband, there must be some middle term offering hope for the free couples who outwit fate and settle down after the happy ending. Surely Godard's married woman [156, and 124] is not *all* married women? Does the bourgeois couple need the stimulus of jealousy and murder [80] to survive? Can true love only exist in the criminal underworld of *La Balance* [149]?

There are, of course, alternative kinds of love, though in *Pension Mimosas* [102] and *Les Enfants terribles* [167] these too are a recipe for tragedy. Comradeship can supply support and fulfil some emotional needs. In the cinema, with its bias towards action and violence, this usually means friendship between men; and the preference for romantic themes also often leads to women being presented as rivals for the love of the central male character. But if you read the secondary plots, you can find the occasional recognition of the support that women give to each other, in contrast to this (masculine) image of women struggling for a mate.

As for friendship among men, it is probably prized above any other form of relationship. Its essential quality is tenderness, one that distinguishes the really seductive heroes, from Gabin to Depardieu, from the mere seducers (Jules Berry is the prewar archetype) whose charm is more superficial, based on a way with words, power, money or ambiguous sexual appeal. The solidarity of *La Belle équipe* [87] is more important than any woman. The songs of Georges Brassens (whose only screen appearance was in *Porte des Lilas* [123]) celebrate 'Les Copains d'abord', and it is significant that René Clair's much earlier film, *A nous la liberté* [85], ends on the truly happy image of Emile and Louis free and reunited, dancing away from the divisive influence of money and respectability, singing that the earth is round and you can find women anywhere.

This fundamental tenderness in relationships with others, which one finds in the great screen heroes, is valuable socially and personally. It makes them protective towards women and loyal to the friends with whom they may be asked to face the dangers of war and resistance. They are often in conflict with the state authorities which are too impersonal to command affection: what matters is the solidarity of a sub-group (gang, cell, 'family'), its superiority proved precisely by this quality in its members. We side with Max [131] and Tony [133] because they are prepared to risk their lives for their friends.

Tenderness also creates a set of altruistic values which may be personally liberating: these men are not slaves to sex, money or similar imperatives and, once more, Emile and Louis, rediscovering this affection that is *the* important thing in life, also attain Nirvana. Freedom is for us, not for me: *à nous la liberté*, not *à moi*. The most important lesson you learn in school is not the classical literature or maths that enable you to advance in the meritocracy, but the comradeship that unites Antoine and his friend despite differences of background [169]. In Truffaut's film, the oppressive nature of the system to which Antoine is subjected is proved by its separation of the two friends, and one of the most poignant images in the film is Antoine standing behind the glass door at the reformatory, able to see René, but not allowed to talk to him.

Maréchale and Rosenthal [34], Max and Riton [131]: brought together by war or crime, these masculine couples (with Gabin as the dominant figure in each case), show a nostalgia for the simple values of the playground, at times exploited to conservative ends in military comedy or farce. More often, though, the friends belong to, or form, a sub-group against the authorities, like the schoolboy groups where 'Them' means teachers and *surveillants*. Freed, like pre-adolescent children from sexual desire, or simply experimenting with it like adolescents (*A nous les p'tites anglaises*, Michel Lang, 1975), they reconstitute their own version of the ideal family. Members of an adolescent gang; they recognize that serious commitment to a woman (*La Belle équipe, Les Enfants terribles*, *Jules et Jim*, and many, many others) threatens to undermine their solidarity. It is because of a woman that the best-laid plans of gangsters are undermined.

As contemporary critics of *Le Salaire de la peur* [95] observed, there is an element of sublimated homosexuality in this, as well as more general sublimation of sexuality or a desire to return to the 'pre-sexuality' of childhood. Max [131], as Colette Audry observed at the time, prefers to sleep alone at his age. The old man of *Un Dimanche à la campagne* (Bertrand Tavernier, 1984) holds the family together because he is an old man, released from urgent desires, while his daughter's affair with her unseen lover in Paris threatens to divide the group.

Homosexuality is acceptable when sublimated, as it is in the thrillers, and, like other expressions of sexuality, it leads to the constitution of a new family. Cocteau realized this in *Les Enfants terribles* [167]: unable to write directly about his own homosexuality, he obliterates it by elevating the brother-sister relationship to the status of myth, while at the same time showing that this 'unnatural' couple form a solid unit against threats from outside. The homosexual couple in *La Cage aux folles* [160] are a genuine family (there is even a child whose mother, a successful businesswoman, further reverses the male-female stereotype by setting out to seduce her man with typically 'male' aggression). In contrast to the bourgeois couple in the same film, the two gays possess the tenderness, affection, sympathy and solidarity of the heroes of French cinema and, while we laugh against the bourgeois family, our laughter at Ugo Tognazzi and Michel Serrault is complacent of their eccentricities and thus acknowledges their tenderness for each other.

* * * * *

'For a few days, I felt I was a young girl like other young girls,' says Suzanne, the night-club hostess of *L'Entraîneuse* (1938). Excluded by circumstances or sexuality (see, as well as homosexuals and others, the hermaphrodite in *Mystère Alexina* [27]), the majority of outsiders want only to return to the group. They can do it by constituting an ideal family outside the norm, by changing the repressive attitudes that have excluded them and (a theme of several recent films) returning to the nuclear, bourgeois family to establish healthier relationships within it. The trouble with the family is precisely that it serves as a transmission belt for repressive patterns from parents to children. Juliette's fate [161] is determined not only by the SNCF regulations which mean that her family loses its tied railwayman's cottage, or the accident of marrying an unsuitable husband who becomes an alcoholic, but by attitudes towards wives and children which are carried from one generation to the next. Setting out to look for their son, the two 'fathers' of *Les Compères* (Francis Veber, 1983) find out about him and about themselves, to arrive at a more balanced view of paternity and of the needs of children. The son (Pierre Beuchot), who made the documentary *Le Temps détruit* [53] to resurrect his own father and two others killed in the 'phoney war' (the writer Paul Nizan and the composer Maurice Jaubert) was impelled by a desire to abolish the fateful cycle of generations and to encounter a young man like himself: time destroyed.

In Alain Cavalier's *Un étrange voyage* (1981) a man's mother disappears during a routine journey; convinced that she has fallen off the train before arriving in Paris, he enlists the help of his daughter and in the course of their search they come to know one another as people for the first time. Maurice Pialat's *A nos amours* (1983) has a similar father and daughter coming to terms with each other (the father played by Pialat himself) and Claude Sautet's *Un Mauvais fils* (1980) examines the same process of re-education between father and drug-addict son. There is nothing facile about these films: their conclusion is arrived at without underestimating the generation gap and they show that crossing it requires as much revision of the child's stereotypes and preconceptions about his or her parent(s), as vice versa. Where the 'teenage-delinquency' films of the 1950s and 1960s assumed an older generation immobile in its attitudes, these suggest that there can be movement from both directions.

All very encouraging, the more so since these films suggest a genuine escape from the old stereotypes. From *Marius* [99] in 1931 to *Les Parapluies de Cherbourg* [112] in 1964, young men yearned for somewhere else, leaving their pregnant women to choose between becoming social outcasts or the wives of men they did not love in a 'safe' marriage that could as easily fail as succeed (*Le Miroir à deux faces* [154]) and leave them thinking of murder, like Bébé Donge [151] or Thérèse Desqueyroux [77]. 'Do you think one can be happy for more than an hour, or a night?' asks Suzanne, the night-club hostess. Perhaps the question itself is wrong. Perhaps the issue is not happiness and misery, inside the old categories of comedy, melodrama and tragedy, but wisdom. Perhaps we can escape from the fatalities of history and geography, learn a mature tolerance of others and infiltrate the structures of the repressive family with those qualities of tenderness and solidarity that gangsters and *résistants* find against their common enemies. Perhaps we can make here the 'elsewhere' to which we have always longed to escape. I doubt it. But the cinema's mission, beside that of reflecting the societies in which we live, is also Utopian. Its ideal couples and reconstituted families, its stereotypes of social categories, its parables of political struggles, its geographies of idyllic provinces to which we can escape from the archetypal urban environment of the Paris of René Clair and Marcel Carné, its mythical revivals of the past and its recollections of childhood games and the dreary courtyards of school, are a transformation of the chaos and disorder of everyday experience. The French cinema may have little to say on the subject of the future: science fiction is not one of its favourite genres; but it is still somewhere to dream.

Conclusion

Having reached the heart of French society, the family and the relationships that hold it together, I have still not come to any conclusion about the French character or any definite 'idea of France'. I hope to have shown, at least, that the films French men and women have made over the past 90 years may contribute to our understanding of the society in which they lived. The early efforts of Lumière did not preserve reality entire, as some people naively expected they would. They remain valuable historical documents which, like all films, incidentally contain a mass of information about the physical appearance of people and things at the time when they were made. And, as the cinema develops its own strategies of story-telling and its own genres, it allows us a less literal, but more profound insight into the world beyond the camera.

However, there are many dangers in trying to 'read' such messages. The Italian woman who came out of the cinema at the Venice Biennale in 1938 after seeing *Quai des Brumes* [2] and exclaimed: 'that's France!', made the same mistake as Vittorio Mussolini, the dictator's son, who walked out of a screening of Luchino Visconti's *Ossessione* four years later angrily insisting: 'that's not Italy!' In retrospect, we may feel that Visconti's film did, indeed, have a great deal to say about the state of Italy in 1942, even if it was not something that Vittorio Mussolini wished to hear.

As for Carné's sombre story about yet another 1930s hero caught up in corruption and denied his simple dream of happiness by the workings of evil men and blind fate, it reflects the state of mind of its director and his scriptwriter, Jacques Prévert, not the state of their country. They made films on this theme before, during and after the war, and the Venetian spectator who interpreted this particular example as an accurate image of French prewar society, was suffering a delusion which belonged to her own society, that of Fascist Italy, with its beliefs about the weakness and corruption of the European democracies. Certainly, these repeated stories of frustration and the desire for escape may guide us towards asking reasonable questions about the social or political mood of the time; and, with hindsight, the false hopes of the heroes and heroines in the Carné-Prévert stories of the 1930s do appear quite apt as a metaphor for the false hopes of the period; but the coincidence is just that and the meanings that we read into these films about the state of society are not to be taken too literally.

On the other hand, the cinema does give evidence about the way people lived, thought and felt; sometimes negative evidence, for example in the failure of almost all films during the 1950s to deal with the colonial wars that dominated the political scene. But even in that period, films of social comment, literary adaptations, crime thrillers and comedies add to our understanding of how audiences wished to see the world. We can learn a great deal, too, from the Popular Front cinema of the 1930s and the 'anarchist' films which reflect the events of 1968. Where, except in the cinema, is it possible to know so fully the aspirations of these times or to share their vision of a better, freer and more equitable society?

Perhaps, to see the French through their films, we should not try to look through the screen, but instead examine the audience. The French, like other people, go to the cinema because it gives them pleasure. They enjoy the visual spectacle, the architecture of Paris in films from René Clair to *Subway*, the landscape of Burgundy in *La Veuve Couderc* or that of Provence in the films of Pagnol or in *Jean de Florette* (1986), a recent adaptation of a novel by Pagnol which was a splendid and highly successful tribute to his work. Sometimes, they enjoy these landscapes because they remind them of paintings. Part of the pleasure of the cinema is that it also gives intellectual stimulation and can refer to other forms of art. Many French people, it is true, are proud of their country's cultural heritage and the popularity of literary adaptations and historical films may be the reassurance they give of continuity with the past.

The 'well-made film' of the 1950s had its strengths, even though it was despised by the young directors of the New Wave. One was the talent of the actors, and especially the mature actors of French cinema. Scriptwriters, like Aurenche and Bost, set designers like the great Alexandre Trauner, photographers like Eugen Schüfftan and musicians who might include Georges Auric or Joseph Kosma contributed to making films which deserved the label 'cinema of quality', but without the sneer that was given to the phrase.

What the audience enjoys, too, is laughter. It is said that French comedy tends to be verbal, rather than visual. Tati is certainly the exception, but there are others. There is a tradition of comedy, right down to Francis Veber (*Les Compères/Father's Day*, 1983) and beyond, in which situation, script and slapstick combine to make hilariously funny films. What one can say, perhaps, is that these comedies are on the whole reassuring rather than disturbing. Just as the audience likes to see people on the screen enjoying a meal, because eating symbolizes friendship and a warm family environment, so the most popular comedies derive from sympathy with the victims of disaster and an affectionate look at the foibles of mankind. Comedies end with a slightly sentimental return to a norm of affection and simple pleasure in the good things of life. Here, as elsewhere in French cinema, friendship and companionship are among the most valued qualities, often triumphing over passionate love, despite the belief among foreigners that *l'amour* is what most interests the French.

There are certain things that the cinema takes for granted, because film-makers or audiences take them for granted, but which, at a distance, appear less self-evident. At times when a large percentage of the French population lived on the land and belonged to the peasantry or the working-class, the norm represented in the cinema was overwhelmingly Parisian and bourgeois. The exceptions, films in which rural or provincial or working-class life was salvaged from this neglect, take on a particular significance. Rural society often appears to offer an illusion of escape from 'reality' or an ideal, anarchistic society. In the Pétainist films of the 1940s, there is a reaction: life in the country is officially promoted as spiritually and physically healthier than life in the city, so that the depiction of peasant life as brutish and retarded takes on a subversive meaning. And, in reaction to all these interpretations, there were attempts in the postwar period to unload all this ideological baggage, and to return to rural or provincial France for locations that were specific and characters whose hopes and feelings were shown to be little different from those of anyone else.

In this way, in dealing with the various geographies or histories of French society, the cinema sets up a kind of 'dialogue of myths'. For a time, one image becomes established: an image of the peasant, of life in a provincial town, of the behaviour of medieval knights and ladies, of the Revolution, of the honest worker or the good wife or the femme fatale or the seductive male. Then, because the cinema is a medium which has always had a peculiar pretention to 'realism', the image is challenged. *Remontons les Champs-Elysées* [16] offers us one version of history, *La Marseillaise* [15] or *Danton* [26] another. Gérard Depardieu is not the same kind of seducer as Jules Berry, and the films in which he appears suggest an entirely different attitude to seduction. And, while none of these films says everything about the time when they were made, together they suggest some of the many, often contradictory frameworks in which French people have constructed their images of reality.

It is this diversity and these contradictions that I want to expose. Like all societies, that of France is built on the conflicting interests and aspirations of individuals, belonging to a bewildering mixture of groups and classes, with their own priorities, their own interpretations of the society and its aims. If I have given no single idea of France in my chapters on the mood of the times, the histories and geographies of the country, and the various concepts of the family and other social institutions, I am glad. Any single notion of these would certainly be false. What I have tried to do is precisely what is indicated in the title of this book: to show, not the French, but the French as they appear in their films. I hope that cinemagoers will be encouraged by it to look again at these films and to consider them in the context of the times when they were made. Most of all, I hope that the book will give its readers some clues towards a better understanding of French cinema today and its place in the continuing dialogue through which film-makers tell us something – but not all – about the world beyond the screen.

References

ARMES, Roy, *French Cinema*, Secker and Warburg, 1985.

JEANCOLAS, Jean-Pierre, *Le Cinéma des Français*, Stock, 1979.

JEANCOLAS, Jean-Pierre, *Quinze ans d'années trente*, Stock, 1983.

PREDAL, René, *La Société française 1914–45 à travers le cinéma*, Armand Colin, 1972.

SADOUL, Georges, *Le Cinéma français*, Flammarion, 1962.

Readers should refer to Armes for an extensive bibliography of books in English and French.

The Filmographies

A NOTE ON THE FILMOGRAPHIES

The reference material that follows consists of entries on 183 films arranged under 12 headings:

    I. CULTURE
    II. HISTORY
    III. WAR AND EMPIRE
    IV. POLITICS AND RELIGION
    V. THE MIDDLE CLASS
    VI. WORKING CLASS AND INDUSTRY
    VII. PROVINCIAL AND RURAL LIFE
    VIII. PARIS
    IX. CRIME AND THE LAW
    X. WOMEN AND THE FAMILY
    XI. CHILDHOOD AND YOUTH
    XII. FANTASIES

The attribution of any given film to one of these categories is necessarily arbitrary: most films could have qualified for more than one category, some for almost all; so I do not intend to suggest in any case that the meaning of a film can be reduced to what it has to say about a particular topic. Within each category I have tried to include a wide range of films, and I hope that within the categories and between them there are some suggestive comparisons and stories of changing attitudes or consistent themes.

The first category, 'Culture', lists ten films which I have put under that head partly because they did not fit neatly into any other list, but also because they illustrate particular moments in French intellectual life. The other headings should be self-explanatory, with the possible exception of 'Fantasies' (science fiction, horror and a couple of popular spy films). As for 'Women and the Family', I would not like this title to be taken as indicating that I consider women's role to be confined to the family circle. The films I list there and my comments on them should tell quite a different story.

The films are numbered consecutively from [1] to [183] and, in each section, listed chronologically, with the exception of Franju's documentary on Méliès [174]. After the title and date of each film, the credits are given, using the following abbreviations:

    d   director
    p   producer

pc	production company
ph	photography
m	music
sc	screenplay/script
ad	art direction
with	leading actors

It is usual to attribute a film to its director. I accept this convention, while recognizing that it ignores the co-operative nature of film production. The star system means that some actors (Gabin is an obvious example) determined a good deal of the meaning of any film in which they appeared: that is what makes them 'stars', not 'character actors'. When a director does not write his own script, the scriptwriter also makes an undeniable contribution to the work: the names of Charles Spaak, Jean Aurenche, Pierre Bost and others recur in many of the films listed here. The team of Aurenche and Bost was unfairly criticized for its part in what the New Wave disliked about *le cinéma de qualité* – too much literature, too little spontaneity. But the Aurenche-Bost credits include *Les Jeux interdits, Gervaise,* and several other films that would not be on the supporting programme of anyone's history of French cinema.

A study of the filmographies reveals the important contribution of cameramen like Eugen Schufftan, Claude Renoir, Henri Decae, Léonce-Henri Burel and Raoul Coutard; of musicians like Maurice Jaubert, Joseph Kosma, Georges Auric and Michel Legrand; of designers like Alexandre Trauner, Max Douy, Georges Wakhévitch and Léon Barsacq. A piece of music may achieve recognition because it can take on an independent existence, but it is very rare for photographers or art directors to get the acknowledgement they deserve beyond a credit on the film. When the National Film Theatre in London devoted a season to Alexandre Trauner in October 1984, it was almost a unique occasion and a tribute to the versatility and longevity of the designer, who was born in 1906 and has worked in European and American cinema for some 50 years.

The filmographies are followed by passages of commentary on each film. These contain a summary of the plot or an indication of the main themes and suggest why a particular film has been included and why it has been put under that heading rather than any other. There are also in some cases translations, of varying length, from critical articles.

These critical extracts have been chosen almost exclusively from contemporary reviews. Because this is a book about film and society, I have also avoided quoting comments on the aesthetic qualities of the film – 'beautifully edited', 'excellent performances', 'fine photography', and so on. Readers who want this kind of evaluation can find it in the many histories of French cinema and in the collected articles of critics. What interests me here is comment that situates a film in the context of the time and society at the moment when it was made, or first shown. For the same reason I have turned principally to newspapers and reviews with a marked bias, either moral or political, which will encourage their critics to judge films in those terms; and I have deliberately sought out evidence of bias in the review.

This has not proved as simple as it might appear. The Catholic Office du Cinéma and other related organizations have graded films according to the age groups for which they were deemed suitable and, ultimately, according to whether they were appropriate for showing to people of any age; and their judgements, at least until the period following the Second Vatican Council, were gratifyingly free of the usual aesthetic considerations. Films which were blasphemous, sexually suggestive or which failed to give the necessary moral uplift to the audience were condemned more or less regardless of artistic worth. I have quoted some of these grades and the comments that accompanied them. However, from the mid-1960s onwards the Church became much more liberal in its attitudes at the same time, paradoxically, as films became more sexually explicit and less morally uplifting. Nowadays, only pornography which has clearly been made with the sole purpose of exploiting the market is condemned. When a poor sequel to a comedy about homosexuals [160] can be graded 'suitable for adult audiences', with only a regret that the topic was not given more serious treatment, at a time when (as far as I know) the Church still deplores homosexual relationships, it makes one wonder whether the Catholic Office is taking its task seriously.

Something similar applies to the political press. Reading Maurice Bardèche and Robert Brasillach's history of the cinema, published in 1935, it is possible to find quotes illustrating their right-wing views and their dislike of the 'internationalism' of French cinema; but it is not that easy. The critics of the Communist daily *L'Humanité*, whom one might expect to carry on a ferocious campaign against the product of a capitalist industry in a bourgeois society, prove, in the main, to offer judgements very little different from those to be found in the pages of *Le Figaro*, with only the occasional denunciation of 'a Fascist work', etc. Films, being an art object, are usually treated as being outside the range of the moral, social or political judgements that would be applied to, say, historical studies or political speeches, unless they have been produced with a clear message. Brasillach, whom it is surely not unfair to describe as a Fascist, shot in 1945 for collaboration with the German occupier, once wept with frustration when he was unable to get into a ciné-club showing of Eisenstein's *Battleship Potemkin* (which is like a Communist begging to be allowed to see *The Triumph of the Will*).

Despite this, I have managed to dig out some comments which illustrate how contemporary critics saw the films in relation to the society of their time. This search has not only been motivated by the fact that extreme comments are more entertaining than trite appreciations of artistic worth. Like the measurement of the water level of the Seine against the Zouave on the Pont de l'Alma, looking at extremes can be instructive, especially in a country where moderation has seldom been the most prized quality in political and social life. Not all French Catholics thought or felt like the Office Catholique du Cinéma, but when it was shocked by a film, one can be sure that many other French people also found that film shocking. The judgements of right- and left-wing newspapers reflected the opinions of at least a fraction of those on the political Right or Left, as well as the opinions of the author who signed them.

The periodicals or newspapers from which I have drawn most of this material, then, are those with a marked tendency: for the Left, *L'Humanité*, *Les Lettres françaises* and *Les Temps modernes*; for the Right, during the war years, *Je suis partout*, and in the prewar period the conservative *Revue hebdomadaire* and occasionally *L'Action française*; for Catholic opinion, *Télé-Ciné*, *La Croix* and the ratings of the Office Catholique. I doubt if any of them fully represents my own views, and, in some cases, I should be very sorry if they were thought to do so. Only in one (François Vinneuil's attack on Cocteau in [3]) have I let myself be carried away to the extent of commenting on an opinion.

The translations, except in a few instances where an English source is indicated, are my own. I regret that space has not allowed me to give the French originals, even when this would demonstrate the inadequacy of my attempt to translate a particularly well-turned phrase or apt comment. Out of it all, I hope, will come some interesting stories of changing attitudes and past polemics, providing further evidence of the part that cinema has played in French life and culture.

I   CULTURE

[1]   *Un Chien andalou* (1929)
  d Luis Buñuel, Salvador Dali *p* Buñuel *pc* Studio-Film *ph* Albert Dubergen
  sc Buñuel, Dali *with* Simone Mareuil, Pierre Batcheff, Jaime Miravilles, Dali,
  Buñuel.

'A commitment to violence, sadism and morbidity,' was how Lucie Derain described Buñuel's 17-min. short in *Cinématographie française* (23 Nov 29), concentrating 'all the harm that Freud could do with his psychoanalysis'. *Pour Vous* saw it appealing to the artistic circles of Montparnasse where 'scandal is theoretically accepted as a necessity'. *La Revue du Cinéma* (15 Oct 29), describing it as 'astoundingly logical', took a similar view: it would enjoy 'un succès de snobisme' in art houses; and later, in its 'review of reviews' for 1 Feb 30 cited Henri Ghéon's remark in *Latinité* that the film was stupid, but that 'stupidity is forgiveable', adding: 'Henri Ghéon is wrong: let him re-read his articles and he will see that, beyond a certain point, stupidity is unforgiveable'.

Un Chien andalou, the best-known Surrealist venture into cinema, remains a powerful assault on bourgeois and cinema conventions.

[2]   *Quai des brumes*/US: *Port of shadows* (1938)
  d Marcel Carné *pc* Rabinovich *ph* Eugen Schufftan *m* Maurice Jaubert
  sc Jacques Prévert, from the novel by Pierre MacOrlan *ad* Alexandre Trauner
  with Jean Gabin, Michèle Morgan, Michel Simon, Aimos, Pierre Brasseur.

The insane violence of the Great War, the subjection of human beings to the implacable operation of fate and the inhumanity of the machine age found expression in the 1920s in Surrealism (*Un Chien andalou*, Léger's *Ballet mécanique*). The 1930s brought a sense of impending disaster: Gabin, the ordinary man aspiring only to individual happiness, is hounded to death within sight of the ship that offers escape to a new life. As the deserter in Carné's film, 'disgusted by people and things ... he is not a "miserable wretch" because, despite doubt, stupidity and fear, he retains some character and self-respect', Bernard Barbey wrote in *La Revue hebdomadaire* (June 1938). 'From all this horror, these haggard or debased faces, emerges ... an impression of purity, which is essentially the purity of art.' Earlier (*RH*, Apr 1938) Barbey quoted an Italian woman who, after seeing the film at the Venice Biennale, exclaimed 'with pity or reproach': 'That's France!' The remark 'shows what may be considered abroad as the dominant or obsessive theme in the inspiration of French artists: sordid milieux, criminals, the lower depths, pimps and whores'.

The Carné-Prévert films fell out of favour with critics after the war, perhaps because they no longer reflected the postwar mood. Jean Cau, writing in *Les Temps modernes* (Feb 1952), saw the film with an appreciative student audience but said that, for him, 'time has not been kind to the work'.

[3]   *Orphée/Orpheus* (1950)
    d Jean Cocteau *p* André Paulvé *pc* Films du Palais Royal *ph* Nicholas Hayer
    m Georges Auric *sc* Cocteau *with* Jean Marais, Maria Casarès, François Périer,
    Marie Déa.

Partly in response to a dislike of Surrealism, Cocteau attempted to revive and modernize themes from Classical mythology and the legend of Orpheus, with its images of art, death and love, particularly appealed to him. The messengers of the underworld are sinister motorcyclists who suggest the uniformed agents of the Nazi occupation, but Cocteau's ambition is to create a timeless myth, as free as poetry.

In 1943, Cocteau scripted a version of the legend of Tristan and Isolde, *L'Eternel retour*, in which some English critics saw Fascist overtones. Admittedly, the film did appeal to François Vinneuil, critic of the Fascist *Je suis partout* (15 Oct 43): 'a rejuvenation of old myths has nourished literature and the arts in all ages ... [Delannoy's film] has reopened a window on the domain of the supernatural ... Our cinema is re-learning that pre-eminently French language, poetry, at the moment when it is cut off from Hollywood ...' But his approval did not extend to Cocteau: 'it is not that [your critic] has discovered any sudden liking for that morbid and now bedraggled clown called Jean Cocteau, for the grimaces of that perpetually inverted intelligence, for that aged weathercock of the third sex who turns in his female capriciousness from Surrealism to the most hackneyed imitation of Henri Bataille, for this mountebank ... like a frenzied coquette ...', etc. The attack, especially that on Cocteau's homosexuality, is worthy of the writer and of *Je suis partout*.

[4]   *L'Année dernière à Marienbad/Last year at Marienbad* (1961)
    d Alain Resnais *pc* Terra *ph* Sacha Vierny *sc* Alain Robbe-Grillet *with* Delphine
    Seyrig, Giorgio Albertazzi, Sacha Pitoeff, Françoise Bertin.

The New Novel of the 1950s challenged the conventions of chronological storytelling and of character in the 19th-century naturalist novel, so it is not surprising that writers like Robbe-Grillet and Marguerite Duras (*Hiroshima mon amour*) were interested in the opportunities provided by cinema. Their films may hint at some of the disquiets of postwar France (political turmoil, colonial wars), but they reflect mainly the tastes of an increasingly prosperous cultured middle-class, able to enjoy such intellectual enigmas. In *Marienbad*, the characters meet, couple and part in a timeless environment, to give a feeling of musical abstraction.

'The anti-novel ... now the anti-film', wrote Gérard Bonnot in *Les Temps modernes* (Dec 1961); *Madame Express* says 'everyone' is playing the *Marienbad* game, 'meaning ... that bourgeois fringe ... no less proud of its secondary culture than of its bank account ... As I write, men whose only crime was to have the wrong kind of face, and show it, are being thrown into the Seine [a reference to murders of Algerians in Paris during the Algerian war, for which the French police were held responsible] ... In the most austere, the most abstract work by Beckett, for example, there is a hidden awareness of our daily struggles and pains ... while in a long analysis of *Marienbad*, I have the feeling that I am betraying, not a particular cause, but the very possibility for mankind still to defend any cause whatever.'

[5] *Trans-Europ-Express* (1966)

d Alain Robbe-Grillet *pc* Como *ph* Willy Kurant *sc* Robbe-Grillet *with* Jean-Louis Trintignant, Marie-France Pisier, Nadine Verdier, Christian Barbier, Robbe-Grillet.

A further advance in the undermining of traditional narrative: a film about a man making a film about the railway train. 'The New Novel version of the Christian myth of original sin,' Didier Anzieu wrote in *Les Temps modernes* (March 1967); or perhaps 'a denial of the Christian myth: despite the myth, that is to say, despite the feelings of guilt evoked in us by any enterprise in love or artistic creation, happiness is possible on this earth; you can accomplish many things, like a happy love affair or even a film ...' Decidedly, *Les Temps modernes* has taken to playing the *Marienbad* game: 'the success of *Trans-Europ-Express* derives from the fact that the film actualizes at the same time the fantasy of the obsessed man and the defence mechanisms of the conscience against the human subject's complacency towards his fantasies and against the resulting agony of guilt.'

On a more prosaic level, it may be said that the film exhibits some of the sadism evident in Robbe-Grillet's later novels, as well as the cinema's perennial love of trains. But, while films like *La Roue* and *La Bête humaine* longed to be train-drivers, *TEE* is with the passengers.

[6] *La Chinoise* (1967)

d Jean-Luc Godard *pc* Annouchka/Prod. de la Guéville/Athos/Parc *ph* Raoul Coutard *with* Jean-Pierre Léaud, Anne Mazemsky, Juliet Berto, Michel Semeniako.

The Vietnam war, the Chinese Cultural Revolution, the Third World were beginning to penetrate the French national consciousness by the late 1960s. Godard was among the directors who contributed a sequence to *Loin du Vietnam* (1967), though the film also included Claude Lelouch's notorious hymn to the beauty of American bombers. *La Chinoise* is quintessential Godard: splendid colour photography and wordy conversations among a group of students who set up a Maoist cell in a Parisian apartment.

Its precise political orientation is hard to pin down and *Les Temps modernes* had still not decided to like Godard. An article by Jean Pouillon (Sept 1967) said 'this film is in reality perfectly conservative, not to say reactionary, but its originality of form makes the traditionalism of content acceptable'. It gives 'a stereotyped picture of youth' and an unthreatening one of revolution: 'Godard has for him those who do not hate to be worried and those, often the same, who want to be reassured.'

[7]   *Jeu de massacre*/US: *The Killing Game* (1967)
d Alain Jessua *pc* AJ/Coficitel/Films Modernes/Francinor *ph* Jacques Robin
m Jacques Loussier *sc* Jessua *with* Jean-Pierre Cassel, Claudine Auger, Michel
Duchaussoy.

This story of a strip cartoon artist who becomes absorbed by the fantasy world of his
creations (drawn for the film by Guy Pellaert), acknowledges an important sub-culture.
Especially before 1968, French schoolchildren were subjected to an academic regime
that demanded rigorous application and left little room for creativity or imagination.
Not surprisingly, they would escape into comics like *Spirou* or *Tintin*. *Astérix* made the
genre more respectable and by the 1970s there was a rich literature of *dessins animés*
from the traditional children's stories to pornographic comics. I have put Jessua's film
here, rather than under Childhood and Youth, because the year after it was made the
country was shaken by the repressed products of that school system who turned the
walls of Paris into a comic strip with slogans like: 'Creativity, Spontaneity, Life!',
'Society is a carnivorous plant' and 'I believe in the reality of my desires'.

[8]   *Themroc* (1973)
d Claude Faraldo *pc* Filmanthrope/FDL *ph* Jean-Marc Ripert *sc* Faraldo
with Michel Piccoli, Béatrice Romand, Marilu Tolo.

In *Themroc*, a production-line worker, disgusted with his mindless existence, reverts to
the stone age, taking his neighbours with him. Eventually, they turn to cannibalism
and (since this is France) eat a policeman. Jean-Louis Bory in the *Nouvel observateur* (6
March 73) saw Themroc's anarchism as 'a gut rejection, provoked by disgust with actual
experience ...', and a loss of faith in progress: 'persuaded that progress is not
civilization, instead of a step forward, he suggests taking a thousand steps back.'

[9]   *Sans soleil*/*Sunless* (1983)
d Chris Marker *p* Anatole Dauman *pc* Argos *ph* Sana Na N'Hada, Danièle
Tessier, Jean-Michel Humeau *sc* Marker

A testament by one of France's most original film-makers, *Sans soleil* is a personal
documentary that travels from a road in Iceland to Cape Verde and Japan, and ranges
across themes of individual happiness, the variety of human cultures, the struggle for
political liberation, information technology and the cinematic vision of reality. Marker
is concerned, too, with time, as experienced by people and by peoples. He has something
important to say about what it means to be a human being and so a Frenchman, in the
last quarter of the century.

[10]   *Péril en la demeure*/*Death in a French Garden* (1985)
d Michel Deville *p* Emmanuel Schlumberger *pc* Gaumont/TF1/Eléfilm
ph Martial Thury *sc* Deville, Rosalinde Dammame, from René Belleto's novel

Sur la terre comme au ciel, with Christophe Malavoy, Nicole Garcia, Richard Bohringer, Anémone, Michel Piccoli.

A murder story, set in leisured, upper-middle-class surroundings, with a penniless student as the central character involved in a complex game. The narrative leaves a lot of work for the audience to do. Technically polished, refined, somewhat heartless, it appeals, like some contemporary French literature, to a mathematical side of the intellect and contrasts with the avid curiosity and openness of *Sunless*.

II HISTORY

[11] *L'Assassinat du Duc de Guise* (1908)
d André Calmettes, Le Bargy *pc* Le Film d'Art *sc* Henri Lavedan *m* Camille Saint-Saens *with* Le Bargy, Albert Lambert, Huguette Duflos.

The best-known production of the Film d'Art, shown to a score specially composed by Saint-Saens, it depicts an episode (1563) in the struggle for power of the Guise family during the minority of King François II. Distantly anticipating popular television historical dramas like that on Mazarin shown in the 1970s, it was one of the first films to give some attention to the development of character and to use experienced actors (Le Bargy of the Comédie Française).

[12] *Napoléon* (1927)
d Abel Gance *pc* Les Films Abel Gance/Société Générale de Films *ph* Jules Kruger *sc* Gance *ad* Alexandre Benois *with* Albert Dieudonné, Gina Manès, Alexandre Koubitzky, Antonin Artaud, Gance.

Gance's excessive, often self-indulgent masterpiece is visually astounding with its use of split-screen effects, etc., and at moments very moving (for example, in the college snowball fight). Its view of French revolutionary and imperial history is epic and Romantic. Norman King's selection of criticism (in *Abel Gance*, 1984) shows that, though the majority of critics praised the film as an artistic achievement, there were doubts about its historical accuracy and its political tendencies. *Candide* (14 Apr 27) compared Bonaparte in one scene to Mussolini, Léon Moussinac, in *L'Humanité* (24 Apr 27) called him 'a Bonaparte for budding fascists', but praised the film's technical brilliance: 'a pernicious work', he concluded in a second article (1 May 27). The accusation of historical inaccuracy centred on Gance's depiction of the Revolution as a bloodbath from which Napoleon had saved the country. There is in France no definitive view of the revolutionary period, such as the one established for most Britons by Burke and Carlyle, and it is not hard to find admiration of Robespierre and intense hatred of Bonaparte, as well as the opposite.

[13] *La Passion de Jeanne d'Arc/The Passion of Joan of Arc* (1928)

d Carl Theodor Dreyer *pc* Société Générale de Films *ph* Rudolphe Mate
sc Dreyer, Joseph Delteil, from novels by Delteil and records of the trial
ad Hermann Warm, Jean Victor-Hugo, Valentine Hugo *with* Maria Falconetti
Eugène Silvain, Michel Simon, Antonin Artaud, Alexandre Mihalesco.

Dreyer stresses the authenticity of the film with a prefatory sequence showing the documentary record of Joan's trial and concludes with a screen title stating that her memory will live on in the hearts of her countrymen. But this Joan is no nationalist, but a peasant girl standing up for her individual beliefs against the authority of the Church, a Protestant Joan, if you like.

Pierre Audard (*Revue du cinéma*, Feb 1929) said that suffering had never before been shown so nakedly on the screen, 'so close to physical terror'.

[14] *La Kermesse héroique/Carnival in Flanders* (1935)

d Jacques Feyder *pc* Tobis *ph* Harry Stradling *m* Louis Beydts *sc* Charles Spaak,
Feyder *ad* Lazare Meerson *with* Françoise Rosay, Louis Jouvet, Jean Murat,
Alfred Adam.

The staid bourgeois of a Flemish town flee before the arrival of the Spanish army, leaving their wives to entertain the troops in their own way. A witty comedy, well-written, lavishly produced, it was considered risqué when first shown. Henri Jeanson described it as a 'Nazi' film.

[15] *La Marseillaise/The Marseillaise* (1938)

d Jean Renoir *ph* Jean Bourgoin, Alain Dovarinou *m* Joseph Kosma,
Sauveplane *sc* Renoir *ad* Léon Barsacq, Georges Wakhévitch *with* Renoir,
Louis Jouvet, Aquistapace, Gaston Modot.

The Popular Front view of the Revolution, in a film financed by public subscription: 'Politics first!', Bernard Barbey commented in *La Revue hebdomadaire* (Feb 1938), and 'in the narrowest and least generous sense'. The bias and left-wing patronage of Renoir's film obliged him to show us Louis XIV as 'indecisive, mediocre, a slave to the tasty dishes that his valets serve him at the most affecting moments in French history' (here, Barbey may have misjudged Renoir's feeling for gourmets), but why show Marie-Antoinette with 'the bored features of Mlle. Lise Delamare'? This is not 'a revolution, or even a revolt; an anecdote, at the most', copying 'the worst American school'.

Other critics appreciated Renoir's sympathetic portrait of the King and, later, his depiction of the Revolution through the reactions of ordinary people (which Barbey condemns as 'anecdotal').

[16] *Remontons les Champs-Elysées/Let's All Go Up the Champs-Elysées* (1938)
d Sacha Guitry *pc* Cinéas *ph* Jean Bachelet *m* Adolphe Borchard *sc* Guitry
ad René Renoux *with* Guitry, Raymond Galle, Germaine Demoz.

A very different view of French history, with Guitry playing six parts, including Louis XV, Napoleon and Napoleon III, as well as the schoolmaster who provides the link for this light-hearted romp down the most famous boulevard in Paris. Its qualities, wit and insouciance are typical of Guitry and sometimes considered 'typically French'. The most interesting aspect of the film now is its picture of French school life before the war.

[17] *Les Visiteurs du soir* (1942)
d Marcel Carné *p* André Paulvé *ph* Roger Hubert *m* Maurice Thiriet, Joseph Kosma *sc* Jacques Prévert, Pierre Laroche *ad* Georges Wakhévitch, Alexandre Trauner *with* Arletty, Marie Déa, Jules Berry, Fernand Ledoux, Alain Cuny.

The devil sends his emissaries in human form to tempt the inhabitants of a fifteenth-century château, but human love defeats his schemes. In the trappings of a purely conventional, legendary Middle Ages, this could be seen as an allegory of resistance. 'Nothing to do with France under the occupation,' Jean-Henri Roy said, categorically, in a review of Carné's later film, *Juliette ou la clé des songes* (in *Les Temps modernes*, Sept 1951), complaining that it was not concerned with any contemporary theme. 'At that time cinema was simply a drug.' If there was an allegory, it was well hidden. *L'Action française* (François Daudet, Jan 1943) was only concerned with its technical qualities, while *La Nouvelle revue française* (Jean Fougère, March 1943) criticized the dialogue ('too literary'), the acting of Arletty and Jules Berry (typecast, because of their previous work, as elegant, disenchanted Parisians) and the tone of the film (Carné is better suited to the realism and 'grey light, the faubourgs with their damp paving-stones').

[18] *Les Enfants du paradis/*US *Children of Paradise* (1945)
d Marcel Carné *pc* Pathé *ph* Roger Hubert *m* Maurice Thiriet, Joseph Kosma *sc* Jacques Prévert, Carné *ad* Léon Barsacq, Alexandre Trauner *with* Arletty, Jean-Louis Barrault, Maria Casarès, Pierre Brasseur, Marcel Herrand, Pierre Renoir.

Everyone's favourite French film? Rivalries in art and love, Parisian low and high life, and murder, against an early-nineteenth-century background beautifully re-created in Trauner's sets. Certainly the most successful of Carné and Prévert's collaborations, *Les Enfants du paradis* (the title refers to the 'gods' in the theatre) owes part of its 'authenticity' to a subtle re-working of literary sources, even though the central characters of the mime Debureau (Barrault), the actor Frédéric Lemaître (Brasseur) and the villainous Lacenaire (Herrand) were historical. Lacenaire bears a strong resemblance to Vautrin in Balzac's *Comédie humaine*, and a number of other features of the film suggest a Romantic literary background that is familiar to everyone from the classroom. All this was patched together in impossible circumstances (Trauner and

Kosma, 'non-persons' under the occupation, worked clandestinely, the actor Robert le Vigan had to flee France because of his collaboration with the Germans, the Italian production company originally involved withdrew and only two parts of the film were shot), to make an enchanting and compelling whole. Before the closure of the Academy Cinema, Oxford Street, London in 1986, they seemed to show it annually and it can afford to be seen over and over again.

[19] *Le Procès de Jeanne d'Arc/The Trial of Joan of Arc* (1962)
  d Robert Bresson *p* Agnès Delahaie *ph* Léonce-Henri Burel *m* Francis Seyrig
  sc Bresson, from records of the trial *ad* Pierre Charbonnier *with* Florence
  Carrez, Jean-Claude Fourneau, Roger Honorat, Marc Jacquier.

'For someone like myself, who is indifferent to [the Christian] myth,' wrote Georges Sadoul in *Les Lettres françaises* (21 March 63), 'the film shows above all ... national resistance in an occupied country.' I doubt if Bresson saw it that way, though Sadoul's remark illustrates how a national 'myth', like Joan's, can sometimes serve Right and Left equally. He continues: 'if anyone had been unwise enough, during the Hitler occupation, to project Dreyer's work, he would have been sent, if not to the stake, at least to the crematorium. Despite this, the Danish director, who believes in God, the immortal soul, vampires, warlocks, miracles and the resurrection of the dead, had an even more mystical argument to his film than Bresson.'

[20] *L'Enfant sauvage* (1970)
  d François Truffaut *p* Marcel Berbert *pc* Les Films du Carrosse/Artistes Associés
  ph Nestor Almendros *m* Vivaldi *sc* Truffaut, from Jean Itard's *Mémoire et
  rapport sur Victor de l'Aveyron* (1806) *ad* Jean Mandaroux *with* Jean-Pierre
  Cargol, Truffaut.

Based on the true story of Dr Jean Itard's attempt to educate Victor, a boy who lived wild in the Aveyron until adolescence, Truffaut's film tackles the themes of education, childhood and 'civilization' in the context of the eighteenth-century Enlightenment (which produced not only the rationalism of Voltaire and Diderot, but also Rousseau's myth of the Noble Savage). Truffaut, himself playing Itard, leaves open the issue of nature *v.* civilization. He asks the question, Christian Zimmer said in *Les Temps modernes* (Apr 1970), 'if all education is a form of dressage/training, what is the use of education?'

[21] *Lancelot du Lac* (1974)
  d Robert Bresson *pc* Mara/Laser/ORTF/Gerico *ph* Pasqualino de Santis
  m Philippe Sarde *sc* Bresson *with* Luc Simon, Laura Duke Condominas, Hubert
  Balsan.

A revised version of the Middle Ages: brutal, tragic and austere, illustrating the

Bressonian theme of divine grace (and its absence). For Jean-Louis Bory (in *Le Nouvel observateur*, 16 Sept 74) it gave 'a more accurate picture of the Middle Ages than all past and future Cecilbedemilleries ... an interior picture: savagery and folly of honour and faith'. And the critic – if not necessarily the film – reflects the influence of the fashionable science of semiotics: '... in harmony with medieval civilization where everything was *sign*, from banners to scarves, from the Graal to the sword-hilt, in the shape of a cross ...'

[22] *Stavisky* (1974)

d Alain Resnais *pc* Cerito/Ariane/Euro-International *ph* Sacha Vierny
m Stephen Sondheim *sc* Jorge Semprun *with* Jean-Paul Belmondo, Anne
Duperey, François Périer, Charles Boyer, Gérard Depardieu.

'Resnais, si! Belmondo, no!' was the title of Jean-Louis Bory's article in *Le Nouvel observateur* (27 May 74), which suggested that the star did not have the right kind of charm for Stavisky, involved in a major scandal of the 1930s. The theatrical elements and the evident pleasure that it takes in period details, made it part of the 1970s fashion for *le rétro* (like granny dresses), despite the political sub-plot involving Trotsky in exile. But this is not how Youssef Ishaghpour and Pierre Samson interpreted it in *Les Temps modernes* (Oct–Dec 1974): 'a film about our own time, about the meaning of inflation and the motive power of the police, in a crisis-ridden society'. They recalled *La Règle du jeu*, 'totally misunderstood at the time: there, too, a story in the style of Beaumarchais ... masked the *danse macabre* of a whole society'.

[23] *Moi, Pierre Rivière ... /I, Pierre Rivière ...* (1976)

d René Allio *pc* Arquebuse/Polsim/SEP/Inst. Nat. de l'Audio-visuelle *ph* Nurith
Aviv *sc* Allio, from a text published by Michel Foucault *with* Claude Hébert,
Joseph Leportier, Antoine Bourseiller, Jacques Debarry.

The full title, 'I, Pierre Rivière, having cut the throats of my mother, my sister and my brother ...', tells most of the story. Allio, who made *Les Camisards* (1970), went to the actual site of the crime in Normandy, used peasant actors and meticulously reconstructed the period detail (1835) with the help of Rivière's own confession, the police dossier and other documents. 'He does not judge, he analyses,' Jean-Louis Bory wrote in *Le Nouvel Observateur* (25 Oct 76), to give 'an explanation on several levels', psychological and social, of a crime committed by a solitary, 'savage' man. 'Hence the care he gives to noting a kind of peasant ruthlessness, clarifying, à la Balzac, the mechanisms of money and the harsh material conditions of [peasant] life.' Despite Bory's reference to Balzac, this is at the opposite pole from the literary nineteenth century of *Les Enfants du paradis* and demonstrates the influence and prestige of French historians and sociologists, like Foucault and the group associated with the historical journal *Annales* (Emmanuel Le Roy Ladurie is the best-known), whose work consisted in minute statistical and documentary investigation of the lives of ordinary people, rather than historical generalization or what is usually understood by 'political' history.

[24]   *Perceval le Gallois* (1978)

> *d* Eric Rohmer *pc* Losange/Gaumont/FR3/RAI/ARD/SSR *ph* Nestor Almendros
> *m* Guy Robert *sc* Rohmer, from the verse novel by Crétien de Troyes
> *with* Fabrice Luchini, André Dussolier, Pascale de Boysson, Marc Eyraud,
> Marie-Christine Barrault.

Another version, again, of the Middle Ages, taken from Chrétien de Troyes's twelfth-century poem on the Graal. Fantasy and enjoyment of the past as a pasture for the imagination coexisted with the sociological work of the *Annales* school.

[25]   *Les Uns et les autres/The Ins and the Outs/Bolero* (1981)

> *d* Claude Lelouch *pc* Films 13/TF1 *ph* Jean Boffety, Jacques Lefrançois
> *m* Francis Lai, Michel Legrand *sc* Lelouch *ad* Jean-Louis Poveda *with* Robert
> Hossein, Nicole Garcia, Geraldine Chaplin, James Caan.

Lelouch's sweeping survey of European and American history through and beyond World War II, shows the enduring temptation of the Hollywood epic school. Superficial, sentimental, loud and colourful, it is closer to Michael Cimino's *Heaven's Gate* (especially in its final scene) than to anything else in French cinema.

[26]   *Danton* (1982)

> *d* Andrzej Wajda *pc* Losange/Production Group X *ph* Igor Luther *m* Jean
> Prodromides *sc* Jean-Claude Carrière, from the play *Afera Dantona* by
> Stanislawa Przybyszewska *ad* Allan Starski *with* Gérard Depardieu, Wojciech
> Pszoniak, Anne Alvaro, Roland Blanche, Patrice Chéreau.

Strictly speaking, perhaps, *Danton* is not a French film, since it was made by a Polish director and, as most critics noted at the time, had as much to do with the struggle of Solidarity in Poland as with the French Revolution. Nonetheless, its contrast between the intellectuality of Robespierre and the earthy passionate nature of Danton, also suggests some of the persistent ideological meanings of the Revolution and the application of its message to contemporary Polish history shows the continuing relevance of those events in France 200 years ago.

[27]   *Mystère Alexina/The Mystery of Alexina* (1985)

> *d* René Feret *ph* Bernard Zitzermann *sc* Jean Gruault, Feret, based on the diary
> edited by Michel Foucault *with* Vuillemin, Valérie Stroh.

The film's punning title (Mister/Mystère) is the only false note in its investigation of the case of a near-hermaphrodite in the 1850s. It questions social attitudes towards sexual identity (Alexina, wrongly classified at birth, is a teacher in a girls' school), but treats the past in a way that does not allow us to be complacent about contemporary society and its attitudes. Intimist history, showing the pervasive influence of Foucault and other socio-anthropologists on the movement of ideas during the past 20 years. It is impossible to imagine such a film being made at any previous time in the history of cinema.

III   WAR AND EMPIRE

[28]   *Le Bled* (1929)
d Jean Renoir *pc* Société des Films Historiques *ph* Marcel Lucien *sc* Henri Dupuy-Mazuel *with* Arguillière, Manuel Raaby, Enrique Rivero.

Renoir's last silent film was commissioned by the government to commemorate the centenary (1830) of the French conquest of Algeria.

[29]   *Verdun, souvenirs d'histoire* (1928)
d Léon Poirier

Poirier's sound version of *Verdun, vision d'histoire* (1928), a reconstruction of the battle of 1916 with a pacifist message, preaching Franco-German rapprochement. There was little documentary material from the fronts of the Great War and by the 1930s, in France as in Britain, cinema was beginning to turn from celebration of military heroism to pacifist themes. Poirier went on to make a number of films set in the French colonies, including *L'Appel du silence* (1935), based on the life of Charles de Foucault.

[30]   *Le Grand jeu/Card of Fate* (1934)
d Jacques Feyder *ph* Harry Stradling, Maurice Forster *m* Hanns Eisler *sc* Charles Spaak, Feyder *with* Pierre-Richard Wilm, Marie Bell, Françoise Rosay, Charles Vanel.

A Foreign Legion melodrama, remarkable chiefly because Marie Bell plays two parts, one dubbed with the voice of another actress.

[31]   *La Bandera* (1935)
d Julien Duvivier *sc* Charles Spaak, from the novel by Pierre MacOrlan *with* Jean Gabin, Pierre Renoir.

Another legionary drama and Gabin's first major film. *La Revue hebdomadaire* (Sept 1935) praised Gabin ('a great actor') and Renoir ('a fine figure of a Christian soldier, ready for sacrifice') and suggested that children should be taken to see it, not because it is a good idea to show them scenes of war, but because 'they can be taught to learn lessons of generosity, self-denial, courage, all those fine and lovely things necessary to the education of the soul which, in a great people, can be engendered in peace as well as in war.'

[32]   *Pépé-le-Moko* (1937)

d Julien Duvivier *pc* Paris Film *ph* Jules Kruger *m* Vincent Scotto *sc* Henri Jeanson, Roger d'Ashelbe, from d'Ashelbe's novel *ad* Jacques Krauss *with* Jean Gabin, Mireille Ballin, Gabriel Gabrio, Lucas Gridoux.

'You don't need a PhD to see a link between the many deaths scriptwriters and the public made Jean Gabin die from the Autumn of 1936 (*Pépé-le-Moko*, ending with his first suicide, was released on Jan 28, 1937) and the disillusionment of the failures and divisions in the [Popular] Front ...' (Jeancolas, *15 ans d'années trente*, 1983). Perhaps not quite how contemporary audiences saw this story of the Algiers casbah, with Gabin as the first in a line of doomed heroes. The colonial setting is present, but merely as a location.

[33]   *J'Accuse* (1937)

d Abel Gance *pc* FRD/Star *ph* Roger Hubert *m* Henri Verdun *sc* Gance *with* Victor Francen, Line Noro, Marcel Delaître, Jean Max.

Sound version of Gance's silent film of 1918–19. His melodramatic story of a poet and another man in love with the same woman and reconciled on the battlefield, is a visionary denunciation of war, using experimental camera techniques.

The title is taken from Emile Zola's open letter (1898) defending Dreyfus in the 'affair' which continued to divide left- and right-wing opinion up to World War II. The film inspired an interesting attack by Bernard Barbey in the *Revue hebdomadaire* (Feb 1938), mixing aesthetic and political comment. 'The more art tries to be realistic,' he wrote, 'the more it must know how to adopt artifice and fiction,' expressing 'distress' and 'shock' at Gance's use of live veterans of the Great War as extras. 'It is incredible, at this time of strikes and broken contracts, that a troupe of actors ... and a team of technicians could have been retained long enough to complete the work' (this was written in the aftermath of the Popular Front). More sinister is the comment 'but then, if *J'Accuse* is not a French work, what is its nationality? ... Monsieur Abel Gance's manner, his style, if you like, has no homeland.' The accusation of 'internationalism' at the time, had Fascist overtones. Barbey concludes that the film either 'provokes the spectator to those crude jests to which a Latin public is only too inclined, or else ... creates a neurotic horror of war ... which will only inspire unease, panic and confusion in the minds of our contemporaries.'

[34]   *La Grande illusion/Grand Illusion* (1937)

d Jean Renoir *sc* Charles Spaak, Renoir *p* R.A.C. *ph* Christian Matras *m* Joseph

Kosma *with* Jean Gabin, Pierre Fresnay, Erich von Stroheim, Dalio, Gaston Modot.

By a stroke of genius, Renoir set his film on the futility of war, not on the battlefields, but in a POW camp where French and Germans meet às enemies but non-combatants. Among the French prisoners, Gabin, Fresnay and Dalio discover a common national culture that overrides differences of class and ethnic background; while von Stroheim and Fresnay, on the other hand, realize that class crosses national boundaries. From this paradox, the message is that we share a common humanity, the dialectical argument supporting a warm, funny and moving story.

For right-wing critics, it was a problem: an undeniably great French film by a director close to the Communist Party. In their *Histoire du cinéma*, Maurice Bardèche and Robert Brasillach insist that, though 'made by an internationalist', it is a nationalist film. Renoir had fought in the Great War and, 'perhaps before returning to his errors, did not want to betray the truth' of this youthful experience. Bernard Barbey declared that *La Grande illusion* confirmed 'the arrival of a great school of French cinema' (*Revue hebdomadaire*, July 1937), distinguishing between M. Renoir's political ideas, 'apparently identical with those of the organizers of the rather insipid spectacles and celebrations' [of the Popular Front], and his rounded characters: 'the subtlety in the make-up of Maréchal [Gabin], the average Frenchman, de Boeldieu [Fresnay], the aristocrat, Rosenthal [Dalio], the Jew, and Raufenstein [von Stroheim], the Prussian warrior, actually conditions their strength and their humanity; yet they remain typical . . .'

[35] *La Bataille du rail* (1946)
> *d* René Clément *pc* Coop. Gén. du Cinéma Fr. *ph* Henri Alekan *m* Yves Baudrier *sc* Clément, Colette Audry, Jean Daurand *with* Désagneux, André Laurent, Daurand, Jean Clarieux, Leroy.

In a period of six years, France experienced the phoney war, the occupation, the liberation and the postwar purges. The country needed to unite behind a single version of recent history and, in this context, Clément's film is the most authentic record of the Resistance, a fictionalized documentary filmed on actual locations, with a largely non-professional cast.

[36] *Le Silence de la mer* (1947)
> *d* Jean-Pierre Melville *pc* OGC/Melville *ph* Henri Decae *m* Edgar Bischoff *sc* Melville, from the novel by Vercors *with* Howard Vernon, Nicole Stéphane, Jean-Marie Robain.

Vercors's story of passive resistance to the occupier (a cultured German officer, billeted on an old man and his daughter, who eventually force him by their silence to question Nazism and effectively to choose suicide), is full of closely observed details of provincial home life. As a film, Raymond Barkan (*Les Lettres françaises*, 26 Apr 49) found it monotonous and 'the antithesis of cinema' because of the inevitable silence of two leading characters.

[37] *Les Portes de la nuit* (1947)

> *d* Marcel Carné *pc* Pathé *ph* Philippe Agostini *m* Joseph Kosma *sc* Jacques
> Prévert, Carné *with* Pierre Brasseur, Yves Montand, Nathalie Nattier, Jean
> Vilar, Serge Reggiani.

Sadoul (*Le Cinéma français*, 1962) speaks of the disharmony between 'outmoded poetic
themes and up-to-date reality' after the early scenes and Carné's first postwar film was a
commercial disaster. Adapted from a ballet by Prévert, it mixes realism and fantasy and,
in retrospect, may translate the atmosphere of the immediate postwar years rather
better than its critics have allowed.

[38] *Jeux interdits/Forbidden Games* (1952)

> *d* René Clément *pc* Silver-Film *ph* Robert Juillard *m* Narciso Yepes *sc* François
> Boyer, Jean Aurenche, Pierre Bost, from the novel by Boyer *with* Brigitte
> Fossey, Georges Poujouly, Lucien Hubert, Suzanne Courtal.

An antiwar film, at the time, might have been impossible and, like *La Grande illusion*,
Clément's film becomes all the more powerful because it does not attack war directly. A
peasant boy and a Parisian girl orphaned by the war, create a cemetery for dead
animals, caricaturing the behaviour of grown-ups. 'The first "forbidden game" is war,'
Clément said. 'A film like no other,' Colette Audry wrote in *Les Temps modernes* (July
1952). 'Next to this profound and serious life of the children, that of the adults
(peasants, priest, nun), all well-meaning people, seems elementary, mechanical and
often ludicrous. Powerless before the drama of their own lives, ignorant, separated from
their own reality by external rituals and a concern for order, they unwittingly devastate
the children's lives.'

   Catholic opinion was divided. In the *Revue int. du cinéma* (No. 14, 1952), there were
mainly favourable reviews by R. M. Arlaud and Stanislas Fumet (who said the film was
only disrespectful of 'prejudices which should not be confused with religious
convictions'). But Mario Verdone, in the same issue, denounced 'the perverse
cleverness of the script' and spoke of 'necrophilia, moral laxity and profanation of
sacred symbols'. In *Téléciné* (No. 34, 1952) Paule Sengissen and Claude-Marie Tremois
described it as 'the work of intellectuals': 'its message is not pure, but ambiguous and
disturbing. The blasphemy . . . in *Jeux interdits* is treated with a complacency that makes
the authors part accessories to the evil they denounce. Their reaction is not a fruitful
opposition to spiritual and moral decay, but a gloomy, secret delight in the spectacle
offered by it.' Undoubtedly, the sensibilities of many French Catholics were wounded by
the children's parody of Catholic ritual in the film.

[39] *Ali Baba et les quarante voleurs* (1954)

> *d* Jacques Becker *pc* Cyclope *ph* Robert le Febvre *m* Paul Misraki *sc* Becker,
> Marc Maurette, Cesare Zavattini *with* Fernandel, Dieter Borsche, Henri
> Vilbert, Samia Gamal.

A colonial film? In 1954, the war in Indochina ended at Dien Bien Phu and that in

Algeria began, while the French public went to see *Ali Baba*, 'the French cinema's New Year present' (*Le Figaro*), 'the best colour photography' (*Paris-Presse*), 'best direction' (*Le Monde*), Fernandel proving he can 'identify as easily with fairy-tale bedouin as with Don Camillo' (*Dimanche Matin*).

For Catholic and some left-wing opinion, however, the film seemed less innocent. 'Not a film for children,' declared *Téléciné* (No. 45, 1955), mentioning violence and belly-dancing, while Raymond Borde (*Les Temps modernes*, Jan 1955) found it 'highly significant that the only evidence the cinema can produce on the Arab World at a time when its consciousness is awaking ... is a re-working of the *Thousand and One Nights*'. 'Exploitation, hunting down, massacre, then filming jolly tales in which one takes on the clothes of the victim – this is the master's ultimate insult to the slave. Even the Germans behaved better in the worst years of the occupation; but, for us, it is not a matter of one insult more or less towards the "bicots". The joke is a pleasant one and very French. We raid Tunisia, rape native women, burn *douars*, let the witnesses of Oudja die and shoot "sidis", while Fernandel sings "I am Ali, Ali, Ali, Ali, Ba-ba" with that aggressive vulgarity that is uniquely his own.'

[40] *Nuit et brouillard/Night and Fog* (1955)
      d Alain Resnais *pc* Argos/Como *ph* Ghislain Cloquet, Sacha Vierny

A short documentary on Auschwitz and one of the first to reveal the full horror of the Nazi concentration camps.

[41] *La Traversée de Paris/Pig Across Paris*/US: *Four Bags Full* (1956)
      d Claude Autant-Lara *sc* Jean Aurenche, Pierre Bost *with* Jean Gabin, Bourvil.

'A distorted picture of the war,' Armand-Jean Cauliez called this humorous tale of efforts to transport a black-market pig across occupied Paris (*Téléciné*, No. 63, 1957), showing a conservative Catholic distaste for 'a somewhat cynical reaction to an excess of heroism' in other war films. Sadoul, on the other hand, liked it a lot (*Les Lettres françaises*, 1 Nov 56), comparing it with Maupassant's novel *Boule de Suif* as a 'reflexion of the reality of a country at a given time'. The Gabin character was 'sickening', 'suggesting those anarchist artists whose taste for "absolute freedom" eventually led them in 1942 to Weimar (at the gates of Buchenwald) while their pictures were sold, for good prices, to the gentlemen of the black market and aesthetes in grey-green uniforms ... This intellectual is not imaginary. His like are to be found, now as then, in positions of authority.' The film had a lesson for 1956, then: 'satisfied profiteers, investing in antisemitism (the Arabs are semites, after all) did not disappear with the German occupation, but continue to uphold the established order ...'

[42] *Un Condamné à mort s'est échappé/A Man Escaped* (1956)
      d Robert Bresson *pc* Gaumont/NEF *ph* Léonce-Henri Burel *m* Mozart

sc Bresson, from André Devigny's account of his escape *ad* Pierre Charbonnier *with* François Leterrier, Charles Le Clainche.

'As a record of the Resistance, his film was antagonistic, but as true as *La Bataille du rail*,' Sadoul wrote in *Le Cinéma français* (1962) about Bresson's painfully detailed film, an interior monologue where the prison becomes a monastery and the escape an achievement of religious salvation.

[43] *Hiroshima mon amour* (1959)
     d Alain Resnais *pc* Argos/Como/Pathé/Daiei *ph* Sacha Vierney, Takahashi Michio *m* Giovanni Fusco, Georges Delerue *sc* Marguerite Duras *with* Emmanuelle Riva, Eiji Okada, Bernard Fressor.

'Great film, great director!' (Georges Sadoul, *Les Lettres françaises*, 18 June 59), though with reservations about Marguerite Duras's script. A postwar love affair with a Japanese man evokes memories of a wartime affair with a German: is this a right-wing film, was one question raised in the round-table discussion on it organized by *Cahiers du cinéma* (translated in the first volume of selections from *Cahiers* published by Routledge and Kegan Paul and the British Film Institute in 1985). The general conclusion, in any case, was that it was a landmark in French cinema.

[44] *Jules et Jim/Jules and Jim* (1961)
     d François Truffaut *pc* Films du Carrosse/SEDIF *ph* Raoul Coutard *m* Georges Delerue *sc* Truffaut, Jean Gruault, from the novel by Henri-Pierre Roché *with* Jeanne Moreau, Oskar Werner, Henri Serre.

Truffaut's story of a triangular relationship created a cult ('Jules et Jim' caps, and so on), because of its enchantment with friendship, youth and physical love. Maybe it also had to do with the Franco-German rapprochement and the feeling that old animosities had been buried: the First World War is a mere episode in these three lives, Nazism an irrelevance from another tragedy. 'The characters ... have no awareness of society,' Claude Tarare remarked (*Les Temps modernes*, March 1962). 'They live only to please themselves and for pleasure. Their jobs (writers, musicians, artists) can be done for amusement like a game ... The only thing which they deign to approach with seriousness – and more than seriousness – is love. Play and love: it's a child's world.' On the other hand, he noted that Truffaut's treatment of sex was moving: 'in France where, if not an excuse for blue jokes, physical love is a taboo subject, this is a *tour de force*.' Georges Sadoul (*Les Lettres françaises*, 25 Jan 62) felt the film was less about *joie de vivre* than about 'the disquiet of our century and some of its basic preoccupations'.

[45] *Le Petit soldat/The Little Soldier* (1963)
     d Jean-Luc Godard *pc* Georges de Beauregard/SNC/Impéria *ph* Raoul Coutard *sc* Godard *with* Michel Subor, Anna Karina, Henri-Jacques Huet, Laszlo Szabo.

Made in 1960, the film was censored until after the end of the Algerian war. This story of a Fascist terrorist is the early, apolitical Godard: Right and Left are identical. This message did not appeal to left-wing critics, though they were in principle sympathetic to the film's problems with the censor. 'Disappointing and outmoded,' concluded Michel Capdenac (*Les Lettres françaises*, 31 Jan 63). 'We see a good deal of torture, but it is the [Algerian] FLN which applies it ... We might applaud a courageous condemnation of torture if the Algerian fighters and those who tried by every means to prolong the war, were not deliberately set on the same level.' Gérard Bonnot, who had seen the film before the censor got to it, described it in *Les Temps modernes* (Nov 1961) as 'quite repulsive, not because of the "realism" of these scenes [of torture], as the stupidity of our censors would have us believe, but, on the contrary, because of their abstract character. The result is that this film which tries to raise the problem of torture in an open manner, seems like an insult to all the victims whose sufferings have not been purely intellectual but very real ...'

[46] *Paris brûle-t-il?/Is Paris Burning?* (1966)
d René Clément pc Transcontinental/Marianne ph Marcel Guignon m Maurice Jarre sc Gore Vidal, Francis Ford Coppola, from the book by Dominique Lapierre and Larry Collins with Jean-Paul Belmondo, Charles Boyer, Claude Dauphin, Bruno Cremer, Alain Delon, Kirk Douglas.

The heroic and spectacular view of the liberation.

[47] *L'Armée des ombres/The Army in the Shadows* (1969)
d Jean-Pierre Melville pc Corona/Fono ph Pierre Lhomme m Eric de Marsan sc Melville, from the novel by Joseph Kessel with Lino Ventura, Paul Meurisse, Simone Signoret.

Melville's account of the activities of a resistance group was 'more brilliant and more exact' than Pierre Kast's *Drôle de jeu* (1968), according to Jeancolas (*Le Cinéma des français*, 1979), 'and doubtless remains the best film on ... the élitist, urban resistance'. Jeancolas also notes the precise depiction of Lyon, as part of a new awareness of the reality of provincial towns.

[48] *Le Chagrin et la pitié/The Sorrow and the Pity* (1971)
d Max Ophuls

With the massive documentary *Français, si vous saviez* three years later, this had an enormous impact, challenging accepted myths of the occupation period through the direct testimony of *résistants*, collaborators and ordinary French men and women. Writing in *Les Temps modernes* (May 1971) Christian Zimmer described it as 'history being written and rewritten, alive, continually confronting the present, engaging in a kind of dialogue with it' and giving the image of a France 'cut in half and rising up against itself' (instead of a country united against the occupier), an image that 'bears a strong resemblance to present-day France' in the class realities covered by the terms 'Left' and 'Right'.

[49] *Lacombe Lucien* (1974)

d Louis Malle *pc* Nouvelles Ed. de Films/UPF/Vides/Hallelujah *ph* Tonino delli Colli *sc* Malle, Patrick Modiano *with* Pierre Blaise, Aurore Clément, Therèse Giehse.

Malle's sympathetic treatment of the young collaborator ('a bastard, but one whose heart is revealed', Jean-Louis Bory, *Le Nouvel Observateur*, 28 Jan 74) divided left-wing opinion. Lucien is a brutal peasant who, when his approaches to the resistance are rejected, joins the Fascist *milice* which offers him a feeling of importance and power. His persecution of a Jewish girl develops into love and their brief idyll, before Lucien is executed, illustrates the ambiguities of the period (revealed on another level by the documentary evidence of *Le Chagrin et la pitié*).

Bory described it as 'the first real, true film on the occupation', praising Malle's attention to the details of life in the Toulouse region: 'this was the daily experience of the time and it was appalling. I know. I was there.' As for Lucien, he sees him as a typical peasant, 'knowing that you have to deceive nature ... It is by chance, not conviction, that he finds himself on the wrong side of the fence', taking 'the revenge of the peasant against the town, the poor against the rich, the humiliated against the proud.'

Christian Zimmer (*Les Temps modernes*, July 1974) saw the film from a different angle. 'The fashion for *le rétro* is not a morbid attraction towards a sinister period of history, but the reflexion and manifestation of a political trend. Gone are the "great designs": the resistance was one, Gaullism another.' Malle's film belongs to the world of de Gaulle's successors, Presidents Pompidou and Giscard, illustrating 'that eminently Giscardian faith in the supremacy of technique ... The only problems are *technical* ones, which is to say, in no way moral ones ... Consequently, good and evil are ideas apparently void of any meaning when set under the pitilessly *realistic* light of circumstances: *Lacombe Lucien* hardly implies anything else: the final scene – that kind of idyllic, paradisiac parenthesis, a remission from history, a utopian arresting of time, in which the young *collabo* and the young Jewess love each other in freedom, under nature ... – is, in brief, an image of the reconciliation preached by the Right.'

[50] *Le Dernier métro/The Last Metro* (1980)

d François Truffaut *pc* Les Films du Carrosse/Andrea/SEDIF/SFP/TF1 *ph* Nestor Almendros *m* Georges Delerue *sc* Truffaut, Suzanne Schiffman *ad* Jean-Pierre Kohut-Svelko *with* Catherine Deneuve, Gérard Depardieu, Jean Poiret, Heinz Bennent, Andrea Ferréol.

Truffaut's film about a theatre company under the occupation marginalizes the events of World War II as *Jules et Jim* [44] dismissed those of World War I. In *Les Temps modernes* (Sept 1981), Françoix Garçon compared it to Fassbinder's *Lili Marlene* and saw it as 'a reverse reply' to Ophuls [48], an attempt 'to ennoble' a shameful page of history. 'The nationalist revival evident in Europe in recent years following the worsening of the economic crisis, partly, at least, explains this fundamental change ... The time has now apparently come for a retreat into an epic vision of past events ... These films are at once the first sign and a warning of this.'

Don Allen (*Finally Truffaut*, Secker and Warburg, 1985) quotes Truffaut's introduction to the published script: 'The Fascist critics regularly denounced "the Jew-ridden plays of Bataille and the effeminate plays of Cocteau" ', and adds that 'the character of Daxiat [Jean-Louis Richard] is based on an episode related by Jean Marais in his autobiography, where he recalls how to beat up the critic of *Je suis partout*, Alain Lambeaux, for his review of Cocteau's *La Machine infernale*.' See my note on [3] above.

[51] *Coup de torchon/Clean Slate* (1981)

> *d* Bertrand Tavernier *pc* Les Films de la Tour/A2/Little Bear *ph* Pierre William Glenn *m* Philippe Sarde *sc* Jean Aurenche, Tavernier, from the novel by Jim Thompson *with* Philippe Noiret, Isabelle Huppert, Jean-Pierre Marielle, Stéphane Audran, Eddy Mitchell.

The story of a police chief in French West Africa during the 1930s who turns mass murderer is a satire on the anomalies and inherent injustices of colonialism, with elements of black comedy.

[52] *Fort Saganne* (1984)

> *d* Alain Corneau *pc* Albina/A2/SFPC *ph* Bruno Nuytter *m* Philippe Sarde *sc* Henri de Turenne, Corneau, from the novel by Louis Gardel *with* Gérard Depardieu, Philippe Noiret, Catherine Deneuve, Sophie Marceau.

A left-wing attempt to make a colonialist epic? Corneau's film certainly appears to want it both ways. Saganne is an old-fashioned, swashbuckling hero of the Sahara who comes to realize the limitations of that ethic on the battlefields of the Great War. But the film harks back to the more innocent colonialist dramas of the 1930s, like Léon Poirier's *L'Appel du silence* (1936).

[53] *Le Temps détruit/Time Destroyed* (1985)

> *d* Pierre Beuchot *pc* Inst. Nat. de l'Audiovisuelle/Ministère de la Culture *ph* Jacques Bouqin, Bernadette Marie *m* Maurice Jaubert.

Beuchot's documentary is constructed around letters written by his father, Roger Beuchot, a signwriter, the composer Maurice Jaubert (whose film scores include *Quai des brumes*, *L'Atalante* and *Zéro de conduite*) and the Communist writer Paul Nizan, all three of whom were killed in the 'phoney war' in 1940. The letters, to women they love, describe conditions at the front, their hopes for the future, their longing to be reunited. The extracts are read over documentary footage from the period and later film of the places where the letters were written. A film with no vast ambitions, but among the most moving and poignant indictments of the idiocy of war.

IV   POLITICS AND RELIGION

[54]   *Les Nouveaux messieurs* (1929)
d Jacques Feyder sc Charles Spaak, Feyder, from the play by Robert de Flers and Francis de Croisset ad Lazare Meerson with Albert Préjean, Henri Roussel, Gaby Morlay.

Political satire, acceptable on the stage in the play by de Flers and de Croisset, came up against the censor when transferred to the screen. Feyder's film tells the story of a worker who goes into politics, becomes a minister and is involved with a dancer, the mistress of a Royalist *député*. As Sadoul (*Le Cinéma français*, 1962) remarks, there were several Socialist politicians whose careers followed a similar course. But Feyder, surprised by his troubles with the censor, considered that the film was mild in its attack on the parliamentary regime. Even so, it was partly responsible for his removal to Hollywood for the next four years.

[55]   *A Propos de Nice* (1930)
d Jean Vigo ph Boris Kaufman dist Pathé-Nathan.

Almost an amateur documentary, in which Vigo stresses the contrasts between luxury and poverty in the Mediterranean town.

[56]   *Le Dernier Milliardaire/The Last Millionaire* (1934)
d René Clair pc Pathé-Nathan ph Rudolph Maté m Maurice Jaubert sc Clair with Max Dearly, Renée Saint-Cyr, Marthe Mellot, Raymond Cordy.

One of René Clair's failures, at a time when he was undoubtedly the most popular director in France. Its success was not helped by the assassination in Marseilles a few days before it opened of King Alexander of Yugoslavia and a French minister, Louis Barthou: the film, set in the imaginary country of Casinario, is a satire on the economic crisis of the depression. Later commentators tend to find Clair's style of parody ineffectual.

[57]   *Topaze* (1936)
      d Marcel Pagnol *pc* Les Films Marcel Pagnol *ph* Albert Assouad *m* Vincent
      Scotto *sc* Pagnol, from his play *with* Arnaudy.

At least four other versions were made of Pagnol's play about a schoolteacher who
realizes, after being dismissed for over-honesty, that he can succeed in public life if he
abandons all moral principles. Louis Gasnier filmed it in 1933 with Louis Jouvet and in
the same year a version was made by Harry d'Abbabbie d'Arrast in the USA. Pagnol
tried again in 1951 and Peter Sellers in 1961. The play, and the early films, were
indicative of popular disillusionment in the 1930s with business and politics and the
naive schoolmaster provides a yardstick against which to measure the sophisticated
cynicism of industrialists and administrators.

[58]   *La Règle du jeu/The Rule of the Game* (1939)
      d Jean Renoir *pc* Nouv. Ed. Fr. *ph* Jean Bachelet *sc* Renoir *with* Marcel Dalio,
      Nora Gregor, Gaston Modot, Renoir, Roland Tutain.

The Renoir team gathered in 1938 to make this story of a country-house shooting-
party which is the most penetrating study of French society of the 1930s. La Chesnaye,
the aristocrat, causes tragedy because he has, effectively, no standards to hold his
society together.
   It was greeted, on first showing, with incomprehension and indifference, then
banned by the censor when war broke out, with other films described as 'depressing,
morbid, immoral and unsuitable for young people'. Jeancolas (*Quinze ans d'années
trente*, 1983) sums up later judgements of the work: Renoir's masterpiece 'and perhaps
the finest film in 80 years of French cinema'. Setting it in the context of Renoir's political
views in the period, Christian Zimmer wrote (*Les Temps modernes*, June 1965): 'The
Popular Front, however things may appear, is already distant. Returning from political
commitment, but perhaps thanks to it, the film-maker has "found himself". If his
affection for his fellow-men is henceforth without any illusion, if he thinks that
mankind can only be helped individually, not saved collectively, for all this, his affection
is the stronger and more generous: *La Règle du jeu*, above all, breathes a passion for
humanity ...' That this 'morbid, depressing and immoral' film should come to be seen
as 'perhaps the finest' in the history of French cinema, says a good deal about changing
attitudes during the past half-century.

[59]   *La Symphonie pastorale* (1946)
      d Jean Delannoy *pc* Gibe *ph* Armand Thirard *m* Georges Auric *sc* Delannoy,
      from the novel by André Gide *with* Pierre Blanchar, Michèle Morgan.

Gide's scepticism and his preoccupation with the question of individualism and
religious authority make him a representative figure of the interwar period, while
Delannoy's efficient version of his short novel about a Protestant pastor's love for one of
his parishioners is characteristic of the 'quality cinema' of its time and similar in
inspiration to his adaptation of Henri Queffélec's *Dieu a besoin des hommes* (1950). For
obvious reasons, the political and spiritual outlook of the 1940s was austere.

[60]   *Journal d'un curé de campagne/Diary of a Country Priest*
(1951)
d Robert Bresson *pc* UGC *ph* Léonce-Henri Burel *m* Jean-Jacques Grunewald
sc Bresson, from the novel by Georges Bernanos *with* Claude Laylu, Armand
Guibert, Marie-Monique Arkell.

The austerity of the time perfectly suited Bresson's temperament, as did Bernanos's
preoccupation with evil. Generally, the film met with approval from Catholic sources:
the Centre Catholique des Intellectuels Français held a meeting at the Sorbonne in
1951 where a Carmelite, Father Bruno, recorded that he had seen the film after it was
recommended from the pulpit by a priest who expressed 'no reservations' about it (an
unusual attitude by a Catholic to any film at this time). Father Bruno was jeered when
he told the audience that he had found the film 'morbid' – 'there is no such thing as a
sad saint' (quoted by Robert Drouguet in his study of Bresson, *Premier Plan*, No. 42).
    So, among Catholics, Bresson separated the happy saints from those who shared his
sin-laden outlook on the world. It was a question of temperament, not of ideology. *Les
Temps modernes*, not necessarily sympathetic to religious works, published two articles.
In one (Apr 1951), Jean Pouillon used it as the starting-point for an examination of
cinema adaptations of novels and an attack on Bernanos's novel in particular: 'this diary
which would seem simplistic and composed entirely of clichés if it were not that of a
priest' had inspired 'a film as dreary as the book it adapts' (not to speak of the
'mediocrity' of the acting). In March, however, the review had published Jean-Henri
Roy's study of 'Bernanos and the Cinema'; 'no thesis is imposed on us. We are not forced
to choose sainthood ... [the film] makes us feel the fundamental ambiguity of every
vocation ... Never has such fervour been expressed in the cinema and Bresson has
translated it magnificently. But it was entirely contained in a book that surely
represents the most valid example of the contemporary Christian novel.'

[61]   *Le Joli mai* (1962)
d Chris Marker *p* Cathérine Winter *ph* Pierre Lhomme *m* Michel Legrand
sc Marker.

Marker returned from China (*Dimanche à Pékin*, 1955), Russia (*Lettre de Sibérie*, 1957)
and Cuba (*Cuba Si!*, 1961) to make this example of *cinéma-vérité* about one month in
Paris. Sadoul called it 'a great work of art [which] opens a new route for French cinema'
(*Les Lettres françaises*, 9 May 63), rightly pointing out that the camera was 'not a
machine to record indifferently the best and the worst'.
    For various reasons, film-makers in the 1940s and 1950s had not been able or
willing to examine the political and spiritual concerns of the period directly (which is
not to say that their films do not, indirectly, give a clue to most of those concerns).
Marker's documentary is a fascinating and convincing portrait of its time. It reacts to
such events as the trial of General Salan and includes testimony from a variety of
people, including that of the worker-priest who describes the reasons for his decision
not to obey the Church's order to leave the movement and return to the priesthood.
    Cinéma-vérité is a term particularly applied to the work of Jean Rouch during this
period.

[62] *La Guerre est finie* (1966)
　　　d Alain Resnais *pc* Sofracima/Europa *ph* Sacha Vierny *m* Giovanni Fusco
　　　sc Jorge Semprun *with* Yves Montand, Ingrid Thulin, Geneviève Bujold.

A portrait of a Spanish political activist, Resnais's film showed a new form of realism in the treatment of contemporary political themes.

[63] *Suzanne Simonin, la religieuse de Diderot* (1966)
　　　d Jacques Rivette *pc* Rome-Paris Films/SNC *ph* Alain Levent *m* Jean-Claude
　　　Eloy *sc* Jean Gruault, from Diderot's novel (1760) *with* Anna Karina, Liselotte
　　　Pulver, Micheline Presle.

Attacked by Catholic organizations even before it was made, this story of eighteenth-century convent life was selected for Cannes, then banned by the Ministry of Information. Even after the *aggiornamento* of the Second Vatican Council, which began to make profound changes in Catholic attitudes, the Church remained particularly sensitive to screen representations of religious subjects. Georges Sadoul (*Les Lettres françaises*, 2 Aug 67) said that the affair had 'unleashed ultra-reactionary forces, against Diderot, against Rivette and against a film which is 'an exemplary and faithful adaptation of a masterpiece of our literature': his defence of the film leads him to a considerable exaggeration of the quality of Diderot's novel.

[64] *Weekend* (1967)
　　　d Jean-Luc Godard *pc* Copernic/Ascot *ph* Raoul Coutard *m* Antoine Duhamel
　　　with Mireille Darc, Jean Yanne, Jean-Pierre Kalfon, Jean-Pierre Léaud.

A bleak Godardian vision of France and Western civilization as a wasteland of industrial and technological debris.

[65] *Z* (1968)
　　　d Costa-Gavras *pc* Reggane/ONCIC *ph* Raoul Coutard *m* Mikis Theodorakis
　　　sc Costa-Gavras, Jorge Semprun, from the book by Vasilis Vassilikos *with* Yves
　　　Montand, Irene Papas, Jean-Louis Trintignant, Jacques Perrin.

Méliès's 15-min. film about the Dreyfus affair (1899) was effectively censored until 1950, Feyder ran into difficulties with *Les Nouveaux messieurs* [54] and direct government censorship; and other factors such as libel laws and public indifference have meant that direct representation of parliamentary life and directly political films have been rare in cinema history. But, at the same time, France has long been a land of exile for political activists from abroad (comp. [62]) and, consequently, is involved on more than one level in foreign politics. The Colonels' regime in Greece aroused feelings expressed through demonstrations, petitions and other ways. Costa-Gavras's film popularized a notable sub-genre of political thrillers.

[66] *La Faute de l'abbé Mouret/The Sin of Father Mouret* (1970)
  d Georges Franju *pc* Stephan/Films du Carrosse/Valoria/Amati *ph* Marcel
  Fradetal *m* Jean Wiener *sc* Jean Ferry, from the novel by Emile Zola
  with Francis Huster, Gillian Hills, Ugo Tozzi, Margo Lion.

In a political film, the period setting might have dulled the force of the attack; but the Church preaches an unchanging doctrine and, as some of its spokesmen insisted at the time of the Vatican Council less than ten years earlier, more than half believes that it has no need to adjust to the 'modern world'. Consequently, Franju's film about a young priest's discovery of love in an earthly paradise, could be seen as a direct assault on religious values, intensified by the gradual relaxation of censorship.

[67] *Aux urnes, citoyens!* (1971)
  d Edouard Bobrowsky.

A documentary on the campaign in Arras for the municipal elections, revealing the mechanism of French parliamentary politics in the Pompidou era. 'The spectacle is horrifying,' writes Christian Zimmer (*Cinéma et politique*, 1974). 'Of course, everything was done to prevent the film being released.'

[68] *Tout va bien* (1972)
  d Jean-Luc Godard *p* Jean-Pierre Rassam *ph* Armand Marco *sc* Godard, Jean-
  Pierre Gorin *with* Jane Fonda, Yves Montand, Vittorio Caprioli.

Godard's questioning of the forms of communication was as loaded as the satire of a factory-owner or the discussions of the strike committee in perhaps his most overtly political film. It shows his best and worst qualities and, in retrospect, is a telling document about the left-wing conscience at a time of ferment. Jean-Louis Bory (*Le Nouvel observateur*, 8 May 72) found Montand and Fonda extraordinarily truthful 'because, beyond the characters they play ... they rediscover their own personal concerns'. But: 'the provocative analysis of contemporary France is softened into a Gospel According to Saint Jean-Luc. What a relief! At last, we can file away the once-fearful Jojo in a drawer with what is today a quite reassuring label: Brecht.' The film was not a commercial success.

[69] *Coup pour coup/Blow for Blow* (1972)
  d Marin Karmitz *pc* MK2/WDR-Cologne *with* the workers of Elbeuf.

A drama-documentary about a strike in a textile factory in Elbeuf.

[70]   *Je vous salue, Marie/Hail Mary* (1985)
d Jean-Luc Godard *sc* Godard.

This, on the other hand, really is the Gospel According to Jean-Luc. Joseph is a taxi-driver, Mary works in a petrol station, and the film concentrates on Joseph's very human response to her immaculate conception. The photography is splendid. The Catholic newspaper *La Croix* praised its 'respect for the mysteries of the supernatural and the irrational' and called it 'a great Christian film', but other Catholic voices showed that, in this area at least, they could still be shocked. There were riots in Nantes and elsewhere, demonstrations outside cinemas and calls for the film to be banned. Monseigneur Marcel Lefebvre expressed his disgust and had support from one very influential quarter: Pope John Paul II stated that the film 'distorted and reviled' the spirit of the gospel story and deeply wounded the feelings of believers. Godard replied by acknowledging that the Pope had rights over the original story.

V   THE MIDDLE CLASS

[71]   *Un Chapeau de paille d'Italie/The Italian Straw Hat* (1927)
d René Clair *pc* Albatros *ph* Maurice Despassiaux, Nicholas Roudakoff *sc* Clair, from the play by Eugène Labiche and Marc Michel *ad* Lazare Meerson *with* Albert Préjean, Olga Tchekova, Marise Maia.

Updating Labiche's play from the 1850s to the 1890s, Clair satirizes the pretensions of a petty bourgeoisie which is closer to that of his own time, but still divided from it by the war. The satire is without malice, conveyed by visual gags and the careful construction of the narrative.

[72]   *L'Argent* (1928)
d Marcel L'Herbier *pc* Cinégraphic Cinéromans *ph* J. Kruger, J. Letort *sc* L'Herbier, from the novel by Emile Zola *ad* Lazare Meerson *with* Alcover, Henri Victor, Alfred Abel, Antonin Artaud, Jules Berry.

L'Herbier's masterpiece, with exteriors filmed at the Bourse, the Opera and Le Bourget emphasizing the updating of Zola's novel and consequently the continuing relevance of its analysis of Capitalism. Noel Burch points out that this interference with a literary 'classic' was the focus of criticism when the film was released (*L'Herbier*, Seghers, 1973). 'Speculative fever has developed prodigiously,' Maurice Sarlat wrote in *Paris-Soir*, 'and the men described by Zola would now look like apprentices, if not fossils.' A number of commentators related it to the collapse of the Gazette du Franc in 1928, which Robert Spa suggested (*Le Figaro*) may have made the events of the film pale by comparison. Jean Fayard (*Candide*) 'would like to have met Armenians, Jews and Levantines' in L'Herbier's bank and stock exchange, 'which could just as well be a large department store' – 'in the cinema, one must not be afraid of stylization'.

[73] *Boudu sauvé des eaux/Boudu Saved from Drowning* (1932)
d Jean Renoir *pc* Michel Simon/Jean Gehret *ph* Marcel Lucien *sc* Renoir, from
the play by René Fauchois *ad* Laurent and Jean Castanier *with* Michel Simon,
Charles Grandval, Marcelle Hainia, Jean Gehret, Jacques Becker.

A respectable gentleman rescues a tramp (Simon) from drowning and takes him to his
home. The tramp responds by continuing to behave as a tramp and seduces the man's
wife and maid, before deciding that he prefers the freedom of the road to the comforts of
a middle-class home. Renoir pokes fun at refined manners and morals, but is not cruel.
The men retain an affection for each other, despite their differences. This is one of
several French films, from *A nous la liberté* [85] to *Vagabonde* [163] in which the
tramp's freedom from social constraints is equated with freedom itself.

[74] *Drôle de drame*/US: *Bizarre, Bizarre* (1937)
d Marcel Carné *pc* Corniglion-Molinier *ph* Eugen Schufftan *m* Maurice Jaubert
sc Jacques Prévert, from the novel by Storer-Clouston *ad* Alexandre Trauner
with Michel Simon, Françoise Rosay, Louis Jouvet, Annie Cariel, Jean-Louis
Barrault.

The middle classes in this Prévert-Carné collaboration are, in fact, the English middle
classes, and eccentric with it; but the farcical goings-on involving a novelist (Simon), a
bishop (Jouvet), a murderer (Barrault) and a character called Mrs Pencil are a 'very
French' (i.e. inaccurate) view of the English side of the Channel.

[75] *Lumière d'été* (1942)
d Jean Grémillon *pc* Discina *ph* Louis Page *m* Roland Manuel *sc* Jacques
Prévert, Pierre Laroche *ad* Max Douy *with* Madeleine Renaud, Paul Bernard,
Pierre Brasseur, Madeleine Robinson.

A love story in which the heroine has to choose between the honest world of the
workmen on a site constructing a dam, and the shallow world of *château* society. She
chooses the former, but it is the scenes of upper-middle-class society that are
memorable: as he showed in such earlier films as *Dainah la métisse* (1931), Grémillon is
admirable when conveying the emptiness of the pleasures of the rich, in contrast to the
working life of the poor. *Dainah*, recently restored by the Cinemathèque, is set in the
engine-rooms and saloons of a luxury liner and contains an extraordinary scene at a
ball suggesting that the passengers are taking part in a dance of death.

[76] *Mon Oncle* (1958)
d Jacques Tati *pc* Specta/Gray/Alter/Centauro *ph* Jean Bourgoin *m* Franck
Barcellini, Alain Romans *sc* Tati, Jacques Lagrange, Jean L'Hôte *ad* Henri
Schmitt *with* Tati, Jean-Pierre Zola, Alain Bécourt, Lucien Frégis, Dominique
Marie.

Tati delights in the eccentricities of the Old Paris and mocks at the pretensions of the new suburbs and the new rich, but the family relationship noted in the title shows that both are aspects of the same class. In the old quarter, we have the traditional lower middle class of tradespeople and employees; in the new suburb, the rising middle class of *cadres supérieurs* who are enjoying the prosperity of the postwar years and exhibiting their culture in their cars, their gadgets, the decoration of their homes, their Franglais and their smart entertainments. 'The ceremonial of the Arpels is, after all, that of the Sun King,' Georges Sadoul wrote in *Les Lettres françaises* (15 May 58), 'and their pitiful fountain the pitiful counterpart of those at Versailles.'

He notes that the film had a mixed reception in Cannes: 'provided one is witty enough, it is possible to make fun of Bernadette and the holy water of Lourdes ... But make fun of the coachwork of the latest Jaguar, the chrome on the DS or the Rolls engine – that really is a sacrilege ... This film is for you, good people, men in the street, who, unlike the others, do not have a Frigidaire for a heart.'

[77] *Thérèse Desqueyroux* (1962)

d Georges Franju *pc* Filmel *ph* Christian Matras *m* Maurice Jarre *sc* Franju, Claude Mauriac, François Mauriac (from his novel) *with* Emmanuèle Riva, Philippe Noiret, Edith Scob, Sami Frey.

Franju brings Mauriac's novel into the present, which some critics found inappropriate: 'in the age of the DS and the 404', Jean Douchet wrote in *Cahiers du cinéma* (Oct 1962), 'the situation could not have developed in this way', and other critics have tended to agree that the provincial bourgeoisie had evolved since 1927, when Mauriac's novel was published.

The film is an encounter between an atheist director (Franju) and a Catholic novelist (Mauriac) – though Mauriac's faith, with its oppressive sense of sin, represents a distinctive current in French Catholicism, if not the only one (see the objection raised to Bresson [60]). The two men met in their strong aversion to the provincial bourgeoisie. The film was 'anti-bourgeois, anti-religious and anti-society', according to Douchet, and Franju considered that he would have had still more trouble with the Office Catholique du Cinéma had it not been for Mauriac: as it was, the Office expressed reservations.

Thérèse, trapped in a loveless marriage, poisons her husband (Philippe Noiret, in one of the first of his roles as an amiable but insensitive middle-class husband). Liberated, she escapes to Paris.

[78] *Un Homme et une femme/A Man and a Woman* (1966)

d Claude Lelouch *pc* Films 13 *ph* Patrice Pouget, Jean Collomb *m* Francis Lai *sc* Lelouch *with* Anouk Aimée, Jean-Louis Trintignant, Pierre Barouh, Valérie Lagrange, Antoine Sire.

The answer to Tati [76], with an equally catchy and not dissimilar theme tune (now, appropriately enough, used in a TV commercial), this represents the lifestyle of a younger version of the Arpels from *Mon Oncle*. He is a racing driver, she is the widow of a stuntman and their previous marriages have given them two lovely children. Free of all other constraints, they agonize over the past.

It won three prizes at Cannes, including the Grand Prix of the Office Catholique International du Cinéma. 'I defy you to find, throughout the length of the film, a single character who is even slightly unlikeable', François Chevassu wrote in *Image et son* (July 1966). 'Lelouch gives us a sugary world beside which *Les Parapluies de Cherbourg* looks like the perverted child of Dante's Inferno ... As for the children, I offer them to grandmas, infertile women, childless couples and naive virgins. They will love them.' The motor car, apparently, takes up around one-third of the total running time and Chevassu points out the 'elegantly rustic' surroundings, 'very *Maison française*' (i.e. *Homes and Gardens*), which the characters inhabit. Nostalgia is a keynote of the film, whether for past loves or for the genuinely rural furniture of the grandparents of this New Class.

[79]   *Belle de Jour* (1967)
   d Luis Buñuel *pc* Paris Film/Five Film *ph* Sacha Vierny *sc* Buñuel, Jean-Claude
   Charrière *with* Catherine Deneuve, Jean Sorel, Michel Piccoli, Geneviève Page,
   Pierre Clémenti.

From *Belle de Jour*, through *Le Charme discret de la bourgeoisie* (1972) to *Cet obscur objet du désir* (1977), Buñuel relentlessly exposed the inadmissible desires behind the façade of conventional society, with a particular hostility to the middle class and the Church. His cinema was also about cinema: 'like each of Buñuel's films, *Belle de Jour* confronts the critic with the problem of the relationship between the mechanism of dreams and that of cinema', Claude Hodin wrote in *Les Temps modernes* (Aug 1967) in a long article on this study of a young woman's sexual fantasies.

[80]   *La Femme infidèle*/US: *Unfaithful Wife* (1969)
   d Claude Chabrol *pc* Les Films La Boétie/Cinégay *ph* Jean Rabier *m* Pierre
   Jansen *sc* Chabrol *ad* Guy Littaye *with* Stéphane Audran, Michel Bouquet,
   Maurice Ronet.

The surface of middle-class life (television, good food, nice children) represses passion, causing a rupture between real feelings and 'civilized' manners. A husband discovers his wife's infidelity and, going to see her lover, ends by killing him. This act of jealousy is also a revelation of love and, as a result of it, she realizes for the first time emotions that have until then been unable to penetrate the façade of their marriage.

[81]   *La Truite*/*The Trout* (1982)
   d Joseph Losey *pc* Gaumont/Partners/FT1/SFPC *ph* Henri Alekan *m* Richard
   Hartley *sc* Monique Lange, Losey, from the novel by Roger Vailland
   with Isabelle Huppert, Jean-Pierre Cassel, Jeanne Moreau, Daniel Olbrychski.

'A social comedy with bitter and sometimes tragic overtones', was Losey's tentative description of this adaptation of Vailland's novel about the impersonality of big business. In fact, it illustrates how far, since the early 1960s, certain middle-class milieux had become the 'natural' setting for the study of sexual relationships.

[82]   *Pauline à la plage/Pauline at the Beach* (1983)
       d Eric Rohmer *pc* Losange *ph* Nestor Almendros *m* Jean-Louis Valero
       sc Rohmer *with* Amanda Langlet, Arielle Dombasle, Pascal Greggory, Féodor
       Atkine, Simon de la Brosse.

Rohmer followed his series of Moral Tales with one of Comedies and Proverbs, of which this is the third. Marion and her 15-year-old cousin, on holiday, become entangled with Pierre, Henri and Sylvain. The class to which the central characters belong is, once more, treated as 'natural'. In the cultured Parisian middle class, their proper environment, these people would pass merely as 'people', with no salient social background at all, as their counterparts do in so many other films of the time. Here, in a 'foreign' setting (a Breton resort) where Henri becomes fleetingly involved with a working-class girl who sells peanuts on the beach, we have some yardstick by which to situate them: but the film constitutes an episode, distinct from 'real' life (it starts and ends with Marion and Pauline's arrival and departure by car).

One indication of changing standards: the Office Catholique Français du Cinéma which, 20 years earlier, would have almost certainly condemned such a film for immorality, merely recommended it as suitable for adolescents: 'Rohmer emphasizes the contrast between the amorous discourse and reality.'

[83]   *Notre histoire/Separate Rooms* (1984)
       d Bertrand Blier *pc* Sara/Adel/A2 *ph* Jean Penzer *m* Laurent Rossi *sc* Blier
       with Alain Delon, Nathalie Baye, Michel Galabru, Geneviève Fontanel.

A frenetic tale which 'lays bare the social and sexual hypocrisies of French middle-class society', in the words of Derek Elley's programme note when it was shown at the London Film Festival. In fact, it is more remarkable for its use of the devices of narrative fiction (stories within stories), though the climax in the bedroom could be construed as a satire on bourgeois standards.

VI   WORKING CLASS AND INDUSTRY

[84]   *La Roue* (1923)
       d Abel Gance *pc* Les Films Abel Gance *ph* Léonce-Henri Burel *sc* Gance
       with Séverin-Mars, Ivy Close, Gabriel de Gravone, Pierre Magnier.

The version of Gance's film eventually released cut out much of the social comment in the original. His railway-driver hero is elevated to the stature of a figure from classical myth, but the real hero is the railway engine. Gance's early critics praised his visual poetry and René Clair, in an article several times reprinted, wished that he would abandon fiction altogether and stick to 'pure film'.

[85]   *A nous la liberté* (1931)
>   *d* René Clair *pc* Tobis *ph* Georges Perinal *sc* Clair *ad* Lazare Meerson *with* Henri Marchand, Raymond Cordy, Rolla France.

Emile and Louis start as comrades in jail, but in the world outside Louis's success separates them and Emile finds himself as the production-line worker, Louis as the boss. In the end, reduced to the same level as tramps, they rediscover happiness and comradeship.

Clair's satire on industrial life (the factory is explicitly compared to the prison) inspired Chaplin's *Modern Times*. Its use of song and other vaudeville elements softens the satire, but Claude Aveline (*La Revue hebdomadaire*, 6 Feb 32) was pleased that Clair had not chosen the form of a political tract. ' "Let's have freedom" ', he wrote, 'is not only the cry of the escaping prisoner ... or of the worker whose submission to discipline and to work on a production "chain" – the word is significant – is almost indistinguishable from prison; it is also the secret wish of the boss whom wealth, acquired too quickly, has thrown into a life that stifles him.' Interestingly, Aveline makes a point about the inadaptability of the *nouveau riche*, when most spectators would understand Clair to mean that wealth and class in themselves are as alienating as poverty or prison.

[86]   *L'Atalante* (1934)
>   *d* Jean Vigo *pc* Gaumont *ph* Boris Kaufman, Louis Berger *m* Maurice Jaubert *sc* Vigo, from a story by Jean Guinée *with* Dita Parlo, Jean Dasté, Michel Simon.

Vigo's film about a couple on a working barge, travelling through the industrial landscape of France during the depression, is a classic of 'poetic realism': that is to say, it transforms everyday reality.

In *L'Humanité* (7 June 34), Emile Cerquast expressed indignation at the fact that Gaumont, having acquired the rights to Vigo's 'very fine film', had tried to popularize it by adding a theme song and re-titling it *Le Chaland qui passe* ('The Passing Barge'). Even 'poetic realism' could be too close to reality for popular consumption.

[87]   *La Belle équipe* (1936)
>   *d* Julien Duvivier *pc* Ciné Arts *ph* Jules Kruger, Marc Fessard *m* Maurice Yvain *sc* Charles Spaak, Duvivier *with* Jean Gabin, Charles Vanel, Viviane Romance, Raymond Aimes, Robert Lynen.

A 'Popular Front' message? Five workmen win some money on the lottery and decide to invest it in a co-operative venture, a riverside cabaret. Spaak and Duvivier preferred the unhappy ending of the first version, but the producers persuaded them to adopt a happier one, apparently after a poll taken when the film was previewed. In either case, the 'co-operative' idea is weak and Duvivier's original ending would have brought the film closer in spirit to the pessimistic melodramas in which Gabin usually starred at the time, than to the optimism of Le Crime de Monsieur Lange.

Georges Sadoul (Commune, Nov 1936) said that, in any case, 'five cannot create a little world of happiness. Happiness is an affair concerning the whole world, millions of men'; but, despite this limitation of the film, 'Duvivier does not disguise his indignation at the fate of the unemployed'.

[88] *Le Crime de Monsieur Lange/The Crime of Mr. Lange* (1936)
  d Jean Renoir pc Obéron ph Jean Bachelet m Jean Wiener sc Jacques Prévert
  with René Lefèvre, Jules Berry, Florelle, Nadia Subirskaia.

'Irony and feeling are indistinguishably mixed', Bernard Barbey wrote in *La Revue hebdomadaire* (Feb 1936) of Renoir's film which tells the story of a small printing works whose manager absconds, leaving his workers faced with unemployment. Instead they decide to run the enterprise as a co-operative and do so with the help of Lange, a writer of pulp fiction. When the manager threatens to return and destroy the co-operative, Lange kills him. It was premiered three months before the elections that brought the Popular Front to power.

Both Renoir's film and that of Prévert and the Groupe Octobre, it encapsulates the spirit of the Front and Renoir's political leanings at the time. The political importance of cinema and the debate on its significance can be judged by Renoir's assertion two years later that Quai des brumes [2] was a 'fascist' film because it showed morally tainted and dishonest characters, making you feel that a dictator was necessary to restore order.

For a writer like Barbey, not sympathetic to the Front, the film was 'an important stage in cinema technique' and marked 'a great moment in the uncertain and painful history of French cinema'. He felt, however, that to be counted a masterpiece it needed 'some of that pity which one finds in the works of Tolstoy' or in German films like *The Blue Angel*.

[89] *La Bête humaine/Human Beast/Judas was a Woman* (1938)
  d Jean Renoir pc Paris ph Curt Courant m Joseph Kosma sc Renoir, from the
  novel by Emile Zola with Jean Gabin, Simone Simon, Fernand Ledoux, Carette.

Another film banned by the censor at the start of World War II as 'depressing, morbid and immoral'. Renoir updates the story from the nineteenth century to 1938, but retains the theme of fatality: Zola's railwayman is a sex murderer because of a tainted heredity. Most of all, the film is interesting because of the picture it gives of life on the railways, as Sadoul remarked (Regards, 5 Jan 39): 'Renoir may even have surpassed Zola ... Zola, as Abel Gance was later to do in La Roue, allowed himself to be too often carried away by the "lyricism" of the railways ... From the first images we are transported into the noise of the locomotive on its way to Le Havre; then we enter the staff dormitories and changing-rooms at the express terminus, the station-master's apartment . . . We also see the obsessive and tragic shunting yards where night conceals the clandestine love of Jacques and his mistress; we go with them to the railway-workers' ball . . .'

[90]   *Le Jour se lève* (1939)

> *d* Marcel Carné *pc* Vog/Sigma *ph* Curt Courant *m* Maurice Jaubert *sc* Jacques Viot *with* Jean Gabin, Arletty, Jacqueline Laurent, Jules Berry.

Honesty against corruption. What is remarkable about Gabin's working-class hero is that he is credible both as an individual and as a representative of the 'ordinary man', which at the time meant a workman with a bicycle, not a racing-driver. Carné takes us inside the machine-shop where Gabin works, shows us where he lives, his entertainment and his dreams. At the end, when he is surrounded by the police, the crowd tries to defend him.

[91]   *Remorques*/US: *Stormy Waters* (1940)

> *d* Jean Grémillon *pc* SEDIF *ph* Armand Thirard *m* Roland Manuel *sc* Jacques Prévert, André Cayatte, from the novel by Roger Vercel *with* Jean Gabin, Michèle Morgan, Madeleine Renaud, Fernand Ledoux.

An eternal triangle, with Gabin between Morgan and Renaud. It is interesting chiefly because of the scenes on the waterfront and at sea: though the effects are appalling (the model of the tug-boat looks like a bathtime toy), the film shows the life of sailors which was Grémillon's passion.

   As a director, Grémillon was unlucky. His films of the 1930s are flawed, but demonstrate his talent. Work on *Remorques* was interrupted by the outbreak of war.

[92]   *Aubervilliers* (1945)

> *d* Eli Lothar.

Lothar's shocking documentary on the slums of a Parisian suburb.

[93]   *Le Sang des bêtes* (1949)

> *d* Georges Franju *pc* Forces et Voix de la France *ph* Marcel Fradetal *m* Joseph Kosma.

Franju's documentary, on the Paris abattoirs, is singularly unpleasant to watch: it describes systematically the method for killing different kinds of animal for meat. It suggests, too, the burden that society imposes on those who do necessary, but disagreeable jobs.

[94] *Le Point du jour* (1949)

    d Louis Daquin *ph* André Bac *sc* Vladimir Pozner *with* Desailly, René Lefèvre, Loleh Bellon.

'With the films of Renoir,' Sadoul wrote in *Les Lettres françaises*, 12 May 49, '*Le Point du jour* is one of the few French films to have gone beyond the facile travesties of populism to show the reality of popular life.' He compared Daquin's film, set in a mining community in northern France, to Ford's *How Green Was My Valley*: 'Ford, in his paternalistic and sermonizing adaptation of Richard Llewellyn's novel, imagined his miners living in smart apartments and the mine itself was chiefly an excuse for him to show the subtle interplay of lifts.'

[95] *Le Salaire de la peur/The Wages of Fear* (1953)

    d Henri-Georges Clouzot *pc* CICC/Filmsonor/Vera/Fono Roma *sc* Clouzot, Jérôme Géronini, from the novel by Georges Arnaud *with* Yves Montand, Charles Vanel, Véra Clouzot, Folco Lulli.

A brilliant suspense film with a sardonic ending, set in an imaginary South American country from which the four central characters try to earn their escape by driving lorries packed with nitroglycerine up a bumpy mountain road. Industry? Working-class? Yes, if only because of Montand. Most popular singers in Britain or the USA, whatever their background, projected an image of suave gentility. Montand, as singer and actor, was resolutely working-class.

    B. Dort analysed the film at length in *Les Temps modernes* (June 1953), praising it for its use of cinematographic effects to achieve suspense, and its depiction of character: these are not 'the abstract heroes of Westerns', though in the second part Clouzot sacrifices character to action. He notes, too, the implied homosexuality in the bond between the men. 'He never defines them as homosexuals, but merely shows them, at times, acting as such.' The ending is 'debatable in terms of simple credibility, but an astounding metaphor, carrying us from the realm of necessity to that of myth'.

    However, the film attracted a hostility that seems surprising today, notably from the Catholic press. The Centrale Catholique du Cinéma rated it 4A ('For adults, with reservations'). In *Télé-Ciné* (Nos. 40–41, 1954), Gilbert Salachas quoted Pierre Kast's description of it as 'a great atheist film': 'we share that opinion'. It gives, he said, 'a deliberately negative and unhealthy moral picture' and exhibits 'a conscious determination to exclude any spiritual dimension'. The cult of the *unhappy end* had become systematic and no more justifiable than the opposite and Clouzot's work was 'the expression of a *mal du siècle* far more harrowing in its aggressive, nihilistic despair than the tears of the Romantic generation'.

[96] *Gervaise* (1956)

    d René Clément *pc* Agnès Delahaie/Silver/CICC *ph* Robert Juillard *m* Georges Auric *sc* Jean Aurenche, Pierre Bost, from Emile Zola's novel *L'Assomoir* (1877) *with* Maria Schell, François Périer, Suzy Delair, Mathilde Cassadessus.

'That rare thing: a successful adaptation of a great novel,' Jean Pouillon wrote in *Les Temps modernes* (Apr 1957). Should it have been updated? 'In choosing to recreate, very precisely, a period and an atmosphere, Clément has undoubtedly achieved a *tour de force*, but at the expense of dating the plot, distancing it from the spectator and making what was polemical in the novel, aesthetic in the film.' On the other hand, 're-read the book and ask yourself if the current conformism of French cinema (and not only cinema) could have tolerated such a violent and profoundly pessimistic indictment! "Reconstructing" was surely the only way not to soften Zola's message. And if you think that is a pity, it is not Clément who should be blamed.'

Even a historical film about the working-class, especially one that depicts its life so convincingly, could not be consigned merely to the status of 'literature' and 'history'. In *Télé-Ciné* (No. 60, 1956), Claude-Marie Tremois described Clément as 'a moralist who adopts an authoritative language to express appalling realities which will remain an insult to humanity until all trace of them has disappeared'.

[97] *Le Bonheur* (1965)

d Agnès Varda *pc* Parc *ph* Jean Rabier, Claude Beausoleil *sc* Varda *with* Jean-Claude Drouot, Claire Drouot, Sandrine Drouot, Marie-France Boyer.

This story of an eternal triangle is set in a working-class family but uses the working-class as a 'neutral' background. 'The tone . . . is uniformly idyllic' and 'nothing could be further from social realism than the make-believe world it constructs' (Roy Armes, *French Cinema*, Secker and Warburg, 1985).

[98] *La Dentellière/The Lacemaker* (1977)

d Claude Goretta *pc* Action/FR 3/Citel/Janus *ph* Jean Boffety *m* Pierre Jansen *sc* Pascal Lainé, Goretta, from Lainé's novel *with* Isabelle Huppert, Yves Beneyton, Florence Giorgetti.

One of the few films to suggest that class divisions might still persist in French society, it tells the story of a love affair between a middle-class student and a working-class girl which eventually drives her to insanity. Her exclusion from his intellectual world is well-observed.

VII   PROVINCIAL AND RURAL LIFE

[99] *Marius* (1931)

d Alexander Korda *pc* Marcel Pagnol/Paramount *ph* Ted Pahle *sc* Pagnol *with* Raimu, Orane Demazis, Pierre Fresnay, Alida Rouffe, Charpin.

The first part of the Pagnol Marseilles trilogy. It was followed by *Fanny* (1934), directed by Marc Allégret, and *César* (1936), directed by Pagnol, with the same actors in the leading roles. Together, the three films established an image of Provençal life: the bittersweet story of the love affair between Marius and Fanny and the older generation of 'characters' in César's waterfront bar recreated on film by the actors who had played them on stage. In 1937, *La Cinématographie française* (12 March 37) published its first poll showing *César* as the most popular film of the year and the trilogy enjoyed considerable success abroad. Dilys Powell (*Sunday Times*, 18 Feb 51), quoting a colleague who regretted, after seeing *César*, that there were no more of them, wrote: 'I find myself forgetting the editing and the camera angles and all the other narrative devices of the cinema, and thinking only that here is an entrancing tale, at once funny and touching, about people.' That, perhaps, is the answer to the argument about Pagnol's films being simply 'filmed theatre'.

Claude Berri's adaptations of *Jean de Florette* and *Manon des Sources* (1986) show the continuing popularity of Pagnol's stories of Provençal life.

[100] *Angèle* (1934)

d Marcel Pagnol *pc* Les Films M. Pagnol *sc* Pagnol, from Jean Giono's novel *Un de Baumugnes* with Orane Demazis, Fernandel.

Like *Jofroi* (1934), another Giono adaptation, this was filmed on location in Provence from Pagnol's Marseilles studios – a phenomenon at a time when the French cinema industry was otherwise totally centred on Paris-Joinville. *L'Humanité* (7 Nov 34) criticized the film for having 'too much dialogue': 'there is also in *Angèle* a bias towards aestheticism not to be found in Giono'.

[101] *Toni* (1935)

d Jean Renoir *pc* Les Films Marcel Pagnol.

Set among immigrant workers in southern France, *Toni* is often seen now as a precursor of Italian neo-realism. 'The subject of the film is taken from an incident which actually happened in part of southern France ... This region is inhabited mainly by immigrants of Italian origin, half-workers, half-peasants. Among these uprooted people, passions run high and the men who served as my models in *Toni* seemed to me to carry with them that heavy atmosphere which indicates the fatal destiny of the heroes of tragedy, or indeed of popular song' (Jean Renoir, in *Comoedia*, 8 Feb 35).

[102] *Pension Mimosas* (1935)

d Jacques Feyder *pc* Tobis *ph* Roger Hubert *sc* Feyder *with* Françoise Rosay, Paul Bernard, Alerme, Lise Delamare, Arletty.

In *L'Action française* (25 Jan 35), François Vinneuil compared the theme (the undeclared love of a woman for her godson) with Greek tragedy and with Racine's

Phèdre, pointing to Feyder's boldness in tackling such a subject with 'the still scanty resources of the cinema', but feeling that it lacked the 'sombre poetry' of characters from Feyder's *Le Grand jeu* (1934), who would hardly be found 'in the limiting environment of a small, middle-class hotel, among its humble or weak-minded guests'. Bernard Barbey (*La Revue hebdomadaire*, March 1935), noting that the film had been criticized for neglecting the landscape of the Côte d'Azur, wrote: 'I cannot share these reservations ... it is indeed a fact of life in a *pension*, even in the sunniest part of the Riviera, that its guests, and still more its proprietors, barely see beyond the entrance hall, the veranda and the palm trees in the garden. Their horizon is limited to the terrace of the casino.'

Recalling the problems Feyder had experienced with *Les Nouveaux messieurs* [54], Emile Cerquast described it as 'morally clean' (*L'Humanité*, 25 Jan 35), demonstrating that 'directors who have remained "independent" are obliged to limit their imagination and to weigh carefully every part of a script'. He considered the film excessively sentimental in parts, 'a simple concession to the supposed taste of the audience'.

[103] *Regain* (1937)

d Marcel Pagnol pc Les Films M. Pagnol sc Pagnol, from the novel by Jean Giono *with* Orane Demazis, Gabriel Gabrio, Fernandel.

An abandoned Provençal village is brought back to life by Panturle (Gabrio) and Arsule (Demazis) who was formerly the mistress (almost the slave) of an itinerant knife-grinder. Jeancolas (*Quinze ans d'années trente*, Stock, 1983) describes it as 'naive cinema, like naive painting' and 'medieval', with scarcely any reference to contemporary society or events; 'in its picture of women, Pagnol's cinema is not medieval, but neolithic. Woman is not an object, but merchandise. In *Angèle*, Jean Servais and the father negotiate her fate in her absence. In *Regain*, Panturle reimburses Gedemus the amount which represents Arsule's upkeep. Arsule is an animal.'

Jeancolas also discusses the question of the relationship of the film to the doctrines of Vichy's wartime Révolution Nationale: *Regain* 'would be, three years in advance, the ideology of the Révolution Nationale were it not so clearly distinguished from the "priest-ridden" dimension' of Vichy. I discuss this question above [pages 40–41]. Giono's anarchism seems to me quite distinct from the ideology of Vichy, and the non-Catholic dimension a significant one. But some aspects of Giono did appeal to Vichy. The documentaries *Manosque, pays de Jean Giono* and Maurice Labro's *Le Pain* appeared during the occupation and were praised in *L'Action française* by Ed. Michel in lyrical terms: the first celebrated 'the joy of the earth, the song of the water and the wind', the second was 'a fine hymn to the basic foodstuff of Frenchmen and the virtues of the race'. But to make Pagnol and Giono responsible for Vichy's promulgation of peasant and family life, is an attempt to establish their guilt by association.

[104] *La Femme du boulanger* (1938)

d Marcel Pagnol pc Les Films M. Pagnol sc Pagnol, from Giono's novel *Jean le Bleu*, with Raimu, Ginette Leclerc.

When the village baker's wife runs off, he refuses to work and the villagers are pressed into helping him to secure her return. 'A very broad farce,' according to Georges Sadoul (*Regards*, 22 Sept 38), 'in the good old tradition of Molière and peasant humour', but at the same time tragic in its depiction of the betrayed husband: 'an admirably French work'. There is a curé, caricatured perhaps rather too much by 'facile and conventional anti-clericalism' but 'we defy all Herr Goebbels' directors to make a film as completely German, all those employed by Sig. Mussolini to create a work as utterly Italian, as this *Femme du boulanger* is French, for all it was produced in a France still in the hands of the Judeo-Marxists, the half-castes and the Slavonic hordes of the Popular Front.'

[105]   *Goupi-Mains-Rouges*/US: *It Happened at the Inn* (1943)

> *d* Jacques Becker *pc* Minerva *ph* Jean Bourgoin, Pierre Montazel *m* Jean Alfaro *sc* Becker, Pierre Véry from his novel *with* Fernand Ledoux, Blanchette Brunoy, Robert Le Vigan.

A peasant family, hostile to outsiders, with the conventional traits of rapacity and greed, settles its own scores. This is no idealized view of country life. Becker's next film, *Falbalas*, was set in the very different world of *haute couture* and made just as the war ended.

[106]   *Le Corbeau*/US: *The Raven* (1943)

> *d* Henri-Georges Clouzot *pc* Continental *ph* N. Hayer *sc* Louis Chavance, Clouzot *with* Pierre Fresnay, Ginette Leclerc, Pierre Larquey, Roger Blin.

Inspired by a case of poison pen letters in Tulle, this would have passed as a conventional thriller had it been made 20 years later. In the event, it caused a scandal and was banned after the war.

The criticisms were moral and ideological. The Office Familial de Documentation Artistique rated it grade 6. Grade 5 was not recommended even for adult audiences, so grade 6 was indescribably bad. François Vinneuil, who had expressed his own aesthetic reservations about it in *Je suis partout* (9 Oct 43: 'we are becoming more demanding of Clouzot's brilliant gifts'), wondered in the same paper (15 March 44) just what the Office *did* consider suitable for French audiences. The Centrale Catholique du Cinéma's ratings did not go beyond grade 5 ('proscribed'), so that is what the film got. 'What people find unpardonable in Henri-Georges Clouzot,' Roger Régent wrote in *Les Nouveaux temps* (Oct 1944), 'is his talent.'

Ideologically, the film did not appeal to the Right (despite Vinneuil): 'It is clear that, throughout the length and breadth of his script, M. Louis Chavance has been seized by the desire to scandalize,' wrote *L'Action française* (3 Oct 43). '*Le Corbeau* has deliberately infringed the most elementary principles of the most common morality.' Still less to the Left: in the clandestine *Lettres françaises* (15 Apr 44), G. Adam and P. Blanchar compared it unfavourably to Grémillon's *Le Ciel est à vous* (1944): 'The Germans can rub their hands: after many mistakes in judging the worth of their French valets, they have finally dug up two who, under cover of a spotless and sometimes even attractive piece of merchandise, will be superb standard-bearers for the enemy's cleverly-concealed ideology ... In contrast to the morally crippled, abnormal and corrupt characters who, in *Le Corbeau*, dishonour one of our provincial towns, *Le Ciel est à vous* offers characters full of French vigour, genuine courage and moral health in whom we rediscover a national truth which will not and cannot die.' Hurray! Unfortunately, the (non-clandestine) Fascist press was also claiming *Le Ciel est à vous* for its own (which just shows how careful you have to be in assigning an ideological tendency to works of fiction).

[107] *Premier de cordée* (1944)
d Louis Daquin *sc* from the novel by Roger Frison-Roche.

Like Grémillon, the work of a left-wing director who had no intention of upholding the ideology of the Révolution Nationale, this story of man's battle against the mountains was also later accused of 'Pétainism' in its preference for the countryside over the town, etc. 'I was, after all, in charge of the clandestine trade union organization,' Daquin wrote in his own defence (*Cinématographe*, May 1978), while accepting that there are 'elements of Pétainist ideology in *Premier de cordée*: whatever one is, one is always subject to the influence of the dominant ideology.'

[108] *Farrebique* (1946)
d Georges Rouquier *pc* L'Ecran Français et Les Films *ph* André Dantan *sc* Rouquier.

See next entry.

[109] *Biquefarre* (1982)
d Rouquier *pc* Midas/Mallia *ph* André Villard *m* Yves Gilbert *sc* Rouquier with the inhabitants of Goutrens (Aveyron)

Rouquier's two documentary dramas about Goutrens must be considered together, though they show contrasting worlds, because they make up the most convincing portrayal of peasant life in French (perhaps in European) cinema. The first is a record of the 'unchanging' face of village life and of farming people whose customs and relationship to the soil had hardly changed since the Middle Ages. The second, centring on the sale of a property, does indeed show some 'unchanging' aspects of the outlook of the same characters, but emphasizes above all the profound alterations that have occurred in their circumstances: mechanization of farming, pollution, even the effects of the Common Agricultural Policy. It is a painful and sad film, but at the same time an extraordinarily penetrating examination of the thoughts and feelings of country people.

Of the first film, Georges Sadoul wrote (*Les Lettres françaises*, 21 March 47): 'it is above all a hymn to the "eternal" peasant and to nature, immutable since the beginning of time ... We see, only or almost only, a "family cell", cut off from the rest of mankind and France'; but, 'despite obvious omissions, the peasants of *Farrebique* do not belong to all time: they are farmers and landowners in the Aveyron in 1946. This is why the film is a great work of art, for the eternal can only be reached through the present.'

[110] *Les Vacances de Monsieur Hulot/Mr Hulot's Holiday* (1953)
    d Jacques Tati *pc* Cady/Discina/Eclair Journal *ph* Jacques Mercanton, Jean Mousselle *m* Alain Romans *sc* Tati, Henri Marquet *with* Tati, Nathalie Pascaud, Louis Perrault, Michèle Rolla.

A delightful comedy of manners which tells a good deal about the atmosphere of a holiday resort on the Normandy coast (near to Paris, and so popular just after the war). Needless to say, there are a couple of English tourists.

[111] *Le Beau Serge* (1958)
    d Claude Chabrol *pc* AJUM/CGCF *ph* Henri Decae *sc* Chabrol *with* Gérard Blain, Jean-Claude Brialy, Bernadette Lafont, Michèle Meritz.

In an open letter to Chabrol, Bernard Dort (*Les Temps modernes*, Apr 1959) compared this with the director's second feature, *Les Cousins* (1959), contrasting the 'reality' of the village of Sardent in the first to the artificiality of the Parisian bourgeoisie in the second. 'We see Sardent through your eyes, through those of your hero ... The square in front of the church, the children's games, the inhabitants walking past, the *bistrot*, the hotel room, the bad morning coffee, the hop ... This village, both open and shut, impenetrable, warm and cold, intimate and foreign, is more than just true: we all know it, we have all seen and lived it.' Through the central character we discover Sardent and Serge, 'his wasted life, his drunkenness, his irritability'.

Serge is the provincial who didn't get away, François the one who did. But, starting from this apparently clear-cut distinction, Chabrol makes us question the ideas of success and failure, and operates a 'Hitchcockian' transfer of guilt.

[112] *Les Parapluies de Cherbourg/The Umbrellas of Cherbourg*
    (1964)
    d Jacques Demy *pc* Madeleine/Beta (Munich) *m* Michel Legrand *sc* Demy *with* Catherine Deneuve, Nino Castelnuovo, Marc Michel, Anne Vernon, Ellen Farner.

The plot is similar to that of *Marius*: a girl finds herself pregnant after her boyfriend has gone away and enters a marriage of convenience to someone else. In this case, the boyfriend is called up for military service in Algeria and the film does give a powerful feeling of the times and the everyday life of the city where it is set – incredibly, in view of the fact that all the dialogue is sung. Georges Sadoul recognized this realistic element in a package so obviously artificial: 'If I was a lawyer or an obstetrician, I could tell you fifty stories like this one' (*Les Lettres françaises*, 20 Feb 64). 'I saw people weeping near me at some scenes in the film and I was myself profoundly moved by it.'

[113] *Mouchette* (1967)

d Robert Bresson *pc* Parc/Argos *ph* Ghislain Cloquet *sc* Bresson, from the novel by Georges Bernanos *with* Nadine Nortier, Jean-Claude Guilbert, Marie Cardinal.

Bresson's heroine, humiliated and despised, lives in a tragic world, cut off from love and communication with others. Rural life is depicted as cruel and unpleasant, its timeless dimension (like that of Bernanos' story) being indicated by the deliberate juxtaposition of old and new, neither of which is shown as in any way attractive. Bernanos' sense of sin and of the meanness of human existence, finds a perfect expression in Bresson.

[114] *Le Boucher* (1970)

d Claude Chabrol *pc* Les Films La Boétie/Euro International *ph* Jean Rabier *sc* Chabrol *with* Stéphane Audran, Jean-Pierre Cassel, Jean-Claude Drouot.

The village schoolteacher (Audran) falls in love with the butcher, who turns out to be killing more than dumb animals. In *Les Temps modernes* (Apr 1970), Christian Zimmer wrote of 'the loving way in which he has photographed the little village of Trémolat, teaching us in our turn to love its main street, its school, its church, its square and its war memorial . . .' and said that the film achieved a perfect balance between 'spectacle' and 'meaning'.

[115] *La Veuve Couderc* (1971)

d Pierre Granier-Deferre *pc* Lira *ph* Walter Wottitz *m* Philippe Sarde *sc* Granier-Deferre, Pascal Jardin, from the novel by Georges Simenon *with* Simone Signoret, Alain Delon, Jean Tissier.

In the 1920s, a country widow shelters a man wanted by the police and falls in love with him. Not, perhaps, on anyone's list of the greatest French films, it is enchantingly photographed in the Burgundy countryside and the details of rural life (except for Signoret's accent) carefully reproduced.

[116] *Poulet au vinaigre/'Cop au vin'* (1985)

d Claude Chabrol *pc* MK2 *ph* Jean Rabier *m* Mathieu Chabrol *sc* Chabrol, Dominique Roulet from his novel *Une Mort en trop*, *with* Jean Poiret, Stéphane Audran, Lucas Belvaux, Michel Bouquet, Caroline Cellier.

Chabrol's favourite territory: the darker side of the provincial bourgeoisie, with in this case a very vicious police inspector who seems to believe that anything is justified, provided it arrives at the truth.

VIII PARIS

[117] *Fantômas* (1913–14)

d Louis Feuillade *pc* Gaumont *sc* Feuillade.

Followed by the series of *Judex* and *Les Vampires*, and filmed in the studio and on location in Paris and its suburbs, these helped to reinforce a particular image of the city, derived ultimately from Eugène Sue's novels *Les Mystères de Paris* (1842–43) which were also filmed before World War I. This mythical Parisian underworld thus persists from the popular literature of the 19th century to *Subway* [126], and no doubt beyond.

[118] *Sous les toits de Paris* (1930)

d René Clair *pc* Tobis *m* Armand Bernard, Raoul Moretti, R. Nazelles *ph* Georges Périnal, Georges Paulet *sc* Clair *ad* Lazare Meerson *with* Albert Préjean, Pola Illéry, Gaston Modot, Edmond Gréville.

The first great success of French sound cinema depicts a less sinister underworld Paris than that of *Fantômas*, but still suggests the mixture of classes and professions through the device of the apartment house: cheap lodgings upstairs, more luxurious ones on the lower floors. 'Alas, it looks as if everyone must get there eventually', Pierre Bost wrote in *La Revue hebdomadaire* (May 1930), admitting that Clair's film was the best French contribution to the 'talkies'. 'A fairly average script, not very successfully situated in *bals-musette*, among somewhat outdated characters (the bandit, the shop-girl, the honest street-vendor) once more demonstrates M. René Clair's skill and intelligence.' The comedy was better, though, in the silent scenes and the *genre* could only lead to less brilliant achievements.

[119] *La Chienne* (1931)

d Jean Renoir *pc* Braunberger/Richebé *ph* Theodore Sparkuhl, Roger Hubert *sc* Renoir, from the novel by Georges de la Fouchardière *with* Michel Simon, Janie Marèze, Georges Flamand.

Set in Montmartre, Renoir's early venture into sound was disappointing, but includes some stock characters of French cinema in the period, notably the prostitute played by Janie Marèze.

[120] *Hôtel du Nord* (1938)

d Marcel Carné *pc* Sedif *ph* Armand Thirard *m* Maurice Jaubert *sc* Jacques Prévert, Henri Jeanson, Jean Aurenche, from the novel by Eugène Dabit *ad* Alexandre Trauner *with* Arletty, Annabella, Louis Jouvet, Jules Berry, Jean-Pierre Aumont.

The district of the Canal Saint-Martin provides the setting for the story of two couples which has the doom-laden atmosphere of all the Prévert-Carné films of this time. It is remarkable chiefly for the performance of Louis Jouvet, a leading figure in French theatre who was also a great cinema actor.

[121] *Bob le Flambeur/Bob the Gambler* (1955)

d Jean-Pierre Melville *pc* OGC/Jenner/Play Art/La Cyme *ph* Henri Decae *m* Eddie Barclay, Jean Boyer *sc* Melville *with* Isabelle Corey, Roger Duchesne, Daniel Cauchy, Guy Decomble, André Garret.

Melville's experience of the underworld around Pigalle (as a *résistant* in the war) served him in good stead. The plot has an ironical twist: a plan to rob the casino at Deauville goes wrong. The film was overshadowed when first released by the successes of *Touchez-pas au grisbi* and *Du rififi chez les hommes*, but Jean-Yves Gonte said that it caught the 'poetic truth' of Montmartre (*Cahiers du Cinéma*, Oct 1956).

[122] *French Cancan* (1955)

d Jean Renoir *pc* Franco-London/Jolly *ph* Michel Kelber *m* Georges van Parys *sc* Renoir *with* Jean Gabin, Françoise Arnoul, Maria Félix, Jean-Roger Caussimon.

The history of the Moulin Rouge: a celebration of tourist Paris, perhaps, but filmed with reference to impressionist and post-impressionist paintings, to give a picture of the city's more obvious charm. 'René Clair on an off day,' was the verdict of *Les Temps modernes* (Aug 1955).

[123] *Porte des Lilas/Gate of Lilacs* (1957)

d René Clair *pc* Sonor/Cinetel/Seca/Rizzoli *ph* Robert Le Febvre *m* Georges Brassens *sc* Clair, Jean Aural, from René Fallet's novel *La Grande ceinture* *ad* Léon Barsacq *with* Pierre Brasseur, Brassens, Henri Vidal, Dany Carrel.

'One of the best French films of 1957,' *L'Humanité* proclaimed, in its cinema review of a year that was 'not only that of Brigitte Bardot' (1 Jan 58). 'René Clair takes us back to the films of his youth with his usual affection for the inhabitants of the slums. His romantic crooks are slightly ridiculous: but friendship, the *valse-musette*, the corner *bistrot* and thwarted love are the stars.'

It also marked the only screen appearance of Brassens, a unique figure in French popular music.

135

[124] *Deux ou trois choses que je sais d'elle/Two or Three Things I Know About Her* (1967)
d Jean-Luc Godard *pc* Annouchka/Argos/Les Films du Carrosse/Parc *ph* Raoul Coutard *sc* Godard, from an investigation by Cathérine Vimonet *with* Marina Vlady, Anny Duperey, Roger Montsoret, Jean Narboni.

Godard's study of the satellite housing estates which were growing up around Paris at this time ('homes for the incurable'), suggesting that bored housewives, left alone during the day, resorted to prostitution. This is combined with Godard's habitual reflexions on communication and other matters.

[125] *Playtime* (1967)
d Jacques Tati *pc* Specta *ph* Jean Bourgoin *m* Franck Barcellini, Alain Romans *sc* Tati, Jacques Lagrange *with* Tati, Jean-Pierre Zola.

Tati's most savage attack on the New Paris, centring on a group of tourists who visit this 'anywhere' of glass and concrete, rather than the real city which was still somewhere to be found.

[126] *Subway* (1985)
d Luc Besson *pc* Loup/TFS/Gaumont/TF1 *ph* Carlo Varini *m* Eric Serra *sc* Besson, Pierre Jolivet *ad* Alexandre Trauner *with* Christophe Lambert, Isabelle Adjani, Michel Galabru, Jean-Hughes Anglade, Richard Bohringer.

Subway opens with a splendid car chase that actually finishes in the *métro* where Christophe Lambert escapes from his pursuers to become a latter-day Fantômas brandishing a light-stick and surrounded by a collection of *marginaux* who are supposed to inhabit the passageways behind the subway stations. No wonder Adjani prefers the company of these freaks to the ones in the polite dining-rooms of her husband's friends. It was one of France's most successful film exports of the year.

IX   CRIME AND THE LAW

[127] *L'Alibi* (1937)
d Pierre Chenal *pc* BN *ph* Ted Pähle, Jacques Mercanton *m* Georges Auric *sc* Marcel Achard *with* Jany Holt, Margo Lion, Louis Jouvet, Erich von Stroheim, Albert Préjean, Roger Blin.

'Melodrama and a complete absence of taste', was Georges Sadoul's description of *L'Alibi* in *Le Cinéma français* (Flammarion, 1962), but Chenal is still one of the most varied and neglected directors of the period. He produced documentaries (*Les Petits métiers de Paris*, 1932, on Parisian street life), dramas (*La Rue sans nom*, 1934, an example of 'poetic realism') and thrillers. This confronts a murderer (von Stroheim) with an early type of the unscrupulous and cynical detective (Jouvet). Its chief weakness lies in Achard's script.

[128] *Le Dernier tournant* (1939)

d Pierre Chenal *pc* Gladiator *ph* Claude Renoir, Christian Matras *sc* Henri Torrès, from James M. Cain's novel *The Postman Always Rings Twice ad* Georges Wakhévitch, Maurice Colasson *with* Corinne Luchaire, Florence Marly, Fernand Gravey, Robert Le Vigan, Michel Simon.

One of the many adaptations of Cain's thriller in which the murderer gets away with his crime, only to be convicted of the killing of his accomplice (Luchaire) for which he was not responsible. The seedy American roadhouse is successfully transformed into a seedy French roadhouse, and the American depression atmosphere to France. In neither case is one surprised that the characters will stick at nothing to escape, even if it is fate, rather than justice, that punishes them in the end.

[129] *Justice est faite* (1950)

d André Cayatte *pc* Silver *ph* Jean Bourgoin *m* Raymond Legrand *sc* Charles Spaak, Cayatte *with* Valentine Tessier, Claude Nollier, Jacques Castelor, Michel Auclair.

One of Cayatte's four social dramas: the others are *Nous sommes tous des assassins* (1952), *Avant le déluge* (1953) and *Le Dossier Noir* (1955) which dealt with euthanasia, the death penalty and other topics. On the first two of these films, *Les Temps modernes* (July 1952) carried articles by Jean Cau and Bernard Dort. 'If a family was not forced to live in one room, a tired and overwrought father would not brain his child because it was crying,' Cau wrote. 'And if the Assistance Publique was not a jail for children, the children would not later become adult jailbirds.' Dort replied by questioning Cau's criteria for judging *Nous sommes tous des assassins*, describing it as 'a sensation-seeking film', propagandist and simplistic in construction, and preferring *Justice est faite*.

An interesting reaction in *Télé-Ciné* (No. 35, 1953), in an article by J.-P. Noel on *Nous sommes tous des assassins* – a reminder that Catholic opinion was (and is) divided on the abolition of the death penalty: 'Does not "understanding" the criminal mean absolving him, at least partially? Is this not an implicit encouragement to all other possible murderous acts? ... Major objections can be raised to Cayatte's underlying thesis.'

On the death penalty, see Lelouch's *La Vie, l'amour, la mort* [146]. The treatment of juvenile offenders was dealt with in the documentary fiction *Chiens perdus sans colliers* (1955), Jean Delannoy's adaptation of Gilbert Cesbron's novel, starring Jean Gabin.

[130] *Casque d'Or* (1952)

d Jacques Becker *pc* Speva/Paris *ph* Robert Le Febvre *m* Georges van Parys *sc* Backer, Jacquez Companeez *ad* Jean d'Eaubonne *with* Serge Reggiani, Simone Signoret, Claude Dauphin, Raymond Bussières.

A period piece, set at the turn of the century, this could probably have as well gone under Paris or History; but the period setting is largely incidental, though carefully recreated, like the Parisian sets. 'This Paris 1900 does not come out of a fashion book,' Colette Audry wrote in *Les Temps modernes* (July 1952), adding that Becker 'has a gift for satire which he should exploit'. Georges Sadoul (*Les Lettres françaises*, 18 Apr 52), said that the plot was taken from a celebrated court case of the time. An ordinary working man falls in love with the mistress of a criminal and is eventually guillotined after committing a justifiable murder and being betrayed by the woman's lover.

Sadoul compared Reggiani's role with those played by Gabin in the 1930s: 'Serge Reggiani does not labour under the weight of a destiny that comes direct from old German films and Greek tragedy. He is, to speak the language of 1900, "a victim of society".' As for Becker, 'he has rediscovered the realistic poetry of Paris and its suburbs, the secret of which seemed to have disappeared with Feuillade.'

[131] *Touchez-pas au grisbi/Grisbi* (1954)

d Jacques Becker *pc* Del Duca/Silver/Antarès *ph* Pierre Montazel *m* Jean Wiener *sc* Becker, Maurice Griffe, Albert Simonin, from Simonin's novel *ad* Jean d'Eaubonne *with* Jean Gabin, René Dary, Paul Frankeur, Lino Ventura, Jeanne Moreau, Victor Franken.

Gabin's 'middle period': friendship takes the place of love, world-weariness has at last overcome hope and the ambition is not to escape, but to get enough money to settle down. Colette Audry analysed Gabin's part at length in *Les Temps modernes* (Nov 1954): 'the story of a gangster, a womanizer, cynical, intrepid, who can only finally be defeated by his own heart which is too loyal to his feeble and clumsy friend'. The ageing Gabin becomes the opposite of the stereotype, imagining rest 'because the life he leads seems *ridiculous to him at his age* ... We have reached the moment when the genre still persists and keeps its style, but empty of substance. This is illustrated by the hero's relationships with women. It is nothing new to discover that gangster films are misogynistic, but women were still expected to produce a certain effect on "men". Max has moved beyond that. Perhaps the conversation of little dancing-girls does bore him, that one understands; that he does not, like his friend Riton, risk being taken for a ride, is his bounden duty as a gangster; but that he should prefer to sleep alone, is quite new.'

In *Télé-Ciné*, Gilbert Salachas admitted that, *à la limite*, the film might teach fraternity and humility, but in the main it was 'far from edifying'.

[132] *Les Diaboliques/Diabolique* (1955)

d Henri-Georges Clouzot *pc* Filmsonor *ph* Armand Thirard *m* Georges van Parys *sc* Clouzot, Jérôme Géronimi, from the novel *Celle qui n'était plus* by Boileau and Narcejac *with* Simone Signoret, Véra Clouzot, Paul Meurisse, Charles Vanel, Pierre Larquey.

A shocker: the story of a plot by two women to murder the husband of one of them, with a totally improbable twist in the tail (very similar to the 1985 Boileau-Narcejac adaptation *Les Louves/Letters to an Unknown Lover*, made by the British director Peter Duffell). The shameless audience manipulation was not what attracted critical attention at the time. Gilbert Salachas in *Télé-Ciné* (No. 46, 1955): 'The world described ... is the most sordid, the most base, the most negative in modern mankind. Everything there is unhealthy, tainted, vile or twisted.' Clouzot 'does not seem to be repulsed by the emptiness and the sickening monstrosity of his little world. He appears to enjoy it and to glut himself with horrors ... If *Les Diaboliques* is a joke, it is not a very agreeable one' and 'one can only be amazed ... at the almost collective aberration of journalists and critics who are usually better informed and who have managed to promote such a desperately empty work.'

[133] *Du Rififi chez les hommes/Rififi* (1955)

> *d* Jules Dassin *pc* Henri Bérard *ph* Philippe Agostini *m* Georges Auric *sc* Dassin, René Wheeler, Auguste le Breton, from le Breton's novel *ad* Alexandre Trauner *with* Jean Servais, Carl Möhner, Robert Manuel.

A suspense thriller with all the ingredients of the French version of the genre: friendship, irony and Parisian locations, and a celebrated scene of a jewel robbery filmed in total silence which remains one of the most gripping moments in the cinema.

[134] *Ascenseur pour l'échafaud/Lift to the Scaffold* (1958)

> *d* Louis Malle *pc* Nouvelles Editions de Films *ph* Henri Decae *m* Miles Davis *sc* Malle, Roger Nimier, from the novel by Noel Calef *with* Maurice Ronet, Jeanne Moreau, Georges Poujouly, Yori Bertin, Lino Ventura.

The conventional ingredients of suspense and irony combine in Malle's first film. Moreau plots with her lover Ronet to kill her husband, but it all goes wrong when he gets stuck in a lift (the suspense) and his car is stolen by a young tearaway who uses Ronet's gun to commit another murder. Ronet escapes from the lift, only to be arrested for the crime he did not commit. Georges Sadoul wondered why a young director (Malle was 25) should have to tackle such a ridiculous theme, imposed on him because producers found such subjects 'commercial', though the public was sick of them (*Les Lettres françaises*, 30 Jan 58).

Other critics looked more closely at Malle's treatment of this conventional plot and found the characters and style of the film deeply significant. 'His characters belong precisely to our time, to 1957,' Armand Monjo wrote in *L'Humanité* (1 Feb 58). '... they evoke, in a few gestures or a few lines, the important problems of our age: the ultra-rich arms dealer who has interests in Saharan oil ("How many thousand million francs did you make out of the war in Indo-China? And now, how much from Algeria?", asks his "right-hand man" [Ronet] before killing him); the former parachutist [Ronet] who coldly and meticulously plans the murder of his mistress' husband ...'

In *Les Temps modernes* (May 1958), Raymond Borde went further along the same path to conclude that 'in every sense of the word, *Ascenseur pour l'échafaud* is a Fascist film.' Right-wing critics, 'understandably, have hailed Louis Malle as a new Vadim ... Like Vadim, he is the victim of certain myths ... One can see that he is obsessed by the exterior marks of wealth ... the motorway motel where you drink champagne with former SS officers, now Common Market businessmen ... These monied Teutons take pride of place in the mythology of Louis Malle and Roger Vadim. They have lived through the Hitler "adventure".' But 'the human model which Louis Malle offers for mass admiration is still more suspect and repulsive [Ronet] ... He kills the arms dealer. This noble murder recommends him to the sympathy of the audience ... He is admired: "That bloke, he's covered with medals and wounds ... He's got incredible style." ' Finally, there is 'a young tearaway in a leather jacket ... a future parachutist' – 'a fashionable little tough guy, a 35-year-old ex-officer and a neo-Nazi capitalist, make up the three reference points of Louis Malle's inner dream'.

[135] *En cas de malheur/Love is My Profession* (1958)

> *d* Claude Autant-Lara *pc* Iéna *ph* Jacques Natteau *m* René Cloerec *sc* Jean
> Aurenche, Pierre Bost, from the novel by Georges Simenon *ad* Max Douy
> *with* Jean Gabin, Brigitte Bardot, Edwige Feuillère, Franco Interlenghi.

One of the three films chosen to represent France in Venice, it brought together old and new figures in French cinema, in conventional characters: Gabin as a lawyer, Feuillère as his wife and Bardot as a young prostitute. It was less a herald of the New Wave, however, than the meeting of the commercial cinema and the 'cinema of quality'.

[136] *La Tête contre les murs/The Keepers* (1958)

> *d* Georges Franju *pc* Attica/Sirius/Elpenor *ph* Eugen Shuftan *m* Maurice Jarre
> *sc* Jean-Pierre Mocky, from the novel by Hervé Bazin *ad* Louis Le Barbenchon
> *with* Mocky, Pierre Brasseur, Paul Meurisse, Anouk Aimée, Charles Aznavour.

The central character is a young delinquent whose father, a middle-class lawyer, has him put away after an apparently 'inexplicable' crime. Filmed inside an actual asylum, it questions both the treatment of mental illness and society's definition of it.

[137] *Pickpocket* (1959)

> *d* Robert Bresson *pc* Agnès Delahaie *ph* Léonce-Henri Burel *sc* Bresson
> *with* Martin Lassalle, Marika Green, Pierre Leymarie, Pierre Etaix.

The inspiration came from Dostoievsky's *Crime and Punishment*, but the style and atmosphere are entirely Bresson's. Sadoul (*Le Cinéma français*, Flammarion, 1962) said that the director had advanced still further into Jansenist asceticism, depriving the film of any dramatic artifice, but noted that however 'mystical' his approach, 'he knows how to recreate, intensely, certain contemporary realities'.

[138] *A bout de souffle/Breathless* (1960)

d Jean-Luc Godard pc Georges de Beauregard/SNC/Impéria ph Raoul Coutard
m Martial Solal sc Godard, from an idea by François Truffaut with Jean-Paul
Belmondo, Jean Seberg, Claude Mansard, Daniel Boulanger.

Godard's first feature uses the conventions of the Hollywood 'B' movie and makes them
entirely his own. This new version of the New Wave did not appeal to Georges Sadoul
(*Les Lettres françaises*, 31 March 60); the Left had just started to come to terms with the
old one. 'I prefer the sincerity of *Le Beau Serge* or *Les 400 coups* to this astonishing
success, in which neither the heroes nor the plot appeal to me.'

He goes on to quote Godard's assertion that, since it was 'conformist' to hate the
police, his hero was unconventional when he said 'I like cops'. 'This anti-conformism is
worse than the worst conformism ... Godard declared in these pages: "I have made the
anarchist film I dreamed of." Fine. But one may judge that his rebellion is far from being
a left-wing one.'

In *Les Temps modernes* (Apr-May – 1960), Gérard Bonnet saw the film more in terms
of the influence of Hollywood on society and 'the priority given to effect, this taste for
style pushed if necessary to the point of murder.' 'Conventional opinion has long
wondered whether cinema can express the whole of human reality. Jean-Luc Godard's
film offers an unexpected solution to this aesthetic problem ... It predicts that there will
soon be no other human reality than that which the cinema can express. It
demonstrates this with convincing talent. But should we rejoice?'

[139] *Le Trou/The Hole* (1960)

d Jacques Becker pc Play Art/Filmsonor/Titanus ph Ghislain Cloquet sc Becker,
José Giovanni, Jean Aurel, from Giovanni's novel ad Rino Mondellini
with Michel Constantin, Jean Keraudy, Philippe Leroy.

Becker returns to his favourite themes of loyalty and friendship in this story of a prison
escape, with no background music and non-professional actors. Raymond Borde (*Les
Temps modernes*, Apr–May 1960) called it 'an astonishing "drama of objects"' and
praised its 'micro-sociological' descriptions, using the opportunity for a dig at the New
Wave: 'the film shows a mastery beside which the little audacities of the New Wave are
feeble stammerings'.

[140] *Le Cave se rebiffe/*US: *The Counterfeiters of Paris* (1961)

d Gilles Grangier sc Michel Audiard, Albert Simonin with Jean Gabin.

One of many gangster movies of the period, none of which could equal *Touchez pas au
grisbi* [130] or *Du rififi chez les hommes* [131], though many of them seemed to use Gabin
whose personality dictated the real meaning of the film. 'A million French people have
already seen *Le Cave se rebiffe*,' Claude Tarare wrote (*Les Temps modernes*, Dec 1961),
quoting the distributors' publicity for the film. 'One might more truly say: a million
French people have *already seen themselves* in *Le Cave se rebiffe* ... as they are and as they
imagine themselves to be.' The crooks talk slang, but think as *bourgeois* and live like

bourgeois: 'A documentary on our contemporaries ... average Frenchmen, reading *L'Aurore* and *Le Parisien libéré*.' And Tarare's description of Gabin's 'godfather' role might have suggested some interesting comparisons to his readers: 'The Father has retired from active life, but in his field, he was a master. He *is* a master, so much so that former colleagues come and ... beg him to go back to work. Coquettish, the Father takes a little persuasion; then he accepts, nostalgic for a job well done and irritated at seeing his successors blundering about in the work he loves. Combining authority, calmness, seriousness, prudence, efficiency and humour, the Father sees the job through successfully, defeats and tricks his associates who intended to trick him, then goes back to his distant rural retreat ...'

Three years earlier, de Gaulle had been persuaded (with the support of the Army, which expected him to maintain the French presence in Algeria) to leave his country home in Colombey-les-Deux-Eglises and take over the presidency. Finding that French rule in Algeria was doomed, he granted the country independence, to the dismay of some elements of the Army who rebelled on the barricades of 1960 and later formed the Organisation Armée Secrète for a terrorist campaign which reached its height in 1962. De Gaulle did not return to his country retreat until 1969.

[141] *Le Doulos*/US: *Doulos – The Finger Man* (1963)
> *d* Jean-Pierre Melville *pc* Rome-Paris/Champion *ph* Nicolas Hayer *sc* Melville, from the novel by Pierre Lesou *with* Jean-Pierre Belmondo, Serge Reggiani, Jean Desailly, Fabienne Dali, Michel Piccoli, Monique Hennessy.

'Le doulos' means 'the informer'; so, too, does 'la balance' (see [150]) – and in both films the informer is a woman, though the male lead is suspected. Melville's complex plot is really a morality about appearance and reality, love and betrayal, though Patrick Bureau, in *Les Lettres françaises* (14 Feb 63) saw it as a 'disturbing apology of the informer's trade'. Jean Rochereau (*La Croix*, 16 Feb 63) interpreted it as showing the 'universal implications and tragic dimension' of the police informer. *Le Monde* (Jean de Baroncelli, 14 Feb 63) described the film as 'great cinema', though it found the police mythology questionable.

[142] *Bande à part*/*The Outsiders*/US: *Band of Outsiders* (1964)
> *d* Jean-Luc Godard *pc* Annouchka/Orsay *ph* Raoul Coutard *m* Michel Legrand *sc* Godard, from the novel *Fool's Gold* by D. and B. Hitchens *with* Anna Karina, Sami Frey, Claude Brasseur, Louisa Colpeyn.

The publisher Gallimard's celebrated detective fiction list, the *série noire*, specialized in translations of American thrillers and give its name to a particular sub-genre of the crime novel. French film-makers were attracted to the cynical outlook and sleazy atmosphere of these works, which could easily be translated to a French setting. *Bande à part*, set in the Paris suburbs, is a tribute, with the usual Godardian interjection of reflexions on a variety of apparently unconnected topics.

[143] *Pierrot le Fou* (1965)

> *d* Jean-Luc Godard *pc* Rome-Paris Films/Dino de Laurentis *ph* Raoul Coutard
> *m* Antoine Duhamel *sc* Godard, from a novel by Lionel White *with* Jean-Paul
> Belmondo, Anna Karina, Dirk Sanders, Raymond Devos.

Once more, Godard transforms his basic material to make a completely individual work. Belmondo and Karina meet, fall in love, commit murder and rampage across France, enjoying one of those brief idylls that recur in the genre. Godard is 'consistent in his inconsistency,' Jeancolas remarks (*Le Cinéma des français*, Stock, 1979). '... like a street urchin who does not respect the rules of the game, he expresses the unease of an increasing number of young people in a country ruled by a very old man according to very old principles.'

Pierrot's adventures are 'not absurd'. Georges Sadoul wrote (*Les Lettres françaises*, 11 Nov 65), calling this the 'best French film of the year'.

[144] *Le Deuxième souffle/Second Breath* (1966)

> *d* Jean-Pierre Melville *pc* Montaigne *ph* Marcel Combes *m* Bernard Gérard
> *sc* Melville, José Giovanni from his novel *with* Lino Ventura, Paul Meurisse,
> Raymond Pellegrin, Christine Fabrega, Michel Constantin.

To combat the terrorists of the OAS, De Gaulle's secret service established its own force of *'barbouzes'*, a 'parallel police' working under deep cover and using the same methods as their enemies. The existence of these, and the *brigades territoriales*, formed later to combat organized crime by similar means, caused a great deal of disquiet which crime films began to show through the interrogation methods of brutal inspectors and an implied identification of police and criminals. The inspector in Melville's film, a torturer and a coward, is the double of the criminal he pursues; only an accident puts them on different sides. 'An intuitive policeman ... and an honourable crook,' was Jean Rochereau's conclusion in *La Croix* (5 Nov 66). Marcel Martin in *Les Lettres françaises* (10 Nov 66) wrote that this was 'a work of very high class'.

[145] *Le Samourai/The Samourai* (1967)

> *d* Jean-Pierre Melville *pc* Filmel/CICC/FIDA *ph* Henri Decae *m* François de
> Roubaix *sc* Melville *with* Alain Delon, Nathalie Delon, François Périer, Cathy
> Rosier.

Delon establishing his type as an amoral hired assassin. Melville's concern is with the solitary outsider. 'A masterpiece, precise, painful and ironical,' Samuel Lachize said in *L'Humanité* (28 Oct 67).

Melville's concentration on the technical details of the contract killer's work, Christian Zimmer wrote in *Les Temps modernes* (Dec 1967), 'has something of a religious ceremony and, at the same time, the fastidious routine of a minor civil servant.' Comparing the film to Bo Widerberg's *Elvira Madigan* ('Classical Melville and Romantic Widerberg'), he said that Melville believed exclusively in a Bergsonian notion of time: i.e. time as relative and subjective, not as simple duration. He noted too, in a survey of three recent Melville films, *Le Doulos* [141], *Le Deuxième souffle* [144] and *Le Samourai*, similarities in the contrast between policemen and criminals: 'those who talk, compose phrases, sayings, literature, are the policemen; the crooks do not express themselves either in words or in facial expressions, but in their appearance, their behaviour and their gestures.' And, in Melville's choice of theatre actors to play the policemen, in a theatrical style, and cinema actors for the criminals (Desailly/Belmondo, Meurisse/Ventura, Périer/Delon), he suggested a permanent struggle between 'naturalness and lies' in society.

[146] *La Vie, l'amour, la mort/Life, Love, Death* (1968)

d Claude Lelouch *pc* Ariane/Films 13/Artistes Associés *ph* Jean Collomb *m* Francis Lai *sc* Lelouch *with* Amidou, Caroline Cellier, Janine Magnan.

A polemic against the death penalty (not finally abolished until 1981, though hardly ever applied in the 1970s). The central character is an Arab who kills a prostitute after a sexual humiliation. The inhuman ritual leading to the guillotine is described in minute and gruesome detail. 'There is a new dimension in Lelouch's work, the mature and secret virtue of compassion,' Danièle Heymann wrote in *L'Express* (19 Jan 69).

There were doubts, however, about the evident weighting of the case: the criminal is shown as 'so likeable, outside his lethal crises, that the spectator is in danger of being convinced by a sentimental rather than a rational reaction', Marcel Martin objected in *Les Lettres françaises* (Jan 1971). 'We seem to have returned to the (prewar) Gabin myth', with Gabin as the model working man denied happiness because of the wickedness of others or the blindness of fate. '*La Vie, l'amour, la mort* is a perfect consumer durable ... The problem it raises, being stated in terms of psychology and morality, can only be resolved in terms of feeling and pathos. This is why the case is biased.'

[147] *Le Cercle rouge/The Red Circle* (1970)

d Jean-Pierre Melville *pc* Corona/Selenia *ph* Henri Decae *m* Eric de Marsan *sc* Melville *with* Alain Delon, Bourvil, Yves Montand, François Périer, Gian-Maria Volonte.

The Melville themes taken a step further, to create an enclosed, entirely mythological world. Delon, again, is the criminal: he was to star in Melville's last film, *Un Flic*, made in the following year.

[148] *Diva* (1981)

d Jean-Jacques Beineix *pc* Galaxie/Greenwich/A2 *ph* Philippe Rousselot *m* Vladimir Cosma *sc* Beineix, Jean van Hamme, from the novel by Delacorta *ad* Hilton McConnico *with* Frédéric Andrei, Roland Bertin, Richard Bohringer, Wilhelmina Wiggins Fernandez.

Despite the operatic theme and treatment and the confused and confusing plot, *Diva* resolves itself into a fairly conventional shoot-out. It became something of a cult movie.

[149] *La Balance* (1982)

> *d* Bob Swaim *pc* Ariane/A2 *ph* Bernard Zitzermann *m* Roland Bocquet, Boris Bergman *sc* Swaim *with* Nathalie Baye, Philippe Léotard, Richard Berry, Maurice Ronet.

'Superficial characterization and gratuitous violence', based on the worst American TV series, according to Roy Armes (*French Cinema*, Secker and Warburg, 1985). This is to ignore the film's close attention to its location (Belleville, with a mixed population, mainly from North Africa), and the particular significance for a French audience of the assertion that certain units of the police, in this case the *brigades territoriales*, are, if anything, worse than those they try to bring to justice (compare *Le Doulos* [141]). Even the character of the warm-hearted and loyal prostitute, though a cliché, is a cliché from French cinema going back to the 1930s.

[150] *Vivement dimanche/Finally Sunday*/US: *Confidentially Yours* (1983)

> *d* François Truffaut *pc* Les Films du Carrosse/A2/Soprofilms *ph* Nestor Almendros *m* Georges Delerue *sc* Truffaut, Suzanne Schiffman, Jean Aurel, from the novel *The Long Saturday Night* by Charles Williams *with* Fanny Ardent, Jean-Louis Trintignant, Jean-Pierre Kalfon, Caroline Sihol.

Truffaut's last film was disappointing in some ways, but at the same time a summary of one aspect of his work and a further expression of his admiration for Hitchcock: the plot concerns an estate agent's relationship with his secretary who has to be convinced of his innocence when he is accused of killing his wife (suggesting a number of Hitchcock plots, from *The Thirty-Nine Steps* onwards, as well as the Hitchcock themes of guilt and suspicion). The Riviera and night club locations are conventional, but part of the same celebration of Hollywood *film noir* and comedy. The Office Catholique Français du Cinéma, recommending it for adolescent audiences, described it as 'quality entertainment which does not take itself too seriously.'

X   WOMEN AND THE FAMILY

[151] *La Vérité sur Bébé Donge* (1952)

> *d* Henri Decoin *pc* UGC *ph* Léonce-Henri Burel *m* Jean-Jacques Grunewald *sc* M. Auberge, from the novel by Georges Simenon *with* Danielle Darrieux, Jean Gabin, Daniel Lecourtois.

A wife murders her husband, disillusioned with the stifling environment of her bourgeois marriage. 'There is a dimension of love which seems excluded from this view,' *Télé-Ciné* (Nos. 32–33, 1953) wrote. 'It is that of suffering, of gratuity ... Another "truth" also emerges from the film ... the need for realistic and spiritual preparation for marriage.'

[152] *Papa, Maman, la bonne et moi* (1954)
d Jean-Paul Le Chanois.

A successful comedy (Le Chanois did a sequel in the following year), but, as Raymond Borde noted (*Les Temps modernes*, Jan 1955), the director 'gives his films a social content and at times a political one'. He praised the opening scene showing the typical inhabitants of an apartment house and the portrait of the (typical?) middle-class family, 'the father, science teacher at Saint-Beuve, a sadico-anal type who keeps his money in a tin, the mother, who does translations of detective novels in her spare time ...'

[153] *Et Dieu créa la femme/And God Created Woman* (1956)
d Roger Vadim p Raoul Levy *with* Brigitte Bardot, Curt Jurgens.

Not at first successful in France, Vadim's film did enormously well in the United States and established Bardot's image. France was entering a brief period of 'star fever' which culminated around Bardot's marriage to Jacques Charrier and the birth of their child. The intense interest of the press in such events was bewailed by some cinema-lovers and the films were condemned by Catholics and conservatives who found them immoral. However, in a round-table discussion organized by *Cahiers du cinéma* (May 1957), Jacques Doniol-Valcroze described Vadim's film as 'a very good essay' on his ideas about love and sexual relationships. *Cahiers* liked Vadim most of all because he did not set out to make films of social comment (they condemned Jean-Paul Le Chanois and André Cayatte for doing precisely that). Vadim's films, they felt, expressed deeper truths about contemporary society.

[154] *Le Miroir à deux faces* (1959)
d André Cayatte pc Gaumont/Franco-London/Union/CEI ph Christian Matras sc Cayatte, Gérard Oury *with* Michèle Morgan, Bourvil, Oury, Ivan Desny.

'The young wife has accepted it all: the kids, the money put aside, penny by penny, the bawling-out by her mother-in-law and the passive idiot of a husband. She is the prisoner of these hideous worms. Thousands of women are in her position.' (Raymond Borde, *Les Temps modernes*, Jan 1959). '... an important film ... full of genuine glimpses of the petty bourgeoisie of Le Vésinet or Montreuil ... Some women spectators will, perhaps, on returning home, have the courage to rebel.'

[155] *Cléo de 5 à 7/Cleo from 5 to 7* (1961)
d Agnès Varda *pc* Rome-Paris *ph* Jean Rabier *m* Michel Legrand *sc* Varda
with Corinne Marchand, Antoine Bourseiller, Dorothée Blank, Michel
Legrand.

Cléo waits, around the Luxembourg Gardens and the Parc Montsouris, for the result of
a medical test. She meets a young soldier on leave from military service. Her private
anxieties about cancer, his about being killed in Algeria, suggest more public concerns.
Georges Sadoul (*Les Lettres françaises*, 12 Apr 62) called it 'a real film, modern and
profoundly of our time', telling the story of 'two victims of two cancers, one of them
(which one neither dared nor was able to name) being called "Algerian war"'.

[156] *Une Femme mariée/The Married Woman* (1964)
d Jean-Luc Godard *pc* Annouchka/Orsay *ph* Raoul Coutard *sc* Godard
with Macha Méril, Philippe Leroy, Bernard Noel, Roger Leenhardt, Rita
Maiden.

Originally '*la* femme mariée', but the censor refused this on the grounds that it might be
taken to mean that the film depicted married women in general, rather than just one of
the species. The Godard mixture of parody, quotation, documentary, pseudo-
documentary and fiction is, as with all his films, impossible to summarize in a few
words.

[157] *La Peau douce/Silken Skin/US: The Soft Skin* (1964)
d François Truffaut *pc* Les Films du Carrosse/SEDIF *ph* Raoul Coutard
m Georges Delerue *sc* Truffaut, Jean-Louis Richard *with* Françoise Dorléac,
Jean Desailly, Nelly Benedetti, Daniel Ceccaldi.

The break-up of a marriage, a theme that Truffaut was later to treat as part of his cycle
of films about Antoine Doinel in *Domicile conjugal*. In this case, the man is a middle-aged
academic who falls in love with an air hostess: his feelings and the needs and feelings of
the two women are sympathetically analysed, without moralizing.

[158] *La Fiancée du pirate/US: A Very Curious Girl* (1969)
d Nelly Kaplan *pc* Cythère *ph* Jean Badard *m* Georges Moustaki *sc* Kaplan,
Claude Makovsky *ad* Michel Landi *with* Bernadette Lafont, Georges Genet.

Like the central character in Varda's *Sans toit ni loi* [163], the 'pirate's fiancée' chooses
to live alone, implying that to be free a woman must always be an outsider in a male-
dominated society. Happily prostituting herself, she becomes the exploiter, not the
victim of men, whom she despises as she despises their conformist wives. When finally
they combine against her, she turns the tables on them all and marches off triumphant.
A very funny, anarchistic and anti-clerical film, including a bitter satire on rural life.

[159] *L'Enfance nue/Naked Childhood/*US: *Me* (1969)
d Maurice Pialat *pc* Parc/Les Films du Carrosse/Renn/Para-france *pc* Claude
Beausoleil *sc* Pialat *with* Michel Tarrazon, Marie-Louise Thierry, René Thierry,
Marie Marc.

Pialat's first feature, by a director who also worked in television, was the story of an
unwanted child (see [161]).

[160] *La Cage aux folles* (1978)
d Edouard Molinaro *pc* Artistes Associés/Da Ma Produzione *ph* Armando
Nannuzzi *m* Ennio Morricone *sc* Francis Veber, Molinaro, Marcello Danon,
Jean Poiret, from Poiret's play *with* Ugo Tognazzi, Michel Serrault, Claire
Maurier, Remi Laurent, Michel Galabru.

The family? Certainly. A homosexual couple who run a night club on the Riviera have
to resort to subterfuge when the son of one of them falls in love with the daughter of a
respectable politician and the boy's mother, a successful businesswoman, refuses to join
in the deception. The homosexual couple are caricature gays, but the film did reverse
some other preconceptions as well as finding a wide audience for a comedy entirely
sympathetic to a homosexual relationship. It led to the inevitable sequels and it is
interesting to note that the Office Catholique, which would undoubtedly have
condemned them had they been made earlier, classified *La Cage aux folles II* as grade 4,
'suitable for adult audiences' and regretted that a dull film had been made of a story
'that might, as well as laughter, have provoked reflection on homosexuality, old age
and the way we are seen by others'.

[161] *Le Destin de Juliette/Juliette's Fate/Juliette's Destiny* (1982)
d Aline Issermann *pc* Laura/A2/PR Communication *ph* Dominique le Rigoleur
m Bernard Lubat *sc* Issermann, Michel Dufresne *with* Laure Duthilleul,
Richard Bohringer, Véronique Silver, Pierre Forget, Didier Agostini.

Juliette is forced into marriage with Marcel, a railway worker, so that her family can
keep their SNCF tied cottage. He is frustrated in this loveless match and takes to drink.
The Office Catholique du Cinéma, recommending it for adolescent audiences, said that
it showed the persistence of patterns from one generation to another in the lives of the
working-class and peasantry, and the complex relationships of 'a couple made up of two
solitudes ... A powerful film, without complacency, in which tenderness overrides
melodrama.'

[162] *A nos amours/To Our Loves* (1983)
d Maurice Pialat *pc* Les Films du Livradois/Gaumont/FR 3 *ph* Jacques Loiseleux
sc Pialat, Arlette Langmann *with* Sandrine Bonnaire, Pialat, Evelyne Ker,
Dominique Besnehard.

Pialat examines the nuclear family, centring in turn on the sexual awakening of an adolescent girl, her parents' marriage, her downtrodden mother, her mixed-up and over-protective brother, her boyfriends and her relationship with her father. Where other films on family life have tended to show it in terms of a single conflict (husband and wife, child and parents), he reveals a complex bundle of relationships, each problematic, each impinging on the others.

The Office Catholique du Cinéma recommended it for adolescents with reservations ('some ideas may offend') and called it 'a hard film' which did not set itself up as a model of behaviour. 'It leads to reflection on love and relationships, seeing them as something other than ... conformity with accepted notions, mere appearances and the deceptive "sexual revolution".'

[163] *Sans toit ni loi/Vagabonde* (1985)
    d Agnès Varda *pc* A2/Ministère de la Culture/Ciné-Tamaris *ph* Patrick Blossier
    m Joanna Bruzdowicz *sc* Varda *with* Sandrine Bonnaire, Macha Méril,
    Stéphane Freiss, Marthe Jarnais, Yahiaoui Assouna.

In the style of a documentary-drama, Varda traces the last days in the life of a girl found dead in a vineyard in southern France, uncovering a fiercely independent character, envied by most of those who came in contact with her for her determination to remain free of all social obligations. Filmed on location, using mainly non-professional actors, the film shows, too, the local people, immigrant workers and drop-outs (*les marginaux*) who inhabit the area and has a definite documentary interest (e.g. in recording the Franglais used by the young people with whom Mona associates). The story of her bid for freedom is at times moving, ultimately depressing, because it implies that such total independence is unattainable.

XI CHILDHOOD AND YOUTH

[164] *Visages d'enfants/Faces of Children* (1923)
    d Jacques Feyder *pc* Zoubaloff-Perchet *ph* Léonce-Henri Burel, Paul Parguel
    sc Feyder *with* Jean Forest, Victor Vance, Arlette Peyran.

A boy coming to terms with the arrival of a step-mother. Feyder achieved extraordinary performances from his child actors and Burel's photography explores the scenery of the Valais, in Switzerland, where the film is set.

[165] *Zéro de conduite* (1933)
    d Jean Vigo *pc* Gaumont/Franco/Aubert *ph* Boris Kaufman *m* Maurice Jaubert
    sc Vigo *with* Jean Dasté, Louis Lefebvre, Gilbert Pruchon, Delphin.

Claude Aveline of the *Revue hebdomadaire* (Apr 1933) saw Vigo's film, 'this boarding-school story which is kind to no one and which may upset a lot of people with its pitiless details as well as the imaginative fantasies transposed directly into images, with no commentary of any kind'. He was right: the film was not re-shown until 1945.

Single-sex boarding schools are rare in France, and Vigo's short film (45 mins.) makes this one a society in which the authority figures are ludicrous or corrupt, and the boys' pillow fights develop into wholesale rebellion. It was only a step to see the film as an invitation to a joyous revolt against any form of authority.

[166] *Rendez-vous de juillet* (1949)

d Jacques Becker *pc* UGC/SNEG *ph* Claude Renoir *m* Jean Weiner, Mezz Mezzrow *sc* Becker, Maurice Griffe *with* Nicole Courcel, Brigitte Auber, Daniel Gélin, Maurice Ronet.

In the decade after the Liberation, the jazz clubs of Saint-Germain-des-Prés and a popularized version of the philosophy of Existentialism became the focus of press enquiries into the manners and morals of contemporary youth. Could modern literature, from André Gide's *Les Caves du Vatican* to Sartre's *L'Etre et le néant*, lead to 'gratuitous crimes', *Le Figaro littéraire* asked a panel of writers following a notorious murder case. Becker's young people have not reached that point: they are simply asserting their right to live differently from their staid, middle-class families.

[167] *Les Enfants terribles*/US: *The Strange Ones* (1949)

d Jean-Pierre Melville *pc* Melville *ph* Henri Decae *sc* Melville, Jean Cocteau, from Cocteau's novel (1929) *with* Nicole Stéphane, Edouard Dhermite, Jacques Bernard, Renée Cosima.

Cocteau's poetic novel made difficult material for the cinema, especially given the realistic conventions of the time: Melville was unable to elevate the theme of incest to the symbolic role it plays in the book. What is left is a sometimes pedestrian adaptation of a story about four young people (though there are compensations in the film's use of mirrors and camera angles to suggest a non-literal view of their enclosed world). Jean Fayard (*Opéra*, 5 Apr 50) was among those who regretted the excessive realism of the adaptation: 'dirty rooms, suspect bed-linen and discarded stockings.'

There were stronger objections from other quarters, inspired not by the film's fidelity to its source, but by the hint of an incestuous relationship between brother and sister (and perhaps by unadmitted hostility to Cocteau's homosexuality: see [3]). Suzanne Rodrigue wrote of 'the vulgar little obscenities offered to the spectator' (*L'Ecran français*, 3 Apr 50) and the Centrale Catholique awarded the film its highest rating ('unsuitable for any audience').

[168] *Le Blé en herbe* (1954)

d Claude Autant-Lara *pc* Franco-London *ph* Robert Le Febvre *m* René Cloerec sc Autant-Lara, Jean Aurenche, Pierre Bost, from the novel by Colette (1923) *with* Edwige Feuillère, Pierre-Michel Beck, Nicole Berger.

Colette's novel about a young man's sexual initiation with an older woman could claim to be based on a Greek pastoral romance, but it shocked some readers, particularly because the boy then goes on to apply what he has learned with a girl of his own age and class. Autant-Lara's adaptation, set like the novel on the north Breton coast which was a favourite holiday spot for middle-class families, is described by Roy Armes (*French Cinema Since 1946*, Tantivy-Barnes, 1976) as 'capturing both the embarrassments and the uncertainties of adolescence and the plight of the older woman ... with great delicacy and insight, so that the theme, though disturbing, is never offensive'. This was not the view when it was first shown. Joseph Folliet, in *La Croix* (14 Apr 54), said that in Christian circles the film had been 'almost unanimously condemned' and that screenings in the provinces had caused disturbances, 'especially when sponsored by organizations connected with the Ministry of Education, an indulgence which, I would suggest, was unnecessary, even under the heading of sexual education.' *L'Humanité* (22 March 54) reported a request from a Communist *député* asking the government to explain the measures it was taking to stop 'reactionary groups' preventing screenings of the film. Quoting this, *La Croix* noted that *L'Humanité* had itself called for the banning of the film of Sartre's *Les Mains sales* three years earlier. Colette would no doubt have been amused to see her work becoming a weapon in the Cold War.

[169] *Les Quatre cents coups/The 400 Blows* (1958)

d François Truffaut *pc* Les Films du Carrosse/SEDIF *ph* Henri Decae *m* Jean Constantin *sc* Truffaut *with* Jean-Pierre Léaud, Albert Rémy, Claire Maurier, Guy Decomble, Patrick Auffay.

Truffaut's marvellous first feature is also the first in his cycle of films about his other self, Antoine Doinel. It discarded all the conventional images of childhood to give a totally convincing picture of Antoine: his downtrodden father, his wayward mother, his school-friend, the dingy apartment where he exists and the streets where he lives. The autobiographical elements and the documentary ones (school, the treatment of delinquents at the reformatory in Villejuif) are perfectly integrated in a film that is touching and funny and, in the final frozen image of Antoine on the edge of the sea, tragic. The film is still deeply moving and one of the most accurate pictures of French life in the period, but one can hardly imagine now the impact that it had, in contrast to the literary adaptations that were the norm in French cinema at the time.

[170] *Les Tricheurs*/US: *The Cheaters* (1958)

d Marcel Carné *pc* Silver/Cinétel *ph* Claude Renoir *sc* Carné, Charles Spaak *ad* Paul Bertrann *with* Pascal Petit, Andréa Parisi, Jacques Charrier, Laurent Terzieff.

Marcel Carné tried, with at best partial success, to depict the younger generation of the 1950s, but in retrospect the film has some documentary value as evidence of attitudes.

'We feel almost obliged to defend this moralizing, demagogic and tedious film,' Raymond Borde wrote in *Les Temps modernes* (Apr 1959), 'when it is attacked from the Right. Imbeciles have protested, respectable fathers have deplored the bad example it gives to young people and the Mayor of Nice ... has taken out a banning order against *Les Tricheurs*. Marcel Carné's timid provocations ... have been enough to scandalize unrepentant Pétainists ... We are likely to end by defending what we hate: false daring which hides conformism, and a delight in punishment ... Marcel Carné describes the youth of Saint-Germain-des-Prés in 1958. They go to the café, dance, ride their scooters ... The girls sleep around ... Now, there's something you don't often see. Will *Les Tricheurs* strike a new note in French cinema? No such luck! The girls are punished.' Clo, the rich girl, is pregnant; when asked if she is going to keep the baby, she says 'yes ... I'm a Christian', much to the relief of the bourgeois audience; Mic, her friend, commits suicide at the wheel of her Jaguar: 'you have to pay for pleasure.' 'These clichés flatter the audience with a vague scent of Poujadism' (the 1950s saw the rise and fall of Pierre Poujade's reactionary party of small businessmen). 'These young people are nothing, not Communist, or Fascist, or very busy, or very loose-living, or artistic, or rebellious, or religious, or atheistic.' Carné may have done a lot of research for his film, but 'it is not enough to take a few phrases from the slang of a period' to describe its young people.

[171] *Les Coeurs verts*/US: *Naked Hearts* (1966)
d Edouard Luntz pc Raoul Ploquin/Sodor ph Jean Badel m Serge Gainsbourg, Henri Renaud sc Luntz with Gérard Zimmerman, Erick Penet, Marise Maire, Françoise Bonneau.

Zim (Zimmerman) and Jean-Pierre (Penet) hang around cafés, pick up girls and indulge in petty crime. The contrasting fate of the two boys suggests the narrow line between social integration and delinquency.

[172] *Le Souffle au coeur*/*Murmur of the Heart* (1971)
d Louis Malle pc Nouvelles Ed. de Films/Marianne/Vides/Franz Seitz ph Ricardo Aronovitch sc Malle with Léa Massari, Benoît Ferreux, Daniel Gélin, Michel Lonsdale, Henri Poirier.

Set in 1954, the year in which the Algerian war broke out and also the year of Autant-Lara's screen adaptation of *Le Blé en herbe* [168], Colette's novel of an adolescence far removed from social or political concerns. The wider issues of the time hover on the fringes of Malle's film, seen from the viewpoint of its adolescent central character, but its focus is elsewhere. The mother-son incest is treated delicately, but the director would hardly have expected it not to shock. It did.

[173] *L'Argent de poche*/*Small Change* (1976)
d François Truffaut pc Les Films du Carrosse/Artistes Associés ph Pierre-

William Glenn *m* Maurice Jaubert *sc* Truffaut, Suzanne Schiffman *ad* Jean-Pierre Kohut-Svelko *with* Geory Desmouceaux, Philippe Goldman, Claudio Deluca, Pascale Bruchon.

An affectionate picture of the lives of children, filmed in Triers with what critics have considered an excess of charm and sentimentality. Maurice Pialat's *Passe ton bac d'abord* (1979), also in a provincial town, showing children at a later stage in their school careers, probably gives a more accurate picture of young people at the time. But Truffaut's film, because it is virtually restricted to pre-adolescent children as a group, betrays a particular idea of the child's emotions and mentality, as yet 'uncontaminated' by the adult view of the world.

XII   FANTASIES

[174] *Le Grand Méliès* (1952)
d Georges Franju *pc* Armor *ph* Jacques Mercanton *m* Georges van Parys
sc Franju *with* Madame Marie-Georges Meliès, André Méliès.

Franju's tribute to Méliès shows how the work of this cinema pioneer had been forgotten by the 1950s, and it remains probably the most convenient place to see footage from the Méliès films. The possibility of using the camera to perform conjuring tricks (special effects, in later jargon) was realized from the start and Méliès used it in such films as *Le déshabillage impossible* (1900) where characters find themselves in the frustrating situation of trying to undress while instantly being reclothed, usually in garments belonging to others. Méliès also filmed an imaginary journey to the moon (1902) and numerous other scientific reconstructions or illusions. Also before World War I, the comedies of Boireau and Rigadin used different effects, including one in which time is speeded up.

[175] *Paris qui dort/The Crazy Ray* (1923)
d René Clair *pc* Diamant *ph* Maurice Defassiaux, Paul Guichard *with* Henri Rollan, Marcel Vallée, Albert Préjean, Madeleine Rodrigue, Charles Martinelli.

René Clair's first film owes a good deal to Méliès: it is the story of a mad scientist who paralyses Paris with a ray gun.

[176] *La Fin du monde/The End of the World* (1930)
d Abel Gance *pc* L'Ecran d'Art *ph* Jules Kruger, Roger Hubert *sc* Gance, from a story by Camille Flammarion *effects* Nicolas Roudakoff *sd* Lazare Meerson
with Victor Francen, Colette Darfeuil, Gance, Samson Fainsilber, Jean d'Yd.

The first spectacular French talkie, and a commercial disaster. It was dismissed by Philippe Soupault (*L'Europe nouvelle*, 7 Feb 31) as ridiculous, scientifically improbable and an example of the direction cinema should not take. Soupault compared it, unfavourably, with Clair's *Paris qui dort* [175]. Despite these two films, and the experiments of Méliès, French cinema never took to science fiction as a genre, perhaps partly because of Gance's failure.

[177] *Les Yeux sans visage/Eyes Without a Face/*(dubbed) *The Horror Chamber of Dr Faustus* (1959)

   d Georges Franju *pc* Champs-Elysées-Lux *ph* Eugen Shuftan *m* Maurice Jarre
   sc Jean Redon from his novel *effects* Assola, Georges Klein *ad* Auguste Capelier
   with Pierre Brasseur, Alida Valli, Edith Scob, François Guérin.

A famous Franju horror: plastic surgeon tries to rebuild his daughter's face after a car accident, using faces from girls he has had kidnapped for the purpose. He fails and is savagely torn apart by the dogs he uses for experiments. When it was first shown at the Edinburgh Film Festival, members of the audience fainted.

   As well as the conventional horror elements, it tackles the question of misuse of science (of universal interest in the atomic age) and nature (going back to Franju's exposure of our inhumanity to animals in *Le Sang des bêtes* [93]). Both suggest a narrowness of vision that the film illuminates: this scientist is prepared happily to sacrifice not only animals, but also other human beings for the sake of his own daughter. Perhaps, as Raymond Durgnat says in his book on Franju (University of California Press, 1968) an attack on the right-wing, Pétainist glorification of the family?

[178] *Le Monocle noir* (1961)

   d Georges Lautner *pc* Orex *ph* Maurice Fellous *m* Jean Yatlove *sc* Jacques
   Robert, Pierre Laroche *with* Paul Meurisse, Pierre Blanchar, Albert Rémy.

The first in a series of popular thrillers, with a tongue-in-cheek element that brings them closer to the later James Bond movies than to the conventions of the thriller.

[179] *Alphaville* (1965)

   d Jean-Luc Godard *pc* Chaumiane/Filmstudio *ph* Raoul Coutard *m* Paul
   Misraki *sc* Godard *with* Eddie Constantine, Anna Karina, Akim Tamiroff,
   Howard Vernon, Michel Delahaye.

'Alphaville or Betafilm?', Arlette Elkaim asked in *Les Temps modernes* (June 1965). 'Intellectual hysteria', 'simplicity or banality (in the dialogue)' and 'pseudo-philosophical verbiage', she went on. Most people were far more worried by the present realities inside President Johnson's very human head than by this 'inhuman technocracy': 'True, large housing estates are depressing and in the *métro*, after work, people look dull or moronic. But computers are not to blame.'

In the following month, *Les Temps modernes* returned to the attack with an article by Pierre Samson. The film's 'wholesale culture' was a means to distract our attention from Lemmy Caution's real role, as a cop. 'However, this manifestly reactionary film has succeeded in mystifying left-wing critics in *L'Humanité* and *Le Nouvel Observateur* ... Godard is the product of a society that has chosen Gaullism ...', his 'petty-bourgeois individualism' offering us love as the answer to anxieties about the unknown and the future.

Constantine plays a typical tough guy role in Godard's very untypical SF thriller. Dislike of Godard among the critics of *Les Temps modernes* reached its height around this time, and the fact that the review was prepared to devote two articles to this one film is evidence of how seriously his influence was taken by the 'unofficial' Left. As the two writers quoted above argue, they saw him serving the régime by distracting attention from the real problems of the time and disguising a 'reactionary' message behind a torrent of (pseudo-)philosophy. Ironically, Godard himself converted to the Left after 1968, adopting many of the attitudes of his earlier critics.

[180] *Coplan sauve sa peau/Coplan Saves His Skin* (1968)

d Yves Boisset *pc* Comptoir Français du Film *ph* Pierre Lhomme, Alain Derobe *sc* Boisset, Claude Veillot, from Paul Kenny's novel *Coplan paie le cercueil* *with* Claudio Brook, Margaret Lee, Jean Servais, Jean Topart, Bernard Blier.

Le Monocle, Le Gorille, Le Tigre, O.S.S. 117 and Coplan were among the French answers to the James Bond type of spy thriller. These series may have concealed many political assumptions about the Cold War or the superiority of Whites. They were made entirely for commercial reasons, however, and owed any hidden political message partly to their Hollywood models.

[181] *Fahrenheit 451* (1966)

d François Truffaut *pc* Anglo Enterprise/Vineyard *ph* Nicholas Roeg, Alex Thompson *m* Bernard Herrmann *sc* Truffaut, from the novel by Ray Bradbury *ad* Syd Cain *with* Oskar Werner, Julie Christie, Cyril Cusack, Anton Diffring, Bee Duffell.

Made in English, Truffaut's film is about a society in which books are banned and destroyed (451° is the combustion temperature of paper), and about the value of language and the liberating power of literature – remember Antoine's love of Balzac in *Les quatre cents coups*. Perhaps because of the language difficulties, it was not Truffaut's most successful work.

[182] *Barbarella* (1967)

d Roger Vadim *pc* Marianne/Dino de Laurentis *ph* Claude Renoir *m* Michel

Magne *sc* Vadim, Jean-Claude Forest, Claude Brûlé, Vittorio Bonicelli, Robert Scipion from Forest's cartoons strip *with* Jane Fonda, John Philip Law, Anita Pallenberg, Ugo Tognazzi, David Hemmings, Claude Dauphin.

The cast also includes Milo O'Shea as Duran Duran, a character who gave his name to a 1980s British pop group, indicating that Vadim's film continued to enjoy a cult following. Far from serious SF, it is also a tribute to the comic strip (see *Jeu de massacre* [7]). Fonda travels round the galaxy, making love with everyone and everything, including a pleasure machine which succumbs in the face of unfair competition.

[183] *Le Gendarme et les extra-terrestres/The Policeman and the Extraterrestrials* (1978)
    d Jean Girault *sc* Jacques Vilfrid *with* Louis de Funès, Michel Galabru, Jean-Pierre Rambal.

The Louis de Funès comic policeman starred in a highly popular series which has a good deal to say about everyday life and attitudes, little about police work. The officious, stupid, self-important and, above all, accident-prone policeman satisfies a need to make fun of authority figures without questioning the system. In an earlier film in the series, *Le Gendarme de Saint-Tropez*, de Funès' comic adventures centred on his prudish attempts to ban nude bathing on the Riviera beach. This sample of the type draws on the conventions of another (alien?) genre; perhaps the inspiration of the producers was beginning to flag.

Index of film titles

Numerals in square brackets denote an entry number in the reference material starting on page 91. Numerals in **bold** denote the number of a **photograph**

A

A bout de souffle [138], 61, 76
Age d'or, L', 35
Alerte en Méditerrannée, 37
Ali Baba et les 40 voleurs [39], 43
Alibi, L' [127]
Alphaville [179]
Alsace, 33
A Man and a Woman, see *Un homme et une femme*
Amour l'après-midi, L', 81
And God Created Woman, see *Et Dieu créa la femme*
Angèle [100], 50
Année dernière à Marienbad, L' [4]
A nos amours [162], 46, 85, 80
A nous deux, Madame la Vie, 30
A nous la liberté [85], 34, 37, 68, 69, 70, 83, **14**, **25**
A nous les p'tites anglaises, 83
Appel du silence, L', 35–36, 67
A Private Function, 46
A propos de Nice [55], 73
Argent, L' [72], 34, 59, 67, 68
Argent de poche, L' [173], 80
Armée des ombres, L' [47]
Army in the Shadows, see *Armée des ombres, L'*
Arroseur arrosé, L', 15
Ascenseur pour l'échafaud [134], 10, 43, 60, 72–73, 76, **27**
Assassinat du Duc de Guise, L' [11], 16
Atalante, L' [86]
Aubervilliers [92], 73
Au-delà des grilles, 48
Aux urnes, citoyens! [67], 66
Avec le sourire, 69
A Very Curious Girl, see *Fiancée du pirate, La*
A Window in London, 59

B

Baccara, 30, 32, 34
Baker's Wife, The, see *Femme du boulanger, La*
Balance, La [149], 46, 61, 73, 82
Ballet mécanique, Le, 18
Ballon rouge, Le, 80
Bande à part [142], 61, 76, **36**
Bandera, La [31], 35
Barbarella [182]
Bataille du rail, La [35], 39, 43
Beau Serge, Le [111], 44, 47, 49, 53
Belle de jour [79], 6
Belle équipe, La [87] 37–38, 48, 58, 69, 83, **15**
Bête humaine, La [89], 59, 67, 70, 74, **17**
Biquefarre [109], 46, 49, 52–53

Bizarre, Bizarre, see *Drôle de drame*
Bled, Le, 35
Blé en herbe, Le [168], 32, 52, 79, **44**, **45**
Bob le Flambeur [121]
Bof!, 71, 82
Bolero, see *Uns et les autres, Les*
Bonheur, Le [97]
Boucher, Le [114], 56
Boudu sauvé des eaux [73], 68
Breathless, see *A bout de souffle*
Butcher, The, see *Boucher, Le*

C

Cage aux folles, La [160], 84
Card of Fate, see *Grand jeu, Le*
Carnival in Flanders, see *Kermesse héroïque, La*
Caroline chérie, 65
Carry on Sergeant, 35
Caserne en folie, La, 35
Casque d'Or [130], 49, 59, 73, **11**, **32**
Cave se rebiffe, Le [140], 44
Celui qui doit mourir, 67
Cercle rouge, Le [147]
Chagrin et la pitié, Le [48]
Champion du régiment, Le, 35
Chantecoq, 33
Chariots of Fire, 46
Charron, Le, 52
Chasseur de Chez Maxim's, Le, 30
Cheaters, The, see *Tricheurs, Les*
Chienne, La [119]
Chinoise, La [6], 76, **28**
Choc en retour, 37
Clean Slate, see *Coup de torchon*
Cléo de 5 à 7 [155]
Coeur de française, 33
Coeur et l'argent, Le, 16
Coeurs verts, Les [171], 81
Compères, Les, 84, 88
Confidentially Yours, see *Vivement dimanche*
Cop au vin, see *Poulet au vinaigre*
Coplan sauve sa peau [180]
Coq du régiment, Le, 35
Corbeau, Le [106], 56, 67
Counterfeiters of Paris, The, see *Cave se rebiffe, Le*
Coup de torchon [51], 36
Coup pour coup [69]
Crazy Ray, The, see *Paris qui dort*
Crime de Monsieur Lange, Le [88], 34, 48, 56, 58, 69, 16
Croisade, La, 34
Croisade de l'air, 52
Croix de bois, Les, 35

D

Dame aux camélias, La, 16
Danton [26], 64, 89
Daybreak, see *Jour se lève, Le*

157

General index

IT'S MORE THAN THE MUSIC

IT'S MORE THAN THE MUSIC

*Life Lessons on Friends,
Faith, and What Matters Most*

Bill Gaither
with Ken Abraham

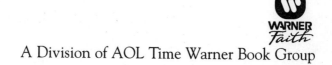

A Division of AOL Time Warner Book Group

EK MW

Ⓦ WARNER*Faith* A Division of AOL Time Warner Book Group

Printed in the United States of America
First Warner Books printing: October 2003

Book Design by Steve Kennedy

10 9 8 7 6 5 4 3 2 1

Library of Congress Cataloging-in-Publication Data

Gaither, Bill.
   It's more than the music : life lessons on Friends, Faith, and What Matters Most / Bill Gaither with Ken Abraham.
     p. cm.
   ISBN 0-446-53041-7
     1. Gaither, Bill. 2. Gospel musicians—United States—Biography.
   I. Abraham, Ken. II. Title.

ML420.G129A3 2003
782.25'4'092—dc21
[B]   2003053519

CONTENTS

PREFACE

BILL GAITHER WILL FOOL
you. At first blush, you may think this fellow with the quick
smile and the self-effacing humor is merely a down-home Mid-
westerner, more comfortable in the company of everyday farmers and factory workers than he is among the top echelons of
businesspeople or among the world's premier music composers.

But take my word for it: As much as he tries to be like the
rest of us, Bill Gaither is no ordinary guy! He is a creative genius, and an astute, savvy businessman. He is a tremendous mo-
tivator, a teacher, coach, and manager with the rare gift of
bringing out the best in everyone around him. He has a passion
for excellence, and he'll settle for nothing less. His ability to see
the potential in an idea and then pull the elements together to
make it work is uncanny. He operates so naturally in the realm
of the supernatural—he thinks it's natural!

Yes, he's down-to-earth, because unlike most of us, Bill
Gaither genuinely knows who he is—he's earthy, yet spiritual
(in the best sense of that word); he's indefatigably creative, yet
extremely practical. He has tremendous faith, yet he believes
faith must go hand in hand with hard work. He's frugal to a

fault, yet generous beyond anyone's expectations. We can learn much from Bill Gaither, and benefit greatly from the life lessons he shares in this book.

And Bill's music is everywhere! In 1978, my brothers and I trekked high in the mountains outside of the Jamaican town of Mandeville. We were making good time—but we were lost! Far from the tourist spots and the sun-drenched, white sand beaches along the shore, the evening air in the dark forests surrounding the inland mountain roads chilled us to the bone. We knew there was a church out there somewhere, and we were determined to find it! We rounded the bend and saw a building, our destination, off in the brush. It was a cement block, a makeshift structure with dirt floors and large windows, but no glass, no electricity, and definitely no heat. Except for the rows of rough-hewn wooden seats inside, the church was indistinguishable from a cattle barn.

Until we heard the music.

A group of about fifty Jamaicans, young and old, had gathered, and as we approached the sanctuary, we heard thickly accented singing at the top of their lungs, "Something happened, and now I know! He touched me, and made me whole!"

I could hardly believe my ears. Here in the backwoods of Jamaica, the family of God was singing a song written by Bill Gaither. It struck me then, as it does now, that Bill Gaither, in his own unassuming, inimitable way, has been preparing us for our primary activity in heaven—praising God. Maybe we'll even sing some of Bill's songs when we get to heaven. I wouldn't be surprised. People around the planet have been singing them for years! Knowing Bill, he'll probably smile and say, "Hey, that's not too bad!"

Bill often jokes about his poor memory. I'm glad he decided to write this book at this point in his career, while he can still remember the key people and events that have shaped his life. Who knows what Bill might have forgotten had we waited any longer to get these insights into print?

But again, don't be fooled. Bill Gaither knows exactly what matters over the long haul; it's seared into the fabric of his being; it permeates his heart, mind, and sinew. And within these pages, he candidly reveals the priorities he has maintained, the reasons behind the pivotal decisions he's made, and the keys to his success with his family, his business, and his music.

It's been a pleasure and an honor, and, most of all, a sacred trust to work with Bill Gaither on this book. He truly is a humble person, with plenty of reasons to boast. He just doesn't.

May you enjoy discovering why he's more than the music.

Ken Abraham
Franklin, Tennessee
April 2003

IT'S MORE THAN THE MUSIC

ONE

HOMECOMING

It seemed as though the big days of my career were over; I could see the handwriting on the wall and it wasn't pretty. I was fifty-five years of age, and after enjoying a successful career writing and performing music for more than three decades, in 1991 the music world was about to pass me by.

I had been a composer and a musician most of my adult life. Making music was all I had ever known; it was all I'd ever dreamed of doing, all I'd ever wanted to do, and now, like the heavy wooden lid coming down on a grand piano, I could see, feel, and hear the music coming to an end.

I was discouraged and slightly depressed as I considered my options, but I wasn't upset. In the music business, change, and making adjustments to it, is the norm. I was accustomed to seeing one aspect of my career wind down while another area of opportunity opened up. Granted, the line between the end and the beginning is sometimes hard to discern, like the line separating the sand from the sea. They seem to run together for a while, and what we think is an ending often becomes a new beginning.

Besides, my wife, Gloria, and I had achieved many of our goals musically, and we were beginning to think about backing off a bit anyhow, slowing down, and living a seminormal life. Oh, we still planned to be involved in music, but more as mentors rather than as performers. We still planned to write and publish music, discover and promote new artists, and even host a few concert events ourselves, but we had been in the spotlight long enough. It was time for us to step offstage and encourage the next generation of writers, musicians, and singers.

One day I told Gloria, "It seems that the Gaither Vocal Band is winding down, but before we quit, we'd like to record a southern gospel classic. I've always loved that style of music, so I'd like to have all my old heroes come in and sing on one song, something we all know. It might be fun, and besides, I'd like to honor some of those people who first got me excited about gospel music when I was a kid."

I called some friends and invited them to join the Gaither Vocal Band—at the time comprised of Mark Lowry, Jim Murray, Michael English, and me—for the recording session to be held at Master's Touch studio in Nashville. One of the first people I called was Hovie Lister, the inimitable leader of the famous Statesmen Quartet, one of the first gospel quartets I had ever heard as a young boy.

Hovie had long since retired and was living in Atlanta, but he was just as energetic as always when I talked to him by phone.

"Hovie, I want to get some friends together to help me out in the studio on an old song. Think you might be interested?"

"I'll be there," Hovie replied. "Just tell me when and where."

"Well, the Vocal Band is recording a new album—I think we're going to call it *Homecoming* or something like that—and we want to include some of the grand old gospel songs. We got to thinking about it and said, 'Wouldn't it be fun to invite some of our friends to sing a song—some of the great gospel singers who influenced us when we first started out in music so many years ago?' We're going to be recording in Nashville, and I'd be thrilled if you could come and help us out on the song, 'Where Could I Go but to the Lord?' We're planning to shoot a video of that song, too. Think you can make it?"

"I wouldn't miss it!" Hovie replied in his usual upbeat style.

"I'm not sure who all is going to show up, but I'm going to ask several other friends, some of the old-timers like Glen Payne and George Younce of the Cathedrals, J.D. Sumner and some members of the Stamps, James Blackwood, and of course, Jake Hess."

"Jake's gonna be there?" Hovie asked excitedly.

"I hope so. You know he hasn't been feeling so well lately, but I'm going to ask him."

"Oh, I sure hope he can come," Hovie answered. Hovie and Jake had worked together for fifteen years as part of the States-men, as far back as the late 1940s. Later, Jake left the Statesmen to start a new "cutting edge" group known as the Imperials. It would be a thrill for me to have them in the same studio again.

"I'm going to invite the Speers and the Rambos, too," I told Hovie, "and who knows who else. We'll just have an old-friends party."

"Sounds good to me," Hovie said. "I can't wait! Where are you going to do this?"

I gave Hovie the details regarding the time and location of the recording session, and he assured me again that he'd be there.

I was off to a good start. I continued contacting a group of gospel music legends including those I had mentioned to Hovie as well as Buck Rambo, Howard and Vestal Goodman of the Happy Goodman Family, the jolly, heavyset couple known for the size of their hearts as well as the size of their physical frames. Eva Mae LeFevre, of the family group by that name, said that she could come, as did several members of the famous Speer Family. My friends Larry and Rudy Gatlin of the Gatlin Brothers heard about the session and said they might drop by as well. Everyone seemed genuinely excited about the idea and willing to help.

These old-time gospel artists were legends to me. They had been the hottest, most popular groups on the circuit when I was growing up. As a young boy, I became obsessed with their music and with them. Now, however, many of the singers were retired, or at least inactive. Some had fallen on hard times. Others were struggling with poor health. For many of them, the tour buses, recording contracts, standing ovations, and deeply moving spiritual moments were fading memories. Although a few of the artists were still able to travel and sing and keep their datebooks relatively full, it was obvious that with each passing year their fans were dwindling. They'd been passed by, ignored by the music industry they had helped to create, and for a number of years now they had been set on the shelf in obscurity. Some had retired comfortably, but others were struggling to survive after pouring their hearts and lives into the music and ministry. Many gospel legends were barely eking out a subsistence living as fewer congregations invited them to sing in their communities. I had hoped that, if nothing else, our recording get-together might remind these heroes that they were not totally forgotten.

On the day of the recording session, we were scheduled to begin rolling tape around ten o'clock to record "Where Could I

Go but to the Lord?," a classic written by James B. Coats. For some strange reason, when I booked the studio time, I had reserved it all day simply to record one song. As it turned out, that booking proved to be providential.

By noon, the foyer of the Master's Touch studio in Nashville was already abuzz with activity. It was like walking into a class reunion. The room was crowded with the friendly faces of people who had sung on shows together all around the country for decades, but in recent years they had hardly seen or talked with one another. There were my dear friends Rosa Nell, Mary-Tom, Faye and Brock, and Ben Speer of the Speer Family. The Speers were one of the first gospel groups I'd ever heard, and in 1960 Ben Speer published the first song I had written, "I've Been to Calvary." Since then the Speers had sung many of Gloria's and my songs, including "Let's Just Praise the Lord," "The Family of God," "The King Is Coming," and "There's Something about That Name." The Speers were singing Bill and Gloria Gaither songs long before anyone else had even heard of us. I was especially glad that they could be here on this occasion.

In another part of the room was Buck Rambo of the Singing Rambos, another family group, and Eva Mae LeFevre, a founding member of one of the most popular gospel singing groups in America for decades. Looking around the room, I saw two of my dearest friends, Glen Payne and George Younce of the Cathedrals. Glen and George had experienced a wonderful resurgence in their careers in the mid-eighties when the younger generation of music artists discovered that "those two old guys can really sing!"

James Blackwood was there, too. James was on the program the first night I ever sat in the world-famous Ryman Auditorium in Nashville, in 1948. He and his family formed the nucleus of the famed Blackwood Brothers Quartet and were true pioneers in this kind of music. James, too, had been sick recently, and I was glad he could make it to the taping.

I was especially excited to see Jim Hill. Jim had sung with the Golden Keys and was the first professional singer to whom I'd ever "pitched" one of my songs. He sang "I've Been to Calvary" shortly after I had written it, and thanks to Jim and the Golden Keys, Ben Speer heard the song, and both groups recorded it. Later, my younger brother, Danny, had sung with Jim as part of the Golden Keys. Jim's own composition, "What a Day That Will Be," had been sung and recorded by hundreds of groups and was already a classic in this genre of music.

Staying close to the coffeepot was J.D. Sumner of the Stamps Quartet, the renowned gospel singers who backed up Elvis Presley during the last few years of his life. The country music artists Larry and Rudy Gatlin did indeed drop by the studio. In the 1970s and 1980s, the Gatlin Brothers had risen to superstardom in country music, and their song "All the Gold (in California)" had even topped the pop charts, catapulting the Gatlin Brothers to performing in Las Vegas, on NBC's *Tonight Show* with Johnny Carson, and in many other places where traditional country music had not yet made significant inroads. The Gatlins' close family harmonies were a pleasant reprieve for many music lovers who didn't care for the heavier rock sounds that dominated radio airwaves at the time. The Gatlin Brothers' rich voices took them around the world to some of the biggest and best music venues of the day. They had grown up listening to gospel music, though, and the brothers had never forgotten their roots.

The atmosphere in the foyer was electric. Everyone was talking, laughing, hugging, and catching up on what each friend had been doing. For years, these folks had seen each other almost every week in concerts around the country. They had worked together so often, most people in the room knew each other's songs by heart. Often, if one group was doing an encore, the other groups on the program would join them onstage for the finale. Frequently, musicians from various groups joined in the fun. It was like one big musical family . . . and now they were together again, in the same room.

I hated to break up the party, but when I noticed the time, I thought, *Hey, this is great, but we have some work to do here.* I held open the large studio door and said, "Let's go in and sing awhile," motioning toward the inner studio. The party eased into the room, and when everyone had assembled I prayed a brief prayer, thanking God for allowing us to be together and asking Him to bless our efforts. Everyone said amen, and I went to work positioning the singers at various places in the oak-paneled studio. Overhead microphones were strategically placed throughout the room, allowing some of our old-timers the luxury of remaining seated while singing.

I explained that a camera crew was on hand to get some footage that we might use for "clips" in the Gaither Vocal Band video of the song. *Camera crew* was probably a grandiose term for the video production team. They had only one video-camera!

"Don't even pay attention to the camera," I said. "Let's just have fun and sing."

We had asked several artists, including Larry Gatlin, Vestal Goodman, and Michael English, to sing solos at certain points, so the three of them gathered around a large Neumann microphone near the center of the room. The only instrument in the studio was a grand piano. I had already recorded the instrumental tracks, which the singers could hear in their headphones as they sang. We waited for the red light to go on in the studio, indicating that we were recording. The excitement was almost palpable, but we weren't really sure what to expect once the tape started rolling. We had assembled a few of the greatest gospel singers in history, but some of the men and women in the studio that day hadn't sung a note in public for several years, much less tried to harmonize with other singers. Worse yet, it suddenly occurred to me that although these artists had performed in hundreds of concerts together around the country, except for the rousing "anything goes" encore numbers, they'd never really sung together seriously. *I sure hope this works,* I thought as the red light came on.

It quickly became clear that my biggest problem was not getting this chorus to sing—my problem was getting it to stop! Everyone was so excited to be together, and was having such a wonderful time, the enthusiasm just kept bubbling up and overflowing! All the singers in the room that day were professionals; they all knew that under ordinary recording circumstances we were to be quiet before the red light was illuminated as the song began, and until the light went out after the song was over, indicating that the recorder in the control room was turned off. And of course, everyone knew that in most recording situations, one was not to give in to any extraneous expressions of praise or worship, no matter how spiritually moved a person might become during a song.

We all knew how to behave in a professional recording session. But these were *not* ordinary recording circumstances. And it became obvious after about ten minutes that this was *not* going to be an ordinary recording. Everyone could sense the Spirit of the Lord was in that studio.

Jake Hess had to sing for a funeral earlier that day so he arrived late for the session, and we were all thrilled to see him, especially Hovie Lister. Hovie nearly wept as the two men embraced in the studio. Jake's smooth-as-velvet voice was the lofty standard that aspiring gospel singers of my generation hoped to emulate.

As Jake listened to the music, he, too, immediately recognized that something unusual was going on. Always the quintessential gentleman, Jake looked over at Vestal Goodman and spoke quietly and reverently, "Something special is happening here. I've never felt such a strong presence of the Spirit in a room in my entire life."

Jake was right. We could all sense it, even if we couldn't describe or control it. Something was happening! *Somebody* other than Bill Gaither was in charge of this session!

We recorded the chorus, and then Vestal, Larry, and Michael sang their solos. It was awesome! The soloists recorded their parts perfectly, and the choir of old-timers sang as though it was their debut. *This is even better than I'd hoped for!* I thought. It was so good, before the bouncing red needles on the recording console had time to lie still, I was gathering everyone together again. "Let's do another take," I said. "That's just too good!"

It wasn't that anyone had sung his or her parts incorrectly or that the recording engineer had made a mistake. I just wanted to hear these people sing some more!

We recorded the song again and "stacked" the vocals—singing the song again and again, putting several "layers" of the same singers' voices on tape, making the chorus sound even larger than it was. While the group sang, the camera guys continued videotaping the entire event—including the comments and expressions between takes.

After a few more takes, we completed the recording, and there was really no reason to prolong things any further, but nobody wanted to leave! Everyone wanted to stay right there and bask in the Presence that had permeated the studio.

We had arranged for a photographer to take a group photo at the close of the session to commemorate our getting together, and possibly to use on the album cover or insert. The entire group gathered around the studio piano for the photo. When the photographer had clicked off his last shot, Larry Gatlin looked over at Eva Mae LeFevre and said, "Eva Mae, play something. Let's sing."

Well into her seventies, Eva Mae could still tickle the ivories like few piano players could. She played the old song "I'll Meet You in the Morning," and her playing was infectious. In a matter of moments, we were all singing along. At the end of the song, Eva Mae stood up and the group gave her a round of applause. "Let's do another!" someone called.

Ben Speer moved over to the grand piano and started playing another favorite old gospel song. With no provocation from me or anyone else, the group spontaneously joined in. Then someone called out, "Hey, what about 'I'll Fly Away'?"

So we sang the old Albert Brumley classic.

"Let's do 'The Eastern Gate,'" someone else suggested. I couldn't help thinking back to a thousand concerts when I'd heard Vestal Goodman or James Blackwood transport an audience to just outside heaven's gates by singing that song. Now, here they were singing it together in the studio, and I got to sing along!

On and on it went, with no preplanned or orchestrated arrangement of who was going to sing what, or even what song we were going to do next. We simply moved from one great gospel number to another.

"Hey, remember that old song . . . let's sing that one!"

"How about that one the Speers used to do? Remember that one?"

"I've got an idea. Let's try this."

Whoever was closest to the piano (and could remember how to play the song) jumped in and began playing. Sometimes the person who used to sing the solo in concerts stood up next to the piano and did so again, just as he or she might have done it years before. The music still carried an unusual power, but this was more than music.

Larry Gatlin leaned over to the cameraman and said, "You better make sure that you're getting this!" The cameraman nodded knowingly.

Most of us had no trouble remembering the words to the songs. An amazing reservoir of spiritual truth was resident in the lyrics of those classics, and with the slightest tug of the Spirit, we were soon reliving old memories while making new ones. We sang the old Stamps-Baxter songs. We sang the old Vaughn Music Company songs. We sang gospel favorites as well as the old hymns.

At one point, almost on a whim, I asked Howard Goodman to recite a reading that he used to do with the Happy Goodman Family. It was a long composition entitled "I Don't Regret a Mile (That I've Traveled for the Lord)." With no advance preparation, Howard movingly recited every word of the poignant poem.

Tears began to flow freely as members of the group recalled the goodness of God and how He had used the words and melodies of our songs to minister to so many people—including us—over the years. One of the singers raised his hand at the end of a song and said, "I want to say something." He then proceeded to give a testimony, telling what God had done in his life recently. He admitted his failures and said something like, "I wish the messages of these songs would have gripped me earlier in life like they do today."

Everyone in the room, including me, could relate. None of us claimed to be perfect Christians. It was only through the love and the grace of God that He put up with any of us! We all could identify with and rejoice over our brother's words . . . and we did!

We had no script, plan, or agenda for anything that we said, did, or sang that day, other than the arrangement we had for "Where Could I Go but to the Lord"? Everything else that happened was totally spontaneous. But the singers in that room possessed a wealth of stories and voluminous experiences with God, not to mention a vast repertoire of great gospel songs. When things got quiet in the studio, it was only a matter of moments before someone spoke up with a testimony of God's goodness and faithfulness. When one person couldn't remember the lyrics to a song, someone else would prompt him. Nobody seemed concerned about the camera that was still in the room. In fact, most of us were oblivious to its presence.

All the while, the recording crew kept the audio and videotape rolling. When someone eventually realized that the tape was on and pointed it out to me, I said, "Just let the tape roll, guys. There's too much good stuff here. Let's get it all."

I really had no idea what we had on tape, but I was glad we had it. I've always been a fan of southern gospel music. I love the music and the people who have performed it over the years. I love delving into the history of the genre. To have these heroes of mine in the studio singing informally around the piano and getting it on tape was a priceless experience I'd treasure for the rest of my life! *What a great souvenir I'm going to have of this day*, I thought. None of us in the studio that day could have imagined just what a role that tape was going to play in all of our lives.

The camera issue settled, we were soon back to singing. Eva

Mae sat down at the piano again, and we began singing some of the old LeFevre songs. Someone suggested a Gaither favorite, so I slipped onto the piano bench. Next it was Rosa Nell Speer's turn at the piano, as we all joined in singing some classic Speer Family numbers. Some of the songs we sang that day were slow, soft, and deeply moving. Others were rousing camp-meeting numbers, the foot-tapping style of songs that these artists had grown up singing literally in church, camp meetings, and gospel concerts all around the country.

It felt almost—I'm reluctant to say it, but it really is true—*heavenly,* as the Gaither Vocal Band and the old-timers sang together. We sang for more than three hours! We were still going strong with no signs that anyone wanted to quit.

We had ordered some food for everyone so we could have lunch right there at the studio, so we took a short break to eat. Fried-chicken-wielding singers were all over the studio and still singing. No doubt the engineers and studio manager were worried sick that their expensive recording equipment might receive an unintentional grease job, but nobody said anything. We were all having too much fun. Larry Gatlin looked over at me with a grin and said, "Gaither, getting us together was a great idea. The only thing that ticks me off, Bill, is that you beat me to it!"

In between songs, we talked about some of the old-timers who were not there. Some had already gone on to be with the Lord; several were ill, so we prayed for them. We sang some more, praised the Lord, and prayed for each other.

Larry Gatlin had recently come out of a rehabilitation center, where he had won a major victory over an addiction problem. He had made a fresh commitment to God and was doing well, but he was scheduled to undergo surgery on his throat to remove nodules from his vocal cords—every singer's nightmare. He didn't know whether he'd be able to sing again when he came out from the operation.

Vestal Goodman had known Larry all his life. "Well, I used to change your diapers," she quipped to him. "Let's just gather around and pray." We all joined in, asking that God would heal Larry completely and give him strength. A sweet Spirit permeated the place, and we knew in our hearts that Larry would sing again.

Jake Hess had been battling ill health for so long he'd almost forgotten what it was like to feel well. His weight had dropped to around 140 pounds, and he had moved to Columbus, Georgia, to be near family when he died. Jake's body was weak that day, but his faith was strong as we all gathered around and prayed for him. Nobody wanted to leave the studio, as everyone was aware that God was doing something extremely special.

One of the most moving moments came when Michael English sang the old favorite "I Bowed on My Knees and Cried Holy." By the time Michael got to the emotionally gripping climax of the song, "I want to see Jesus!" tears were flowing freely down the faces of almost everyone in the studio. It was the heartcry of each of us.

Another highlight for me personally took place when Jim Hill, now in his sixties but still strong of voice, stood up to sing a song I wish I had written: his own composition "What a Day That Will Be." The lyrics talk about heaven, and it was clear by the expressions on the faces in the studio that heaven seemed a lot closer for many of us that day. Memories washed over my mind as I recalled hearing Jim sing that song for the first time back home in Indiana. In those days I started writing music myself and taking my songs to Jim, hoping that he and his group, the Golden Keys, might like them.

At one point in the day, God's presence in the place was so powerful that Larry Gatlin sat down crossed-legged on the studio floor. As various members of the group shared what this day had meant to them, Larry listened in awe. Finally he spoke up and said, "This is the most amazing experience I've ever had!" Then he added, "I was sitting here thinking a while ago, *Lord, please don't let anything happen to the people in this room, because if it does, I'll lose all my heroes.*"

I felt the same way.

It was dark outside by the time our troupe finally sang itself out. As we left the studio, hugging each other and reluctantly calling out our good-byes, we were tired and our throats were nearly raw from singing so long, but we were exuberant. God's Spirit had been with us in an unusual way all day long. It had been a powerful spiritual experience, and like most of the artists in the studio that day, I was deeply moved.

From a practical aspect, I was certain that the video company had plenty of good material from which to choose some special moments. When the producer of the video said he definitely had all the video that he needed, I asked, "What are you going to do with the leftover raw footage?"

"We'll probably just throw it away," he replied.

"In that case, I'd like to have it," I said. I hadn't seen the video footage yet, and I certainly had no plans to release it to the world. But I knew there were two or three hours' worth of my heroes on tape, and if nothing else I wanted to keep it in my own archives.

That night, I called Gloria from Nashville and told her, "Something unusual happened in the studio today. It was almost like a revival. A camera crew caught some of it on tape, and if they have even a fraction of what I experienced, it has to be really special."

When I got home a few days later, I sat down to view the videotape and to relive that special afternoon. As I watched the film, I was astounded. I was absolutely mesmerized by the music, and even more amazed at the supernatural power that seemed to accompany it. Although the music wasn't technically "tight," with people singing whatever melodies and harmonies they wanted, and the camera shots lacked variety and professional lighting effects—we had used only one videocamera and no special lighting—an overwhelming love and emotion came through on the tape. I couldn't tear my eyes from the screen for a moment while the tape was playing. "We've got ahold of something good here," I said aloud, as I continued to watch. "We've got to do this thing right."

As yet, I wasn't sure what "this thing" might be, but I wanted to find out. I called Don Boggs, a friend who was the head of the communications department at Anderson College (now Anderson University), my alma mater. "Don, I have some video from a recording session in Nashville, and I'd like to see if you think we could turn it into some sort of short-form video. Would you have time to take a look at it?"

"Sure, Bill. Bring it over right now," Don replied. "Let's see what you have."

Don and I watched the videotape together, and he, too, was convinced that there was something spiritually powerful about the content. "Let's see if we can edit it to fit into a one-hour format," he said. Don and I did our best to shape up the tape, but in truth, there wasn't much we could do. We managed to trim some of the times when someone would unwittingly stand in front of the camera, or those portions of the tape that were almost too dark to be seen. Apart from that, we left it pretty much the way it happened in the studio.

I added a few still shots of some of the artists when they were much younger, and I tied it all together with a bit of narration. I closed the video with a poem, "There Has to Be a Song," written by one of gospel music's staunchest advocates and one of my dearest friends who had passed away far too soon, Bob Benson. Bob had formerly headed up one of the premier gospel music recording companies, but his true gift was as a communicator of profound ideas through simple words.

The next time I was in Nashville, I showed the tape to a few friends, including Stan Moser, then president of Star Song Communications, our record company. Stan was so moved by the contents of the video that he insisted I allow him to take it to someone at the Family Channel. At that time, the Christian Broadcasting Network operated the Family Channel, and Norm Mintle, a producer at CBN, requested permission to air the tape.

"I'd like to use the tape on the air, and offer it for sale," Norm told me by telephone.

"You've got to be kidding," I replied. "That tape is not network quality. It has a home-movie feel to it."

"I know," Norm said, "but I'd like to run it just as it is."

"Are you serious?" I could hardly believe my ears.

The broadcaster assured me that his offer to air the video was genuine. We worked out the details, and the rough video—with no overdubs and very few musical edits, except those necessary to fit into the format of an hour-long television show—aired on national television. We titled it: *The Gaither Vocal Band Homecoming Video Album.*

Almost immediately CBN's telephones began to ring with requests that the video be rebroadcast. Norm Mintle had developed a commercial at the end of the video by which viewers could call the CBN toll-free number to order a copy of the spontaneous revival. Seven thousand people placed orders within hours after the network showed the tape.

CBN replayed the video three weeks later, and the response was identical. The network received another seven thousand orders, maxing out CBN's response system at that time.

Many viewers recognized some of the gospel greats in the video. To them, groups such as the Happy Goodman Family and the Speer Family were household names. Many audience members didn't know any of the singers, but they sensed that something unusual had been captured on tape. There was an awareness of the presence of God that seemed to show up whenever the tape was shown.

Our office in Alexandria was inundated with telephone calls and letters wanting to know if we had any more videos similar to the one shown on CBN.

We didn't, and I wasn't sure it was possible to create another tape similar to the first *Homecoming* video. But I couldn't help wondering, *What would happen if we did it again, and did it on purpose? What if we had musical arrangements made up in advance? What if we recorded on a twenty-four-track machine that allowed for overdubbing? And what if we had several cameras, with real television-quality lighting, and microphones available to the artists so they didn't have to pass a mike around? Could we do it again? Would it be as good? Or would it seem contrived? Manipulative? Exploitative?*

I didn't know, but the more I thought about it, the more convinced I became. "We've got to do this again," I said.

Before long I was on the phone again, calling the many friends who had participated in the *Homecoming* tape, other gospel music legends who had been unable to take part in the first recording session, and some younger artists, too. In the fall of 1991, the old-timers and the youngsters gathered again in a Nashville recording studio, singing more great songs such as "Peace in the Valley," "Farther Along," "I Will Be There Soon," "I Never Shall Forget the Day," and "Sheltered in the Arms of God."

This time we were more organized—we actually had several cameras on hand for this shoot—but the atmosphere was just as informal. Once again, the Spirit of the Lord took over, and His presence in the room was contagious.

We called the second video *Reunion: A Gospel Homecoming Celebration*, and indeed it was all that and more. The night before we were to film the "reunion" video in Nashville, I asked Gloria to write something that would make the moment special. Although Gloria sometimes felt like an outsider to the southern gospel part of my life, I knew she was articulate enough to sum up our lives in just a few sentences. And she did—beautifully (more about that in chapter 17).

It wasn't long after the release of *Reunion* that we were back in the studio, producing another video in the *Homecoming* series . . . and another, and another! At this writing, we've now done more than one hundred videos, and we're still counting! More than one hundred gospel legends have appeared on the tapes, as well as younger artists such as Janet Paschal, the Martins, Jeff and Sheri Easter, Lillie Knauls, Guy Penrod, David Phelps, and dozens of others. Literally millions of videos featuring the good old gospel music have been sold, and we've designated a portion of the proceeds to help fund the Gospel Music Trust Fund, a much-needed financial safety net for men and women who have given their lives to spreading the Word through music, but who have fallen on tough times. The way the fund came about is an amazing story in itself, and I'll fill you in on the details later in this book.

In 1994, Barry Jennings, the CEO of Gaither Music Company, had created an infomercial drawing material from some of the *Homecoming* videos. We were trying to get the Nashville Network to air the infomercial or some of our videos as specials, and we were running up against a stone wall. A friend suggested that we contact Bill Carter, an interesting character with a varied past, including everything from a stint as a Secret Service agent to President Kennedy, to handling the Rolling Stones when they first toured America. When we first met Bill, he was a manager for country artists such as Tanya Tucker and later Reba McEntire.

Bill had connections everywhere, and although it took nearly a year, we struck a deal with the Nashville Network (TNN) to air some of our programs. The first two that were broadcast were the second most popular programs on that network during the weeks they aired, trailing only the Statler Brothers, who were long established on the network. Today, it's possible to turn on your television almost any hour of the day and find a *Homecoming* session being broadcast.

Even more gratifying than the sales and the popularity of the videos has been the effect they have had on the careers of some of my heroes. The programs reacquainted many people with the artists featured in the *Homecoming* videos, while introducing the artists to a worldwide television audience, many of whom had never heard of groups such as the Blackwood Brothers, the Speer Family, or the Happy Goodman Family. Soon the artists on our tapes were receiving invitations to sing again in churches and auditoriums around the globe. Interestingly, the invitations spanned the spectrum of denominational lines, from overtly Pentecostal and charismatic groups to mainstream evangelicals such as Southern Baptists and Methodists, to Lutherans, Catholics, and so-called high church Presbyterians and Episcopalians.

Additionally, in 1996 we began taking the *Homecoming* family on the road, for the *Homecoming Concert Tour*, performing in cities across America. It's been fun and rewarding to watch the old-timers, along with some of the youngsters, consistently sell out huge arenas around the country, drawing larger crowds in some cities than major rock stars.

Along the way, I've learned a lot of lessons about loving God and loving each other. And we've made a lot of music with our friends. But the real story, I've discovered, is much more than music. Let me tell you about it.

TWO

INDIANA YOUTH

The Gaither family has always had strong ties to the Mid-American heartland. On my mom's side of the family, my grandparents, Burl and Addie Mae Hartwell, settled in the Innesdale neighborhood, a small cluster of homes outside of Alexandria, Indiana. "Mom," as everyone called her whether they were related or not, was Irish and became the unofficial grandma of the entire town. Everyone loved her.

A big man about six foot, five inches tall, with a bald head, "Pop" Hartwell was half Native American and had a rough, gruff, booming voice but a gentle spirit. He enjoyed singing bass in the United Brethren church choir. Orphaned as a child, he worked odd jobs most of his younger years until he could save enough to buy a small farm. "Any honest work is honorable work," Pop liked to say. He was a loving, kind, giving human being who could fool you into thinking that he was a mean fellow at first brush, but not for long. During family gatherings, for example, with children and adults chattering incessantly before mealtime, Pop often startled everyone to attention. "Okay, kids, get quiet!" he'd bellow. (And I do mean bellow!) Then he'd look over at Mom Hartwell, and with a softer voice he'd say, "Mom, pray."

Mom and Pop Hartwell grew much of their food in their own garden, and Mom canned vegetables to use during the cold winter months when little could grow in the Indiana soil. Although they were never wealthy, they always found enough to share, and their home was a haven for many. Anyone who needed a warm meal or a place to stay for the night was always welcome at the Hartwell home.

On my dad's side of the family, my grandma and granddad Blanchie and Grover Gaither were of strong, determined German stock. They also lived in Alexandria, where my granddad provided for his family as a hardworking farmer and a toolmaker in a nearby factory. Their son, George, was my dad, a friendly, easygoing, quiet man. By the time I was born, Dad and Grandpa Gaither were farming about sixty acres on the southeast side of Alexandria—"the other side of the tracks."

Grandma Gaither was a small but rugged woman who preferred to work in the fields with the farmhands than to be cooped up inside doing housework or preparing the meals. Homemaking was simply not her forte. In fact, Grandma Gaither was one of the first women in our family ever to work in a factory, which stirred up quite a bit of gossip in town and made her a popular topic of conversation at the local church socials. Grandma didn't mind the church ladies' gossip one bit!

Grover W. Gaither, my granddad, was the consummate hardworking Middle American farmer. Born in 1892, he lived in Alexandria all his life and was known around town as a man of integrity, a firm but fair fellow in all his dealings, and a man of real character. He had a great sense of humor and he loved to laugh. He enjoyed telling stories about his dad, who bought his first car after going to town most of his life in a horse and buggy. "This is going to be a great invention," my great-granddad said, "but it's going to be real tough on the guys who drink too much on Saturday night, because they'll no longer have the horses to take them home." Grandpa would tell that story on his dad, and then he'd throw his head back and laugh as though it was the first time he'd ever heard it.

Grandpa especially loved to tell "Pat and Mike stories" such as this one:

> Pat and Mike were flying from Los Angeles to New York when the four-engine plane they were on encountered engine problems. The pilot came on the intercom and said, "We just had an engine go out, but don't worry, we have three other engines. I'm sorry to inform you, though, that we will probably arrive about an hour late." A short time later, the pilot came on the speaker again, and said, "Bad news. Another motor has gone out, but don't worry, we still have two more. But it will make us about two hours late." Not long after that, the pilot reported, "Another motor just went out, but don't worry, we still have one more engine. I'm sorry, though, we're now going to be about three hours late."
>
> Pat looked at Mike and said, "I sure hope that other motor doesn't go out, or we're gonna be up here all day!"

Grandpa told that story, and others like it, over and over again. Every time he'd tell a Pat and Mike story, he'd nearly be in tears by the time he got to the punch line. Today people often ask me, "Bill, where did you get your sense of humor?" I immediately think of Grandpa Gaither.

My granddad, my dad, and I have all told those stories to our kids in hopes that they will know that they've come from a long line of storytellers who loved to laugh at life—at its best and at its worst.

The night before my granddad died, he told jokes and laughed so hard he almost cried. He was out in the fields the following day, busy at work on his tractor, when he died suddenly of a heart attack. My dad always said, "Well, at least he died with his boots on!"

I'll never forget the praises that people heaped upon this common farmer at his funeral in 1965. I was especially struck by the things he had done that hardly anyone had known about, not even the other members of our family. An extremely good electrician in town told me, "You don't know this, but I was an orphan. I came here as a boy from Arkansas and your granddad took me in and gave me a place to stay. When I finished high school, I wanted to go to electronics school, and your granddad paid my way. He will always be dear to me."

Repeatedly, I heard my grandfather described with words such as *generous, strong, forgiving,* and *compassionate.* Again and again, people came to me and said, "Your grandfather was a good man."

As a kid, I always wanted to be like my grandpa.

I grew up (and still live) in the small Midwestern town of Alexandria, Indiana, a rural community so quiet, my friend Bob MacKenzie used to quip that he could hear the corn growing. The town had about six thousand residents when I was a boy, and although people have come and gone over the years, the population remains much the same today.

The Gaither homestead consisted of a small farm where we grew corn and wheat and tended a few milk cows. Lela and George Gaither, my mom and dad, were hard workers, and they instilled a strong work ethic in the Gaither children. We attended services regularly at my grandparents' church, and my parents modeled practical spiritual principles. A plaque on the wall of our home summed up Dad and Mom's attitude when it came to faith: "Pray for rain, but keep hoeing!"

Besides struggling to keep up with the farm work, Dad also worked for Delco-Remy, a division of General Motors that made electrical parts used in automobiles. The factory was located in Anderson, Indiana, about ten miles from our home, and the auto industry employed nearly twenty-five thousand workers; today the Delco plant is virtually closed, with just a handful of our townspeople working in the auto industry.

The oldest of the three Gaither siblings—two years older than my brother, Danny, and seven years older than my sister, Mary Ann—I attended grade school at Cunningham School, about a mile from our home. Each morning before school, as the sun came up, Danny and I went to the barn to milk our three cows and to pitch some hay for them. I was allergic to the hay, and it irritated my eyes so badly I often went to school looking as though I had been crying. After school, we fed the chickens, worked in the cornfields, or did whatever chores that needed to be done.

Danny and I shared a small bedroom with purple wallpaper. Mom had chosen the color after badgering me for several days to make my own choice. "Oh, I don't care," I said. "Make it purple!"

I was joking, but Mom took me seriously! After a while, Danny and I actually started to like it. We managed to fit twin beds, with hard, unyielding mattresses, into the small room.

We were typical brothers; we fought over everything, including which side of the room our beds would occupy. It's a wonder we didn't drive each other nuts! But our constant squabbles were rather tame, and they didn't keep us from loving each other. And certainly, anyone outside the family knew better than to pick on either of us, because one brother would be right there to defend the other.

Mom was an artistic sort of person in her own simple way. She played the piano—not well, mind you, but proficiently enough to pick out a few melodies. She must have thought that lessons would have helped her, because she enrolled me in piano lessons at around six years of age. My teacher, Miss Innis, was a traditionalist when it came to teaching music, a taskmaster who insisted that I study basic piano technique and practice playing scales every day. I hated to practice and skipped it whenever I could. Many times over the years, I've wished that I had paid better attention to Miss Innis's instructions and spent more time practicing the basics!

As I took lessons from Miss Innis, I began hearing other music in my mind. Like most kids, I immediately started looking for a shortcut. I'm convinced that children come out of the womb looking for shortcuts! I wanted to play more popular, commercial types of music rather than classical, so I wondered, *Is there an easier way? Do I really need to learn all this classical music to be able to play what I want to play?*

Nowadays, I encourage young musicians to learn the basics. You'll have plenty of time and opportunity to improvise later on, but without a firm foundation in the rudiments of music, you'll always be somewhat limited. You'll be much better off if you master the classic elements that have been used to create great music over the years. I didn't, and I've had to compensate for it all my life.

I enjoyed all sorts of music as a boy and whenever I could, I listened to the popular artists of the day on the radio, including the Mills Brothers, the Ames Brothers, Peggy Lee,

Rosemary Clooney, Pee Wee Hunt, the Four Preps, Patti Page, Andy Williams, the Four Lads, and Ken Griffin on the organ.

I was out working on the farm when my love affair with gospel music began. A dust-covered radio played in the barn while I milked the cows and did my chores, and one day I heard some gospel singers perform live. It was 1948, and the music was vibrant, rhythmic, boogie-woogie style. To be honest, I was drawn to it because of the beat and the sound, rather than the lyrical content or any inspiring theological messages it may have contained.

Nowadays, when people criticize modern Christian music as being "worldly," I remind them that it has always been worldly. Martin Luther wrote tremendous lyrics to what were street tunes of the day. William Booth and the members of the early Salvation Army often injected biblical messages into familiar, secular melodies that their listeners recognized. One day we'll look back on some of the new art forms that we now have trouble accepting in the church, and we'll say, "Wasn't that fantastic?"

Worldly or not, the style of music fascinated me. From that day on, I tuned in the broadcast as often as possible. One day at the close of the show, the announcer said, "We're the Dixie Four Quartet and we're singing today out of the new Stamps-Baxter songbook.[1] If you'd like to have a copy of this book, send fifty cents to the Dixie Four in care of WIBC, Indianapolis, Indiana, and we will send the book to you!"

I saved up fifty cents as fast as I could and ordered the book from the radio show. I could hardly wait to get it; I looked for it in the mailbox every day! When the book finally arrived, I quickly unwrapped the package and gently opened the pages, as though I were opening a priceless treasure or a delicate family heirloom. There were the songs I'd heard on the radio! I started flipping through the pages excitedly. I couldn't wait to try to play some of the notes on the pages.

On the back of the book was an advertisement for more song-books and a gospel music newsletter. "Keep up on the latest news! Subscribe to the *Stamps Quartet News*, our monthly newspaper," the ad encouraged. I ordered the newsletter and when it came, I discovered that a number of other groups were out there performing this kind of music.

On the back of one songbook, I noticed another advertise-ment: "Attend the Stamps Quartet School of Music, the largest school of gospel music in America. Three-week session in June each year in Dallas." I was intrigued and decided to send for more information. Although I was too young to attend the school at the time, I kept it in mind and dreamed of the day that I might be able to go to the Stamps School of Music.

Meanwhile, Grandma Gaither took me to Joe's Record Shop in Anderson, eight or ten miles down the road from our home. "Do you sell records by these guys?" I asked Joe as I held up my Stamps Quartet newsletter for him to see.

"Why, sure we do," Joe replied. "Right here, on RCA Victor and Capitol Records."

Joe took out an enormous catalog about the size of a city tele-phone book and began thumbing through the pages. He found a section of gospel recordings, and I saw the names of groups such as the Dixie Four Quartet, the Blackwood Brothers Quar-tet, and the Harmoneers. Each 78-rpm disk contained two songs, one on each side. I placed an order for one record by the Harmoneers Quartet.

When the recording arrived, I begged Grandma Gaither to take me to Joe's immediately to retrieve my purchase. I took that record home and played it over and over again! I was hooked! Dad paid me a small allowance for milking the cows every morning. It wasn't much of a job, but on a cold Indiana morning, at least my hands stayed warm! More importantly, every time I saved enough money to buy another record, Grandma and I were off to the record store.

I was especially intrigued when I saw a picture of a group called the Statesmen Quartet. With their pencil-thin mustaches and dark, curly hair, they looked more like a Mafia class photo than a group of gospel singers, but their wall-to-wall smiles just wouldn't quit; they sure had pizzazz! I saved up and bought my first Statesmen recording, and could they ever sing! After that, I bought every Statesmen record that came out on RCA Records. I continued to buy more songbooks, too, as well as eight-by-ten glossy photos, and more and more 78-rpm records. While some kids plastered the walls of their rooms with pictures of pretty girls, cars, sports sensations, motion picture stars, or other heroes, I covered the walls of Danny's and my room with photos of famous gospel quartets. Years later when I heard Barbara Mandrell sing, "I was country when country wasn't cool," I could relate, because I was "gospel" long before gospel music was cool! It was a passion for me! I just loved it!

I was as much a fan of the gospel music personalities as any kid my age was a sports fan. I followed the schedules and news about my heroes of the stage just as avidly as most of my friends kept up with the stats of their favorite football, baseball, and basketball teams. The music kept me busy and out of trouble. In fact, I first heard the gospel on the radio and much later on, Gloria and I wrote a song about it:

> Needing refuge for my soul
> When I had no place to go—
> I heard it first on the radio.[2]

While I was a bit out of sync with many of my classmates, my obsession with gospel music occupied so much of my day, I had little time left to get in trouble. Consequently, drugs, alcohol, and nicotine never posed a problem for me as a teenager.

One day I was walking home from school when I spotted a large, multicolored poster tacked to a telephone pole. As I got closer, I realized that the poster bore a picture of some familiar images. Sure enough, there on the poster was a picture of the Dixie Four, and the poster was announcing the fact that the quartet was to appear in concert at Cunningham Elementary School! I hurried home and could hardly wait to tell Mom and Dad.

We attended the concert at the school and from then on, anytime the Dixie Four Quartet was anywhere within reasonable driving distance, the Gaither family was there! Mom and Dad carted us all over the state of Indiana to listen to the Dixie Four. When I think about that today, I am amazed at my parents' love and patience. Mom and Dad were not musicians; nor were they wealthy music connoisseurs. They were ordinary, blue-collar folks eking out a living, yet they always found the time and money somehow to take my brother, sister, and me to the gospel concerts anytime the groups came near. I loved the shows and as I listened to the singers, I imagined myself up on the stage someday.

I had an extremely active imagination, too. One of my favorite things to do was to go upstairs to a small closet off the side of Danny's and my room, and pretend that I was a booking agent in my office, busy scheduling and promoting concerts for famous gospel artists of the day, including myself!

I was a promoter right from the start. I loved putting programs together, too. As soon as Mary Ann was old enough to walk, I plopped her up on the piano bench and got her involved with Danny and me, singing harmony and doing little music shows for Mom and Dad and any relatives who may have stopped by the house. When Danny was around six years of age and I was eight, we often walked or rode our bicycles to the general store, at the end of the street where we lived. We'd walk in the store with our heads barely high enough to see over the counter, and I'd tell the shop owner, "My brother can sing. If you'll give us two pieces of candy, I'll have him sing a song for you."

The shop owner almost always complied. He gave me two pieces of candy, one for me and one for Danny, and I made Danny do the singing! Danny would stand up straight, rear back, and sing, "Let's wemembo Puwl Harbor as we did the Alamo. . . ." He was barely six years old!

See, I was a concert promoter right from the beginning!

My mom owned an old-fashioned "wire" recorder, the precursor to modern tape recorders, so each day while I was at school, I had her record the gospel music programs on the radio for me. When I got home, I'd race to listen to the new songs she'd captured.

Upstairs, in Danny's and my bedroom, I pretended I was a disc jockey as I played songs from the wire recorder as well as my 78 rpm records, and "broadcast" a daily radio show out the upstairs window. I loved introducing the artists and their songs to the cows and a few neighbors who might overhear. "Next we have the Speer Family singing from their brand-new album on Skylight Records . . ." I'd insert "little-known facts" about the singers, usually information I'd gleaned from the Stamps Quartet newsletter, and made it sound as though the singers were my best buddies in the world . . . which, in a way, they were.

Before long I discovered WSM, a famous country radio station broadcasting out of Nashville, Tennessee. One of WSM's most popular programs was a live broadcast from Ryman Auditorium, home of the original Grand Ole Opry. In addition to country and bluegrass music, on the first Friday night of the month WSM also featured gospel music.

I was in the eighth grade when I heard about the show on Fridays, promoted by Wally Fowler, a gregarious fellow with a flair for show business. I just loved to hear Wally introduce the groups, and I loved to hear them sing!

One day while Dad and I were working in the barn, I asked him, "Dad, how far away is Nashville?"

"Oh, it's a good day's drive," Dad replied and kept on working. In 1949, before the interstate highway system was completed, Nashville was at least seven to eight hours away.

"Dad, would you take me to Nashville to go to *Wally Fowler's All-Night Singing?*" I asked, not realizing how ridiculous my request really was.

Dad was a farmer and a toolmaker in an auto parts factory, and Mom was a homemaker who played a bit of piano. Neither of them was musically inclined, and they certainly had no illusions about my one day making a living as a gospel musician. Nevertheless, they recognized that I had a passionate interest in this new phenomenon, and they loved me enough to encourage me even though at the time, my interest made little sense to them.

Amazingly, Dad and Mom consented to take me to Nashville. I was so excited, I could hardly wait! On the day of our trip, I hopped out of bed earlier than usual to get my chores done, so we could leave as soon as possible and arrive at Ryman Auditorium several hours before show time. I wanted to see and hear it all; not just the music, but how the entire show came together.

I nagged, whined, and badgered Dad about leaving earlier than necessary, until I finally wore him down. "For crying out loud, Bill, it's an all-night singing," Dad said. "If we're going to have to go this early, then you are going to stay till the very end."

"Okay, Dad!" I couldn't imagine a better punishment!

We packed the entire family into the car and made the long trek from Indiana to the heart of Tennessee. Sure enough, we arrived early in Nashville, and I was enthralled. There it was— the majestic Ryman Auditorium, a large, red-brick, barnlike former church that was now the home of the Grand Ole Opry . . . and on the first Friday of the month, the home of *Wally Fowler's All-Night Gospel Singing.*

As soon as the doors to the Ryman opened, I was inside the building, gazing in awe at the scenes I had only imagined as I listened on the radio. Our seats were right down front, on the main floor, but tucked behind one of several poles holding up the balcony in the old auditorium. I didn't care. I sat on the edge of my seat, leaning one way then the other, straining to see everything in the place, and to hear every sound. I watched as the microphones were checked, the instruments tuned, the records set up at the front of the stage and outside the auditorium in the foyer. I was fascinated by every detail of the concert.

Headlining the concert that night were the Homeland Harmony Quartet, the Blackwood Brothers Quartet, the Speer Family, and the Harmoneers. It was an awesome program card.

From the time the music began until the last note was sung, my eyes never left the stage. I drank it all in—the sight of the gospel groups' outfits, their commanding presence on the stage, the incredible sound coming out of the Altec-Lansing speakers, the amazing artistry of the piano players—and I relished every bit of it! True to his word, Dad stayed until the last song was sung—at about 2:30 the following morning! Only a few hundred people remained in the audience by then, and I was the most wide-eyed awake of all of them. I didn't want the music to stop or the show ever to be over! From that night on, my goal in life was to become a pianist and singer for a gospel quartet. Although I had lofty dreams, I'm not sure I could ever have imagined how those dreams would one day come to pass.

A few months later, I talked Dad and Mom into returning to Nashville for another program at the Ryman. The Statesmen were on the program that night, and they were in a league of their own. They were incredible singers but beyond that, they were fabulous showmen. When the Statesmen took the stage, they seemed to grab the audience by the heart and never let go. I watched and listened in amazement as Cat Freeman's tenor voice soared into the stratosphere, while Jim "Big Chief" Wetherington's rich bass voice plunged off the scale. Doy Ott's smooth harmonies blended perfectly, and Hovie Lister, the group's pianist and emcee, provided a show of his own. Hovie didn't sing much—although we later discovered that he hummed constantly during the Statesmen's sets—but he was bouncing all over the piano stool and pulling at his pant legs, revealing his trademark red socks, when his fingers weren't flying up and down the keyboard.

Perhaps the most contagious of the Statesmen, however, was the dignified, charismatic lead singer, Jake Hess. Jake seemed literally to radiate the love of God from the stage in every song he sang. I probably didn't recognize at the time the class, grace, and charm that he possessed; all I knew was that his singing performance was mesmerizing and his impact on the crowd was unbelievable!

Jake Hess didn't simply sing a song; he delivered a message to the audience. He did more than hit the notes; he strove to enunciate every syllable with perfect diction and pronunciation. He used gestures, vocal inflections, and facial expressions to communicate the song.

This was also the first time I'd ever heard a singer "croon," a style of singing familiar to fans of Bing Crosby and Perry Como that had to be heard to be appreciated. Jake Hess was the ultimate crooner, later captivating audiences for years with his rendition of "Prayer Is the Key to Heaven, but Faith Unlocks the Door."[3]

During the intermission after the Statesmen's first set, I walked up to the front of the auditorium, where the members of the group were selling records from the front of the stage. I bought a Statesmen album, which gave me my opportunity to speak to the Statesmen's lead singer.

"Mr. Hess, I love your singing," I said.

"Well, thank you very much," the singer replied with a big smile.

"You sound like Bill Kinney of the Ink Spots," I ventured.

"Well, thank you very much! That's quite a compliment," Jake Hess said with another huge smile. Jake immediately became a hero to me. He was so kind and gracious, and his example spawned in me a desire to be like him.

After that, I bought every Statesmen album I could get my hands on. Years later, after the *Homecoming* videos had become best-sellers, I often joked with Hovie and Jake, as well as the Speer Family, James Blackwood, and J.D. Sumner. "You guys just about broke my family's budget when I was a kid. We bought every record you had, not to mention the money we spent on gasoline to go see you. I can't tell you what a joy it is at this time in my life to get some of that money back from you!"

Back home, I found a few fellows in my school who liked to sing, and we attempted to form an amateur group. It was one of my first lessons in learning how to sing in harmony. We sang at school programs, and then my voice changed, dropping lower and lower until it finally landed somewhere between a solid baritone and a high bass. I enjoyed performing and people seemed to like my singing. I once even received a standing ovation for my rendition of "Old Man River" in a program at school. *Hey! I must be pretty good!* I thought. The ovation fueled my already active imagination concerning the possibilities of making a living as a singer.

The band and choir teacher in my high school was a young fellow named Carroll Copeland. Mr. Copeland had recently completed a tour of duty with the military, and it showed in the way he ran his music program. A fantastic showman with an engaging smile, Mr. Copeland directed his high school musicians as though he were commanding a military unit. He was a strict disciplinarian and I responded positively to his approach. He was tough, but he made the music exciting.

Once, Mr. Copeland told me, "Bill, you have a lot of talent, but you're lazy." That was one of the most motivational statements I ever heard. I set out to prove to Mr. Copeland, whom I respected so much, that I was a hard worker. I appreciated his striving for excellence even in a small school like ours, and I wanted to show him that I would settle for nothing less in my performance as well.

About the same time, I was singing with my brother, Danny, and my sister, Mary Ann. I was a slave driver, too! As the older brother, I constantly drilled them on harmony parts, and it's a wonder they didn't clobber me.

Somewhere around my freshman year in high school, Danny's voice really came into its own. It was obvious he was developing into a sensational singer, and I began to dream that someday he and I might be able to perform together on the gospel stage.

Throughout high school, I worked at Cox's Supermarket, our local grocery store, where I earned enough money to finance my ever-expanding record collection. I listened to WSM on Friday nights, often sitting by myself out in our family car because I got better reception on the car radio than on the one in the house. I played basketball in junior high and I loved the game, but I wasn't a good ballplayer; I was the seventh man on the team. I'd go to the games, sit on the bench and feel rejected, maybe play a few minutes here and there when the score got lopsided, then come home and sit in the car till eleven o'clock, hoping to get a strong signal out of Nashville.

Outside in the dark, I'd fiddle with the knobs on the car radio, tuning in WSM through the static, until I could pick up the sounds of my favorite gospel artists. While the guys on the basketball team were out celebrating a victory or drowning their sorrows over a loss, I was straining to hear the harmonies of a gospel quartet. My friends may have dreamed of loping down the court with Bob Cousy, Wilt Chamberlain, or Bill Russell; meanwhile, I was leaning my head back on the car seat, dreaming that I was performing on stage with Hovie Lister, Jake Hess, or James Blackwood.

I was moderately popular in our small high school, although I was extremely shy. I dated a few fine young ladies, fell in love a time or two, and got my heart crushed once or twice as well. Gloria and I attended one of my class reunions not long ago, where I picked up a yearbook and began showing Gloria some of my classmates. Flipping through the pages, we came to a picture of me in my closely cropped crew cut along with the caption "Most Popular."

"You could have fooled me!" I quipped to Gloria.

My brother, Danny, on the other hand, had as full a social calendar as he could handle while in high school. He was a handsome young man, and all the girls wanted to be seen on his arm. Me? I wasn't good-looking, and I never thought I was supposed to be. When friends or potential dates gave me the cold shoulder, I was hurt but not devastated. After all, I still had my "friends" Hovie, Jake, James, Big Chief Wetherington, and the other gospel greats I introduced in my imagination.

During the summer of 1953, my junior year of high school, I decided I wanted to attend the Stamps School of Music that I'd seen advertised on the gospel songbooks. The school was located in Dallas, Texas, and I had never before been away from home by myself. Nevertheless, I believed that the three-week school would prepare me for a career in gospel music, so it was worth the risk. I talked Mom and Dad into allowing me to go, started saving my money, and sent in the application.

I traveled by train from Anderson to Dallas, where a song-writer working at the school picked me up and took me to the boarding house where we were to stay. Fourteen boys bunked in a cramped boarding house with no air conditioning, and only a window fan for ventilation in the middle of the summer in Dallas. Night or day, the temperature never dropped below a hundred degrees in that tiny house, but I didn't care. I was in my element, with other boys who loved gospel music. To me, I was in Jerusalem and it was just one step away from heaven!

We attended classes at Bethel Temple, a church located in the Oak Cliff section of Dallas. It was an area that a few years later became infamous as the home of Lee Harvey Oswald, the man accused of shooting President John F. Kennedy.

When I arrived at the Stamps School of Music, I looked around in awe. Nearly six hundred other like-minded young men and women about my age, with a similar passion for performing gospel music, were gathered in one location! We started early each morning, learning music theory, harmony, chords, and other elements of music. I learned a lot. In fact, when I later studied music theory in college, I earned straight A's largely because of what I'd learned years earlier at the Stamps School of Music.

At 9:30 each morning we had group singing, then around 10:30, the students took private piano or vocal lessons. During the afternoons, we'd get together as a group to sing. In the evenings, various professional groups, as well as groups pulled together from the students, performed. I was part of a quartet including Glenn Creaseman from Asheville, North Carolina, Virgil Lovett from South Georgia, Finis Barr from St. Louis, and Charlie Hodge from Decatur, Alabama, who later sang in a group with me after I graduated from high school. Charlie eventually went into the Army and was stationed in Germany, where he met a young singer from Memphis. His name was Elvis Presley. Charlie and Elvis struck up a friendship and a professional relationship, and Charlie went on to play rhythm guitar onstage with Elvis for many years.

I met many friends—some of whom turned out to be lifelong ones—at the Stamps School of Music. One of the professional groups that performed during the school included a tremendous young piano player, Henry Slaughter, and an incredible lead singer, Glen Payne. Both men would later become two of the dearest friends I've known in my life.

I had such a great time at the school, I stayed there for three weeks and never once called home to talk to Mom or Dad. My only disappointment was that I had to leave.

THREE

FALSE STARTS AND
BETTER BEGINNINGS

I COULD HARDLY WAIT TO
finish my final year of high school, and I worked every spare
hour to save enough money to return to the Stamps School of
Music the following summer after graduation in 1954. Once
again, I sang with Charlie Hodge at the Stamps school, and
with all the enthusiasm three weeks of solid gospel singing can
evoke, Charlie and I came back home convinced we could develop a career in gospel music. Charlie had a friend from Alabama who sang bass, so they, Danny, and I formed a gospel
singing group known as the Pathfinders.

We sang at churches, fairs, and just about anywhere anyone
would invite us in Indiana. Sometimes we got paid, sometimes
we didn't. Often when we sang in churches, the congregation
would take up a freewill love offering on our behalf. I learned
quickly that it's hard to live on love!

We heard that Illinois held some good opportunities for a

group like ours, so we made the big jump across the state line. When we found that things were no better there, we later moved to Columbus, Ohio. When we made the first move, Danny had to drop out of the group because he had two years of high school remaining. We replaced him with another fellow who was a good singer, but not nearly as good as Danny. I knew I'd miss singing with my brother, but it was time to get out of the cornfields and into the big time. I was nineteen years of age and ready to conquer the world.

In an effort to duplicate the success of the Dixie Four, we talked our way onto a fifteen-minute radio show that Pennington Bread sponsored on WRFD in Worthington, Ohio. We hoped that people would hear us on the show, invite us to sing at their churches or civic functions, and throngs of excited gospel music lovers would turn out.

They didn't.

In fact, they avoided the Pathfinders in droves. Looking back, I can see that the Pathfinders were four young guys with a lot of enthusiasm, a little potential, and even less raw talent. When I compare our sound to the Statesmen or Blackwood Brothers, we left a lot to be desired. But at the time, we thought we were hot stuff and even shared the stage with some big-name quartets as the opening acts when they came to town.

For more than eight months, the Pathfinders struggled along, hoping and believing that around the next turn we were going to make it, yet not knowing where our next meal was going to come from. On more than a few occasions, I recall surviving on nothing more than toast and coffee. We worked hard, we promoted ourselves aggressively, but the success we sought continued to elude us. For some reason, the group just wasn't working. We weren't good enough for any concert promoters—what few there were in those days—to get excited about us as musicians;

we weren't entertaining showmen; we didn't have a deep, powerful spiritual impact. We were just four young guys who loved to sing. We didn't have that intangible quality that athletes refer to as "chemistry" or show people call "magic." We were missing whatever it took to make us more than music.

One August afternoon at a county fairgrounds in the small town of Van Wert, Ohio, the Pathfinders were at a dead end. Broke, dejected, and discouraged, we were scheduled to perform a concert at the 4-H building that night. When we heard how many tickets had been sold for our concert, the number was so negligible that had I not been so close to tears, I probably would have laughed uproariously.

But the joke was on us. I felt nauseated and disheartened. As I trudged out behind the 4-H building to get some air and sort through my thoughts, my heart was breaking. All of my lofty dreams, my inflated hopes and plans to be a career gospel singer seemed to be nothing more than hot air. Reality was pinching at my idealism and the balloon was about to pop. Salty tears flowed freely down my face, and I didn't even bother wiping them away. I had never felt so low in all my life. I was an abject failure, with no money, no career, no future.

Reluctantly, yet resolutely, I hung up my dream of being a professional gospel musician. I've always been a realist, and for the first time in my life I had to confront the ugly truth that I was not good enough: not good enough to be a professional singer; not good enough to be a professional piano player; not smart enough or manipulative enough to make it in the real world of professional music.

All I could do was pray.

Nowadays, I'm aware that prayer can be more than my last resort, but back then I wasn't tuned in to God very well. I had grown up going to our home church in Alexandria, and I believed in God. I'd asked the Lord to come into my life nearly every summer at church camp, as well as several times when traveling preachers had come by our town to conduct revivals. I tried to live in a manner pleasing to God as best I knew how. But my spirituality was based mostly on emotional experiences rather than a commitment to, and a genuine relationship with, God. Undoubtedly, for a while after each revival or similar spiritual event I attended, I felt energized. I tried to live a little better. But I was still the one in control. I called the shots; I did what I wanted to do and made my own decisions. Even my dreams of being a gospel musician were more about me than they were about God or the gospel. I just wanted to make a living doing something that I enjoyed.

But behind that 4-H building that day, I came to the end of myself, my way, my ability or lack of it, my trying to make something happen. And for the first time, I truly placed my life in God's hands.

I prayed, "God, there has to be more to life than this. I don't know what you want me to do, but evidently, it's not music. So I don't know how I'm going to make a living, but I'm not going to do this anymore." I committed myself to doing whatever God had planned, even though at that point I had no clue what that might be. "God, if music is not what you want for me, I'm willing to give it up," I said. I winced at the words. Even as I prayed, I was convinced my music career was over.

I was confused and perplexed, but I wasn't angry with God. After all, I hadn't really consulted with Him about entering the music field; I'd just followed my dream the way everyone says a person is supposed to do. Now that my reality check had decimated me, I laid down my dreams, never imagining that my utter failure could be the beginning of the fulfillment of His dreams for me.

Today, as one of the more seasoned members of the music community, I'm often approached by young artists asking questions about how they can succeed in their careers. Sometimes I wish they could be more realistic about their gifts, talents, and calling.

Great singing performances or incredible musicianship do not always lead to a successful career in music. It's not just how talented a person is. Another dimension is involved. Many less-than-great singers have achieved astounding success as music artists; others who are far less musically gifted have received a special touch from God that sets them apart to be used in some powerful way, and millions of lives are impacted. It's always been more than music.

Yet a realistic appraisal of one's gifts might be extremely revealing. When I'm asked by fledgling artists whether they should continue trying to make it in this difficult, horrendously competitive field, I usually respond, "I can only tell you what I did. I tried to carve out a career in music as a nineteen-year-old kid. I gave it everything I had. I worked as hard as I could, sacrificed as much as I had to give. I ate, slept, and breathed music. I poured my life into it. But there came a point where I had to take a long look in the mirror and say to myself, 'This just isn't working. And it's not going to work.' It hurt me deeply, but I had to admit that it was time to move on to something else."

Over the years, I've watched and listened to numerous artists getting angry at their recording companies. "They're not selling my products," the artist complains. "They're not getting my songs, albums, or videos aired. They just aren't promoting me or marketing my products correctly."

I've even heard of some artists becoming so disgruntled and disillusioned because their careers were not working, they were ready to give up their faith in God. "There must not be a God," one artist said, "or people would be responding to the message I'm trying to convey."

That's nonsense! That's sad.

I've often wanted to respond (and in more recent years have done so), "At some point, you have to ask yourself, 'Do people really want what I am creating?' And if they don't, find some other way to make a living while you pursue your music for artistry's sake."

"That's easy for you to say," the more outspoken artist may respond, "because you are successful."

"Now I am, perhaps," I respond. "But I've had to come up through the ranks the same way you do, and I've had to ask myself those hard questions again and again throughout my career. 'Do people really want what I'm offering?' If they don't, I need to reevaluate what I'm doing. Possibly I need to work more on a local or regional level, rather than on a national scale. Maybe there is another place where I can perform or minister, and fill a real need. Perhaps the problem is my pride. I don't really want to use my gift and talent in some obscure or mundane manner or place. But trust me on this, there is *always* a place for someone who is willing to serve. And if I truly want to be successful, I must find something that either meets a need or fills a gap that no one else is filling. Keep in mind, too, that *success* is a relative term. Successful compared to what?

"Imagine that you've written a song, but maybe it's not for the whole world. Maybe it's not for the whole nation. Possibly it isn't for the entire denomination, movement, church, or even for the choir. Maybe that song was intended for you and a few people close to you. That doesn't diminish the importance of the song; it simply narrows the scope of influence, and even that may change with time."

Beyond that, I explain, there is the element of historical timing. By that I mean that within every historical context, the culture cries out to see and hear particular styles or artists for which there is no rational explanation. In the 1940s, for example, the world swooned at the sounds of Rudy Vallee singing "My Time Is Your Time"; then came Perry Como and Bing Crosby crooning "Racing with the Moon." Then it was time for the Everly Brothers, Elvis, Bobby Vinton, the Beach Boys, the Four Seasons, the Supremes, the Four Tops, the Carpenters, and some incredible groups and solo artists in the 1960s. Suddenly, the Beatles shook up the music world, and it goes on and on. What was once the latest sensation is now a footnote in music history.

Consequently, I often tell creative young artists who may be slightly ahead of their time, "Be patient; your time will come. If this music is something you want to do, go for it. Do it with all your heart, do it even if nobody wants to hear it, but be realistic enough to recognize that if there is no market for it, you must find some other means to make a living."

Where do you go when your dreams have been dashed, when your hopes are all gone? Where do you go when you have nowhere else to go?

You run to those who love you unconditionally.

At the lowest point of my nineteen years, I decided to go home. The morning after the Van Wert concert disaster, I told the rest of the guys in the group, "I'm going home."

At first the guys tried to talk me into staying a little longer. "Things are just starting to gel, Bill," one of the guys said. "Don't give up now."

"We're almost there, Bill," another guy said. "A few more concerts and we'll be over the hump."

I had been hearing such things for months now, but the truth was there was not a large enough audience that wanted to hear what we were doing. It didn't make me a bad person, or the guys a poor group. It was simply a matter of timing and talent.

I got in my car and drove back to Alexandria, where Mom and Dad welcomed me. They didn't criticize, condemn, or chastise me. My folks were so supportive! They didn't say, "Bill, we told you that music thing wasn't going to work." Nor did they say anything like, "Well, it's about time you came to your senses!" I can never remember any attitude from my parents other than loving support, open arms, and acceptance.

That's not to say that other people within our circle of friends and family members didn't regard my dream-chasing as foolish. Although he never mentioned it to me at the time, Dad took quite a razzing from people who wondered why I wasn't out looking for a real job. Frequently friends or relatives who didn't quite understand my passion to perform gospel music asked Dad, "How's Bill doing?" They *knew* how Bill was doing. He was falling on his face! But Dad was always kind and gracious.

Dad was cool. "Well, he's struggling," he replied. "And he's struggling pretty hard. I don't think they're going to make it."

"What's he going to do?" the relatives asked.

"I don't know," Dad answered pensively. "We'll just have to wait and see."

But when I stepped through the doors of our little home, Mom and Dad were right there for me, eager to help me pick up the pieces and start over again. Mom and Dad never really stated it, but all the Gaither kids knew: no matter where we'd been or what we'd done—good or bad—we could always come home.

I returned to my hometown and to my job at Cox's, the local grocery store, waiting on shoppers and working as a meat-cutter in the butcher shop. It didn't take me long to figure out that I was not born to be a meat-cutter, so I did one of the smartest things I've ever done in my life. I decided to enroll in college. I applied to and was accepted at Taylor University, a Christian liberal arts school in Upland, Indiana, but I kept my job at Cox's to help pay my tuition.

I knew nothing about college; I knew little of the joy of learning, grappling with new or controversial ideas, or approaching life from a philosophical worldview. Nobody else in the Gaither family had ever gone to college. My only interests outside of music were in English literature; in high school, I had been an average student in most other courses, but in music and English, I excelled. So when it came time to choose a college major, I wrote down "English Lit."

I continued living at home in Alexandria and commuted every day to Taylor. It was a half-hour drive, so to pass the time each morning I tuned my car radio to WOWO, the fifty-thousand-watt blowtorch broadcasting a show featuring the Weatherford Quartet from Fort Wayne, Indiana. That was about the only gospel music I heard during my tenure at Taylor, since southern gospel was not considered an acceptable style of church music at that time. But even if it wasn't in the churches or the school curriculum, the music was in my blood. I listened to gospel music like a castaway craving water.

While I enjoyed studying English and literature, I found the rest of my academic studies somewhat boring. Nevertheless, I worked hard and tried to make the most of my college experience.

I was just getting comfortable with the whole idea of college when one day, out of the blue, Earl Weatherford and his wife, Lily, stopped by Alexandria and offered me a job playing piano for their group. They had heard me play at the Stamps School of Music and then later with the Pathfinders, and they were convinced I could contribute to the Weatherfords.

I could hardly believe my ears as I listened to their offer. The Weatherford Quartet wanted me! Better still, they were willing to pay me more money to play piano for them than I made cutting meat at the grocery store. I told the Weatherfords that I'd talk it over with my parents and call them as soon as possible.

When I broached the idea of leaving college to travel with the Weatherfords, Dad was clearly troubled. An easygoing father who rarely declined any reasonable request from his children, Dad surprised me. "No, Bill," he said. "You've started at Taylor and you're going to finish."

That was some of the best advice I've ever received in my life. I tell aspiring artists something similar today: "Finish your education first. Even though the lure of diesel smoke is strong and enticing, the tour bus will still be there after you get your education."

I tell parents of talented offspring the same thing.

Truth is, I am able to operate at the level I do within the music community not because of luck or unusual musical ability, but largely because I stayed in school and finished my formal education. Many talented artists discover too late that it takes more than an attractive appearance, hot vocal licks, or cute little ditties to last in the music business, especially once you pass certain age milestones.

I respected my dad immensely, and I knew better than to argue with him. As much as he had always supported me in pursuing my dreams of being a gospel musician, we had already been down that road and it had gone nowhere. He had seen how difficult and unstable making a living could be in that line of work. Not surprisingly, he wanted me to complete my college education before heading out on any more wild goose chases—

even if it meant turning down the offer of going with the Weatherfords.

I reluctantly called the Weatherfords and declined their kind offer. When I got off the phone, a sick feeling ran through my stomach. *I've just closed the door on an offer of a lifetime,* I thought. Most of my friends from the Stamps School of Music would have been thrilled to be onstage with the Weatherfords, and what had I done? I'd turned them down to study English literature and poetry!

It's often said that for a Christian the tough decisions are not so much between good and bad, but between *good* and *best*. I didn't know it then, of course, but to have gone with the Weatherfords would have been a great honor, lots of fun, and probably an exhilarating experience for me . . . but it would not have been God's best for my life. As much as I will always be grateful for Earl and Lily's confidence in me when I had so little confidence in myself, I'm thankful to Dad and to the Lord for keeping me in school. God had a much bigger plan in mind than I had!

Oh, sure, I was disappointed that Dad hadn't seen the light, but I had already resigned myself to the fact that I had probably no possible career in gospel music, so I went back to college and tried not to think about what might have been.

My sophomore year, I transferred to Anderson College, another Christian liberal arts college closer to my home. Maybe it was because I had passed the true test—the Weatherfords' offer—that I was more contented about being in college. I actually began to enjoy school. I majored in English and minored in music. I got involved in the college volunteer choir and eventually became the director. It was my first experience at organizing duets, trios, quartets, and other ensembles into one compact, tightly knit program.

While pursuing my teaching degree from Anderson, I met many wonderful, bright Christian people, and a few brilliant ones. Two men who left an indelible impression on both my heart and mind were Dr. Robert Nicholson—my choral conducting teacher, who later became the academic dean at the institution, and who eventually became president of Anderson—and Dr. Karl Kardatzke, my professor for adolescent psychology.

Dr. Nicholson modeled how it was possible to feed both your mind and your spirit. He showed by his daily life that a person did not have to park his or her brain outside the academic classroom simply because he or she was a Christian. Quite the contrary, Dr. Nicholson combined a keen intellect with a passion to live more fully for God. He talked a lot about servanthood, and he modeled it. I often thought, *Now, that's the kind of man I want to be like.*

Years later, I realized that I had patterned many of my own personal teaching attitudes and habits after those of Dr. Nicholson. I especially emulated him in the realm of classroom discipline. He fostered a positive attitude toward learning in a classroom. He wasn't harsh or threatening toward the challenging students or the class clowns, but instead he chose to engage them and harness their energy in positive ways. Later, when I taught high school, I incorporated a similar approach to discipline in class. I attempted to make the classes fun and entertaining, yet informative and demanding. And kids responded incredibly well! I've used much the same technique with the young music artists I've tried to teach over the years. My goal is to make the program so entertaining, and the experience so enriching, artists don't want to leave.

Dr. Kardatzke was another brilliant professor in a field that some Christians discounted, while others regarded it as being spawned by the devil himself. In an era when Christians viewed psychologists as just slightly better than atheists, Dr. Kardatzke dared to deal with human personality and emotional problems from a clinical perspective as well as the spiritual. More importantly, Dr. Kardatzke had a heart for God, and he wasn't ashamed to show it. One night at a midweek prayer service, I saw tears streaming down Dr. Kardatzke's face as we sang the well-known hymn "The Old Rugged Cross." I couldn't help being impressed that this highly intelligent man, with more degrees after his name than I could keep track of, was weeping over what the Lord had done for him on the cross.

Another strong, early influence in my life was Dr. Robert Reardon. Dr. Reardon was the president of Anderson during the time I was in school there. He was extremely open and honest in his approach to faith. *Doubt* was not a bad word to Dr. Reardon; in fact, he taught us that any thinking person will eventually have moments of extreme doubt, and that doubt is simply a stepping stone on the pathway to real faith. Moreover, Dr. Reardon taught me that many times life comes down to simply doing the right thing, and doing it simply *because* it is the right thing to do.

He also taught me how to establish and maintain integrity in dealing with other people. Dr. Reardon never concealed any hidden agendas. Once, long after Gloria and I were well established in the music business, Dr. Reardon visited to invite me to serve on the board of trustees and to get a major donation. "Bill, we're here today to get as much money out of you as we can!"

I had never before seen that sort of fund-raising technique . . . but Dr. Reardon walked out of my office with a major commitment.

Thanks to men such as Dr. Nicholson, Dr. Kardatzke, and Dr. Reardon, my own faith grew much stronger. I began to see the Christian life more as a matter of the will than the emotions. I love the old chorus "I Have Decided to Follow Jesus," because it succinctly summarizes what it has always meant for me to be a Christian. My relationship with God is not based on my feelings or even my perfect performance. It is based on commitment: His commitment to me, and my commitment to Him. It may sound simple to some people, but for me, that was a major revelation, and it was worth far more than the price of my education at Anderson just to discover it!

One of the advantages of living at home while attending college was that on weekends, I could sing together with my brother, Danny, and my sister, Mary Ann, now a teenager. We called ourselves the Gaither Trio, and sang for churches, fairs, and various civic groups. I wasn't a great singer; I wasn't even a good singer! But Danny had developed a smooth-as-silk, clear voice, and Mary Ann and I blended well with him. I played the piano and emceed the program. We sang all "cover" songs, material other artists had written or made popular. At this point, I hadn't yet tried to write a song, let alone dared to think that one day people around the world might actually sing something I had written.

Soon the make-believe concert-booking that used to occupy my time upstairs in my "office" became a reality. The phone started ringing, and people were calling with invitations for us to sing.

"What do you charge?" many wanted to know.

"I don't know," I replied. "Just pay us whatever you think it's worth."

I carried a date book in my shirt pocket everywhere I went, because somebody might ask us to sing! Before long, the Gaither Trio started getting better dates than the Pathfinders did.

By the end of the year, I went to my dad and said, "I think that I could quit my job at Cox's and just sing to pay my way through school."

Dad was hopeful, but still skeptical. "Are you sure?" he asked. "We've already been down this road."

"Yes, I think I can do it," I replied. "People really like our trio."

"Okay," Dad acquiesced.

I went to the local radio station and struck a deal to do a daily broadcast, sponsored by Cox's Supermarket. The announcer at the station was Mort Crim, who later became a major media personality for NBC News, on a par with Chet Huntley, David Brinkley, or, in my opinion, any current news anchors. Soon we started receiving invitations from churches, farm bureaus, and other civic organizations. We put together a little show in which we sang gospel songs as well as some secular numbers such as "Back Home in Indiana," "Sugar Time," and "Old Man River."

For someone who had no experience at booking a group except what I had imagined, I quickly became a pretty good agent. By the end of my sophomore year in college, the Gaither Trio was busy. We entertained a lot of people, and we even made a bit of money. When the Trio took off, I was able to sing my way through college, buy a new convertible, and still have a few extra dollars in the bank. I booked programs at farm bureaus and service clubs on Tuesdays and Wednesday evenings; on Saturdays we often sang for a church youth rally somewhere, and on Sundays we usually sang in a church service or two. We sang our way throughout Indiana, Illinois, Ohio, the southern part of Michigan, Kentucky, and Tennessee.

When I graduated from college, I got a job teaching junior high English in the Anderson school system. Meanwhile, I went back to school to get my master's degree in guidance and counseling, which required a thorough knowledge of psychology. Looking back over the years, I've come to appreciate my studies in psychology even more. It has been a tremendous tool to help me deal with a wide variety of people. More importantly, I've discovered that good theology is also good psychology.

I loved teaching, especially when I could see by the expression on the kids' faces that they really were getting the ideas that I was trying to communicate. Although I've done many things since then, I've always considered myself first and foremost a teacher. To this day, it remains a thrill for me to teach young musicians and artists how to do something, or how to improve a presentation. In my heart, I will always be a teacher.

About that time, as kids are apt to do, my brother, Danny, went through a rebellious age. A strong, talented, fun, easygoing, good-looking guy with loads of personality, Danny was a prime target for every enticement. I could see trouble coming, but it was tough to confront a brother who was making what I thought were unwise choices. I wanted to be gracious and kind; I didn't want to embarrass or discourage him. Nor did I want to sound self-righteous. Yet once I became aware of Danny's situation, I couldn't ignore the responsibility we had as gospel singers with a public platform, onstage and offstage. When I saw the red flags waving, I simply had to say, "We need to be consistent with the message we are presenting in our music." We weren't espousing a message of perfection, but we did believe that what we were saying from the stage and what we were saying through our daily choices should match closely.

I loved my brother dearly, but when he seemed impervious to Mary Ann's and my pleading that he make some changes, I said, "Okay, if that's the way it's going to be, let's just forget it." We disbanded the Gaither Trio, and when the pastor asked if I would direct the choir at our local church, I said, "Why not?"

I wasn't trained in formal choral music, and it certainly wasn't my forte, but I did my best trying to direct the choir for about a year and a half. I have tremendous respect for choir directors, because it is not an easy job. The best directors are not always the best singers or musicians themselves, but they have learned how to bring out the best in their people.

Working with the choir provided an opportunity for me to see and hear firsthand the new church music that believers were writing, as well as the deep well of old favorites from the hymnbooks. I noticed, however, that there was a void when it came to combining sound theology with real-life experiences expressed through music. I loved the old hymns, but many of them were difficult to sing, and the new songs seemed to fall into two main categories: they were either about meeting the Lord and "getting saved," or they were sugar-sweet, syrupy pictures of life in heaven.

Wait a minute, I thought. *I believe in getting saved, and I'm glad that someday I'll go to heaven, but in between, we have a lot of living to do in this old world! I think I can write better songs than that!*

With more than forty years of experience as a songwriter, a few gray hairs, and a lifetime of travel, ministry, and music, I'm now appalled at my youthful audacity. To think that I could add a drop to the wonderful wellspring of great Christian music was probably the height of arrogance! Even today, when I see my name on music in books along with music written by songwriting giants such as Charles Wesley, Fanny Crosby, Martin Luther, George Handel, A.B. Simpson and others, I still shudder.

But fresh out of college, with a few years as a "road warrior"—and singing with my brother and sister—under my belt, I really thought that I could write something that would benefit the church and people everywhere. Keep in mind, at this point, I had never yet written a song!

One day in 1960, after hearing about a friend's trip to Israel, I got to thinking, *Well, I've never been to Jerusalem. I've never taken the ten-day Holy Land tour, in which special guides herd you from one part of the country to the next.* (Sort of "Today I ran where Jesus walked!")

But in a spiritual sense, I *had* been to Jerusalem, to the foot of the cross where Jesus died. I sat down and began to scribble some ideas on paper. To me, great songs always start with great ideas. Occasionally, a melody or tune will simply compel a songwriter to create lyrics for it, but in Gloria's and my songs, the idea almost always has led the music.

Slowly, my ideas came together and melded with the music I heard in my mind. Within a few hours, I had all the pieces together and I had composed my first song: "I've Been to Calvary." When I finished playing and singing the completed song through for the first time, I sat back and thought, *You know what? This is pretty good!* To this day, I believe that the sense of accomplishment we feel when we create something with God's help is instilled by, and is a reflection of, our Creator. I felt just a flicker of what God must have felt when He created the world, and "God saw that it was good."[1]

Looking back at that song now, I think, *Oh, my! I could have done this or that to make it better, or I should have written it this way or that.* Truth is, though, for that time in my life, "I've Been to Calvary" was a good song. I'd like to think that I've grown as a composer over the years, and I'm absolutely positive my lyrics have greatly improved thanks to Gloria's writing skills, but for me, that first song was a landmark.

And to think it came about largely because I had failed as a singer and a piano player. God took the very setback that I thought of as the end of my musical career, and He used it to send me to college where I would study English literature and poetry, and discover a much broader spectrum of music than that to which I had previously been exposed.

Now that I had written the song, though, I was stumped. What should I do with it? The Gaither Trio was no longer singing together, so it was tempting to simply put the song in a drawer and forget about it. But I couldn't do that.

I had a friend, Jim Hill, the founder of the Golden Keys Quartet, from Portsmouth, Ohio, whom I had met while singing with the Pathfinders. In 1955, Jim had written a song, "What a Day That Will Be," that was destined to be a classic. I decided to take my song to Jim in hopes that he might sing it. I drove to Ohio from Indiana so I could personally teach "I've Been to Calvary" to Jim. When Jim heard the song, he loved it! He encouraged me to write more, and he became a tremendous booster of my early material.

What a thrill it was for me to hear Jim Hill sing "I've Been to Calvary" for the first time! A few weeks later, the Golden Keys performed the song in concert. Afterward Jim called me and said, "Bill, your song tore the place up. The people loved it!"

I wrote a few more songs for Jim and the Golden Keys, and then one day, I received a phone call that changed the course of my life.

"Hello, Bill? This is Ben Speer."

I nearly dropped the receiver. I didn't really know Ben Speer, but I knew who he was. Ben had been onstage with the Speer Family when I attended my first gospel music concert in Nashville's Ryman Auditorium as a boy of eight. Now, here he was calling *me*!

"Ah, yes, sir, Mr. Speer. This is Bill. What can I do for you?"

We exchanged some small talk, and then Ben got to the point. "The other night I heard the Golden Keys sing 'I've Been to Calvary,' Bill. Do you have a publisher for that song?"

A publisher? I didn't even have a printer! I barely had the notes and lyrics written out on music paper.

"Ah, er, well, no, I don't," I stammered. I was so excited I could almost hear my heart pounding in my chest.

"Would you be interested in our company publishing your song?" Ben Speer asked. "We'll print and distribute your song, and pay you a royalty for every piece of sheet music we sell. If someone records your song, you'll get some royalties from that as well."

I could hardly believe my ears! Ben Speer was offering to publish my song! I was ecstatic to think that someone of Ben's stature in the world of gospel music considered my song worth publishing. That would be tantamount to an established artist and songwriter such as Paul McCartney or Paul Simon calling a young songwriter today and saying, "Hey, kid, I hear you write some music. Would you be interested in my company publishing your song?"

I didn't need to think or pray about that decision for a long time. "Are you serious?" I asked Ben.

"Sure am," Ben replied. "Let me draw up a simple contract to cover that song and a few others, and I'll get it in the mail to you right away."

Within a few days I received the contract from Ben, and the Speer Family (as well as the Golden Keys) recorded "I've Been to Calvary." Before long, a number of other groups had also recorded the song.

So I wrote three more: "In the Upper Room," "Lovest Thou Me More Than These?" and "Have You Had a Gethsemane?" I boldly proclaimed to myself, *Now these are better songs than those other songs I've been hearing!*

Ben agreed and quickly offered me another publishing contract, but I was reticent to sign it.

"Ben, I think I want to go a slightly different direction," I said.

"What do you mean?" Ben asked.

"I think I'm going to start my own publishing company."

"Oh, you don't want to do that!" said Ben. "That's a lot of work, and we already have established you as a writer on our publishing company. There's no need for you to take on the publishing responsibilities, too."

"You'll still sing my songs, even if you don't publish them . . . won't you?" I asked.

"Well, I don't know about that," Ben replied.

I wasn't sure if he was serious or not. I knew it was risky to reject Ben's offer. I had no way to promote my songs, and I had no guarantee that anyone would ever sing them if the Speer Family didn't. But I felt strongly that something good was about to happen, that my songwriting career was about to take off, and I wanted to be sitting in the pilot's seat rather than a passenger's.

I've always been grateful to Ben and his family for initially singing and publishing my first songs. We've enjoyed a long and close friendship and working relationship over the years. But taking control of my own copyrights was probably a major turning point in my career. An even more significant turning point came about when I bumped into an attractive young woman with blonde hair.

FOUR

GLORIA

In September 1961, I took a job teaching English in my hometown at Alexandria High School. One cold morning at the beginning of the second semester, I noticed an attractive young woman I hadn't seen around the school before. Her eyes seemed to sparkle, and her blonde hair gently grazed her shoulders. I nearly did a double take when I first saw her because the young woman looked so much like Doris Day, one of my favorite celluloid stars.

I asked a female teacher down the hall about the new woman. "That's Gloria Sickal," the teacher told me. "She's from Battle Creek, Michigan. Her dad's a pastor there, and she's a student at Anderson College."

"A student?"

"Yes, she's still in school, but she's substituting for our French teacher, who was scheduled to have surgery during Christmas vacation."

"Oh," I nodded. "Is she married?" I surprised myself at my uncharacteristically bold inquiry. Why should I care whether the blonde was married or not? Marriage was not even on my mental list of goals and priorities. I wasn't a social recluse, but at twenty-six, I wasn't really looking to settle down anytime soon. Besides, being a bachelor allowed more time for traveling and singing. Still, the substitute French teacher was pretty cute. . . .

"Nope," my colleague's voice pulled me out of my thoughts. "Single and free as a jaybird. Want to meet her?"

"Er, ah . . . yeah, ah . . . why don't you introduce us sometime?"

"I'll be glad to," the teacher said with a smile as she turned back to her classroom.

Later that morning, I was rounding the corner in the hallway near the front office when I saw the blonde again. She seemed to be a bit frazzled as she hurried to the office holding what looked to be the day's attendance sheets. Nearing the office, I dropped my pencil and it rolled right in front of the Doris Day lookalike. I stopped, picked it up, and looked up right into the young woman's eyes.

"Ah, oh . . . excuse me."

"Quite all right," she replied as she waited for me to stand upright.

"Hello, what's your name?" I asked matter-of-factly.

"Gloria Sickal," she answered. "Who are you?" she asked in an equally perfunctory manner.

"My name is Bill Gaither," I told her. "I teach English here. Actually, I've been teaching junior high English for three years at another school, and I just started here this year."

"Oh, yes!" the blonde's eyes brightened and an interested look came over her countenance. "Bill Gaither. . . ."

I was surprised she'd heard of me and was about to say so when Gloria Sickal said, "You're the one who has a good-looking brother that my friend is dying to meet!"

I picked my ego off the floor and shrugged. "That's the story of my life," I said with half a grin. "All the pretty women want to meet my brother."

The substitute teacher smiled at me. We talked briefly and I began to understand why she looked so rattled on her first day at school. She'd walked into her classroom just as a six-foot, four-inch basketball player tossed a typewriter over the heads of his fellow high school seniors to his cohort on the other side of the room. The blonde's first job was to restore order to the classroom—which she managed to do—before she could begin her teaching career.

Just as my friend down the hall had said, Gloria was only nineteen years of age and still a junior at Anderson College. But when the French teacher at Alexandria High had to have surgery, qualified French teachers were not readily available in our rural community, so the administration appealed to Anderson. Gloria's professor felt that she could handle the responsibility along with another college student, and the experience of student-teaching three classes would benefit her greatly.

Gloria and I talked often in the hallways or in the cafeteria at lunch, and I quickly discovered that besides teaching French, she was also an articulate, well-read English major. We shared a love for great literature, and we both loved to talk sociology and politics. Inevitably, our conversations took on a spiritual tone, and we frequently discussed our faith in God. We spoke passionately about eternal truths, grand ideas, and social changes that could transform society.

Ironically, we rarely discussed music. Gloria said that she was not a musician or a singer, so I let it go at that. I never mentioned that I had written a few songs. Nor did I tell her about my stint with the Pathfinders. For her part, Gloria loved poetry, but she was equally reluctant to say anything about the poetry she had been writing. At that point, we could never have guessed that in the future we would write more than six hundred songs together, and she would become one of the best Christian lyricists of all time.

As the Indiana snow began to melt, so did my heart. I asked Gloria out a few times, first to lunch, then to some Indiana basketball games. The better I got to know her, the more I liked her. After several dates, we both felt that we had discovered a soul mate.

A few dates later, I finally mustered the courage to play and sing a few songs for her at the house. Gloria noticed my name on the music.

"Did you write this stuff?" she asked.

I was almost afraid to answer. "Um . . . yeah, I did."

"It's pretty good," she said with a smile.

We got engaged that same summer.

The summer before Gloria and I married, she went home to Battle Creek, where she worked at Kellogg's to earn enough money to return to Anderson College that fall. I frequently drove up to Michigan to see her on weekends, and when Gloria got off work at midnight on Friday, I'd be waiting for her in my red convertible.

She came out of work dead tired, wearing her baggy green Kellogg's uniform, her face drawn by fatigue, with a few cornflakes still stuck in her hair, but she looked like an angel to me! She was the most beautiful woman in the world, and she loved me!

One night, when she crawled into the car after a long, hard shift, I had a surprise for her. I had purchased an engagement ring, and it was burning a hole in my pocket.. "Gloria, I . . . ah . . . we really need to cement this relationship. Would you, er . . . I have something for you . . . would you marry me?" I took the ring out of my pocket and placed it on her finger.

"Oh, yes, Bill!" she said as tears filled her eyes.

"We're officially engaged now," I said. We'd talked about marriage for months, and in our hearts and minds we were "unofficially engaged," but I'd never given Gloria a ring until now. It wasn't much of a ring, because I've never really cared for big, gaudy diamond rings; besides, on my salary as a high school teacher, I couldn't afford too much. Personally, I preferred a simple, plain, gold wedding band, the kind most married folks in my family wore. But I knew that Gloria wanted a more significant symbol so her friends and family in Michigan could tell that we were truly engaged, and this ring fit the bill.

We married on December 22 of that year and spent only one night in Fort Wayne as our honeymoon. We wanted to get back home to celebrate our first Christmas with our families! Over the years, we've visited all sorts of exotic locations and have enjoyed them immensely, but we've always been grateful for that first Christmas as newlyweds with our families.

On our wedding day, I gave Gloria the wedding band matching her engagement ring, but I never really cared much for those rings. Every once in a while, I'd glance at Gloria's rings and blurt something like, "Those are the dumbest-looking rings!" (For you newlywed husbands, I don't recommend this!) "What I really wish I'd given you is a plain gold wedding ring. A plain gold band looks so . . . so *married*."

Gloria smiled lovingly, hugged me, and gave me kiss. "I love my rings, Bill," she'd say. But I could tell it bothered her that I didn't like her rings.

One evening two or three years into our marriage, Gloria and I stopped at Kmart to do some shopping. I ambled toward the music department while Gloria scoured the building looking for bargains. As she walked near the jewelry department, she heard the announcement over the store's public address system: "Attention, Kmart shoppers. We're having a Blue Light Special in our jewelry department." Gloria looked up and sure enough, there was a blue light revolving above the jewelry cases.

She quickly hustled in that direction and discovered that they were having a sale on wedding rings. There in the case she spied a plain gold wedding band for only $13.95! She took what little money she had left over from grocery shopping and bought one. She took off her pretty rings and put the band on her finger.

When Gloria and I got in the car, I pulled out the latest album of music I had just purchased. "How do you like this?" I held up the album for her to see.

"Fine," she replied nonchalantly. "How do you like this?" She held up her hand, displaying the plain gold band on her left ring finger.

"Hey! I like that!" I said. "I really like it. It looks so . . . so, *married!*"

Gloria wore that $13.95 Kmart Special ring for the next seventeen years. During that time, we saw a number of our friends and colleagues flashing huge diamonds on their fingers, only to have their marriages crash on the rocks within a short period of time. Meanwhile, our plain gold band and all that it symbolized concerning our commitment to each other remained intact. All the glitter in the world won't make up for a relationship that is not founded on something more substantial and lasting than material things.

Although Gloria was satisfied and content with the ring she bought for herself, I wanted to do something more lavish for her. In 1982, while our music group was in Israel, we stopped by a jewelry store in Jerusalem. There I spotted a beautiful, twenty-four-karat-gold ring. The ring bore the inscription in Hebrew, "Arise my love, and come away," a quote from the Song of Solomon, one of Gloria's favorite books in the Bible. Without her knowing, I bought the ring for Gloria and had it sized for her.

The following February, right around Valentine's Day, just as our family sat down for supper one night, I paused before giving thanks for the food. The kids were bantering back and forth while Gloria was trying to get them to settle down. "I want everyone to be quiet," I said. "I have a presentation to make."

That got everyone's attention instantly.

I took out a small blue box and handed it to Gloria. "I bought this for you in Jerusalem," I said.

Gloria excitedly opened the blue box and the expression on her face told the story—she loved the ring! She took off her $13.95 Blue Light Special and put on the gorgeous gold ring, and she's worn it ever since.

Truth is, though, Gloria and I were just as married with that inexpensive little ring. Our marriage is not based on trinkets we can buy for each other. It's grounded on commitment and unconditional love. We both know each other's strong points and weak points, our triumphs and our failures. What a joy it is to be loved by someone who knows me at my best *and* at my worst!

To me, marriage is one of the clearest symbols of God's love for us. He knows us even better than our marriage partners, and He *still* loves us unconditionally. Many people are reluctant to risk reaching out in love for fear of rejection. Knowing that we are loved unconditionally by God frees us to love each other regardless of our insecurities or personal circumstances.

More than fifteen years into our marriage, Gloria and I put those thoughts into a simple yet extremely profound song:

> I am loved!
> I am loved!
> I can risk loving you,
> For the One who knows me best
> Loves me most.
> I am loved,
> You are loved,
> Won't you please take my hand?
> We are free to love each other;
> We are loved.[1]

When you know you are loved unconditionally, the substance of the wedding ring on your finger won't matter; the size of the house in which you live, the style of car you drive, the amount of money in your checkbook, or the fashion statement your clothes make will all fade to the background. Only one thing will matter—*somebody loves me!*

FIVE

MORE THAN THE MUSIC

GLORIA WAS TWENTY YEARS of age and I was twenty-six when we married. We wed at the church her father had once pastored in Michigan. We returned to Alexandria and rented a little house from my parents, right next door to their home. Living in such close proximity to parents or in-laws can be a pain for some young couples, but not for us, largely because Mom and Dad left us alone unless we needed their help. Mom and Dad loved Gloria. Although they couldn't relate to her artistic nature or her passion for books and poetry, they appreciated her work ethic. Any woman who got out of bed and started working before sunup was okay in my parents' book. And Gloria loved Mom and Dad, too.

Dropped into the small town where I grew up, and knowing only the people she had met during her stint as a substitute high school teacher, Gloria immediately set about learning everything she could about my upbringing, my school activities, my high school friends, and so on. One day my mom asked, "Gloria, would you like to see Bill's old scrapbooks?"

"I sure would!" Gloria replied. She and my mom pored over my high school yearbooks and scrapbooks for hours. She wanted to know all the things I had done as a boy, the hobbies on which I had spent my time, and all the influences that had shaped me into the person I am today. To Gloria, it was like filling in all the blanks about the person she had married.

Gloria graduated cum laude from Anderson College in 1963, with majors in English, French, and sociology. She, too, got a job in the Alexandria school system, teaching English as well as French. Even before we were married, Gloria began helping me with some lyrics to my songs, offering suggestions, a better word or phrase here, or an idea there. Before long, she became an integral part of my creative process, a sounding board who patiently worked with me to find just the right way of expressing what we wanted to say.

Most of our songs grew out of our daily experiences, or a perceived need, often in response to a sermon, something we'd read in Scripture, or an event in the lives of the people around us. Many times we'd say, "There ought to be a song that says . . ." When we couldn't think of an existing song that expressed the ideas we were looking for, we wrote our own.

I continued teaching high school English with no real thoughts of a music career, apart from my songwriting and leading the church choir. But I was interested in spreading my music to a larger audience, so I asked our church board to consider underwriting the expenses to produce an album of choir music, including several songs I had written and arranged. The church considered the idea and decided against it. If I wanted to record an album with our choir, fine, but I'd have to finance it some other way.

I chose to pay to record the choir myself. The church was located on South Meridian street, so we called the album *The South Meridian Sings*. The custom album—an album not produced or distributed by a major recording label—sold more than a thousand copies and we used the proceeds to finance *The South Meridian Sings, Volume 2*. The two choir albums were my first ventures into the recording business.

When we think back, Gloria and I have to smile at our simple beginnings in the music industry. Often Gloria and I would work on a song, and I'd write it out by hand on music paper. Then we'd run off a few copies on a mimeograph machine and take it to Wednesday night choir practice. If the choir responded positively, we knew we were on to something. If not, I told them that the well-known Christian composer John Peterson wrote it! (Years later, I "confessed" to John, and he thought it was hilarious.)

About that time, Paul Hart, the assistant pastor, introduced me to a big man with a big voice who had begun dropping in to our church services. It was impossible for the fellow to be inconspicuous sitting on the back row. His name was Doug Oldham. The Oldham name was well known in Central Indiana church circles. Doug's dad, Dr. Dale Oldham, was a great preacher and singer, and a bit of a poet. He had formerly pastored the large Park Place Church close to Anderson College, and had been the host of a national radio broadcast sponsored by the Church of God, whose headquarters were in Anderson.

Doug had been a soloist with his father's ministry and was known not just for his great singing voice, but also for the way he delivered a song. When Doug sang, it was almost like listening to a master storyteller.

But when I first met Doug Oldham, he had lost almost everything he'd ever held dear—his wife, family, friends, ministry, reputation, as well as many of his earthly possessions. He had become so depressed that one night he loaded a revolver and drove around town trying to muster the nerve to shoot himself. At his lowest point he cried out to God, "If you're there, either give me something worth living for or the guts to pull this trigger!"

Thankfully, Doug Oldham did not commit suicide. Instead he turned to God and began the slow and painful process of putting his life back together. Doug sought forgiveness from the people he had hurt, including his wife, children, and his father. The healing of those relationships wasn't immediate, but Doug was committed to the process.

As Doug and I developed a friendship, it was only natural that we discussed music. Before long I began sharing with him some of the songs I had written. He especially liked a new one called "Have You Had a Gethsemane?" It alluded to Jesus' submission to God's plan, even though He knew it would cost His life. The night before Jesus was crucified, after what we now call the Last Supper, Jesus went to an olive garden, the Garden of Gethsemane. Knowing in advance what cruel torture He faced on the cross, Jesus prayed, "Father, if Thou art willing, remove this cup from Me; yet not My will, but Thine be done."[1]

For Jesus, Gethsemane was a place of absolute surrender to His heavenly Father's will. Maybe that's why Doug Oldham related to the song so well. Doug had experienced his own personal Gethsemane, submitting to God's will. Doug learned the song and recorded it.

A few months later, he and Laura reconciled and slowly began rebuilding their marriage and their life as a family. Doug was invited to sing at the annual convention of the Church of

God. When he sang "Have You Had a Gethsemane?" it was as though God invaded the place, breaking down walls of pride, arrogance, bitterness, and self-righteousness, bringing people to a place of brokenness in their own lives.

"Have You Had a Gethsemane?" was the first song Gaither Music Company published. The poignant irony of that has never escaped me. Out of surrender comes victory, out of death comes new life.

Doug Oldham went on to sing many of our songs, including "In the Upper Room with Jesus," "Lovest Thou Me More Than These?" and a song that we wrote a few years later especially with Doug in mind.

As a sign that they had truly started a new life together, Doug and Laura Oldham sold the house they had been living in when their marriage had fallen apart. They purchased a new home where they could rebuild without the haunting memories of the past. During the moving process, on a trip to pick up some of their belongings back at the house where they used to live, one of Doug and Laura's little girls ran and hid behind the door. She'd done something similar many times before when she'd heard her daddy angrily stomping into the house.

When Doug saw his daughter cowering behind the door, it broke his heart. He knelt down, scooped her into his arms, and said, "Honey, you don't have to be afraid. You've got a new daddy now." Then he whispered almost as much to himself as to his little girl, "Thanks to Calvary, we don't live here anymore."

Not long after that, Doug and Laura told Gloria and me about the incident. As soon as we heard it, we knew we had to put it into a song. When we first played it for Doug, he wept. "Thanks to Calvary" became somewhat of a theme song for Doug. He's sung it around the world for more than thirty years.

Doug Oldham became a conduit through whom I could pour

my music to the world. Gloria and I wrote the songs, and Doug sang them. In his own style, sometimes singing, sometimes speaking the lyrics, Doug communicated our music in a powerful way and probably became known for singing our songs more than any other artist. Interestingly, the idea for one of our most popular songs didn't come from Doug, but from his father.

Back during the days of restoration in Doug's life, Dr. Dale, as we called him, asked Doug to sing for some of his revival services and to tell what God had been doing in his life. Doug agreed and asked me to accompany him on the piano. Doug planned to perform a number of my songs, including "I've Been to Calvary" and "Have You Had a Gethsemane?" Sometimes I even sang with Doug during his father's services.

One Saturday night in 1963, on the way back from a service in Huntington, Indiana, Doug, Dr. Oldham, and I were driving along, talking about God's power to touch and change a life. Dr. Dale looked over at me and said, "Bill, there's something about that word *touch*. You ought to write a song about how God touches lives."

The idea was a gift right out of heaven. The next morning, before the Sunday service, I couldn't get the idea out of my mind. I went into the back room, sat down at our old spinet piano in our little rented house, and wrote:

> Shackled by a heavy burden,
> 'Neath a load of guilt and shame . . .

I had noticed that no matter what a person has done, no matter how deeply the scars have been cut into a person's soul, when that person cries out to God in simple faith, he or she can be set free from the hurts of the past.

With that in mind, I wrote:

> Then the hand of Jesus touched me,
> And now I am no longer the same.

The chorus welled within me as a declaration of freedom:

> He touched me, oh, He touched me.
> And, oh, the joy that floods my soul.
> Something happened and now I know,
> He touched me and made me whole.[2]

In a short time, I scrawled the lyrics to two verses and the chorus. The melody line to the music was simple, eminently singable, and seemed fraught with power, emotion, and a sort of spiritual ecstasy. The following Tuesday, before another of Dr. Oldham's revival services, I handed Doug a copy of the handwritten music. "Let's see if we can sing this one tonight," I suggested.

Doug and I rehearsed "He Touched Me" a few times, and he picked up on the innate power of the song. That night, when he sang it for the first time in front of the congregation, it was obvious that God was using the song to connect with the people. As Doug was prone to do, he returned to the chorus of the song several times throughout his set. Before long, the audience was singing the chorus along with us, and people have been singing it ever since.

Doug Oldham was the first to record "He Touched Me." Actually, about that same time, I sent a mimeographed copy to George Beverly Shea, the great soloist for the Billy Graham Association, in hopes that he could use the song in a crusade or record it on an album. Unfortunately, my letter to Mr. Shea and the music got lost in the mountain of correspondence the beloved singer received.

What an honor it was for me a few years later when I received a Dove Award from the Gospel Music Association, presented to me that night by none other than the highly esteemed George Beverly Shea. Since then, Gloria and I have been privileged to sing at several Billy Graham crusades, and we've had more than a few good laughs with Bev Shea over our upstart efforts at pitching songs.

Demand for the printed music of "He Touched Me" really picked up when Kathryn Kuhlman began using it on her radio and television broadcasts. Before long, the Speer Family and several other popular gospel groups started singing it. Ben Speer called one day and ordered three hundred copies of the sheet music. Gloria and I hastily counted out and packed up the copies.

In the early days of the company, we usually printed each song in lots of one thousand copies, which we then stored in the "warehouse" of Gaither Music Company (the back room of our tiny house). Gloria's mom and dad had retired from active ministry due to her dad's health, so they moved from Michigan to Alexandria to help us with the packing, shipping, and other responsibilities involved in the publishing business. By this time we had our own logo, a backward note that Gloria had designed, and the one-color logo was printed on all our white sheet music. Then, when we really wanted to get fancy, we'd reverse the print, making a white logo on a colored backdrop, printing each song with a different colored backdrop. The "professional" logo was our only similarity to larger established music publishing companies; that, and the fact that we had a few songs that people wanted to sing. The next day, Ben called again. "Send us five hundred more. We're sold out!"

Bev Shea eventually got around to recording "He Touched

Me," as did many other artists as varied as Kate Smith and Jimmy Durante. In fact, "He Touched Me" has been recorded more than any other song Gloria and I have written. It's been translated into dozens of languages and sung in far-flung nations around the world.

Every once in a while, I'll tease Gloria by reminding her that I wrote the song without her help.

With the sudden explosion of interest in "He Touched Me," people soon began to discover other songs that I had written. Of course, I worked every spare minute I could to help get our fledgling little music company off the ground. I taught school all week, then on weekends, if we weren't singing somewhere ourselves, I went from one gospel concert to another, carrying a batch of songs, some so new they hadn't even been printed in sheet music yet. With the success of "He Touched Me," most of the gospel artists were at least willing to listen as I pitched my songs to them. The Speer Family and a few other big-name groups were especially kind to me.

Others were convinced that they could write their own songs, every bit as good or better than the ones I was pitching. "We'll write our own; we don't need to pay anyone to write for us," one quartet boss told me bluntly.

Another quartet leader who owned a publishing company made me what he considered a generous offer. After looking at one of our new songs he said, "I'll give you fifty bucks for it."

"Ah, no, thanks," I said and promptly swiped our song out of his hands. Our songs were not for sale. Gloria and I had already made a decision that we were going to keep our own copyrights rather than selling off our creations, and hopefully receive a royalty. Disappointed but undaunted, I'd head off to the next concert where the performers might show a more receptive attitude.

Anytime a gospel group passed within a hundred miles of our home, Gloria and I attended the concert and then invited them to the house for dinner. We'd fill their stomachs with Gloria's good home cooking, then I'd usher the singers into our family room and say, "Have a seat, fellas. I have a few songs I'd like you to hear." Most of the visiting artists were gracious enough to pretend they were interested in my songs, even if they weren't.

One group that we were always delighted to have in for dinner was the Speer Family. The Speers sort of adopted us, and we adopted them as family. Rosa Nell, Mary-Tom, Brock, and Ben Speer, as well as Harold Lane, who sang with them and arranged some of our early sheet music, became lifelong friends. Gloria's cooking must have been doing the job, because the Speers sang a lot of our songs!

I was especially nervous the day the Imperials came to our home. The group was relatively new, but the guys were already stirring up tremendous excitement in the music world with their innovative, contemporary arrangements and style. Beyond that, Jake Hess, who had sung lead for the Statesmen for fifteen years, had launched out on his own in 1963 and formed the Imperials. Now, here was one of my lifelong heroes, sitting in my living room, listening politely to one of my songs! I thought that maybe I'd died and gone to heaven!

Jake had assembled an incredible array of talent in his new group, including Sherrill Nielsen, the fabulous tenor; Armond Morales singing bass; Gary McSpadden singing baritone; and Henry Slaughter on piano. The Imperials didn't sound like any of the country-gospel groups on the circuit in those days. They were in a class all by themselves.

Around the time the Imperials came to our house, I had just recently planted some new grass seed in our yard, and a few trees. After dinner, while I was showing "He Touched Me" to

Henry Slaughter, I looked out the window and to my chagrin noticed Gary McSpadden hitting golf balls on my beautiful new sod, scooping out huge divots of grass with every shot! I wanted to run outside and yell at him to get off my grass, but I didn't have enough nerve. Besides, I wanted Henry to see the song much more than I wanted our grass to grow. Years later, I told Gary about that incident and my reluctance to miss the chance to pitch a song. He laughed heartily, but to this day, I won't allow Gary anywhere near my lawn with his golf clubs!

The Imperials loved "He Touched Me" and not only did they record it, but they sang it night after night in concert. One of the people sitting backstage listening to the incredible opening act was Elvis Presley. Elvis was so moved by the song and impressed with the audience response the Imperials received when they sang it, he recorded it as well.

Before long, I started receiving invitations from churches to come sing and talk about some of my songs. That created a dilemma for me. I knew that I was not a strong singer on my own, and Danny had joined the Golden Keys Quartet, so he wasn't available to help. I used every ounce of persuasion I could muster and finally talked Gloria into joining Mary Ann and me on the platform.

Growing up in a pastor's home, Gloria had sung all her life. She had a soft, pleasant voice, but she certainly didn't claim to be a professional singer. Nor did she have any desire to stand on a stage and exhibit her inadequacies for all to see and hear. Speaking, writing, or teaching would have been a natural for her, and over the years, she has excelled at all of those; but I was asking her to do something she was not naturally good at, something that didn't come easily for her. I knew that the only reason Gloria acquiesced and consented to sing was because of her love for God and her love for me.

We did okay for a while, but then one day Gloria gave me some exciting news. "Bill, we're going to have a baby," she said.

I was overjoyed that we were going to be parents, even though as the pregnancy progressed it became more and more obvious that Gloria was going to have to drop out of our singing group before the baby arrived. About that time Danny returned, and it seemed we were stable again. Shortly after that, however, Mary Ann informed us that she was getting married and wanted to start a family of her own. She'd be leaving the group. Danny and I auditioned several other singers, but for one reason or another, none of them seemed to fit with us. The Gaither Trio disbanded again.

Nevertheless, prior to Mary Ann's departure, I had made a commitment to do a concert at a church in Springfield, Ohio. To me, a person is only as good as his or her word, and I had promised that the Gaither Trio would be in Springfield. I felt compelled to keep the commitment.

There was only one person who could help me pull it together: Gloria. I literally begged her to sing with Danny and me, but Gloria wanted nothing to do with getting back on the platform.

"Please, Gloria, you've got to sing with us, just this once. I need you there."

"Bill, you know I'm not a singer."

"Yes, I know," I teased, hoping that a bit of reverse psychology might prompt her to take up the challenge. "But you're pretty, and you can talk on pitch! You're a great communicator, you're my wife, and I need your help. So let's go. Please, Gloria!"

Gloria reluctantly agreed. That night, I experienced the first of what I came to recognize as God working through my wife. We opened the concert with "I Never Loved Him Better Than

Today," a bouncy song our friend Henry Slaughter had written. From there, we moved right into Doris Akers's worshipful number, "Sweet, Sweet Spirit." Then, only two songs into the program, I stopped and said, "Gloria, please pray for us."

Gloria would rather have prayed than sung anytime, so that part wasn't unusual. But as she prayed that night, she was articulating the corporate thoughts and needs of the people and of her own heart. Most of the people in the church bowed their heads and closed their eyes as Gloria prayed.

Gloria prayed . . . and prayed . . . and prayed. I honestly don't remember the words she said, or even the tenor of her prayer. All I know is that when I opened my eyes and raised my head, people all over the sanctuary were in tears. Without a formal invitation, numerous people converged on the front of the church and knelt to pray. Others simply sat in their seats, basking in the presence of God.

The pastor told us later, "We haven't seen that kind of response for some time in this church, not even in evangelistic crusades."

During the drive home, I pondered what had occurred that night. I said almost jokingly to God, "Are you trying to tell me something here?" I came to a startling realization: *what we are doing is definitely about more than the music.* I also began to understand a truth that I have shared with new artists many times since then; namely, the most-talented singers and musicians are not necessarily the people who are getting the job done. Often people who are less talented musically are more effective communicators in other ways. Sadly, too often these people sit on the sidelines and watch as the more aggressive, confident, or flamboyant performers lead the parade. All the while, the less-talented singers wonder why they aren't even in the parade.

Clearly, God had used Gloria to touch the hearts of people in that audience in Springfield. Something about her demeanor, her down-to-earth, sincere concern for the people, and her passionate belief that God was the only answer they needed, encouraged the congregation to experience Him in a fresh way.

I was actually ashamed of myself. In my intense desire to promote our songs, I had been obsessed with trying to find just the right "sound" for our trio rather than the right person . . . and Gloria was the right person. I should have known better.

That night in Springfield, Ohio, radically changed the direction of what Gloria and I were to do for nearly the next two decades of our lives. For me, it meant that I was going to sing with a person who might seem inadequate musically, yet God used that very weakness to touch people's lives. Gloria was always quick to admit, "I'm not a singer! I'm a writer, a speaker, a communicator." God didn't seem to mind. In fact, He used all of the gifts that He had given her, but she had to sing—the area in which she felt the least confident—to use the other talents in which she had tremendous ability. It is the irony of our lives, yet it is the key to understanding Bill and Gloria Gaither, that God chose to use not our strengths but our weaknesses to take our music to the world. Neither Gloria nor I would have guessed that she and I would sing together onstage for the next twenty years!

SIX

BEGINNING OF A LEGACY

OUR LIVES TOOK A MAJOR turn when our first baby was born in 1964. We'd been married nearly three years and were as prepared as any couple can be for the cataclysmic changes that take place when a tiny newborn person suddenly takes control of the family.

I was teaching school one morning when I received a message that Gloria had called the office from home. "I'm ready," she said.

"Gloria's *ready*!" I called to the school principal. "I've got to go!" I hurried through the school halls, burst out the door, ran to my car, and raced to the hospital in Anderson, about a ten-minute drive ordinarily. I think I made it in five that day. When I got there, I realized I had forgotten something.

Gloria was still at home!

I jumped back in the car and raced the nine or ten miles back to our little rental home in Alexandria. I ran through the back door and there was Gloria standing calmly in the kitchen. "Where have you been?" she asked.

"Well, I'm sorry. I thought you were already at the hospital."

"How was I going to get to the hospital?"

"I don't know . . . but maybe we should head in that direction now."

Gloria rolled her eyes as if to say "Good idea!"

Later that day, our first child was born, a beautiful baby girl. We named her Suzanne Reneé. We named her Suzanne because Gloria and I were big fans of the singing group the New Christy Minstrels, who had a song that said, "Good-bye, Suzanne, don't cry, Suzanne, for I'm goin' away."[1] We chose the middle name, Reneé, because Gloria taught French. Suzanne grabbed my heart that day, and she's held it ever since.

Suzanne was a doer; she was a perfectly contented little baby as long as she was doing something! No putting her to sleep and taking the afternoon off. No way. Suzanne kept Gloria hopping. As she grew up, she wanted to be right in the middle of everything. If Gloria was washing dishes, so was Suzanne, splashing suds and water all over herself and chattering the entire time. If Gloria was making cookies, Suzanne was sure to be covered in cookie dough. She was always building something, painting, or writing. We quickly discovered that if we could just give her enough projects to do, she'd be happy. I don't know where she ever got that trait!

We continued to travel and sing on weekends, writing songs during the week, sometimes with Suzanne propped on Gloria's hip. In the early days, we simply took Suzanne with us to the churches where we were singing. I didn't see that as a problem since she was easily transportable!

No one was more proud of Suzanne than my grandma, Mom Hartwell. She beamed as she held Suzanne in her maple rocking chair and sang to her. Sometimes she'd look over at me and say, "Play something, Billy Jim," as she nodded toward the slightly out-of-tune piano up against the wall.

Shortly after Pop Hartwell died, Mom's health began to go downhill. It was as though she felt that her work on earth was done, that she'd completed what God wanted her to do. In her latter days, Mom had a stroke and slowly slid into delirium, but she never lost touch with God. Even while bedfast and only semiconscious, she'd often softly whisper His name. Her eyes would flutter open and she'd sing, "Oh, He is so precious to me."

On her best days, Mom Hartwell could sit up and talk with us for a while. One day Gloria and I sat in Mom's bedroom, holding Suzanne so Mom could see her. The sight of our baby elicited all sorts of stories from Mom's deep well of memories.

Near the close of the conversation, I posed a question to her. "Mom, you've lived a long time. Gloria and I are just starting out with our baby and our family. Tell me, has it been worth it, serving God all these years?"

With her Irish eyes still twinkling with life and with hardly a moment of hesitation, Mom reached over and touched my arm. "Oh, Billy," she said, "the longer I serve Him, the sweeter He grows."

That was one of the last cogent conversations I ever had with Mom, and even that day I knew that we wouldn't have her with us much longer. But her testimony would be a living legacy forever. "The longer I serve Him, the sweeter He grows."

Not long after that, Mom Hartwell went on to heaven. One day I sat down at the piano and with her in mind, scribbled the rough lyrics to a song. The second verse especially reminds me of the way Mom and Pop Hartwell lived:

> Ev'ry need He is supplying;
> Plenteous grace He bestows,
> Ev'ry day my way gets brighter—
> The longer I serve Him, the sweeter He grows.[2]

After Gloria and I had been married a few years and she had given birth to Suzanne, we decided we wanted to build a home where we could raise our family. Being frugal money managers, we prayed and patiently kept looking for just the right place.

Gloria had given up her teaching job when she became pregnant, so our decision about what to buy had to be based on my income alone. The songs we had written were beginning to take off, and the demand for sheet music was increasing. Besides that, I still had a relatively secure income from my high school teaching position. All that notwithstanding, we'd have rather remained in our tiny rental home had we not had a healthy down payment. Gloria and I had saved fifteen thousand dollars in the bank, so I went to our local bank's loan officer, and naively asked, "We have plans for a $25,000 house. Would this $15,000 be enough for a down payment?"

The banker nodded agreeably, "Yes, I think so."

Nevertheless, we resisted the temptation to think too grandiosely, continued looking for something we could afford, and refused to plunge ourselves into a debt from which we might never surface.

It frightens me nowadays when I meet many young artists who have achieved a modest level of success in their careers, and the first thing they want to do is go out and buy a new tour bus or a house with a hefty payment, or a new car that they really don't need. Don't misunderstand; those things are fine when you have a stable income and savings and can purchase them without debt or strain on your budget. But all too often, Gloria and I see young people who feel they must present the appearances of wealth, because supposedly "money attracts money." In doing so, they fail to consider the fickleness of the music business (or any business, nowadays!), the public's taste, or the amount of stress they place on themselves to maintain

the appearance that they are successful. Sadly, they would probably be much more successful if they could learn to be content
operating on a balanced budget, avoiding debt, and investing in
their futures by saving. Gloria and I were obsessed with being financially solvent before moving out of the tiny house that we
were renting from my parents.

We finally found a fifteen-acre parcel of pastureland close to
town that seemed just right. The land featured gently rolling
fields, a few mature trees, and a drainage ditch that Gloria and
I jokingly referred to as a "river." Only one problem: a man
named Mr. Yule, a ninety-two-year-old retired banker, owned
the land, and he had no intention of parting with it. Although
he had no need of the land himself, Mr. Yule altruistically allowed the farmers nearby to graze their cattle there. He used
this as an excuse not to sell the property.

Gloria and I visited Mr. Yule at the bank, which he still visited each morning, ostensibly to read his newspapers, but more
likely to make sure that the newcomers were maintaining his
high standards. Gloria had dressed Suzanne in a cute little outfit, complete with bonnet and bow, and we stepped up to see
Mr. Yule as a family.

I introduced myself and our family to Mr. Yule and told him
of our desire to purchase a piece of his land.

The retired banker peered at us over the top of his bifocals
and said nonchalantly, "Not selling." He focused his attention
back on the newspaper as if there were nothing else to consider.
"Promised it to a farmer to graze his cattle," he added.

"Yes, I understand that, Mr. Yule, but I teach school here in
town, so we thought that maybe . . . you might be willing to sell
it to someone who was planning to stay here and settle in the
area."

Mr. Yule appeared intrigued. He looked up from his paper

and squinted slightly as he looked me in the eyes. "What did you say your name was?"

"Gaither. Bill Gaither . . . and this is my wife, Gloria, and our daughter, Suzanne," I said, just in case he needed reminding.

I needn't have worried. Mr. Yule's mind was sharp and alert. "Hmm, Gaither, huh. Any relation to Grover Gaither?"

"Yes, sir. Grover Gaither was my granddad. He passed away a few years back."

"Yes, I recall. I attended his funeral." Mr. Yule took off his glasses and laid down his newspaper. He seemed to be looking at us, yet seeing something far away, in the distant past. When he finally spoke, his voice was quiet and extremely kind. "Grover Gaither was the best worker I ever had on my farm. Always gave me a full day's work for a full day's pay. He was an honest man, too. . . ." Mr. Yule seemed caught up in his memory. Then he snapped back to the present. "What did you say you wanted?"

I explained again that Gloria and I were looking for some property where we could raise our family.

"Let me think on it," Mr. Yule replied. "Come back and see me again."

About a week later, I returned to see Mr. Yule. He seemed to be expecting me. "I had the property appraised since the last time we talked," he said.

"Oh?" Several scenarios streaked through my mind. Maybe the appraisal would cause Mr. Yule to want to keep the property, or if he did want to sell it, perhaps the price had just gone up. I didn't know what to expect.

"How does thirty-eight hundred sound?"

I was ecstatic and scared stiff at the same time; ecstatic that Mr. Yule was willing to sell his property to us, yet bowled over by the price. Thirty-eight hundred? *Thirty-eight hundred!* And we wanted to buy fifteen acres! At thirty-eight hundred per acre, that would be nearly sixty thousand dollars, which in the mid-1960s was a large amount of money, especially on a schoolteacher's salary!

"Thirty-eight hundred," I repeated thoughtfully, my brow furrowed.

"Yup, fifteen acres for thirty-eight hundred dollars," said Mr. Yule matter-of-factly. "That's my best price, take it or leave it."

"I'll take it!" I nearly shouted. I wasn't a real estate agent, but I knew that Mr. Yule's land had to be worth much more than that! Gloria and I purchased the fifteen-acre tract, built our first and only home there, and have lived there ever since. We raised our children there, and now we're enjoying our grandchildren in that same location. Oh, sure, we've been tempted to move a few times, but in our modern, transient, disjointed society, in which people are constantly moving from place to place, separated from family and friends, there's something wonderful about stability, about being able to put down some roots and say, "This is home."

One of the first things I did after we built our home was to get busy planting trees on the property. I've always felt strongly about replenishing the earth; that when we use trees and other natural resources for our benefit, we have a responsibility to help leave something behind for the next generation. I loved learning about trees and horticulture, and although some people probably wondered if I had a Johnny Appleseed complex, the tree-planting and nurturing have been a wonderful diversion from the music business. Today those trees tower over our house, and I'm still planting more every chance I get. Besides being a great hobby for me, planting trees, flowers, and shrubs has transformed Mr. Yule's pasture into a great place for grandkids to come and play.

Eighteen years later, our son, Benjamin, was leaving for the summer to work in Philadelphia with an inner-city ministry headed by Dr. Tony Campolo. As Benjamin looked around the backyard one day, he suddenly realized how much he was going to miss home and the property on which he had grown up. Benjamin's eyes swept over the now lush green grass, the beautiful trees, and the gently flowing creek where the drainage ditch had once been. "Dad, this is a beautiful place. How did you and Mom ever get this property?"

"I thought you'd never ask," I said. Benjamin and I sat down on the grass and I told him the story of Mr. Yule. I had probably told him the story before, but Benjy had never really heard it. Now, as a young adult, he had a genuine appreciation for his heritage. I couldn't resist the temptation to preach a bit. "Benj, you've had a great place to grow up and to have fun with all your friends, not necessarily because of anything you or I did, but because of the kind of person your great-granddad was. He was a man who led a good, honest, honorable life. A man's reputation is worth far more than gold."

SEVEN

ENTER, BOB MACKENZIE

By the mid-1960s, Gloria had become much more involved in our songwriting, progressing from simply supplying a word or two here and there, to offering a phrase or a line that might work better in my songs, to creating entire pages of lyrics from the ideas we talked about. Eventually, Gloria became the primary lyricist and I composed the music for most of our songs, although we both contributed suggestions for the other's consideration.

Gloria was an incredibly talented lyricist, and the poetry that she loved so much finally found expression in our songs. The inevitable chicken-or-egg question—Which comes first, the melody or the words?—was irrelevant to us. We both worked from the *idea*. The idea drove the process. When it comes to actually putting the pieces together, it's easier for us to have a melody, a context, in which to place the lyrics, rather than having the lyrics and hoping to find a musical home for them. But we've started songs from every possible perspective. The goal isn't to guard our turf. When it comes to Gloria and me working together on a song, we're both committed to making the end product something that will honor God, and something about which we can feel a sense of satisfaction.

The Gaither Trio recorded many of our early songs on four or five custom albums, which we produced in Indiana using only a grand piano and organ accompaniment. Not surprisingly, the records were rather "churchy" in sound and style. We sold them primarily after our concerts, and people who enjoyed our concerts usually enjoyed the albums as well.

Then in 1964, I promoted a concert date in Alexandria with Jake Hess and the newly formed Imperials; the Gaither Trio would perform as the opening act. It was a Thursday night stopover date for the Imperials as they passed through Indiana on their way to Chicago for their big weekend concert programs.

I thought, *Promoting this concert will be a piece of cake! All I have to do is tell the folks that Jake Hess and the Imperials are coming, and the crowd will pour in.* I booked a five-hundred-seat elementary school auditorium and printed up some posters and flyers announcing the concert. Then I sat back and waited for the tickets to fly out the door. They didn't. I distributed more flyers and waited . . . and waited.

After a few days, I realized that I was in trouble. The tickets simply weren't selling. *What am I going to do?* I thought frantically. I decided to start beating the bushes, telling everyone I could about the upcoming concert. I visited pastors, youth leaders, newspaper editors, and all sorts of "opinion makers." I went to all the local schools and asked them to announce that the Imperials were coming. At that time in our country's history, most public schools in our area were quite cooperative in promoting local events. Only one school principal expressed concerns. "Could you call it something else, such as a folk-music concert, instead of a gospel concert?"

"Well, no, not really," I answered. "It's a gospel concert."

"Oh, all right," he replied, taking the announcement from my hand.

I announced the concert in all of my classes as well, raving to my students about the Imperials. "They're young guys, their music is upbeat and cool, and you'll really love them," I said. "And besides that, if you want to get a good grade in English this year, you better show up!" The classes knew that I was kidding, but their interest was piqued. We had a full house for the Imperials, and the concert was the talk of the school the next day.

The Trio opened the program that night, singing two or three songs, and then we got off the stage. We were excited about singing in front of the hometown crowd, but we were no dummies. We knew that on a Thursday night in Alexandria, the people had not paid hard-earned money to hear the Gaithers. They wanted to hear the Imperials!

In the audience that night, however, was Bob Benson of the Benson Company, the Nashville recording company founded by his father, John T. Benson. Bob was the company's main Artist and Repertoire director and record producer—the person who helped select the songs for the group's albums and directed the recording sessions. After the concert, Bob approached me and said, "Hey, you guys are pretty good."

"Do you think so?" I asked tentatively.

"Yes, you are," Bob replied. "Have you ever thought about recording in Nashville?"

"Well, yeah," I said, "but we really can't afford those kinds of musicians and studio fees."

"We could take care of that for you," offered Bob. "Why don't you come on down, and we'll work out a contract?"

I could hardly believe my ears! When I told Danny about Bob Benson's offer, he was ecstatic. "Bill, we've got to do it!" he said.

It was a major turning point in the Gaither Trio's career when we walked into RCA Studio B in Nashville. To be in that studio, the same one in which Chet Atkins, Elvis Presley, the Statesmen, the Blackwood Brothers, and other well-known artists had cut so many great records was awesome enough. But that was not the most important or pivotal factor that day. What changed our lives and our music was the introduction to one of the most amazing music personalities I've ever known.

Bob Benson came in and along with him was a short fellow with animated features, horn-rimmed eyeglasses, and an athletic build. "Bill, this is Bob MacKenzie. He's just moved here from the Northeast. He's going to be producing your album," Bob said matter-of-factly.

"Good to meet you, William," MacKenzie stuck out a hand. "Let's get started."

"But I . . . ah . . . I, I thought . . ." I looked at Bob Benson like a little boy who had just had his candy stolen from him. "I thought *you* were going to produce our music," I said.

"No, no. Mac will take good care of you," Bob assured me.

"Are you sure this is the guy you want to produce our album?"

"Oh, yes, I'm sure."

I wasn't so sure. What did this MacKenzie guy know about our music? Who was he to be telling us how to sing our songs? But I trusted Bob Benson, and he was, after all, the man who had brought us to Nashville to record.

I talked briefly with Mac, and my misgivings were not dispelled in the least. To be absolutely honest about it, I didn't like him at first. He was just so brash, outspoken, and opinionated. I could tell it was going to be his way or the highway when it came to recording.

Nevertheless, Bob MacKenzie had hired famed studio engineer Chuck Sykes and assembled some of Nashville's "A Team," top studio musicians who played on hit records for a multitude of big-name artists. And he was a master at getting the best music possible out of them. I soon began to understand why Bob Benson regarded Mac so highly. A highly intelligent, talented trumpet player who grew up in Boston and then migrated from New York to Nashville to manage the symphony, Bob was also a brilliant producer who knew how to package a musical product when he found one. He was a hands-on type of producer, hovering over the studio board, listening carefully to every note.

For our part, the Gaither Trio was as prepared as it could be as we set about recording our first album on the Heartwarming label, one of the music divisions the Benson company owned. We included some of our best songs, such as "He Touched Me," "Joy in the Camp," "I've Been to Calvary," as well as three or four songs Mr. Benson owned, as stipulated by our recording contract. Mary Ann sang on that first album along with Danny and me, and when it was done, Bob MacKenzie was quite complimentary. More importantly, through the recording process I learned to trust Mac's musical judgment, and we established a strong, enduring friendship.

One of Mac's greatest gifts was his ability to ask the tough but right questions. "What are you trying to say with your music? Who are you trying to reach? Why are you doing what you are doing?"

To Bob MacKenzie, the "why" question was the most important. There will always be people who know *how* to do something, but those who understand their motivations are rare. One sage said it well: "The people who ask the question 'how?' will always be working for those who ask 'why?'" Bob's blunt honesty with his artists was his strongest suit. He refused to tell artists half-truths simply because he knew that was what they wanted to hear. He opened windows in the realm of Christian music, room to allow a fresh, new breeze to blow through. Before long, he was not only producing southern gospel quartets, but he became one of the leading proponents of a new style of gospel music that became known as "contemporary" Christian music.

Bob Benson and Bob MacKenzie titled the Gaither Trio album *Sincerely*. They didn't really ask my opinion. Later, when people asked me about the title, I told them, "I guess they just thought we looked sincere." We didn't dress ostentatiously or put on any pretense; we were truly a "What you see is what you get" sort of group.

The album sold respectably, although compared to the numbers of albums artists sell today, our figures were minuscule. Still, the record company was convinced that we could grow our sales, so before long we were back in the studio again. Our second album was titled *When God Seems So Near*. By the time we were ready for the third album, *I Am Free*, Mary Ann had left the group, so Danny and I auditioned several female singers we thought might fit with us. Nobody seemed to blend the way we wanted, and the recording date was approaching, so we asked Gloria to sing with us.

Convincing Gloria to sing onstage was one thing; trying to persuade her to sing in the studio was harder still. The recording process can be brutal; it is not the place for wavering confidence or fragile egos. Singers can sometimes get away with a less-than-perfect performance in a large church or concert hall, but in the studio, every flat or sharp note, slurred word, or other musical miscue is blasted through the speakers for all to hear.

Singing in a soundproof vocal booth or in a windowless studio tends to deaden a voice anyhow, and hearing your voice "dry," with no reverb or other electronic "sweeteners" can be a disheartening experience. The tape (or modern digital) machine captures both the good notes and the bad ones.

Gloria knew that, and that's one reason why she wanted no part of making recordings of our music. "I just don't feel confident enough to do the recording, Bill. Please get someone else," she begged.

Mac suggested bringing in someone who sounded similar to Gloria. "I know just the person," I told Mac. "Betty Fair, a friend of ours from college, lives nearby. She's working with her husband, who is serving as a minister of music at a church, and her voice is like Gloria's."

Both Gloria and Mac encouraged me to call Betty. When I explained to Betty what we wanted to do, she happily agreed to sing with Danny and me on the record. Gloria sang harmony parts as well, and we included two songs in which Gloria recorded some special spoken narrations. Because of Betty's style and spirit, she blended beautifully with us; so well, in fact, we pictured all four singers on the album cover. Betty joined us in concerts occasionally, but she and her husband were committed to their work with the church, so we didn't expect her to sing with us full-time. She did, however, join us on three albums for the Heartwarming label.

At Mac's insistence, we always included one song on each side of the album that contained a special part spoken by Gloria. These portions would come to be known as Gloria's "readings," some of which were actually recitations or narrations of her own writings, and others that were spontaneous, extemporaneous insights she shared during our concerts.

Mac insisted on this because one weekend, he traveled with us to Elkhart, Indiana, where he heard the Gaither Trio do some-

thing during a Sunday morning worship service that blew him
away. It was Gloria—not her singing ability but her gifts for communicating a message to an audience through spoken words—
that left such an indelible impression on Mac's heart and mind.

Gloria and I had written a new song, "There's Something
about That Name," a slow and forceful acknowledgment of the
supernatural power resident in the name of Jesus. During an instrumental interlude in the song, Gloria stepped to the microphone and began to speak with deep emotion:

> Jesus. . . . The mere mention of His name can calm the
> storm, heal the broken, raise the dead. At the name of Jesus,
> I've seen sin-hardened men melt, derelicts transformed, the
> lights of hope put back into the eyes of a hopeless child. . . .
>
> At the name of Jesus, hatred and bitterness turn to love
> and forgiveness; arguments cease.
>
> I've heard a mother softly breathe His name at the bedside
> of a child delirious from fever, and I've watched as that little
> body grew quiet and the fevered brow became cool.
>
> I've sat beside a dying saint, her body racked with pain,
> who in those final fleeting seconds summoned her last
> ounce of ebbing strength to whisper earth's sweetest
> name—"Jesus, Jesus. . . ."
>
> Emperors have tried to destroy it; philosophies have tried
> to stamp it out. Tyrants have tried to wash it from the face of
> the earth with the very blood of those who claimed it. Yet
> still it stands.
>
> And there shall be the final day when every voice that has
> ever uttered a sound—every voice of Adam's race—shall rise
> in one mighty chorus to proclaim the name of Jesus, for in
> that day "every knee shall bow and every tongue shall confess
> that Jesus Christ is Lord!"
>
> So, you see, it was not mere chance that caused the angel
> one night long ago to say to a virgin maiden, "His name shall
> be called JESUS."

Jesus . . .
Jesus . . .
Jesus . . .
There is something—something about that name.[1]

What an impact Gloria's recitation had! It was more than just music.

Since that morning, we have performed the song "There's Something about That Name" hundreds of times in auditoriums around the globe. Inevitably, when we come to the portion of the song in which Gloria does the recitation, something special happens in the audience. I'm convinced that it has something to do with the truth Jesus told His disciples, "If I be lifted up, I will draw all men unto myself."[2]

Bob MacKenzie recognized that something more than music came across in Elkhart. When he heard Gloria's performance that morning he said, "I want to get *that* on record."

"I don't think we can get that on a record," I said.

"I'll help you," Mac replied. Mac intuitively realized that it was imperative that Gloria be on the next album; not merely her part, but her presence. He looked at Gloria and spoke matter-of-factly, "And you're going to sing this time."

"Bob, you know I'm not a singer," Gloria protested.

"I know, but I'll help you. Trust me. It will be good. Besides, when people buy your albums, they want to hear you. You've got to sing on the records. You're good enough in concert; we'll make you good enough in the studio."

Every artist needs someone to believe in him or her, and Gloria knew that Bob MacKenzie believed in her. He would never ask her to do anything that would be foolish; challenging, maybe; difficult, certainly; but Bob knew how to make great recordings. Gloria trusted Bob. Beyond that, Mac's confidence was contagious, and Gloria consented. Good thing, since I doubt that Mac would have taken no for an answer anyhow.

I'll be forever grateful to Bob MacKenzie for pushing us beyond our comfort level. He had much more spiritual insight into what we could do than we did; he simply said, "I'm not going to let you get by with less."

Our relationship with Bob MacKenzie and his wife, Joy, continued throughout the years, and Mac and I became much more than friends; we became like family. In fact, our families frequently vacationed together. Often during those trips Mac and I would spend hours on end dreaming and talking about some of the things we could do together musically. Eventually, those dreams developed into a company known as Paragon Associates, which we formed in the mid-1970s. Because of Mac's vision and his unwillingness to remain locked into the status quo, Paragon soon signed some incredibly talented songwriters, such as the recently converted Grammy Award winner, Gary S. Paxton. Gary had written such hits as "Monster Mash" and "Alley Oop" and now wanted to use his talents to express his new-found Christian faith.

One of Mac's first projects on Paragon was Gary's album, *The Amazing, Incredible, Outrageous, Unbelievable, Different World of Gary S. Paxton*, which was nominated for a Dove Award. Gary accompanied Mac to the awards program wearing a bright red jumpsuit and red cowboy boots. Gospel music traditionalists stared in shock and wondered if Mac had lost his mind. But Mac didn't care. He knew that Gary S. Paxton and others like him could create incredible music and express things that needed to be said in the Christian community.

Soon Mac had rounded up a stable full of innovative young writers such as Michael W. Smith, Scott Wesley Brown, Eddie DeGarmo, and Dana Key. Throughout the 1970s, Paragon writers and artists continued to create new music, expressing their sincere faith in God in ways few of us could have imagined before Bob MacKenzie put his own reputation, money, and energy on the line to help make it happen.

To help us run Paragon, Bob brought in another Northeasterner, Wayne Erickson. Wayne was a great people person, and our writers and artists on Paragon related to him well. Wayne understood the business world, but he had an artist's heart. Eventually, he became the president of the Benson Company when it was being sold. Wayne was another person in Mac's network of friends who became a close friend of mine.

Mac's incredible creativity could be matched only by his equally awful management skills. Details such as budgets, board meetings, and costs of doing business bored Bob. To him, the only thing that mattered was the artistry. Not surprisingly, after about seven years, we discovered that working together in business wasn't as much fun as we thought it might be, and we sold our holdings in Paragon. Yet we remained the closest of friends. That's no small feat: to part company as business partners without bitterness or rancor. But to Mac and me, our friendship was worth far more than money.

Bob's brain was always miles ahead of everyone else's, so much so that Bob sometimes even outdistanced himself. Once, for example, he took a trip to Atlanta, and upon his arrival back at the Nashville airport he couldn't find his car in the airport parking lot.

Frustrated, he called home and said, "Joy, where did I park the car at the airport?"

"Bob, the car isn't at the airport," Joy replied sweetly. "You drove to Atlanta." That was classic Mac.

———————

Bob MacKenzie was probably one of the best networkers in the music business. For our fifth album on the Heartwarming label, Mac wanted to put a full orchestra behind us. Prior to this, the background music on our albums had been mostly a rhythm section with some minor overdubbing. Now Mac wanted to go all-out.

I was a little worried about the orchestrations and said so. "Don't worry, William," he said, "I have just the guy for you. His name is Rick Powell, he's a great arranger and producer, and you'll love him."

As usual, Mac was right. Rick was great. With Mac producing and Rick arranging, we formed a musical partnership that reached some major milestones in the music business. Along the way, Rick, too, became a lifelong friend.

In the late sixties, early seventies, Mac introduced us to Ronn Huff, another extremely talented arranger. Mac said, "Bill, your music is good, but the churches uptown don't know about it. Ronn Huff is the guy who can take you there." Once again, Mac scored big-time with his choice. Ron knew how to take my simple melodies and put them in a much better musical setting. I had some basic musical insights and could compose, but Ronn Huff took our songs to an entirely new level of performance with his tremendous arrangements and productions. Soon churches all over the country began singing Gaither songs. One of the most significant projects we did together was *Alleluia: A Praise Gathering for Believers*, which resulted in the first bona fide million-selling Christian album. I'll tell more about that later, but my point here is that it might never have happened had it not been for the great facilitator, Bob MacKenzie, pulling the right people together.

Bob also connected me with Fred Bock, another key person in our musical career. A funny, gregarious guy, Fred was the choral director at Hollywood Presbyterian Church, pastored at the time by Lloyd John Ogilvie, now chaplain of the U.S. Senate. Fred was also an accomplished organist, conductor, composer, arranger, and publisher of Christian music.

Fred was active in a whole other world of Christian music that I hardly knew existed: the more formal, liturgical church circles. He was a walking hymnody, as easily conversant in the great old hymns of the church as a football fan might be with all the statistics of his favorite teams.

Fred, Ronn, Mac, and Gloria and I came up with an idea for a new, nondenominational church hymnal (Remember hymnals?), a collection of the best of the grand old songs, but also some of the new, contemporary compositions that were already popular in many circles. We called it *Hymns for the Family of God*. We included a wide spectrum of songs, many of which had never before been published in a hymnal, such as "How Great Thou Art," "The Lord's Prayer," "Let There Be Peace on Earth," "This Is My Country," as well as some of Gloria's and my songs, "He Touched Me," "Fill My Cup, Lord," and others.

It took us more than two years to develop the innovative hymnal. Altogether, we chose 699 hymns, gospel songs, spirituals, folk tunes, and classics for the book, as well as Scripture passages from ten separate translations or paraphrases. We also included challenging devotional readings from Christians past and present, people such as Billy Graham, C. S. Lewis, Martin Luther, Dietrich Bonhoeffer, Malcolm Muggeridge, Catherine Marshall, and Robert Schuller. Under each hymn, we printed a Scripture verse that lent itself to memorization.

The book was organized neatly into four sections, (1) God's love for us; (2) our love for God; (3) our love for the family of God; and (4) our love for others.

Our goals were lofty: we wanted to revitalize the experience of congregational singing, and we wanted to change the definition of "hymnal." In many ways, we succeeded far beyond our expectations. *Hymns for the Family of God* became the best-selling hymnal ever published that was not tied directly to a particular denomination. Nowadays, of course, with the proliferation of praise-and-worship choruses, coupled with new technology that can quickly and beautifully project the lyrics of songs onto a screen, many churches hardly even use hymnals anymore. But for its time, *Hymns for the Family of God* was a groundbreaking project and another of the many great concepts spearheaded by Bob MacKenzie.

During the last ten years of his life, Mac's body began to betray him. His health deteriorated and it was difficult to watch the once vibrant, highly energetic embracer of life slowly lose the strength he had always known. He endured two rounds of open-heart surgery, and then during the last year of his life, diabetes began to take a severe toll on his body. His eyesight began to fail.

I called him frequently just to check up on him, and his attitude was amazing. "Mac, how are you doing?" I'd ask.

"Well, William . . ." he started. From the earliest days, Mac always called me William. Part of the reason for that no doubt stemmed from Mac's formal Northeastern upbringing, but more significantly, it was Mac's way of instilling confidence in a person. By calling me William, he was saying, "You're better than Bill." It was part of his emphasis on the dignity and value of the person. "You may be Bill to some folks, or you may be Gaither to others, but to me, you are *William!*" Sometimes, Mac even called me Sir William.

When I asked Mac how he was feeling, his answer was always the same. "Well, William, what can I say? I just have a bad body! But I can blame nobody but myself, because I haven't taken care of the fine body God gave to me."

Immediately Bob would shift the conversation away from his poor physical condition. He was quick to ask me, "How are *you* doing? How are the *Homecoming* videos selling?"

The *Homecoming* video series was the first major musical success that I had experienced since Mac and I had parted company in business together. Nevertheless, Mac was one of my greatest encouragers and the biggest fan I had. Sometimes Mac came into the studio while I was recording sound tracks for a *Homecoming* project, and he'd say, "William, I don't envy your success. I don't even envy the money you are making from it. But I am jealous of the fun you are having doing it! And I applaud you!"

Mac was also my staunchest defender. I once heard from a third party who had been listening in on a conversation between Mac and another person in the music industry. The person was criticizing me after the *Homecoming* videos began to take off. "Gaither really knows how to chase success," the music-biz person said, implying that I was capitalizing on the success of the old songs and artists featured in the videos.

MacKenzie's face became flushed. "Wait a minute!" he interrupted. "Have you ever been to the Gaither home?"

"No," the person acknowledged.

"Well, if you ever go, sooner or later, he will take you into the family room, and he'll drag out those old quartet albums from the 1950s and 1960s. He will play that stuff over and over again. Don't tell me about him chasing success. This is the love of his life, and he's doing it out of his heart. If someone else likes it and wants to pay some money for it, God bless 'em."

The last year of Mac's life, he went back to the East Coast, seeking a new treatment method that could restore heart tissue and muscle. Sometimes on his day off from treatment, Joy took him out to the beach so Mac could listen to the waves rolling in from the sea. By then, he was almost totally blind and had to get around in a wheelchair.

One day I called him on a mobile phone at the beach. "How're you doing, Mac?" I asked as always.

"William, today in listening to the waves come in, I said to myself, 'I guess this is about as good as it's going to get.'"

"Are you okay with that?" I asked.

"I'm going to have to get okay with it. But to be honest with you, it's not fun," Mac admitted.

It was the first time I'd ever heard even a slightly negative attitude come from Mac's mouth. For as long as I'd known him, Mac was perpetually optimistic. He was always the guy who, as we approached the midnight hour—at five till—was still saying, "Wait! Wait! There's still a way. We can make this happen!"

It was tough to hear the resignation in his voice as he acknowledged, "This is going to be it. . . . This is the best I can hope for, and it's probably not going to get any better."

I have been blessed with wonderful family members and many close friends, and in recent years I've attended the funerals of many dear loved ones. But letting go of Bob MacKenzie was one of the saddest experiences of my life.

Mac was one of the greatest representatives of Christian music that we've had in the past fifty years. When the definitive history of Christian music is written, Bob MacKenzie must be included as a key player during the twentieth century because of his vision and his openness to new ways of performing. Did he have weaknesses, drawbacks, or failings? Sure he did! But his pluses far outweighed any minuses he may have had. As one music wag put it, "Mac wasn't always right, but he was never in doubt."

EIGHT

BACK HOME IN INDIANA

OUR SECOND DAUGHTER, Amy, was born in 1969, just about the time many people thought the world was going to hell in a handbasket. Apocalyptic preachers were pronouncing with assurance that Jesus was about to part the skies any day. Indeed, many students of prophecy saw great significance in recent events. Specifically, in 1967 the Israeli army beat back an onslaught by its Arab neighbors. Against overwhelming odds, in only six days, the Israelis reclaimed control of Jerusalem for the first time since A.D. 70, when the Romans had destroyed the city. "Surely," many Christians declared, "it won't be long now before we see King Jesus face-to-face."

Gloria and I believed in the second coming of Christ, but we tended to focus more on serving God in this life than on speculating about the future. Besides, we were parents of young children; we were singing on weekends, writing songs, and teaching school during the week; we were too busy keeping up with the hectic here and now to pay much attention to the sweet by and by!

During the summer of 1970, our good friend Gene Braun, a preacher, stopped by our house. Gene told us about another preacher named James Crabtree, who had been speaking about the return of the Lord. The preacher closed his message by walking through the congregation as though he were Paul Revere or a town crier alerting the people at the top of his voice, "The King is coming! The King is coming!"

When I first heard that phrase, I thought, *What a great hook for a song!* In songwriting, as in other forms of writing, a good "hook" is essential; a hook is a phrase that captures the listener's imagination, that reaches out and grabs the heart or mind and says, "You have to hear the rest of this song!" When I first began writing music, I disliked talking about a song's hook because it seemed so contrived to me. But the more I honed my craft, the more I realized that the hook is what the rest of the song hangs on. Once the hook catches the listener, the writer can explain other details throughout the song; but without a good hook, no matter how great a tune or lyrics a composer writes, the song is doomed to obscurity.

Think of some of the great hymns of the church: "Blessed Assurance," "It Is Well With My Soul," "O for a Thousand Tongues," "A Mighty Fortress Is Our God," "The Old Rugged Cross," "All Hail the Power of Jesus' Name," "I Love to Tell the Story." Each one has a great hook!

Gloria and I began to ruminate about that hook "the King is coming!" How could we get that idea to the street? How could we communicate that sense of urgency and the need to be prepared for His coming? Could we do something in a song similar to what James Crabtree had done in his sermon?

We began working on a song and had it nearly completed

when another evangelist friend of ours, Chuck Millhuff, dropped by our home. When we told him what we were working on, Chuck was excited. He, too, had heard about the sermon by James Crabtree.

"Bill, you ought to put some phrases in that song talking about how the saints of God in heaven are dressed in regal robes. Imagine the sight and sound of the greatest choir ever assembled! I can almost hear them singing 'Amazing Grace.'" Chuck scribbled down all sorts of ideas, most of which we couldn't use, but it was marvelous to imagine what such a heavenly gathering might be like.

In the days following, Gloria and I continued to talk about the Second Coming. We didn't regard Christ's return as something to be feared but rather something to be anticipated; it would be an exciting celebration day. It would be the day we'd see our Savior, Lord, and King for the first time, face-to-face. No doubt, it would be *awesome* in the truest sense of the word!

I took the hook "the King is coming" and began working with it some more, writing and rewriting until I was able to distill the essence of what I wanted to say into a simple chorus:

> The King is coming! The King is coming!
> I just heard the trumpet sounding, and now His face I see.
> Oh, the King is coming! The King is coming!
> Praise God, He's coming for me!

Gloria took it from there and wrote some of the most powerful lyrics ever put to music. Interestingly, rather than dwelling on the frightening judgment of God at the end of time, Gloria focused on God's wonderful redeeming power. She created a scene of the King walking through the coronation gallery, viewing the many lives that His goodness and grace had touched.

Happy faces line the hallways—
Those whose lives have been redeemed,
Broken homes that He has mended,
Those from prison He has freed. . . .

For the last verse, she penned the stirring words:

I can hear the chariots rumble,
I can see the marching throng.
The flurry of God's trumpets
Spells the end of sin and wrong.

She also incorporated some of Chuck Millhuff's suggestions as she wrote:

Regal robes are now unfolding,
Heaven's grandstand's all in place,
Heaven's choirs, now assembled,
Start to sing "Amazing Grace"![1]

When Gloria brought the words to me, even though we had worked independently for the most part, the melody and the lyric matched almost perfectly. Over the years, when I've been a part of something that I recognized as better than what I could possibly do on my own, I've referred to it as a "God thing." I'm convinced that "The King Is Coming" was one of those "God things" in our lives. I say that carefully, because I know that God gets credit or blame for a lot of things that were much more human than divine.

One of my favorite songwriting stories along this line came from Bob Benson. A young writer approached Bob, saying, "God gave me this song."

Bob looked at the song and said, "I believe that God gave you the inspiration for this song, and God did a wonderful job on His part. You just haven't finished your part yet."

Our friends the Speer Family were singing at a camp meeting nearby, so I took a copy of "The King Is Coming" over to them and let them try it out. When the Speers got ahold of "The King Is Coming," they started singing it every night. Each time they performed the song, the audiences responded ecstatically, often rising to their feet and applauding long before the song was concluded. When our producer, Bob MacKenzie, heard it, he knew that the Gaither Trio had to record it.

In 1970 we went into the studio to begin work on an album we called *Back Home in Indiana*. Bob produced the recording and had the fantastic arranger Rick Powell create the orchestrations for the album. After we did the basic rhythm tracks, Rick recorded incredibly beautiful instrumental tracks in London, then brought the tracks home so Gloria, Danny, and I could add our vocals. We all sensed that we were a part of something special. We recorded "There's Something About That Name," "The King Is Coming," and other new songs that we had just written.

We had no idea just how groundbreaking that album would be.

"Bill, you're not going to believe this!" I recognized the voice on the phone as that of Wayne Buchanan, marketing director at the Benson Music Group. "*Back Home in Indiana* has sold ten thousand units!" Wayne gushed.

Wayne was right: I didn't believe him. Our best-selling album to date had barely sold eight thousand units. Christian albums in those days rarely sold more than ten thousand copies total. Anything in the twenty-five- to fifty-thousand range was considered a megasuccess! But now Wayne was calling to let us know that in the first few weeks after the album released, it had already surpassed our wildest expectations.

A few weeks later, Wayne called again. "Bill, you're not going to believe this!" he said excitedly. "*Back Home in Indiana* is at twenty thousand sold!"

I began to look forward to hearing Wayne's voice on the phone. Each time he called, he'd begin, "Bill, you're not going to believe this," and he was always right! Before Wayne stopped calling me regularly, the album surpassed 350,000 sold, the best-selling album in the Benson Company's history at that time.

Certainly we were thrilled with the sales of our music—but not because we wanted to run to the bank or build a new house. Gloria and I still live in the first home we ever built, and the mortgage has been paid off for more than thirty-five years. We had no desire to move into a posh gated community, or to buy a Rolls-Royce. We've been quite content with our lifestyle. But we were excited that the music and the message were connecting with an audience far greater than we ever dreamed.

Moreover, right from the start, when *Back Home in Indiana* caught on, we took some of the profits from our music ventures and invested them in other music projects or in the staging, production, or equipment that has helped us present our music at a level of professionalism that is comparable to any other artist's.

When people questioned us about the prosperity we enjoyed from our careers, Gloria and I never tried to put on a "poor boy" routine. I often responded, "Yes, we've been blessed, and we hope to be very generous."

I am always quick to point out that when sales are the primary motive for artistry, a project is almost bound to fail. Reporters frequently ask me, "With the increased marketing and sales potential of Christian music today, isn't there a danger that people will get involved for the wrong reason—simply to make money?"

The answer is yes! Sure, it is possible that people will get involved in Christian music or any other creative expression merely to make money. They may last for a short while, but they won't remain in the arts for long. Money is not enough of a motivation for a truly creative person. To last out on the road for ten, twenty, thirty years or more, it has to be more than the money and more than the music that keeps a person going. You have to believe in the idea, the message.

One of the things that always helped keep us "honest" about our music, ministry, money, and motivations has been our practice of paying our own way. From the time the Gaither Trio first started singing in public concert halls, we sold tickets and products to pay the bills. We didn't depend on donations or charitable gifts to keep the ministry going. Oh, sure, when we first began singing in churches, we were often "paid" by means of a "freewill love offering," which was basically passing the offering plates, and whatever anyone wanted to put in (or not!) was what we took home as remuneration for our singing.

I was never really comfortable with the "freewill love offering" system of financing gospel concerts or other special church programs. Many nights, I felt as though we were being sold by the pound, auctioned off to the highest bidder. I'd sit on the platform and cringe as a pastor or emcee listed all the needs we had, or the reasons why the congregation should support our ministry. At times, I felt sure the leader was manipulating the people, trying to coerce them to give through guilt or browbeating, or some promise that if they gave exorbitantly to us, God was going to give back exorbitantly to them. I hated that.

But once we started performing in concert halls and auditoriums—even when the concerts were extremely small compared to the scale of the productions we do nowadays—we sold tickets. If people didn't want to hear us, they didn't have to buy tickets. If a promoter booked the Gaithers and the public did not purchase enough tickets to pay the expenses, I told the promoter, "Don't worry about it. Don't pay us." As far as I know, no promoter ever lost money on the Gaithers. If one did, it was only because I was unaware of the situation.

Although I understand the need for certain legitimate ministries to operate as nonprofit, tax-exempt organizations, we chose instead to operate on a for-profit basis. We moved our concerts out of the churches, and never again accepted donations as our means of support.

Moreover, once we began singing in auditoriums, only on extremely rare occasions did we accept invitations to sing in churches. Part of the reason for this was due to the crowds that were showing up for our concerts. Most churches, even modern megachurches, were too small to hold the number of people who wanted to come unless we did multiple programs. Rather than trying to sing in a dozen churches in a particular city, we announced that we'd be performing at the civic center.

Two unanticipated fringe benefits occurred as a result of our concerts taking place in the neutral, nonchurch environment. For one thing, people from all church denominations gathered under one roof to hear the music and the message. Before long, Baptists, Methodists, Presbyterians, charismatics, Catholics, and Pentecostals were all praising the Lord together. Subtly, the walls between denominations began to crumble, and Christians began to realize that they had more in common than they had ever imagined.

Second, the nonchurch concerts provided an excellent opportunity for believers to invite unbelievers to a nonthreatening, neutral location where they could hear the gospel. All our concerts had an emphasis on the power of Christ to change a life, but we did our best never to make anyone feel uncomfortable with the presentation of the message.

I still love to sing in churches—I just like the feeling I get when we sing in church—and over the years, we've undoubtedly missed something by going to the auditoriums. I've never enjoyed it when the house lights come down in an auditorium and the stage lights come up. I can't see the people anymore. Although we know there are thousands of people out there, we can't see more than a few past the front row because of the bright spotlights onstage.

I know that we can turn any location into "the house of God" simply by having the family of God show up, but there's just something special about singing God's praises in His house.

Once a friend of mine, who pastors a large church in Kansas City, said to me, "Bill, I'd really like for you and your troupe to come to our church to sing. How much would you charge us?"

"Well, we don't have a charge," I replied, "because we normally just sell tickets. If people come, we get paid, and if they don't buy tickets, we go home empty-handed."

"Please, won't you consider coming to our church?" the pastor asked.

"Okay, we'll come on one condition," I answered.

"What's that?"

"That you will not make a big offering pitch. But that you will simply pass the hat. And don't say that we could be making a whole lot more money doing something else, because that makes me feel like a piece of meat, and I'm not really sure I could be making a whole lot of money doing anything else!"

The night of the concert, we had a marvelous time. When it came time for the offering, the pastor told his congregation during intermission, "You're not going to believe what the

Gaithers charged us to come and sing at our church. Bill said just to pass the hat, and whatever comes in, they'll take home. 'If the people are moved and blessed, they'll give, and if they aren't, they won't.'"

After the service, the pastor came to me with a check. "We don't have all the money counted yet," he said, "so we'll give you a check for what we have so far and send another check when we get it all counted. Tonight's offering is the largest in the history of our church!"

I smile when I think of that offering, not so much because of the large amount, but because it reminds me of the generosity of God's people. I don't believe that it is necessary to put people on a guilt trip so they will finance the kingdom of God. Arm-twisting, manipulation, begging, or other gimmicks to get people to give are superfluous when God's people recognize the value or the need. I'm convinced that Christians are the most generous, giving people in the world and will respond above and beyond what is expected when the opportunity is put in the proper context.

When it came to financing our music ministry, I've believed from the beginning, as the Scripture says, "The worker is worthy of his support."[2] If God is in it, He'll take care of it, and if He's not, you're wasting your time and you might as well forget about trying to make it work anyhow!

When our music business took off, and we actually started making more money than we needed to live, most of our friends and financial counselors gave the same advice: diversify; don't lock yourself in to one business area, but spread your investments around. With all respect to the financial advisors, Gloria and I decided to stick to what we know. We've kept our investments within the realm of music and publishing. Most people would consider these high-risk ventures, but for us, they were not nearly as risky as businesses we knew nothing about!

The success of *Back Home in Indiana* also was the catalyst for a wonderful relationship that Gloria and I have enjoyed for more than thirty years with Wayne Buchanan and his outspoken and hilariously funny wife, Sue. The Buchanans became and remain some of our dearest friends in the world. Gloria and I look forward to seeing them each year at Family Fest in Gatlinburg, when we can spend four or five days tromping the mountains, having picnics along the mountain streams, and shopping till we drop in Gatlinburg's many specialty stores.

Sue Buchanan has an outrageous sense of humor. For my fiftieth birthday, Gloria threw a surprise party for me in Anderson. I thought she was taking me out to dinner, but then I walked into a room to discover friends from all over the country. I was truly surprised!

Everyone at the party had a Bill Gaither story. When it was Sue Buchanan's turn, she rose from her chair, looked around the room, and said, "I don't know why I'm here." The room grew extremely quiet as Sue paused for effect. "Because I am the 'other woman.' You may wonder why we're never seen in public. I ask you . . . the way he dresses? Would *you* want to be seen with him? Bill isn't a GQ type of man. Bill thinks semiformal means new tennis shoes. He dresses like he just ran from a burning building. His clothes look like they were designed by the fashion editor of a seed catalog. He bought a new suit last week. The jacket looks good . . . but the pants are too tight across the chest!" Sue looked in my direction. "When are you going to tell her?" Sue nodded in Gloria's direction. "How long are you going to let this go on, Bill? To be honest, I'm really angry about it." Sue stomped out of the room in a huff, as everyone in the room roared in laughter. A few moments later she returned to

BACK HOME IN INDIANA

her table, as though she had been out trying to regain her composure.

Just then, Bev Darnall, sitting next to her husband, John, leaped to her feet, looked at Sue, and said, "I don't know why I'm here. I thought I was the other woman!"

Once again, the room convulsed in laughter. With friends like these. . . .

Along with the success of our album came an increased demand for sheet music of our songs. For several years after we started Gaither Music Company, I kept track of every piece of sheet music we sold—noting the date, the number of copies sold, and the group to whom we sold them—in a small spiral-bound notebook. Those old ledgers are interesting to look back at now—although my accountant would shudder, no doubt, at my elementary accounting system. Nevertheless, it's easy to trace the path of Gloria's and my songwriting career simply by tracking the sales increases over those early months and years.

I continued to teach high school English even after we had achieved some level of success as songwriters. I still considered myself a full-time teacher and a part-time singer, with a sheet-music company on the side. After getting home from school each day, I usually worked in our publishing company another four to six hours before bedtime. But the pace was starting to get to me. Thanks to the success of *Back Home in Indiana*, our concert schedule was increasing and we were busier than ever, singing and writing new songs. Something was going to have to give soon.

Nevertheless, I had taught for ten years, and I was reluctant to give it up. I remembered all too well those days with the Pathfinders when we could barely scrounge together enough money for a meal. Besides, I loved teaching and interacting with the students.

One of my favorite high school English classes was the section I taught on Edgar Allan Poe, the nineteenth-century American author whose short stories could still scare the daylights out of a generation not yet satiated with images of television violence and Hollywood gore. Sometimes I'd put on a recording of one of Poe's horror stories, such as "The Murders in the Rue Morgue" or "The Masque of the Red Death," or his frightening poem "The Raven." Then I'd leave the classroom and sneak outside to an obscured window, through which I would howl haunting sounds while the class listened to Poe.

The window came in handy for class discipline as well. Because of its location I could see the classroom, but the students couldn't see me. Sometimes when I had to leave the class briefly for some reason, I'd tell the class, "Stay in your seats. I'll be back shortly."

Before returning to the room, however, I'd stop by to observe through the window. Often I'd discover a mischievous student causing trouble. I'd return to class and say something such as, "Jack, I thought I told you to stay in your seat." Jack gazed at me in awe. "How did you know I was out of my seat?" he'd ask, amazed at my omniscience. I'd have few discipline problems with him ever again!

Both Gloria and I thrived in the classroom situation. We threw ourselves into teaching just as we did anything else— with the attitude "If we're going to do this, we're going to do it *right!*" Looking back, I can honestly say we were good teachers, too. Outside the classroom, we enjoyed working with the students on school projects and we directed the high school plays. During our tenure there, we did such productions as *Our Town* and *Arsenic and Old Lace,* and with the help of some bright young students, we put on a pretty good show!

After about four years in a row in which our concert and sheet music sales vastly surpassed the amount of money I was making as a schoolteacher, our accountant, Jim Wilson, said, "Bill, I think this is here to stay. I think you can trust it, so why don't you take the jump, and do your music business full-time?"

I had great confidence in our accountant, so I agreed it was time to lay down my teaching job before I fell down from exhaustion. I went to the high school principal, Shorty Burdsall, and told him, "We are spending so much time on our moonlighting job that I am not giving you my best in the classroom anymore. I apologize for that, but I know I can't keep up this schedule any longer. I'll be resigning my position at the close of the semester."

. Shorty was a good friend and was extremely gracious. He said, "Bill, I understand, and I'm sorry to see you go, but if you ever decide to return to teaching, there will always be a job here for you. Anytime you or Gloria wants to come back, we'd take you in a minute."

I was honored at his kind words, and there've been a few times over my career when I considered taking him up on his offer!

I've always regarded teaching as a noble profession—or at least it should be. As I look back today, after more than forty years of communicating with audiences across America and in various places around the world, I believe we did a good job of sweeping into a city, presenting an uplifting program, and then sweeping back out or on to the next venue. We also wrote some songs that encouraged many people and helped multitudes through some difficult places in their lives.

But I often think of the impact that a good teacher can have on a student, not simply for one night, or for the time it takes to listen to a recording. A teacher can affect a student for a semester, a year, or even a lifetime. In my more philosophic moods, I sometimes wonder if teaching is not yet the higher calling.

In some ways my heart never left the classroom, because to this day, I enjoy being a teacher and a coach to the professional singers and musicians with whom I work. Recently, the *Homecoming* touring group gave a rather lackluster performance in one city. Nobody would have guessed it by the audience's response. The crowd rose to its feet and applauded enthusiastically at the end of the program. Most of the people who attended the program went home talking about what a great evening of music they had experienced.

But I knew better. And so did my coworkers on the *Homecoming* tour.

I could hear the voice of the late Bob MacKenzie in the back of my mind: "B is a great grade, B-plus is better yet, but an A is a whole lot better."

The following weekend, before our concert in another city many miles away, I called all the artists together at four o'clock in the twelve-thousand-seat arena where we were to perform that night. Without scolding, I said to the professional singers, musicians, and crew members, "Last Saturday night, we lost our focus. We are like a good sports team; we have so much individual talent here that it's easy to start depending on routine, abilities, and raw talent rather than focusing on what we are trying to do, whom we are singing about, and whom we are trying to please."

I looked into the faces of the thirty or more people with whom I would soon be going onstage and said, "I'm just as guilty as you. So let's go into this arena tonight recognizing that these twelve thousand people have chosen to spend their Friday night with us. They are busy people. Many of them are trying to pay off their mortgages, some are scrambling to buy clothes for their children, pay medical bills, put their kids through college, and some of the people who will be here are doing all of those things. But they chose to make us a priority this night, from seven o'clock to eleven o'clock. They deserve our very best."

The professionals listening to me nodded in agreement.

"The people coming tonight have made a sacrifice in time, effort, and money to be here, so we need to pay the price as well. We need not only to look good and sound good, but we need our minds and hearts here tonight, fully engaged in all that we are doing."

Standing in the same cavernous arena that was home to one of the National Basketball Association's top teams, I couldn't resist using a basketball metaphor. "Trust me," I said, "as an Indiana basketball fan. It will make a difference between winning or losing the game tonight. Most games are lost not because of missing fancy slam dunks or long three-pointers outside the key, but because of lack of hustle, not going after loose balls, not going up for a tough rebound, not being willing to take a charge from an opposing player, or sacrifice for the good of the team. Most games are lost because of some players' momentary lapse of concentration, focus, or effort, not because of a lack of ability. Let's not lose the game tonight. Let's give it everything we've got!"

The *Homecoming* performers responded fantastically, turning in one of their finest performances in a long time.

Shorty Burdsall would have been proud of us.

Prior to the release of *Back Home in Indiana*, the Gaither Trio was singing primarily in churches with a few civic functions thrown in, along with an occasional gospel concert in a local school or hall. Each weekend, we'd load our scrappy sound system into our little white bread truck that we had converted for travel, with sleeping quarters in the back, and we'd head off around the countryside. Eventually we purchased better sound equipment to make our presentation more professional, and a motor home to make travel more convenient.

Following the phenomenal success of *Back Home*, we began booking concerts in high school auditoriums with a seating capacity of around one thousand people. We put together a concert package of Doug Oldham, Henry and Hazel Slaughter, and the Gaither Trio. We sold tickets to these concerts, unlike those we conducted in churches. Soon the requests for tickets indicated that crowds wanting to attend were larger than the high school auditoriums could accommodate, so we moved our concerts to small civic auditoriums, seating two to three thousand people. We performed all across the country for seven years.

We hired a team to promote concerts out of our own office and worked with local radio stations around the country to advertise the program. With all respect to the many wonderful concert promoters who are doing great work nowadays, handling our own concert promotions was one of the best moves we ever made. We learned early on that we couldn't safely trust that the myriad concert promotion details were properly taken care of unless we kept a close watch on them. I grew weary of going into a different town each evening, working with a different concert promoter, expecting that the details were covered, only to discover that more often than not, they weren't. I came up with a saying: "He that has no plan becomes the victim of other people's plans." I realized that each promoter in each town had a plan for my life while I was in his city, but it may not have been the plan that was consistent with my own!

Beyond that, I discovered that our concerts were not always promoted at the level and with the same energy and enthusiasm that I would have used myself. So often, after arriving in a town and being met by the concert promoter, I'd ask, "How are the ticket sales going for tonight's concert?"

Rather than answering my question, the promoter would say something like, "Well, ahhh, we have a lot of advertising out. We've got posters in all the churches, and ads on all the radio stations. We've been doing a lot of hard work in getting the word out."

"Yes, that's great, but how many tickets have you sold?"

By the time we got to the building where the concert was to be held, the promoter would confess that few advance tickets had actually been sold.

I determined in my heart and mind that as a responsible husband and father, I could not leave home without knowing that when we arrived at the concert venue, the promoter had done the best job possible. We worked extremely hard on our end to provide a stellar program. Why should we relegate our success or failure to someone who might do a less-than-top-notch job? That's when we decided to create our own concert promotions team. My sister, Mary Ann, who understood my desire for excellence in every part of our operation, came on board to head up our concert promotions.

Soon we moved to larger venues, eventually booking arenas, but setting up the seating capacity only as we needed it. At first, we set our stage on one end of the arena and sold only half of the seats. Then as the crowds grew larger, we began selling out fifteen-thousand-seat arenas and larger. All along the way, we

were careful not to speculate, to overstep our budget, or to exaggerate our ability to draw people into the arena seats. We
went to a larger venue only when the demand absolutely dictated the move, and it made good financial sense to do so.

Of course, along with the larger venues and more elaborate
productions came larger expenses for bigger and better sound
systems, publicity, and logistics. Every new step spawned another. When we started using larger sound and lighting systems,
we started our own sound reinforcement company. Then we
needed a way to transport the equipment, so we bought our own
trucks and hired our own drivers. Then when we moved to
arenas, we had the added concerns of union regulations, lots
of parking attendants, local taxes, and concession fees to be
paid to the arena for the privilege of selling our own products. As the size of the venues grew larger, our expenses grew
commensurately.

Still, I'd be less than honest if I didn't admit that we were
awed by our success. One day I was talking with our orchestra
arranger and friend Rick Powell, and in my exuberance over the
latest album sales reports and concert attendance figures I
gushed, "Rick, the crowds at our concerts are unbelievable!" I
rambled on about how many people were coming, how enthusiastic they were, and how much of our product they were pur-
chasing after the performances.

Finally, Rick motioned for me to move closer. "Bill, let me
give you a bit of advice: don't take it too seriously. You're not as
great as you think you are, and you're not as bad as you'll think
you are somewhere down the road."

Rick wasn't trying to rain on my parade. He'd been around
the music business a long time, and he'd seen success ruin many
fine artists who had started from scratch as we had. He was simply saying, "Don't get caught up in reading your own press re-

ports. Keep it all in perspective. Keep your feet on the ground and your head out of the clouds."

May I always have people like Rick Powell around me who are willing to say, "Gaither, don't take it too seriously."

One of my favorite poems, which I have prominently mounted on a plaque on my office wall, is Rudyard Kipling's classic "If." The poignant piece begins with the statement:

> If you can keep your head when all about you
> Are losing theirs and blaming it on you;
> If you can trust yourself when all men doubt you. . . .

The poet provided a profound insight when he said,

> If you can meet with Triumph and Disaster
> And treat those two imposters just the same. . . .

Interesting, isn't it, that Kipling regarded both triumph and disaster, success or failure, as imposters. Kipling also described keeping one's head in the face of success, which is sometimes the more difficult task:

> If you can talk with crowds and keep your virtue,
> Or walk with Kings—nor lose the common touch,
> If neither foes nor loving friends can hurt you,
> If all men count with you, but none too much;
> If you can fill the unforgiving minute
> With sixty seconds' worth of distance run,
> Yours is the Earth and everything that's in it,
> And—which is more—you'll be a Man, my son.

More than any other poetry or literature outside of the Bible, Kipling's insightful piece has helped me keep our music career in perspective. Gloria and I especially knew that we were not great singers, and that Danny carried us along musically. But it was clear from the beginning that God was not merely interested in our talent to perform or our singing ability. He had placed a gift in our hands to communicate His message through music, and we were well aware that the songs didn't simply flow from our own ingenuity. Certainly we had the responsibility to work hard, to develop kernel ideas, to study our craft, and to be good caretakers of the talent He had given to us; but when it came right down to it, apart from His blessing we could easily have been just a couple of schoolteachers putting some words to some tunes.

I realized that once success started happening, many people were prone to telling me what they thought I wanted to hear. Sometimes I had to work hard to get the truth from some people. I guess that's another reason I respected Bob MacKenzie so much. Bob made it a practice to tell me the truth . . . in fact, Bob *enjoyed* telling me the unadorned truth!

One day, a colleague of Mac's and mine commented, "I can't believe that he works for you and you put up with his being so blunt!"

"What do you mean?" I asked. "I pay him big money to be that blunt!"

I believe that I'm being honest with myself when I say that I have never gotten caught up in my own success, enamored with it, or fooled into thinking that I am somebody special because of it.

Today, I often tell young artists who come to me when they are discouraged, "No matter how it looks or feels, things are not as bad as you may think. You're not losing as much as it seems you are right now, even though you feel as though everything you've ever hoped or dreamed for has gone down the drain." I watch as the younger artists' eyes light up, and then I'll say, "And can I tell you something else? You weren't nearly as hot as you thought you were a short time ago."

Most of them smile and say something such as, "You're right. I thought I was bigger than I really was."

I'm convinced that God looks at us much the same way. He doesn't get overly impressed with our successes, nor is He overly depressed by our failures. He is still the same whether we are on the mountaintop or trudging through the valleys of life. I love stories of faith about real people who have had hard times as well as great times, because that is more true to form for most of us. Most people don't live perpetually on the triumphant experiences of life. Similarly, I love songs such as the one written by Tracy Dartt, "God on the Mountain," because it helps me to keep the good times and the tough times in perspective:

> Life is easy when you're up on the mountain
> And you've got peace of mind
> Like you've never known,
> But when things change
> And you're down in the valley,
> Don't lose faith for you're never alone.

> We talk of faith when we're up on the mountain,
> But talk comes easy
> When life's at its best,
> But in the valley of trials and temptations,
> That's when faith is put to the test.

> And the God on the mountain is still God in the valley,
> When things go wrong
> He'll make them right,
> And the God in the good times is still God in the bad times,
> The God of the day is still God of the night.[3]

Practically speaking, we've been able to keep our careers in perspective because early on, Gloria and I made some key decisions about our priorities. We set some firm boundaries around our career. First, we decided that we would not become slaves to our own success. Just because the phone was ringing off the hook with invitations to sing in various parts of the country, we didn't have to accept every opportunity that presented itself. If you think that it is God's will for you to run every time the phone rings, you're going to run yourself ragged.

Plenty of people are experts at putting spiritual guilt trips on others. I've had people say to me, "Can you please come to our city? You've got to come!" They cite the high crime rate, the horrible sin running rampant, and all sorts of other things as evidence of the need for spiritual renewal. Then they say, "And you're the only one who can save this city."

Who, me? I can't save a soul.

"God told me that you are to come," I've been told multitudes of times. My response has always been, "I'll pray about it, and if God tells me that we should come, we'll be there. Otherwise, you better call someone else." One of the hardest words I've had to learn to say during my forty-plus year career has been *no*.

I quickly discovered that our daily decisions weren't so much between good and bad, but between *good* and *better*. I often had to say, "Your invitation is a good one, but there is a better invitation for me," and it usually involved my wife and three children.

We imposed strict limits on how much we'd perform and travel away from home. That sounds easy. But when your childhood dream was to stand on a stage and sing, you gave that dream up to God, and now, by all appearances it seems He is giving it back, the temptation is to capitalize on the moment and be booked into huge arenas every night of the year. Besides, Gloria and I had left our schoolteaching jobs; if we didn't sing and write songs, our music careers could easily slip away.

Yet somehow, almost instinctively, I knew that *more* was not necessarily better. Gloria and I decided that we'd perform only sixty concerts per year, usually thirty weekends, leaving Sundays open so we could be back home in our own church as much as possible. That decision alone was monumental in maintaining our marriage, our family, and our relationship with God.

A second major decision was our choice to remain in our hometown of Alexandria. Certainly, Nashville and the music business beckoned; it would have been convenient to live and work in Music City, and we were certainly drawn in that direction by people we enjoyed. But Gloria and I felt that there was value in separating our "real lives" from our "stage lives." In a way, we had the best of both worlds. Because of our concert schedule, we were able to travel extensively and take our children with us to a wide variety of places, yet we were always able to come home to the small-town environment where people knew us for who we really were, not "gospel music stars."

A number of years into our careers, Darrell Harris, an executive of Star Song Music, and I were sipping coffee in the Bakery, one of my favorite little coffee shops in Alexandria. Knowing our busy schedule and our many trips back and forth to Nashville, Darrell was intrigued as to why Gloria and I had stayed in the small community.

Just then a grandfatherly-looking man came in and saw me as he shuffled up to the counter. "Mornin', Billy Jim," he said nonchalantly.

I'm not sure that Darrell had ever before heard anyone call me Billy Jim. I looked across the table and said to him, "Everyone needs a place where the people know you well enough to call you by your elementary school name."

That's what Alexandria has always been for us: a place where people have known us well and loved us; a place where we weren't "music biz"; we were family and friends.

Good thing, too, because the discouragement and disillusionment we endured as a result of our "friends" in the music business nearly destroyed us.

NINE

DOWN BUT NOT OUT

"I don't know, Bill. Are you sure you want to do this?" Gloria asked when I got off the phone.

"Why, sure, honey. It will be great. You'll love it."

"But the National Quartet Convention? Why would we want to sing there? We're not even a quartet. Besides, we don't have big-voice singers with big-ending songs."

"Oh, that doesn't matter. The Rambos aren't a quartet, either. But the people love Dottie Rambo's songs, and they'll treat us just the same."

I was flattered by the phone call from J.D. Sumner inviting us to sing at the convention. I had grown up loving southern gospel music and for me, to sing at the convention was like a dream come true. Gloria, on the other hand, grew up in Michigan and had little love for that style of Christian music. From her perspective, the southern gospel performances seemed far too showy, with tenors straining to sing supersonic notes, and bass singers growling notes not too far removed from belches in their attempts to elicit more applause from the crowds.

Funny, when we don't really know people, it's often easy to draw the wrong conclusions from our preconceived notions about them. Certainly the southern gospel field was similar to every other style of music in that it had many good qualities and many fine, upstanding artists. Unfortunately, it also had some fakes, flukes, and flaws. But the counterfeit didn't discount the genuine; the flaws didn't diminish the beauty of the big picture.

Years later, when Gloria got to know many of the southern gospel artists through the *Homecoming* videos, she discovered that many of them were sincere, wonderful, godly people, and she became close friends with most. But in the early years of our career, she wanted nothing to do with southern gospel artists.

It took all of my persuasive powers to convince Gloria that we should accept J.D.'s invitation. After all, Gloria and I had written several songs that had caught on well in southern gospel circles, and a number of groups were singing our songs. I felt confident that the southern gospel music community would accept us. Gloria was extremely reluctant, but she finally gave in and said, "Okay, I'll go."

From the moment we arrived at the Memphis convention, J.D. Sumner and his associates treated us like kings. They could not have been kinder to us. J.D. built us up to his friends and to the audience as though we were the greatest thing since ice cream. He was a smart manager, and he wanted everyone to "hit the ball out of the ballpark" because when they succeeded, he did, too.

We soon discovered, however, that the National Quartet Convention could become extremely competitive, almost a musical "Can You Top This?" At times, it seemed that the focus was on who could get the crowd more excited and on their feet the most throughout the evening. Most of the groups closed with their "big moment," a blow-the-doors-off type of song, usually featuring—as Gloria expected—a high tenor or a gravel-voiced bass singer vibrating the sound system, or both! I understood that. A performance at the convention provided a group with the ideal opportunity to prove themselves to other concert promoters.

J.D. gave us the prime spot on the Saturday night program, and the house was full. At 9:30, the Gaither Trio took the stage.

But the Gaither Trio didn't have any big-moment, blow-out songs. We didn't have a screaming tenor or a booming bass singer. We had Danny's smooth-as-velvet voice and Gloria's readings, and we were three rather nerdy-looking schoolteachers. Nevertheless, we were determined to put our best foot forward. We decided to sing one of our recent favorites, "There's Something About That Name."

Danny began crooning, "Jesus, Jesus, Jesus . . . there's just something about that name. . . ."

I looked out at the audience, and I was totally unprepared for the sight that greeted me. I had never seen the backs of so many heads in my life! I thought that perhaps somebody had called for an intermission and a large number of people in the audience had suddenly decided it was time to go to the rest room. Others looked at us, looked at each other, and shrugged their shoulders as if to say, "What is this?"

The audience wasn't intentionally being rude. After all, the concert began around six o'clock and ran till the wee hours of the morning. Sooner or later, everybody needed to get up and move around a bit. But it seemed that half the audience took a break while we were singing. The fact is, they had no preconditioning for our sort of presentation. Those who stayed, however, genuinely appreciated our music and message. We completed our set and exited the stage as gracefully as possible.

Many people came by our record table later on and expressed kind, wonderful words of encouragement. Several concert promoters came up to me and inquired about booking the Gaither Trio. Al Muusse, who promoted dates in the Grand Rapids area, said, "You are exactly what we have been looking for." I was tremendously excited!

Gloria, on the other hand, was devastated. I chose to look at the glass as half full rather than half empty. Gloria saw it vice versa, and despite the positive feedback we received, she was crushed by seeing the large number of people who had walked out on us. She left the Quartet Convention discouraged, disheartened, and determined never again to subject herself to such foolish, unnecessary humiliation.

I tried to explain to Gloria that competition between the artists was extremely common and could even be a good thing. Over in Fort Worth, for example, gospel concert promoter W. B. Knowlin sponsored a "Battle of Songs," which meant that the singers had to sing harder, faster, louder, higher, or lower than the other groups to win. I'd even heard of "preach-offs" in some churches in which one preacher attempted to outpreach another, all in friendly competition. To Gloria, it was pointless.

Ordinarily, Gloria could relate to almost anyone. She had grown up in a pastor's home and was used to meeting and making friends with all sorts of people, but that weekend at the National Quartet Convention was one of the most miserable of her life. She felt ostracized and rejected by the southern gospel music troupes. It was the continuation of a complicated relationship between Gloria and southern gospel music. The gospel singers respected Gloria for her success as a songwriter (although many of them secretly thought that I was the real lyricist, and I was merely placating my wife by putting her name on the songs), but for many years they regarded Gloria as that "smart Yankee woman," and she regarded them as rude, insolent, arrogant, and ignorant.

I was disappointed that Gloria felt so soundly rejected at the convention, but it was a no-win situation for me. On the one hand I loved Gloria, and on the other, I was still awestruck by many of the big-name gospel quartets, some of whom I'd admired since my childhood. And I thought I could see the good in the southern gospel community. The tension created by my love for Gloria and my love for the music I'd grown up with would not disappear. In fact, it would continue to be the "elephant in the living room" that she and I lived with and had to dance around throughout our marriage. Although we shared a genuine love and passion for each other, we were simply not on the same wavelength when it came to this issue.

After the National Quartet episode, almost by accident we took our music in a different direction, doing what our vocal abilities and performance style permitted us to do. Consequently, over the next twenty years, we developed our own audience, one accustomed to our soft and easy approach to the music. Because our low-key style was still rooted in the simplicity of southern gospel but appealed to a slightly different audience, we met a need that the more raucous music wasn't fulfilling. We were soon busier than ever and drawing large crowds of our own. Some people saw that as the Gaither Trio veering away from southern gospel, but in reality, we were merely doing the only kind of music and program for which we were suited, and in a manner that would allow us to survive on the stage.

For its part, over the next twenty years, the southern gospel community pretty much felt that we had departed the camp

and weren't really part of it. Since we weren't in competition
with them, a lot of groups sang our songs, but we had to accept
the fact that we could not survive on their platforms. Gloria
didn't mind that a bit. She shook the dust off her feet and
moved on. But somewhere deep within me, there was still a
longing to be able to play in that field, and to be accepted in
the company of my heroes.

About this same time, my sister, Mary Ann, went through a
devastating divorce. When I first learned of the impending
breakup of Mary Ann's marriage, it rocked our world. Gaithers
didn't get divorced. Divorce was something awful that happened to other families. I felt utterly helpless to offer any assistance. All I could do was stand by and watch as my sister's life
was shattered.

Against that backdrop, a mere three months after giving
birth to Amy, Gloria and I discovered that she was pregnant
with our third child! We weren't upset that we were going to
have another baby; we just weren't anticipating another little
one so soon! Gloria's body had barely recovered from her last
pregnancy when she again had to endure all the usual stresses,
mood swings, and hormonal upheaval that go along with having a child.

On top of all that, I contracted mononucleosis and was completely drained of energy, enthusiasm, and my usual physical
stamina. I was depleted and down in the dumps most of the
time. I didn't realize that the physical fatigue and the emotional
stress we were experiencing also left us spiritually vulnerable.

The attack came in a way none of us would ever have expected. A close acquaintance, a person that Gloria and I loved
dearly and in whom we had invested a lot of time and energy,
wanted us to become involved in a financial deal that we re-

garded as unwise. He came to our house and tried to persuade us, and he wouldn't take no for an answer. Finally I just had to tell him straight out, "Look, we're not interested."

Gloria and I were shocked at his response. He railed at me, "You're just a phony! You wouldn't believe this Jesus stuff if you weren't making big money at it!"

"What?" I said, taken aback. "What are you talking about?"

No matter what I said, he wouldn't hear of it. He stomped out of our house, slamming the door behind him.

I was devastated. I couldn't believe that this person who knew us so well would impugn our motives. Moreover, as a younger artist, I didn't know how to cope with such unfair criticism as I do now. At that time, it really got to me. In the back of my mind a little voice was saying, "You're a fake. You're a phony, Gaither."

Criticism at almost any other level would not have affected me so severely. Someone could have said, "That's not the greatest singing I've ever heard."

And I'd have said, "You're probably right."

"That's not the greatest song I've ever heard."

"Yes, you're probably right."

"You were trying too hard in that concert that night."

I'd say, "You're probably right."

"There was too much of you out there onstage, and not enough God in it."

And I'd say, "You are probably right."

But when someone criticizes my motives, concerning why I do what I do, that gets my attention like nothing else. I don't like phonies, and I don't like hypocrites, and I don't ever want to be considered one.

Beyond that, my friend's comments were rude and insulting to me as an artist. Any creative person in the arts of any kind would do what he or she does for free. Even those who are successful probably struggled to survive for a long time before they ever made any money from their artistry. To imply that I was motivated merely by money was simply wrong.

Under ordinary circumstances, I may have been able to slough off the accusations with "Okay, if that's the way you feel about it." But I was physically down and emotionally wrung out. The maligning of our motives pushed me over the edge into a pit of depression.

Being an artist, I am prone to battles with depression. I mentioned this to a psychiatrist friend of mine. "I know I've been depressed from time to time," I told my friend. "I've experienced deep depression over certain issues, and this incident was one. But evidently it's never been critical, because I've never had to medicate for it."

The doctor laughed and said, "Don't kid me, Bill. Your pill is your work." I never fully realized the truth of that statement until my friend smacked me in the face with it. I had to admit that *I am a workaholic*; I don't simply enjoy my work, I love to work, and as much as I try to be understanding, compassionate, and aware that I am the person with the problem, I sometimes have difficulty relating to people who don't view their work as passionately.

I justify my workaholic tendencies by telling myself, "Well, it's doing a lot of good for a lot of people. And after all, it is how I make my living." But the truth is, I would do what I do even if I didn't make a dime at it. I love to write songs, I love to create great programs and special worship opportunities, I love to perform onstage, and I love to take the videos I now do and tell inspiring stories with the music and the message. I love to do something that touches people's hearts, especially people who

are going through tough times. Yes, I am guilty. I am a workaholic, and I love being one!

Maybe that's why our friend's accusations concerning my motives bothered me so much. I knew that I was only doing what
I loved.

I still got up and tried to work every day, but the depression
took its toll. I didn't eat well, I slept only sporadically, and I was
a bear to live with much of the time. I often sat in a large chair
in our family room, and analyzed my actions and motives. I've
always felt that in every criticism, even those that are unmer-
ited, there may be a kernel of truth worth considering. We can
always learn from our critics. So I pondered our friend's words
seriously. But as I examined my motives over and over again, I
honestly couldn't find anything that validated our friend's
accusations.

Certainly the Gaither Trio took in money at concerts, and
Gloria and I made money by selling our sheet music, and we
earned royalties from our songs, but making money wasn't what
motivated us. Danny, Gloria, and I worked hard at what we did,
and God had blessed us, so our careers were financially profitable. There was nothing unbiblical about that. Early on, we'd
even met with Dr. Bob Reardon, a good friend of ours from Anderson University, who helped us set financial priorities in
place as well as a generous plan by which we could give money
to causes we wanted to support. We knew that giving and
tithing—giving at least 10 percent of one's income to the
Lord—are built into the fabric of the universe, and we attempted to be faithful managers of the resources God had given
to us. And the more we gave, the more God seemed to dump
into our laps, pressed down, shaken together, and overflowing![1]

Knowing all that, however, did nothing to lift the dark cloud
that had settled over my spirit. Every time I tried to do what my

heart desired to do—to write or perform music—it seemed almost as though a little monkey climbed on my back and whispered in my ears, "Why are you doing this? Do you need some more money?" I knew that money was not even an issue, but for several months, the depression immobilized me. I was down and not able to get back up. I tried to pray, but my words seemed to get stuck on the ceiling. It seemed as though God had suddenly disappeared, or at least, I felt so far away from Him, I couldn't hear His voice in the cacophony around me.

Friends who were aware of my despondency tried to encourage me. "Don't worry, Bill. God is in control."

I believed that, but sometimes those statements just don't mean a lot when you are in the thick of a struggle. Sometimes all you can do is agree with the psalmist's words "Hold on, joy comes in the morning."[2]

Ordinarily I am an eternal optimist, but as I looked at the world during that time, I could find little reason to hope. It seemed the entire world was spinning out of control in a downward spiral. When I looked across the room at Gloria's bulging belly, I fretted even more about bringing another baby into the world.

Nothing could cheer me up: not the news of our album's success, not the kind words of friends such as Bob MacKenzie, Bob Benson, Doug Oldham, or Doug's dad, a man whom I had always respected highly; not the encouragement and heartfelt prayers of my wife.

Ironically, throughout this entire period our lives continued at a breakneck pace. We still traveled and sang and kept up the business. I forced myself to honor our concert commitments, but it was more out of a sense of duty than a passion to perform, or any hopes of being a spiritual blessing to anyone. Yet to the people who heard the Gaither Trio during this dark season, God amazingly used us as a means of encouragement and blessing. Except for our close friends, most people didn't know anything was wrong. I could go out onstage for a few hours, do the concert, and then tumble back into my bunk in our bus until the next performance or until we got back home.

The one thing I could not do was the thing I felt born to do: I couldn't write any songs. Gloria continued to come up with great ideas, catchy phrases, new biblical insights or reminders, but they all washed over me like suds in a car wash. I sat at the piano, plunked around at a few melody lines, but nothing meshed. At times I wanted to bang on the keys with all my might, hoping there might be a song in there somewhere! Nothing came. I felt as though someone were wrapping me in a large, heavy curtain, repeatedly enveloping me in one layer after another, restricting my legs, then my waist, my arms and hands, and soon he would completely cover my head, stifling any air to my lungs. The invisible straitjacket kept getting tighter and tighter around my spirit.

I now know that such feelings of depression are not uncommon in Christian circles, but at the time I thought there must be something unusually wrong with me. I found out later that many devout people deal with depression, especially preachers, teachers, artists, musicians, authors, and other creative types.

Some people might say, "Bill, that's ridiculous! How could you possibly write all those positive, uplifting songs, then find yourself sliding toward depression? You know the Lord; you know the truth; you've read the back of the Book, and you know everything is going to turn out all right. What is there to be depressed about?"

I don't know. All I know is that despite everything I've learned from the Bible, the spiritual truths that have shaped my life, and all that I have experienced with God, something about my emotional makeup makes it easy to get down on myself. Part of the problem, I'm sure, is that I am a perfectionist. I want everything to be right. Maybe that's why the unkind accusations sent me tumbling; in my mind, there must have been some reason why my accuser felt that way. Surely I must have done something wrong, or at least not done everything right.

Regardless, I was trapped in a quagmire and nothing anyone said or did could keep me from sliding deeper into the quicksand of depression. Gloria prayed for me constantly, probably even more than I knew. Then one day, my good friend Dr. Sid Guillen, head of the language arts department at Anderson University, stopped by our house. Sid, Gloria, and I sat down in the family room and talked awhile, then Sid said, "Bill, this is not just discouragement that you are dealing with. This is an attack from the outside."

An attack from the outside? I knew that Sid wasn't the spooky type, or the sort of person who saw demons under every bush. I respected his spiritual discernment. If Sid thought that I was under attack, maybe there was some credence to it.

"Bill, enough of this," Sid said. "Let me pray for you."

Sid prayed a simple, straightforward prayer, commanding the enemy to take his hands off God's property. Then he said amen, gave Gloria and me a big hug, and left. Simple as that. No loud rantings and ravings, no hype or hoopla, no hocus-pocus or spiritual manipulation: just a man who believed God and took Him at His Word.

TEN

"BECAUSE HE LIVES"

It didn't happen over-
night, but in the weeks following Sid Guillen's prayer I began
to feel better. Physically I grew stronger, and emotionally I felt
that I was finally coming out of the dark tunnel in which I'd
been plodding for months.

Although I didn't feel any divine revelations or spiritual sensations, I went back to the piano out of a sheer sense of duty; indeed,
my lifelong work ethic demanded that I get back to work. I began
working at the task of writing songs, getting up each morning and
going to the piano like a farmer goes to the fields, or a factory
worker punches a clock. I knew that our songs depended upon divine direction but at the same time, God expected me to do my
part, too. I decided I wasn't going to sit around and wait for something to pop up in my fertile imagination, but I'd get busy plow-
ing up the fallow ground. When God dropped a seed into my
heart and mind, he'd find soil that was receptive and ready.

Gloria was nearing the end of her pregnancy, and more and

more I felt my optimistic outlook returning. I began toying with a phrase for a song: "Because He lives, I can face tomorrow."

I recalled part of one of my favorite old hymns—"He lives, He lives, Christ Jesus lives today"[1]—and as usual, I wanted to find a way to bring that concept down to the street where people live today. "So what? Why does it matter that He lives?" I'd ask myself. "What difference does it make?" Certainly I would consider all sorts of theological ramifications to the Resurrection, but I kept coming back to the bottom line: "Because He lives, I can face tomorrow."

I went to Gloria and said, "This would be a great hook for a song: 'Because He lives, I can face tomorrow; because He lives, all fear is gone.'" Gloria filled out the lyric: "Because I know He holds the future, life is worth living." We began putting some of those ideas down on paper.

On July 19, Gloria gave birth to a precious baby boy. We named him Benjamin, "most beloved son." Benjy's birth yanked away the last vestiges of the depression in which I had languished for so long. I was thrilled to see our little boy and to sense the elation that comes from knowing that Gloria and I had partnered with God to bring a new human being into the world. As we thought of our own baby, these words poured out of Gloria's heart:

> How sweet to hold our newborn baby,
> And feel the pride and joy he gives;
> But greater still, the calm assurance,
> This child can face uncertain days because He lives.

The chorus to the song rang true in my heart, echoing my

own experience, even as Gloria and I put the finishing touches to the song:

> Because He lives I can face tomorrow;
> Because He lives all fear is gone;
> Because I know He holds the future,
> And life is worth the living just because He lives![2]

The song that came out of that abysmal period in my life became one of the best-known and best-loved songs that Gloria and I have ever written. We recorded it on a new album shortly after Benjamin was born, and before long, it seemed that we were hearing it everywhere. Not since "He Touched Me" had we experienced such phenomenal acceptance of one of our songs.

Although hundreds of artists have recorded it over the years, and thousands of people have sung it, "Because He Lives" has remained our family song. To me it will always have special significance.

A few months after that we were presenting a concert in New Jersey, where we had been cautioned to expect a more "reserved" reception to our music. Much to our surprise, though, the audience was fantastic! They enthusiastically clapped along on some of the up-tempo songs, applauded and cheered, and laughed at my jokes. When the program turned more serious and worshipful, the audience shifted gears right along with us. Whoever had categorized these Easterners as cold, calm, and quiet was wrong!

We closed the program with "Because He Lives" and "The King Is Coming," and the crowd responded ecstatically with thunderous applause, cheering, whistling, throwing things in the air, and calling for more even after we had left the stage. Similar to a rock concert audience, the crowd continued applauding until we sheepishly walked back out for another bow. It would have been simple to have said "Good night, and God bless you!" and walked off the stage with a wave. But as much as we appreciated the enthusiastic applause and accolades, I felt uncomfortable being the focus of such adulation. I felt that we needed to turn the attention back to the Lord, where it belonged.

I slid onto the piano bench, thanked the crowd, and motioned for them to be seated. As I began softly playing and singing the old song "Oh, How I Love Jesus," the crowd quieted down. Gloria and Danny joined in softly and before long so did the audience. Many people shut their eyes and turned their faces heavenward as they sang. Others just bowed their heads. An amazing awareness of God filled the auditorium. It was no longer simply our concert performance; it was a marvelous concert of praise the entire audience offered up to God.

When the Trio got back on the bus later that night, we talked about what had happened, and how we could sense the audience's praise moving away from us to the Lord. "Honey, we need a song that sums up the evening," I said to Gloria, "something that says 'Thank you for being so kind and gracious to us,' but also something that helps make sure the praise goes to God rather than to us."

"Why don't we say exactly that?" said Gloria, already reaching for a yellow notepad on the table. One of our musicians had a guitar aboard the bus, so we began to write:

> We thank you for your kindness; thank you for your love,
> We've been in heavenly places, felt blessings from above.
> We've been sharing all the good things the family can afford,
> Let's just turn our praise toward heaven and praise the Lord.

The chorus begged for audience participation, which was ex-

Music is important in Gloria's and my life, but relationships are what really matter to us—our relationships with God, family, and friends. Here, we are making music with some *Homecoming* friends, Lillie Knauls, Janet Paschal, Lulu Roman, Mark Lowry, J. D. Sumner, Ivan Parker, LaBreeska Hemphill, and Jonathan Pierce.
(Photo by Michael Deitsch, Jr., courtesy Gaither Music Company, Inc.)

I grew up in a typical blue-collar family in rural Indiana. The contented expression on my face at three years of age typifies my childhood.
(Gaither Archives, courtesy Gaither Music Company, Inc.)

My first real suit at age five—just like Grandpa Grover's! I admired and emulated my grandfather and, over the years, I've benefited greatly from his good reputation.
(Gaither Archives, courtesy Gaither Music Company, Inc.)

With my junior high school basketball team, 1949–1950. That's me on the far
left in the back row. I wasn't a great athlete, but I enjoyed the game, and still do!
(Gaither Archives, courtesy Gaither Music Company, Inc.)

Mary Ann, Danny, and me—
the first Gaither Trio.
*(Photo by Tony Lewellyn, courtesy
Gaither Music Company, Inc.)*

During my college years. After I left the Pathfinders, I attended college and majored in English; it was one of the best decisions I ever made.
(Gaither Archives, courtesy Gaither Music Company, Inc.)

Gloria's and my wedding day, December 22, 1962. We were two school-teachers setting out on life's course together. We could never have dreamed where that journey would take us!
(Gaither Archives, courtesy Gaither Music Company, Inc.)

One of the first photos with Gloria as a member of the Gaither Trio. Gloria had no desire to sing onstage. "I'm not a singer," she told me repeatedly. "Yes, but you're pretty, and you can talk on pitch!" I convinced her.
(Photo by Tony Lewellyn, courtesy Gaither Music Company, Inc.)

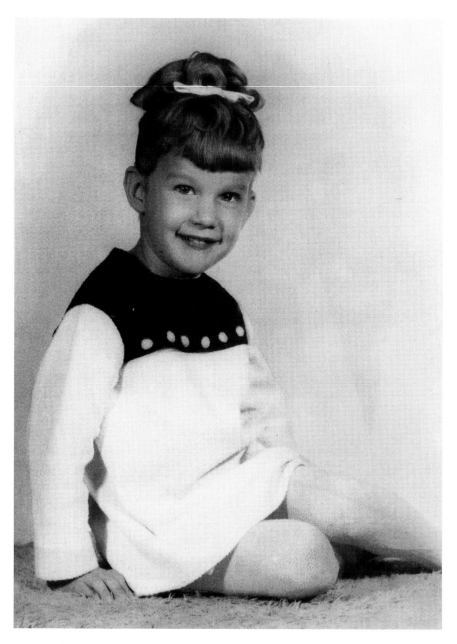

As a child, Suzanne cried every time we took her picture, but she held back her tears long enough for the photographer to snap this special shot, so she could give the photo to me as a Christmas present.
(Gaither Archives, courtesy Gaither Music Company, Inc.)

My first Dove Award, the Gospel Music Association's highest honor, was for
Songwriter of the Year in 1969. The GMA bestowed that award upon me eight
times between 1969 and 1977. I received these two Doves in 1974 for Song of
the Year ("Because He Lives") and as Songwriter of the Year.
(Gaither Archives, courtesy Gaither Music Company, Inc.)

When I first met Gloria we were in our early twenties and she reminded me of movie star Doris Day. Here we are in our "mid-life" years.
(Photo by Tony Lewellyn, courtesy Gaither Music Company, Inc.)

A 1980s Gaither family moment; Suzanne is on the left; that's Amy and Benjamin to the right of Gloria.
(Photo by Mollie Plummer, courtesy Gaither Music Company, Inc.)

My brother Danny, a truly wonderful man and the real singer in the Gaither family! Being estranged from my brother for several years was one of the toughest times of my life, and being reconciled to him was one of God's greatest gifts to me. Danny traveled with us until he lost his battle with lymphoma in 2001, but his velvet voice and his radiant smile can still be enjoyed on several of the *Homecoming* videos.

(Photo by Bill Grine, courtesy Gaither Music Company, Inc.)

We had arranged for a group photo after the "old timers" recording session. Larry Gatlin suggested to Eva Mae LeFevre, "Let's sing something." We did — for the next three hours! Little did we know, it was the beginning of the *Homecoming* series.
(Photo by Ben Pearson, courtesy Gaither Music Company, Inc.)

Doris Akers, composer of "Sweet, Sweet Spirit," and more than five hundred other songs, leads the chorus during a segment of "Old Friends," the third *Homecoming* video, and the first done in our own studio.
(Photo by Dale Pickett, courtesy Gaither Music Company, Inc.)

I first saw Hovie Lister with the Statesmen, at the famous Ryman Auditorium in Nashville. I was just a boy, but I was mesmerized by Hovie's showmanship. In his latter years, though his health was failing, Hovie's spirit remained irrepressible. His death marked the end of an era.

(Gaither Archives, courtesy Gaither Music Company, Inc.)

Cutting up with George Younce and Jake Hess, two of the best friends I've ever known.

(Gaither Archives, courtesy Gaither Music Company, Inc.)

Occasionally, I get to lead a song from the piano during a *Homecoming* taping. What a thrill it is to accompany some of my heroes and friends such as Glen Payne, James Blackwood, Howard and Vestal Goodman, and Faye and Brock Speer.
(Photo by Robin Nelson, courtesy Gaither Music Company, Inc.)

Some of our current *Homecoming* regulars onstage in Sydney, Australia. From left to right: Taylor Mason, Mark Lowry, Guy Penrod, Russ Taff, Charlotte Ritchie, David Phelps, Janet Paschal, Jeff Easter, and me.
(Photo by Russ Harrington, courtesy Gaither Music Company, Inc.)

Mom and Dad, Lela and George Gaither, on Christmas Eve 2001, two days
before Mom passed away.
(Gaither Archives, courtesy Gaither Music Company, Inc.)

In April 2000, ASCAP honored Gloria and me as their Gospel Songwriters of the Century, saying, "The Gaithers are to Christian music what the Beatles are to pop music." Pictured here after the ceremony are: Dan Keen, me, Amy Grant, Vince Gill, Senator (now Attorney General) John Ashcroft, Gloria, Michael W. Smith, and Connie Bradley.

(Gaither Archives, courtesy Gaither Music Company, Inc.)

The Gaither family today.
(*Photo by Dale Pickett, courtesy Gaither Music Company, Inc.*)

Today I still write and perform music, and continue to dream up and produce new video concepts. I spend a large amount of time on the business side, as well as the creative side. One of the great joys of my life is to introduce artists to audiences and then sit back and watch them succeed. One day, when people review my life and career, I hope they will recognize that it has been about much more than the music!

(Photo by Russ Harrington, courtesy Gaither Music Company, Inc.)

of "contemporary" Christian music, much of it linked to the pop-rock culture out of which many of the performers had come after finding a genuine relationship with God. A natural outgrowth of these two phenomena were the "Jesus festivals," a modern version of the old-time camp meetings, only with younger crowds and louder music. Oddly, one of the songs heard frequently at these festivals was written not by some newly converted, youthful longhair, but by a couple of thirty-something conservatives, Gloria and me. The song? "Let's Just Praise the Lord." It was a lesson that we were about to learn in many exciting, new ways: When we stop focusing on ourselves and begin praising God together, barriers come down as the praise goes up. Male and female, black or white, rich or poor . . . none of those things matter when people join together and lift their hands and hearts in praise of Almighty God.

If I had any doubt, I knew that I had left the doldrums far behind me when Gloria and I attended a local high school football game one Friday night. I've always been a sports nut, especially Indiana basketball, but for some reason it struck me that night just how much effort and enthusiasm we, the fans, were exerting on behalf of our teams. And for what? A bunch of guys lugging some pigskin filled with air across some white lines! Oh, of course, they were our local kids, and that gave the game significance on one level, but the fans were going wild over something that, in the long run, really didn't matter that much.

On the way home from the game, Gloria and I talked about the exuberance we'd seen at the ball game. "It's great to see people get that excited about something," I said. "Just think what might happen if we ever got that excited over the Lord."

Gloria was intrigued by the fact that we have the greatest message on earth, and we often sit in church as though we are

actly what we wanted the song to do: lead the audie
praise and worship of God.

> Let's just praise the Lord! Praise the Lord!
> Let's just lift our hands to heaven, and praise the Lord!
> Let's just praise the Lord! Praise the Lord!
> Let's just lift our hands toward heaven and praise the Lo

We began using the song to close our concerts each e
and the difference was astounding. People from all walk
and across the spectrum of Christian denominations su
found themselves immersed in an entirely different t
experience. Rather than singing *about* the greatness o
or His power, love, grace, or some other attribute, the
singing *to* the Lord, exalting Him and extolling Him in
tion and praise. And inevitably, it seemed that God show
as people praised Him.

Two other spiritual and cultural phenomena were t
place in America during the early 1970s. First, an outpouri
the Holy Spirit occurred across the nation, which resulte
many mainstream Protestant and Catholic churches experi
ing God in fresh ways. Many people who were affected by
wave of God's Spirit naturally wanted to express praise bac
God. Although we weren't really aware of it and had little t
with it, "Let's Just Praise the Lord" became almost an antl
for those newly Spirit-filled believers. People were sing
"Let's Just Praise the Lord" in coffeehouses, on college ca
puses, in church fellowship halls, in Full Gospel Businessme
dinner meetings, and a wide variety of places where no one h
heard of the Gaithers!

A second phenomenon took place concomitantly and w
perhaps related to the first: namely, the explosion of new forn

bored stiff. Then we go out into everyday life and talk about all sorts of things that have no eternal significance. We laughed as we thought of all the mundane things we have supposedly serious conversations about: weather, other people, politics, world conflicts, and personal problems. Yet we often ignore the one person who has the solution to all of those situations.

On Saturday morning, as Gloria was making breakfast for the family, I poured a cup of coffee, went in to the family room, and sat down at the piano. I began playing a bouncy little tune that eventually became one of the Gaither Trio's signature songs, "Get All Excited."

The way I figure, if people can get excited for a sporting event, we Christians have every right and indeed every reason to get excited about our Lord!

Ronn Huff, our great producer and music arranger, attended some of our concerts. Ronn was a musical genius, highly respected throughout the music industry. When he heard our songs, and especially the closing with "The King Is Coming," "Because He Lives," and "Let's Just Praise the Lord," he was inspired. An idea clicked in his mind that we'd never even considered. "We ought to put a Gaither type of concert into a musical," he said. Ronn believed that a musical could be tailored around our songs in such a way that churches could perform it.

As he explained his idea to us after a concert one night, we were intrigued and honored, but not exactly sure we could pull off such an adventurous undertaking. Still, we felt it was worth a try. Gloria and I had been writing songs for the church for some time by then, and we were well aware of the pluses and minuses in church music. To think that we might actually be able to contribute a top-quality musical to the church excited us.

We considered how we might be able to create something that churches all over the country could do, something that would allow them to experience the same sort of excitement and participation that we did in our large auditorium and arena concerts.

"Don't worry, I'll help you," Ronn promised.

True to his word, Ronn spent long hours rearranging some of our songs. He worked together with Gloria and me developing the spoken parts in the musical, and then gradually shaped the music and the acting into a cohesive whole, incorporating many of the favorite songs from our "live" concerts. Gloria had been reading a book on the life of Christ, in which one of the characters said, "I don't know anything about Jesus. All I know is that He makes the straightest door in Nazareth. If He makes the door, you can be sure it will be plumb." Gloria began toying with similar ideas, mixing biblical characters with contemporary people who had similar situations or problems to confront. What if Peter told his story about being impulsive, and an impulsive fellow in our church could tell his story, too? What if Mary Magdalene, a known prostitute prior to meeting Jesus, told her account of how Jesus had forgiven her, and a contemporary woman of the world gave her testimony of finding freedom and forgiveness from deep, dark sin as well?

These were the kinds of narrations we created for the characters in *Alleluia*. We also allowed room for choirs to customize the musical to the personalities in their own congregations. For example, we had Doug Oldham tell his story of how God put his family back together, and then we left room in the musical for Doug's local counterpart (and every church had one!) to tell his or her story of a broken home mended by the power of God.

We cast Diane Susek, wife of evangelist Ron Susek, as the young woman who thought life was about being beautiful;

when her life fell apart, she discovered that it wasn't about what she looked like, but what she was like. The characters we created for *Alleluia* were simply models that a choir could personalize and use to bear witness of God's power in their town, in their families, and in their own individual lives. It was a radically different concept for a Christian musical production.

Finally, we were ready. We called some friends and got some singers together, including Dallas Holm, Diane Susek, Bill Grine—a photographer whose scratchy voice was perfect as the apostle Peter's—and went into the recording studio to do a demonstration tape. We planned to package the demo with the songbook, to help choirs catch the vision for how they might be able to use the new musical that we called *Alleluia! A Praise Gathering for Believers.*

When the musical came out, we were amazed at its reception. All sorts of churches began working together to perform the production in their towns. In some communities, churches that had rarely cooperated on *anything* came together en masse to perform the musical and bear witness to what God had done in their lives. As more and more choirs performed the musical, the demand increased for an album of the material. The demo album we produced to promote the musical shot up the sales charts and eventually became the first certified gold record in Christian music, signifying sales of more than half a million copies.

Before long, we started receiving letters from places as far away as Romania. Then we got word that the musical had shown up in China! We received a copy of *Alleluia* as Chinese believers performed it. People all around the world had discovered a vehicle through which they could present the gospel and give testimonies about God's work in their lives.

Years later, I received a copy of an article telling the story of a sociology professor, Wendell Campbell, who had sent a copy of *Alleluia* to former President Richard M. Nixon shortly after his forced resignation following the Watergate scandal. President Nixon had retreated to his home in San Clemente, California, while the public and the press continued to castigate him.

Dr. Campbell doubted that the album would actually get to the outcast president, or that he would listen to it if it did. Nevertheless, he attached a note to it, saying that if the president couldn't play the entire album, he should at least listen to track eight.

One day, three weeks later, while Professor Campbell was teaching his class, an assistant interrupted him with word that he had an important phone call. The professor rushed to his office, picked up the phone, and to his amazement heard the voice of President Nixon's personal secretary informing him that the former president wished to speak with him.

When Mr. Nixon came on the line, he got straight to the point. "Professor, I must ask you not to repeat any part of this conversation for at least ten years."

The sociology professor agreed and Nixon continued. "In an adult lifetime of public service," he said, "I have received thousands of gifts and mementos. None, however, has moved me as deeply or has been as encouraging as the album you so graciously sent. You asked me to listen to band eight. Well, I've played that so many times, that I've about worn out that song on the album."

The song on band eight was "Because He Lives" . . . "Because He lives, I can face tomorrow."[4]

Interesting, isn't it, that the album we produced specifically to help people praise the Lord became one of our best-selling albums. Moreover, *Alleluia* transformed the world of church

ELEVEN

STRESS AND HEARTBREAK

YEARS AGO, I HEARD A STATE-
ment first found in Walt Kelly's comic strip, *Pogo*, that piqued
my interest: "We have met the enemy, and he is us!"

I've used that line many times over the course of my musical
career because, so often, we really are our own worst enemies.
Most of us are tempted to blame something or somebody other
than ourselves when things don't go our way. Some people
blame everything from poor potty training to their upbringing,
their environment, "the system," or even the devil for their lack
of success or other failures. I'm convinced that we don't always
get what we deserve, but we usually get what we expect.

I also believe that far too often our attributing blame to de-
monic entities is a convenient excuse for our own laziness, in-
eptitude, or mistakes. Satan's only power is to tempt; he can't
make a Christian do anything. Nor can the enemy of our souls
destroy what God is doing in and through us unless we let down
our defenses, open the door, and give him an open shot. As

music at the time, crossing musical lines as well as denominational lines.

And to think that it all started out of an awful depression! As my buddy Mark Lowry is fond of saying, "God is good all the time!"

He's good, even when the circumstances in our lives are looking pretty bad . . . which Gloria and I were about to experience again.

of "contemporary" Christian music, much of it linked to the pop-rock culture out of which many of the performers had come after finding a genuine relationship with God. A natural outgrowth of these two phenomena were the "Jesus festivals," a modern version of the old-time camp meetings, only with younger crowds and louder music. Oddly, one of the songs heard frequently at these festivals was written not by some newly converted, youthful longhair, but by a couple of thirty-something conservatives, Gloria and me. The song? "Let's Just Praise the Lord." It was a lesson that we were about to learn in many exciting, new ways: When we stop focusing on ourselves and begin praising God together, barriers come down as the praise goes up. Male and female, black or white, rich or poor . . . none of those things matter when people join together and lift their hands and hearts in praise of Almighty God.

If I had any doubt, I knew that I had left the doldrums far behind me when Gloria and I attended a local high school football game one Friday night. I've always been a sports nut, especially Indiana basketball, but for some reason it struck me that night just how much effort and enthusiasm we, the fans, were exerting on behalf of our teams. And for what? A bunch of guys lugging some pigskin filled with air across some white lines! Oh, of course, they were our local kids, and that gave the game significance on one level, but the fans were going wild over something that, in the long run, really didn't matter that much.

On the way home from the game, Gloria and I talked about the exuberance we'd seen at the ball game. "It's great to see people get that excited about something," I said. "Just think what might happen if we ever got that excited over the Lord."

Gloria was intrigued by the fact that we have the greatest message on earth, and we often sit in church as though we are actly what we wanted the song to do: lead the audience into praise and worship of God.

Let's just praise the Lord! Praise the Lord!
Let's just lift our hands to heaven, and praise the Lord!
Let's just praise the Lord! Praise the Lord!
Let's just lift our hands toward heaven and praise the Lord.[3]

We began using the song to close our concerts each evening, and the difference was astounding. People from all walks of life and across the spectrum of Christian denominations suddenly found themselves immersed in an entirely different type of experience. Rather than singing *about* the greatness of God, or His power, love, grace, or some other attribute, they were singing *to* the Lord, exalting Him and extolling Him in adoration and praise. And inevitably, it seemed that God showed up as people praised Him.

Two other spiritual and cultural phenomena were taking place in America during the early 1970s. First, an outpouring of the Holy Spirit occurred across the nation, which resulted in many mainstream Protestant and Catholic churches experiencing God in fresh ways. Many people who were affected by this wave of God's Spirit naturally wanted to express praise back to God. Although we weren't really aware of it and had little to do with it, "Let's Just Praise the Lord" became almost an anthem for those newly Spirit-filled believers. People were singing "Let's Just Praise the Lord" in coffeehouses, on college campuses, in church fellowship halls, in Full Gospel Businessmen's dinner meetings, and a wide variety of places where no one had heard of the Gaithers!

A second phenomenon took place concomitantly and was perhaps related to the first: namely, the explosion of new forms bored stiff. Then we go out into everyday life and talk about all sorts of things that have no eternal significance. We laughed as we thought of all the mundane things we have supposedly serious conversations about: weather, other people, politics, world conflicts, and personal problems. Yet we often ignore the one person who has the solution to all of those situations.

On Saturday morning, as Gloria was making breakfast for the family, I poured a cup of coffee, went in to the family room, and sat down at the piano. I began playing a bouncy little tune that eventually became one of the Gaither Trio's signature songs, "Get All Excited."

The way I figure, if people can get excited for a sporting event, we Christians have every right and indeed every reason to get excited about our Lord!

Ronn Huff, our great producer and music arranger, attended some of our concerts. Ronn was a musical genius, highly respected throughout the music industry. When he heard our songs, and especially the closing with "The King Is Coming," "Because He Lives," and "Let's Just Praise the Lord," he was inspired. An idea clicked in his mind that we'd never even considered. "We ought to put a Gaither type of concert into a musical," he said. Ronn believed that a musical could be tailored around our songs in such a way that churches could perform it.

As he explained his idea to us after a concert one night, we were intrigued and honored, but not exactly sure we could pull off such an adventurous undertaking. Still, we felt it was worth a try. Gloria and I had been writing songs for the church for some time by then, and we were well aware of the pluses and minuses in church music. To think that we might actually be able to contribute a top-quality musical to the church excited us.

We considered how we might be able to create something that churches all over the country could do, something that would allow them to experience the same sort of excitement and participation that we did in our large auditorium and arena concerts.

"Don't worry, I'll help you," Ronn promised.

True to his word, Ronn spent long hours rearranging some of our songs. He worked together with Gloria and me developing the spoken parts in the musical, and then gradually shaped the music and the acting into a cohesive whole, incorporating many of the favorite songs from our "live" concerts. Gloria had been reading a book on the life of Christ, in which one of the characters said, "I don't know anything about Jesus. All I know is that He makes the straightest door in Nazareth. If He makes the door, you can be sure it will be plumb." Gloria began toying with similar ideas, mixing biblical characters with contemporary people who had similar situations or problems to confront. What if Peter told his story about being impulsive, and an impulsive fellow in our church could tell his story, too? What if Mary Magdalene, a known prostitute prior to meeting Jesus, told her account of how Jesus had forgiven her, and a contemporary woman of the world gave her testimony of finding freedom and forgiveness from deep, dark sin as well?

These were the kinds of narrations we created for the characters in *Alleluia*. We also allowed room for choirs to customize the musical to the personalities in their own congregations. For example, we had Doug Oldham tell his story of how God put his family back together, and then we left room in the musical for Doug's local counterpart (and every church had one!) to tell his or her story of a broken home mended by the power of God.

We cast Diane Susek, wife of evangelist Ron Susek, as the young woman who thought life was about being beautiful;

when her life fell apart, she discovered that it wasn't about what she looked like, but what she was like. The characters we created for *Alleluia* were simply models that a choir could personalize and use to bear witness of God's power in their town, in their families, and in their own individual lives. It was a radically different concept for a Christian musical production.

Finally, we were ready. We called some friends and got some singers together, including Dallas Holm, Diane Susek, Bill Grine—a photographer whose scratchy voice was perfect as the apostle Peter's—and went into the recording studio to do a demonstration tape. We planned to package the demo with the songbook, to help choirs catch the vision for how they might be able to use the new musical that we called *Alleluia! A Praise Gathering for Believers*.

When the musical came out, we were amazed at its reception. All sorts of churches began working together to perform the production in their towns. In some communities, churches that had rarely cooperated on *anything* came together en masse to perform the musical and bear witness to what God had done in their lives. As more and more choirs performed the musical, the demand increased for an album of the material. The demo album we produced to promote the musical shot up the sales charts and eventually became the first certified gold record in Christian music, signifying sales of more than half a million copies.

Before long, we started receiving letters from places as far away as Romania. Then we got word that the musical had shown up in China! We received a copy of *Alleluia* as Chinese believers performed it. People all around the world had discovered a vehicle through which they could present the gospel and give testimonies about God's work in their lives.

Years later, I received a copy of an article telling the story of a sociology professor, Wendell Campbell, who had sent a copy of *Alleluia* to former President Richard M. Nixon shortly after his forced resignation following the Watergate scandal. President Nixon had retreated to his home in San Clemente, California, while the public and the press continued to castigate him.

Dr. Campbell doubted that the album would actually get to the outcast president, or that he would listen to it if it did. Nevertheless, he attached a note to it, saying that if the president couldn't play the entire album, he should at least listen to track eight.

One day, three weeks later, while Professor Campbell was teaching his class, an assistant interrupted him with word that he had an important phone call. The professor rushed to his office, picked up the phone, and to his amazement heard the voice of President Nixon's personal secretary informing him that the former president wished to speak with him.

When Mr. Nixon came on the line, he got straight to the point. "Professor, I must ask you not to repeat any part of this conversation for at least ten years."

The sociology professor agreed and Nixon continued. "In an adult lifetime of public service," he said, "I have received thousands of gifts and mementos. None, however, has moved me as deeply or has been as encouraging as the album you so graciously sent. You asked me to listen to band eight. Well, I've played that so many times, that I've about worn out that song on the album."

The song on band eight was "Because He Lives" . . . "Because He lives, I can face tomorrow."[4]

Interesting, isn't it, that the album we produced specifically to help people praise the Lord became one of our best-selling albums. Moreover, *Alleluia* transformed the world of church much as Satan attempts to interfere or cause trouble among God's people, he is a defeated foe, and he knows it! I truly believe that greater is He who is in me than he who is in the world.[1]

Certainly there are times in life when events take you by surprise, when things happen over which you have no control. You wish that you could snap your fingers and magically change the circumstances, but you can't.

In those times, we simply have to do what we believe is right based on biblical principles. After that, we can only gulp hard, hold our tongues, and turn the situation over to God. Granted, that's especially difficult to do when people don't understand all the details, and you can't really explain matters to them; or they misconstrue your motives even when you attempt to explain. Gloria and I encountered such a situation that threatened to destroy our careers as well as our reputations, and there was little we could do to defend ourselves.

In the mid-1970s and early 1980s, the American Society of Authors, Composers, and Publishers (ASCAP) took a keen interest in the burgeoning Christian music business, especially noting that some Christian radio and television stations were not paying the appropriate fees for using songs ASCAP licensed. To be fair, the majority of Christian stations were complying with the rules and paying the fees just as most secular stations do.

At that time, either Broadcast Music Incorporated (BMI) or ASCAP licensed most recently published gospel songs. A third licensing agency, SESAC, has grown up in more recent years. A songwriter doesn't have to place his or her songs with a licensing agency, but with so many sources using music nowadays, it helps. Here's how the system works: The licensing agencies charge a blanket fee to radio and television (and now, Internet sources) all over the world, granting permission to these outlets to use any of the material in the licensing agency's catalog during the term of the license. The agency then monitors radio, television, and Internet transmissions, noting when songs in their catalog are performed. When a song is aired, the agency credits points to the writer and publisher of the song. Eventually, these points translate into real money, and money received from airplay can become a significant source of income for many professional songwriters and their publishers.

I am so thankful to live in a country where a musician or songwriter is able to make a living doing what he or she loves. Throughout history and in many countries yet today, artists couldn't exist without government subsidies or some other sort of patronage system. Thanks to the entrepreneurial spirit of America, we developed a way that songwriters and publishers can support themselves through the selling of their music. Christian songwriters have as much right to derive income from their craft as their non-Christian counterparts do.

At one time, people making their living in other fields wrote the majority of our Christian music. Wonderful writers such as Stuart Hamblen were also recording artists; Ira Stanfield, another early songwriter, pastored a church, and that was his primary means of support. Certainly, many great recording artists are great songwriters as well. Take Paul McCartney, Lionel Richie, and Paul Simon, who have written much of the material they have recorded throughout their careers. The same could be said for Michael W. Smith, Twila Paris, or Steven Curtis Chapman. Many pastors also communicate through songwriting, such as Dr. Jack Hayford, who wrote "Majesty," a song destined to be a classic.

In recent years, however, we've seen a striking change in Christian songwriting circles. Nowadays people who make their livings strictly from writing are composing much of our Christian music. Everything else they do flows from that primary fountain.

Mosie Lister was my model in this regard. Mosie was one of the first great Christian songwriters who wrote exclusively as his means of supporting himself and his family. Mosie declared, "I am going to make a living writing and publishing my songs." And he did!

Unfortunately, until recently many fellow Christians who wouldn't expect a skilled Christian auto mechanic to constantly give away his services, or a Christian carpenter, dentist, or doctor to work for free, have disregarded the fact that Christians who create "intellectual properties," such as songs, poems, books, designs, or computer programs, receive their income from these sources. Just because a song contains biblically based content or themes doesn't mean the person who owns the copyright should not be compensated when the "product" is used in public.

Part of the problem is that many people regard songwriting as a hobby rather than a skill, let alone a career. Nobody is more aware of that than I am, hailing as I do from a small blue-collar town. In our community, it was almost a given that most males would do some sort of apprenticeship to learn how to be a tool-and-die maker. When I hadn't done so by my sophomore or junior year of school, my relatives began asking my parents, "What's Bill going to do?"

"Well, he likes music," my dad would reply.

"Yes, that's great. But what's he going to do for a living?"

After more than forty years of making my living in music, primarily as a songwriter, I find those questions still common. One day not long ago, Dad was at a feed store in a nearby town to get some feed for his cows. The owner of the store said to

Dad, "Now, I see Bill on the weekend doing those television programs. What does he do through the week?"

Similarly, Glen Payne, the famous lead singer for the Cathedrals, had an illustrious career singing gospel music throughout his seventy-three years. Glen told me the story of an old friend of his father's in Rockwall, Texas, who at the height of Glen's career asked his dad, "Hey, Harry, that oldest boy of yours—did he ever get a real job, or is he still singing?"

Comments such as these sum up the crux of the problem that ASCAP faced. Many people simply don't understand that writing, publishing, and performing gospel songs is a source of income for many people.

On the other hand, many Christian radio and television stations began as nonprofit organizations to spread the gospel, and some station owners did not feel that they should have to pay a fee to use Christian music on their airwaves. "Talk radio" station owners, many of whom aired almost a nine-to-one ratio of preaching, teaching, and conversation compared to a small portion of music, were especially upset. In all fairness, they had reason to be. At that time there was no sliding scale in place for stations that aired a large percentage of music compared to those who aired just a little. Consequently, prior to ASCAP and BMI's insistence, most religious stations considered themselves exempt from these usage fees.

Obviously this was illogical and unfair to the owners of the song copyrights, but many religious broadcasters felt it was okay to use copyrighted material without paying for it because "it was for the ministry."

Of course, if this logic were applied universally, pastors would not be paid. Nor would church custodians, or teachers at Christian schools. Granted, it is sometimes difficult to think of a song as a piece of property in the same sense as the seats or the lights in a church. Yet just as those seats and lights required somebody's labor, the songs we sing in our services involved somebody's labor as well, even though the end product is often used in ministry.

ASCAP wasn't necessarily interested in ministry; the licensing group was primarily concerned about receiving fair compensation for its writers and publishers. Ironically, the fees ASCAP collected often allowed Christian songwriters to pursue their work—and their ministries—and provided the means by which they could support their families without being a drain on the government or the church.

ASCAP pressed the stations for payment. Once confronted with the issue, most Christian radio and television stations recognized what was right and acquiesced. Although they weren't happy to have to pay for material that they had previously used for free, they understood the fairness issue and regarded the fee as simply a cost of doing business. About fifty stations, however, refused to comply.

ASCAP repeatedly warned the Christian stations that they were required to pay a blanket fee to use its enormous catalog of songs. When the stations continued to balk, the licensing organization filed a class-action type suit on behalf of all its copyright owners against the offenders. Listed as parties in the suit were many of the leading Christian music publishing companies of the day, representing writers such as Andrae' Crouch, Dottie Rambo, George Beverly Shea, and a host of other sincere Christian songwriters. Most of the copyrights, however, were held in company names such as Manna Music, Bug and Bear Music, Tree Publishing, and other innocuous-sounding and individual-shielding monikers. The copyrights to Gloria's and my songs were in my name, William J. Gaither. As such, listed there along with all the other publishers on the lawsuit against the Christian stations was my name for all to see.

Almost instantly word got out among the Christian media: "Bill Gaither is suing Christian radio and television!"

In the broadest sense, that was true, since ASCAP licensed our songs, and many Christian radio and television programs frequently aired our songs around the country. But in reality, I was only one member of a large organization whose business it was to represent thousands of songwriters and publishers, and collect the fees for use of their intellectual properties.

Complicating matters further was erosion of copyright concerns: if we gave up our right to earn a living by our music being played on the air, soon further chipping away of the songwriters' royalties would be inevitable. Our choice was either to break ties with ASCAP (or any other licensing organization) and allow the miscreant stations to avoid payment to us and our colleagues, or to be included in a lawsuit against fellow brothers and sisters in Christ. Talk about a rock and a hard place!

Many stations on the air in the early 1980s literally informed their listeners that they could no longer play Gaither music or songs we had written because Bill Gaither was suing their station! Derogatory pamphlets were distributed to churches and other Christian groups that advertised on Christian radio and television stations, decrying the fact that those greedy Gaithers were trying to keep the gospel from going forward because of money! It was ludicrous, but there was little that Gloria or I could do to defuse the nasty things that were being said about us.

A few station managers who understood the awkwardness of our dilemma tried to make a deal with our music company apart from ASCAP. That seemed unethical to me, and I didn't feel right about entering into such an agreement. After all, I had chosen to be a member of ASCAP, and the organization had served me well for the most part, as it had (and does) for most other Christian songwriters. To work out a deal apart from the agency would be cheating it.

One night in the midst of this mess, Gloria and I got down on our knees beside our bed to pray. "God, we've tried to be as honest with this thing as we know how to be. We don't know what to do. We know your Word says it isn't good to be in-volved in a lawsuit against fellow Christians, but what else can we do? If we withdraw, we will jeopardize not only our situation but many other songwriters' ability to make a living."

I wish I could tell you that a specific word of direction came from God as a result of that prayer, but none did. All we could do was to continue to believe that God would work out all things for good, to those who loved Him and were called ac-cording to His purpose.[2] That included us . . . and the stations named in the lawsuit.

Eventually, the suit was settled, with ASCAP's regulations upheld. Both sides came to agreeable terms allowing the writers and publishers the opportunity to make their livings creating music, and an equitable, sliding scale was established for radio stations airing more or less music. A radio or television station owner doesn't have to use songs from the ASCAP, BMI, or SESAC catalogs, but if he or she does, the stations must pay the licensing fees. Today, all concerned—writers, publishers, and users of recorded music—feel that the system is as fair as it can possibly be without attempting to police every single perfor-mance throughout the world.

Gloria and I lost some friends over the issue, but we did what we believed to be right. The good news was that neither the writers nor the radio and television companies harbored harsh feelings. In fact, a number of years later, our company entered into a business relationship with one of the major players in the lawsuit. Life is far too short to carry grudges. When a representative of the media conglomerate's CEO and I met to discuss doing business, he reminded me of his company's role in the ASCAP suit. "My boss was afraid that you wouldn't want to do business with us now because of what happened nearly twenty years ago."

I smiled and said, "Tell him that I have a bad memory."

The ASCAP lawsuit was one of those awkward situations that caused people to ask, "Okay, how should I as a Christian handle such a matter?"

But if we thought that dilemma was a tough one, we soon looked at it as a piece of cake compared to what was coming next.

I'm not quite sure how or when it happened, but early in my music career, I came to grips with the fact that I don't live in a "black and white" world, a world in which every question had one definitive, correct answer, and all others were wrong; a world reminiscent of the old Western movies in which there were "good guys" wearing white hats, and "bad guys" wearing black hats.

Sometimes I wish that I lived in such a world. At times I tried to believe that I did, but then reality would smack me upside the head. I'd be reminded once again that there really were shades of gray to many issues and questions that I had tried to squeeze into my "black" or "white" categories.

If all moral issues were clearly right or wrong with easy, clear-cut answers on what to do and how to do it, our job would be simple: Obey. Do what is right. But I've discovered that not every issue falls neatly into a black or white category, and there are usually good people on all sides of most questions.

Don't misunderstand: I believe in absolute truth. I believe the Bible is that absolute truth on which I can build my life, make my decisions, and place my hope. When the Bible says something is right or wrong, I take that as truth. I don't quibble over semantics or try to find some way to circumvent the obvious. But I also recognize the difference between unalterable biblical principles and my own spiritual convictions.

In the mid-1970s, many Christians regarded divorce as a black-or-white issue: somebody had to be very right and somebody had to be horrifically wrong. Some Christians regarded the "big D" almost as the "unpardonable sin," especially divorce between two Christians. Gloria and I may have shared that opinion, too, had not some of our friends and family members divorced. We realized firsthand that divorce happens sometimes even to good people. That doesn't make it right; it doesn't make it easy. But as a realist, I had to face the truth that even sincere Christians are not immune from the stresses and strains that tear at every marriage.

My sister, Mary Ann, was the first of several loved ones whose marriages broke up. We grieved over the marriage failures of our family members and friends and refused to hide the pain from our children, even if we could. Instead, we faced the fractured relationships around us head-on, attempting to demonstrate attitudes of understanding and compassion. At the same time, we affirmed the biblical standard of marriage—that it is meant to be a commitment of a lifetime—and encouraged our kids to make wise choices in their dating lives and in choosing mates.

We also saw these collapsed relationships as opportunities to remind our family members about the grace of God. We emphasized that no matter how the divorce happened, God hated it, but He didn't hate the people involved. He loved them no matter what. If they would allow Him, He could forgive them, bless them, and rebuild their lives. In Mary Ann's case, that's exactly what happened. Several years later, Mary Ann married Donny Addison, a wonderful man who became dear to our family, and they have lived happily and committed to each other. As tough as the divorce was, God still brought good out of it.

Gloria and I have always tried to be understanding of those who are going through marriage difficulties without compromising our own beliefs. I'm not sure we've always handled things correctly, especially when it involved my own brother.

I'd known for a while that Danny had been having troubles in his marriage. I didn't know all the details, and I didn't need to. Danny didn't want a divorce and would have done almost anything to prevent it. He told me time and again, "Bill, I'm just trying to keep my family together." Danny was a loving, kind, sweet, gentle spirit, and he didn't want to hurt anyone, especially his children. Consequently, he continued to live in a marriage that almost everyone around him regarded as unhealthy. That was typical of Danny. He was always willing to sacrifice his own happiness for the good of others. Gloria had often said, "I could never have asked for a better brother-in-law than Danny."

Danny knew that his failing marriage would not only bring disrepute to him, but to the Trio as well. And that was the last thing he wanted to happen. He went the second mile and beyond, hoping that the situation at home would improve. It didn't. The stress of trying to keep his family together was taking a toll on Danny personally and was beginning to affect our work as the Gaither Trio.

One day he came into the office, and I could tell that he was distraught. I said, "Danny, we can't continue like this. We need to talk about what's going on in your home. We have a house divided here. Maybe you need to take some time off to sort through the issues in your marriage and resolve this thing one way or the other."

I couldn't imagine Danny not singing. He and I had grown up singing together, and after all those years, he was still one of the best vocalists I'd ever heard. More importantly, I knew Danny's heart's desire was to serve God. He was keenly aware that something more than music was taking place in our concerts. He was an integral part of everything we did. Furthermore, it was Danny who actually pushed us to develop Pinebrook, our own recording studios in Alexandria. He loved working in the studio, working on the bus, and just about anything else that required technical know-how.

That day in the office, we talked frankly about what Danny was going to do. I knew that his choices weren't easy and the possible ramifications for the Gaither Trio could be severe.

Danny was never a mean-spirited, belligerent person, and even though we didn't agree on how to remedy the situation, he remained loving and kind, and sensitive to the bigger picture. With tears in his eyes, Danny responded, "Bill, I wouldn't want to do anything that would hurt what we have built up in the last fifteen years. If we have to do this, okay. Fine." Danny turned and left our office.

As I watched my brother walk out the door that day, I knew that life in the months ahead was going to be tough for all of us. I sought the counsel of some close pastor friends and a Christian attorney who understood the issues involved, and I came to the conclusion that our most reasonable option was to dissolve the Gaither Trio. We had done that once before, back in the early days of our career, and I had gone to work directing the church choir. This time, I didn't know what I was going to do.

Over the next months, our family went through a traumatic time, and we all experienced a great deal of hurt and misunderstanding. Living extremely public lives in a small town, as we did, it wasn't surprising that people began to talk . . . and take sides. Had people close to us in our community taken a vote, I would have lost hands down.

Somewhere in the ugliness that followed, I lost my brother. Danny left the Trio, and more importantly, he left the unconditional love of our larger, extended family. As much as Gloria and I expressed to Danny that we would always be there for him, Danny and I became estranged from one another. About three months after Danny left us, he set out on a solo singing career. We still talked when we'd see each other in town, and I tried to keep in touch with him, but it just wasn't the same. There were thick, high, invisible walls between us.

We were so heartsick over Danny's departure, Gloria and I were ready to quit singing ourselves and go back to teaching school. For several months, we did next to nothing. We took some time off and tried to reevaluate, looking squarely and realistically at our options. How could we help anyone else when we couldn't even help keep our own family together?

About that time, Bob MacKenzie came to me and said, "Bill, I don't think it's right for you to give up the platform God has given you simply because of the problems you and the family have experienced. Why don't you try to reestablish your platform and do something else? You and Gloria are still writing good songs, saying good things, and you shouldn't just walk away from that. But you need a platform from which you can present those ideas to people."

In response to Mac's encouragement, Gloria and I reorganized the Gaither Trio and invited Gary McSpadden to join the group. We decided to do a Praise Gathering event in Indianapolis. I'll mention more about that later, but for now, it's important to know that we were at our lowest point, ready to quit.

We didn't realize that we were on the verge of another explosive phase in our career. It really is darkest right before the dawn.

In the meantime, Danny and I didn't communicate very well. I was probably more of a jerk than he was on any given day. When we saw each other at family functions—those that he'd attend—our conversations were stilted, short, and terse. Neither of us wanted it to be that way, yet we felt powerless to bridge the chasm between us.

We went on like that for about five years. Then one Christmas, Danny and his family returned to our Christmas gathering at Mom and Dad's home. Slowly I sensed the walls coming down between us, and the laughter and joy we had always known began to come back. It didn't happen overnight. There was no crisis point at which he and I sat down and said, "You were right; I was wrong." There were no overwhelming emotional moments in which we broke down in tears, apologized to one another, and asked for forgiveness, even though we both felt that. Like most brothers, we simply didn't communicate that way. Most men don't. But when Danny poked me in the arm, or I slapped him on the back, we knew our relationship was back where it had been previously, and we were expressing something real rather than something contrived.

Danny maintained his solo ministry for about ten years, but eventually he and his wife divorced. Shortly after that, in 1986, Danny, Gloria, and I reunited on the road, although not on the stage. Unfortunately, by the time Danny came back, he had developed throat problems; his voice was shot. He could still speak and sing in a soft, raspy tone, but he couldn't sing professionally anymore.

Gloria and I were disappointed that Danny could no longer sing, but we wanted him to be a part of what we were doing nonetheless. I asked Danny if he'd consider rejoining the family business as our bus driver and mechanic. I said, "Come work with us, Danny. You need a job, and we need a bus driver, and you've always been good with engines."

Danny loved the idea. To him, working on the bus was not a demeaning job; it was a joy, and he cared for our vehicle as though it were his baby. Amazingly, when Danny returned, our relationship was better than it had ever been before. He loved me and I loved him, and we had a good time together. When we were on the road, we started going to breakfast like we used to do, at truck stops along the interstate highway. Often we'd sit and drink coffee and tell stories and just laugh and joke together. Danny had the best sense of humor of anyone I've ever known. He'd laugh uproariously, with abandon, until tears nearly ran down his face.

It was like old times. Danny had come back to us a broken person, but in truth, I needed him as much or more than he needed me. I had missed my brother terribly and was glad we were back together.

Danny was happy, too. Every once in a while, though, I'd glance at Danny checking the oil or wiping the dust off our motor coach, and the irony was almost too much for me. While other singers, many of whom were less-talented vocalists than Danny had been, went inside the concert hall to sing, the fellow who formerly had a better voice than most of us went to catch some shut-eye so he could drive us up the road to the next concert venue. In some ways it was heartrending, but I was glad, at least, to have my brother back.

While I am certainly not a marriage counselor, I've been around the music industry long enough to realize that many marriages in our circles are strained. The situation we faced in our family was no different from what many Christian music artists are dealing with today, regardless of the label they put on their music. It is difficult for some people to maintain a thriving marriage relationship and a thriving career. For some, it is tough to bring together their lives onstage, their spoken words and the songs they sing, with the way they live out their faith at home. This has been a perennial problem, and it takes a lot of grace and understanding on the part of everyone involved to deal with it.

Sadly, sometimes those on the sidelines looking on from afar, or those for whom life is going well, are quick to sit in self-righteous judgment on those who are going through the dark night of despair. That attitude does nothing to help people who are struggling with their marriages and often does a great deal of damage. I learned through Danny's situation that I dared not throw rocks at anyone or condemn someone for his actions until I had empathized with him and "walked in his shoes."

Over the years, Gloria and I have sometimes been criticized for being "too soft on sin," too willing to forgive people who have made mistakes in their lives. Maybe we have been too emotionally involved with our friends or family members to see things clearly. I don't know. But God knows our hearts and our motives. We simply refuse to give up on someone we love. That sort of love can be risky to your career and reputation, but it's a risk worth taking.

Danny drove our bus for more than ten years, and during that time, he was a constant cheerleader and an encourager. In the 1990s, when we started recording the *Homecoming* videos, Danny came along with us and often sat in with the "choir." People loved to see him, and he loved being a part of the music again.

In 1991, Danny met a delightfully sweet woman by the name

of Vonnie Furnish. Vonnie loved Danny, and all of our family members fell in love with her. They dated for several years before marrying. Vonnie brought so much joy to Danny's life, and we will forever be grateful to her.

Danny was always extremely strong physically; he had the Hartwell frame in our family, and he could outwork me on the farm any day. He kept himself in good physical condition, too, and was anything but a wimp when it came to enduring pain. That's one reason we were concerned when he mentioned a chronic pain emanating from a slight lump in his shoulder.

Finally in 1996 he consented to see his doctor. "I think you ought to have a biopsy done on that area," his doctor told him. "It looks like lymphoma to me, but I'm not certain."

Danny was his usual optimistic self. "Aw, it's probably not," he said to the doctor. "It's probably just a strain of some kind."

"Okay, let's wait till the biopsy report comes back."

I went with Danny to the hospital to have the biopsy done the Monday before Thanksgiving. The next day I was working with Larry Gatlin in our studio, doing some vocal fixes on a video project we had done on the Gatlins. Larry was with me when the call came from Mary Ann. "It's lymphoma, Bill," she said quietly. "Cancer."

"What are they going to do?" I asked, almost too stunned to speak.

"Danny and Vonnie are going to meet with the oncologists next week to begin chemotherapy treatment."

I put down the phone and muttered, "Oh, brother." I relayed the report to Larry and just stood there, trembling. Larry hugged me and said, "Bill, this is not good news, but we are part of the human race. You've got the Lord, and you have us and a lot of good friends, and we'll help you through it."

Two days later, Gloria and I hosted the family and extended

family for Thanksgiving dinner in our home, just as we had for thirty-eight years. For more than twenty years, Gloria had maintained a family tradition of passing around a basket and having each person place a kernel of corn in the basket as he or she related at least one thing for which he or she was thankful over the past year.

This year, as we went around the room, it was an emotional time for all of us. When Danny's turn came, he valiantly attempted to be strong. "Well, I'm thankful for Vonnie . . . and I'm thankful for a lot of good things in my life." Then Danny paused and said, "But right now, I feel a little bit like the old farmer who had been rained on, and his wheat had been ruined. Then he had a bad winter and lost a couple of cows; then the barn burned down in the springtime, and a bunch of other bad things happened. The old farmer said, 'I still believe in the Lord, but on a given day, I think He does about as much damage as He does good!'"

We all laughed at the story, and although we appreciated Danny's attempt to be upbeat and joke in the face of cancer, it didn't change the reality of the situation. Unless God undertook in some supernatural way, it was possible that Danny wouldn't be with us for many more Thanksgivings.

Danny had incredible faith and he put his faith to work for himself and for others. He stayed active in his local church, attending services every time the doors were open, serving on the board, and inspiring others with his attitude and courage. Occasionally, he came along to a *Homecoming* concert and sang along with the chorus. He was always such an inspiration, and his appearance at the concerts was an emotional experience for us and many of our friends.

For the next six years, Danny and our entire family rode an emotional roller coaster. Anyone who has dealt with cancer knows what a wrenching experience that can be. On any given day, you think and believe that the chemo has done its work, and the cancer is gone. But then it comes roaring back again.

Danny fought hard against the disease, doing the chemo, trying some natural treatments, and considering every reasonable medication and potential cure anyone suggested. He wanted to live so much! Despite Danny's undaunted efforts, his condition continued to deteriorate to the point that his oncologist said, "We can't do anything else for him. But I've never seen such a spirited fighter in my life."

Like many of our friends and everyone in our family, I had been praying for Danny since the first day we learned the news of the lymphoma. I prayed often that God would perform a miracle on my brother's behalf, that God would heal his body. But Danny's condition continued to worsen. One night at a concert in Kentucky, our dear friend Vestal Goodman brought a sweet black woman named Sister Willodeen to see me. Sister Willodeen was a good friend of Vestal's and a powerful prayer warrior. She had prayed for Vestal once when all the doctors had given up on her . . . and Vestal had gotten well!

Vestal asked, "Bill, would you mind if we prayed with you for a miracle on Danny's behalf?"

"Please do," I said softly. "Please do."

The two women prayed . . . I mean they *prayed*! I knew that if God was going to hear anyone's prayer and respond to faith, He'd certainly have to consider theirs. But it was not to be. Danny's condition remained the same. In fact, shortly thereafter, he took a nosedive for the worse.

My own faith was weak and vacillating. I called Gloria from the road and said, "You know, I think I've been the problem. Maybe I am the reason Danny has not been healed."

"What? What are you talking about, Bill?"

"Christ couldn't do miracles in the face of unbelief—and I'm the guilty one!"

At night, alone by my bed, I prayed and repeatedly had to confess my lack of faith to God. "Please, God, help my unbelief," I prayed.

The words of a song Gloria and I had written came to mind. It is one of my favorite songs that we have ever written, and we still sing it a lot.

> I believe, help Thou my unbelief.
> I take the finite risk of trusting,
> Like a child.[3]

If ever I could relate to the message of that song, it was now.

I've always been the quintessential optimist, believing the best in people, in business, and in most areas of everyday life. But when it comes to matters of faith, I've had to wrestle with my skepticism. I was born a doubter and I remained a bit that way all my life. I believed that God had done miracles in the lives of other people; I believed that He *could* perform miracles in my life and in those of my family members. But nothing like that had ever happened to me. It was just plain old hard work, and keep on keeping on. That old sign on our kitchen wall as I was growing up came back to mind so many times: "Pray for rain, but keep hoeing."

We flew Danny and Vonnie out to the cancer center at the University of Nebraska at Omaha. We left them standing there at the air service, waving as we pulled away and took off, and I felt that same awful feeling a parent feels when he or she leaves children behind at summer camp. You know it is good for them, but oh, how it hurts to say good-bye.

The up-and-down emotions that we all felt during those

years were just tough. Encouragement. Discouragement. Hope. Despair. Back and forth. *He's getting better! He's slipping again.*

At Christmas 2001, Danny tried his best to remain positive. He laughed and joked as always. He leaned his head back and closed his eyes as we sang Christmas carols as we had so many times before. Earlier than usual, Danny leaned over to Vonnie and said, "We probably better go home, Hon." He was just too tired to stay with us any longer.

Shortly after that he went into the hospital, where he remained in bed for the next four months. He got out of the hospital long enough to come to a videotaping at the Indiana Roof, where we recorded "Freedom Band." It was obvious to all of us that Danny's body was slipping away, but his spirit was free. Following the taping, Danny returned to the hospital, but his heart was already with the Lord.

A buddy of Danny's and mine went with me to visit with him one afternoon just before I headed for Mobile, Alabama, to tape a special George Younce video. When our friend and I entered the room, Danny raised up on his bed, leaning on his elbow, and smiled. It was the first time Danny had recognized anyone in more than two days.

He pointed at us as if to say, "You two characters!" Then he said simply, "Beaumont, Texas!" I couldn't remember ever being in Beaumont, but apparently something humorous connected in Danny's mind when he saw our friend and me. He laughed and we laughed along with him. Then he lay back down and slipped back into a semiconscious state.

That night while I was in Alabama, I received a phone call from Vonnie, Danny's wife. "Bill, somebody wants to talk to you."

I listened as Danny came on the line and said in a weak voice, "Hi, Bub."

I said, "Hey, Dan, how're you feeling?"

"I think we're making some progress on it now," he replied.

I've never seen such optimism in my entire life. Those were the last words I ever heard him say. A few hours later, after we had shot the video and I returned to my hotel room, the phone rang. It was Mary Ann calling. "Bill, Danny's gone," she said through her tears.

Danny's funeral was one of the largest our little town had ever seen. So many people wanted to pay their respects and offer condolences, our family members greeted people in a receiving line for almost two solid days, every hour the funeral home was open. It was a wonderful tribute to a truly wonderful man.

As the older brother, I did my best to remain stalwart for the benefit of our family, but inside, my heart was breaking. I began to understand even more why the old saints of God sang the songs about heaven with such passion.

TWELVE

WE ALL WIN

THANK GOD FOR GOOD FRIENDS who won't let you quit when times get tough. Although Gloria and I were discouraged enough to quit after Danny's departure, Bob MacKenzie refused to allow us to give up without a fight. "Bill, I don't think you should hang it up. You and Gloria are still writing important songs. You shouldn't give up your platform so easily. I'll help you put together something else," he promised. "Your career can't end here on this down note."

Mac recognized that we had struck a chord in the hearts of many Christians when we had done the musical, *Alleluia! A Praise Gathering for Believers*. He suggested that we create an environment where Christians could come together for a few days to be refreshed physically, but also where they could be encouraged spiritually in an atmosphere of praise and worship. Gloria and I talked about the idea and we liked it. The possibility of providing a worship experience that involved more than music especially intrigued us.

Looking back, it's quite easy to see that in many ways, God used even the awful family circumstances with which we were dealing to open up whole new vistas of opportunity for Gloria and me, as well as for many new artists who needed a place to get started. That doesn't take the sting out of those tough times, but it does help to know that God causes all things to work for good, to those who will trust Him.[1] He really can take what the enemy intends for evil and turn it around for something good.

We had already done one Praise Gathering concert in Indianapolis prior to Danny's leaving the Trio, but Bob MacKenzie suggested, "We can take this thing to a whole other level. We can include special seminars, get some outstanding speakers as well as the great musicians and really make it a special weekend-long event." Mac, Fred Bock, and Bob Benson helped us reorganize the Praise Gathering for Believers in the Indianapolis Convention Center during October of that year. Although the name alluded to an environment in which believers could praise, worship, and experience God in fresh ways through the arts, it was not an overtly "charismatic" sort of gathering. We had people from all denominational backgrounds, and some with no denominational ties, gather together for a weekend filled with special concerts, inspiring speakers, mass choirs, hilarious comedians, as well as varied Christian art forms. From the beginning we tried to break down barriers between Christians who might not see eye to eye on every detail of the faith, but were family nonetheless. We purposely pushed the envelope as we tried to present timeless truth in new packages. Praise Gathering became much more than an uplifting weekend; it became a spiritual event people looked forward to year after year.

As we've conducted the event in downtown Indianapolis at

the convention center, we've featured a wide variety of Christian music artists and speakers, including Corrie Ten Boom, Chuck Colson, Anne Graham Lotz, Max Lucado, Walter Wangerin, Bill Hybels, Richard Foster, Philip Yancey, T. D. Jakes, Gordon MacDonald, Beth Moore, Tony Campolo, Frank Peretti, and Zig Ziglar. We've also featured painters, praise-dancers, and all sorts of other artistic expressions of praise and worship. We never cease to be amazed at the wonderful creativity God inspires in His people when they choose to use their gifts and talents to praise Him.

It was also largely due to Praise Gathering that we began to expand our musical horizons by bringing in a broad spectrum of young artists to share the stage with us in what we called our Gaither and Friends concerts. I found that I really enjoyed pulling together all the elements of the program, almost as much or more than performing myself.

Gary McSpadden was doing a fabulous job singing the lead part in the Gaither Trio. Gloria and I had known Gary for several years and had often heard him sing with Jake Hess and the Imperials. Gary's dad, Boyd McSpadden, pastored a church in Fort Worth. Gary wanted to help him with the music program, but he was on the road full-time with Jake. Since our schedule wasn't as constant as the Imperials', Gary felt that he might be able to work with us and still live in Fort Worth and help his dad in the ministry. It was the beginning of a trend in our group, that the singers who worked with us didn't necessarily have to live in the same part of the country as we did.

Gary was the first nonfamily member ever to be a part of the Gaither Trio for any length of time. Although we've had numerous fine artists share the stage with us, Gary was the person who worked best with the Trio. It was awkward for him and for us at first because everywhere we went, people asked, "Where's

Danny?" But Gary was so gracious and kind, he smoothed things over as best he could. "Danny is doing solo work on his own now," he responded. "Go hear him if you get the chance." Gary did a yeoman's job and sang with us from 1976 to 1988.

In addition to Gary, we introduced a number of new artists such as Amy Grant to Trio audiences. Amy's career was already starting to skyrocket, and when she sang at a few of our concerts, it was easy to see why. Amy captured the crowd's hearts instantly, and I was delighted. To this day, there are few things I love more than to turn the stage over to promising young artists and watch them win with our audiences.

One fellow whom we weren't quite sure whether our rather conservative crowds would accept was Don Francisco. With his acoustic guitar, blue jeans, and sweatshirt or flannel shirt, longish hair, beard, and mustache, Don looked as though he had just stepped out of a commune. But when Don began telling the story of Peter's denial of Jesus in song, the crowds sat in rapt attention. Then as Don's haunting voice led the audience to the cross and beyond to the tomb of Jesus, everyone in the room felt the despair those early disciples must have felt at Christ's crucifixion and burial. Then Don reached the climax of the story, the disciples discovering that Jesus was not in the tomb, and the entire audience leaped to its feet when Don hit the chorus: "He's alive! He's alive! He's alive and I'm forgiven, heaven's gates are open wide! He's alive!"[2]

Once the crowd heard Don sing "He's Alive," we never had to worry about his being accepted again.

Our stage band at that time included stellar musicians such as Billy Smiley and Mark Gershmel, who along with Dann Huff, our fabulous guitar player, and Steve Green, one of our background singers, later started a group known as White

Heart, which became tremendously popular in contemporary Christian music. An incredible tenor singer, Steve had worked with Truth, a mixed vocal group put together by Roger Breland, before coming to us. Steve's wife, Marijean, also sang in our background group. Another singer who traveled with us was Bev Darnall, who today schedules a large amount of the studio session work in Nashville. Playing drums for us was Roger Byrd, a happy-go-lucky guy who sang along on all our songs and had a great time while he played. We got more letters about Roger than almost any other artist, not for his musicianship but because of his great personality. "He looks like he's really enjoying what he's doing," people wrote to us about Roger. He was!

Also in our troupe of great new singers was a young lady with an almost operatic voice. Her name was Sandi Patty. Gloria and I had known Sandi all her life. She and her family lived just down the road from us. Her dad was a singer and a preacher who in his younger years had worked in a singing group with Doug Oldham. Later when Doug went solo, Sandi's dad went to work with former Cleveland Browns football player Bill Glass, conducting evangelistic crusades.

Sandi was a natural singer and one of the best lyric sopranos I have ever heard. When she was just a little girl, her dad stood Sandi and her brother up on chairs to sing, and she'd let it rip! She's been able to belt out a song since she was three years old!

We watched Sandi develop as a wonderfully talented and sincere Christian woman. She was always upbeat, friendly, and had a refreshingly positive outlook on life. When Sandi was working her way through Anderson College, Gloria and I hired her to teach piano lessons to our son, Benjy.

One day I walked into the control room of our recording studio in Alexandria, where a group of young singers was overdubbing background vocals on an album. That wasn't unusual, since we often hired young people to do background vocals for the various artists who recorded in our studios. I noticed one young woman who was singing her heart out, giving 110 percent. "Who is that kid singing in there?" I asked the producer.

"That's Sandi Patty," the producer replied.

"It is?" I could hardly believe it. I hadn't seen Sandi in quite a while and I didn't recognize her. "Boy, she's good, isn't she?" I said.

"She sure is," the producer agreed.

Not long after that, we had some people leave our touring backup group. I was walking down the hall of our studio complex one day when I saw Sandi. An idea struck me. "Sandi, would you be interested in going with us on the weekends to do backup with the Trio?"

Sandi said, "Wait one second. Let me pray about it." Sandi whirled around 360 degrees and said, "Yes!"

"Okay, you're hired," I said with a laugh. Sandi had just signed a recording contract with the Benson Company in Nashville, and they had pitched a new song to her written by Dottie Rambo. The song was called "We Shall Behold Him."

At a Benson Company sales conference that I attended, Sandi sang the new song and tore the house down! The incredible young singer blew away the sales reps. After the conference, I talked with Sandi and asked, "Do you want to sing that song this fall when you come with us on the road?"

"I'd love to!" Sandi gushed.

Every night of our fall tour, Sandi sang in the background group behind the Gaither Trio. Then midway through the program I brought her up to sing "We Shall Behold Him," and she consistently received standing ovations and rave reviews from the audiences.

After a few weeks, a music industry executive said to me, "Doesn't that bother you, Gaither?"

"Doesn't what bother me?" I asked naively.

"Doesn't it bother you that the young kid goes out there and literally stops the program every night?"

"I'm not tracking with you," I replied. "Don't you understand? We are all on the same team. When Sandi wins, I win, too. The whole team wins, and most of all, the audience wins."

The music exec stared back at me blankly. If anybody should understand that concept, we in the Christian music field should; sadly, all too often our pride gets in the way and we don't. We are much better at weeping with those who fail than we are at rejoicing with those who succeed.

Night after night we'd have people approach us and say, "I don't know what you are paying that little gal who sings behind you, but she's worth it. She is into everything you are doing. She is excited about the program, and she just looks like she is having the time of her life."

Over the years, I've often used the example of Sandi Patty during that first tour as a model for young artists. "When you are hired to do a job, it's more than just singing or playing the notes. You need to be involved with what that group is trying to communicate," I tell them. "To be frank, Sandi probably wasn't into the more laid-back, down-home style of music that we were doing, but it didn't matter to her. She was there to help make us sound as good as she could. And she gave it everything she had every night."

Somewhere during that first tour, I was excitedly talking about Sandi with a producer in Nashville. "This kid has more talent than anyone I've seen in a long time," I said.

The producer's answer disappointed me. "I'm not sure that we could sell the image," he replied coolly.

It struck me that he was referring to Sandi's appearance rather than her ability to sing and communicate with an audience. Like many kids, Sandi had always struggled with her weight. To Gloria and me, she was beautiful and a great talent. But the Christian music industry was following the lead of country and pop music in its search for the next slim and sleek artist—guys who all looked as though they had just stepped off the cover of GQ magazine, and young women who looked like fashion models who just happened to be able to sing. Hopefully they had some substance to go with their style, but if not, as long as the style was there, the record companies were happy.

That attitude made me sad then, and it still makes me sad now. I'm convinced that what the world is really looking for is another great heart, and Sandi Patty had a heart that embraced the entire world.

Of course, the producer's argument was a moot point a few months later, when Sandi's album featuring "We Shall Behold Him" hit the record stores. The record company couldn't keep the records in stock. Clearly, the American public was voting with their cash for a great heart and a great communicator.

Sandi Patty had been on the road with us for several tour seasons, singing background and being featured on two or three songs every night, when I said, "Sandi, we need to talk."

Every night, in cities around the nation, people wanted to hear more from the "bubbly little girl with the big voice." I recognized that as much as we were thrilled to have her with us, it wasn't fair to her.

I said to her, "Sandi, I thank God for you, and I thank God that you have given us this part of your life, and you are welcome to stay as long as you want to stay. But I know that you are getting a lot of calls. Your solo career is taking off, you're selling a lot of albums, and anytime you feel that you want to go out on your own, don't feel that you owe us a thing. I want you to go with my blessing."

"Are you serious, Bill?"

"Yes, I am," I replied.

"As long as you're okay with it, I'll go." That fall, Sandi went on tour by herself.

In early August that year, I was at the Christian Artists Seminar in Estes Park, Colorado, and in the early morning devotional session I heard a young man perform in front of about fifty or sixty people. He was a sharp-looking Italian guy and an incredible entertainer. His name was Carman.

Carman did three or four songs, and when the session was over, I went backstage to the small meeting area and introduced myself to the young man. I said, "That was fantastic this morning. What is your last name?"

"You couldn't pronounce it," Carman replied in his thick Bronx brogue.

"Tell me anyway, just for my own information."

"Licardello."

"Nice to meet you, Carman," I said, admitting defeat. "What are you doing these days?"

"I'm just waiting," the young singer answered. "I think I'm close to landing a recording deal."

"Would you mind coming to Indiana and doing a concert so I could see you do an entire evening?"

"No problem," he answered.

I called a pastor in Fort Wayne and asked him if he'd have Carman in for a concert. The pastor wasn't familiar with Carman but took my word that he was good. Gloria and I went to see him, and Carman wasn't good; he was absolutely amazing! He sang his own original songs, he was extremely funny, and he handled a crowd expertly. More than anything, I sensed that he had a great heart.

Afterwards I asked him, "Are you doing anything this fall?"

"Not really," Carman replied.

"Would you like to go with us on tour?"

"You're not going to believe this," Carman said, "but my sister has been praying for two things to happen in my life. One of them was that I would meet you, let alone be on your program."

I never did find out what Carman's sister's second prayer request was, but I asked Carman to join us on tour that fall. By the time we got to Praise Gathering in late October, Carman had found a niche. Carman loved to shock audiences with his offbeat, hilarious comedy routines. For instance, his take on the Abraham and Sarah story in the Bible—"Abraham, you keep away from me!"—was about as far as our audiences wanted to stretch their Bible stories, but he got away with it, and more importantly, Carman got across a great message that nothing is too hard for God to do if we will trust Him.

On the Praise Gathering program that year, we had numerous special guest artists, including Sandi Patty, whom we hadn't seen for a number of months. On Saturday night, Carman tore the place up! After the program, Sandi Patty came up to me and quipped, "Bill, I wished you well, and I sincerely meant it, but I'm not sure I wanted you to do *that* well!" Sandi and I laughed, and we knew that we had both won again.

In all fairness, I must admit that I haven't always been right when it comes to guessing which artists will connect or not connect with an audience. Over the years, Gloria and I have introduced a multitude of new artists at Praise Gathering and other venues around the country. A few of them, such as Don, Sandi, and Carman, have caught on in a big way. Far more young talents have not. That didn't mean they were failures; it simply meant that their ministries or artistry might be more fruitful at a different location, at a later time, on a different level, or in a different manner. The gifts and callings of God are irrevocable; what He chooses to do with them is up to Him, not Bill and Gloria Gaither, or anyone else.

THIRTEEN

BIRTH OF THE VOCAL BAND

IN JANUARY 1981 THE GAITHER
Trio was doing a concert in Florida when during the intermission, Gary McSpadden, Steve Green, Lee Young, and I started singing around the piano backstage, as we often did just for fun. Steve and Lee were still members of the the Gaither Trio's backup vocal group at the time, and anytime the four of us got to sing together, we loved to bring back some of the old four-part-harmony songs. As we were fooling around vocally that night, the group sounded incredible. I said, "Why don't we have some fun? Let's tell the audience that we're premiering a new vocal group tonight, and see how they respond."

After the intermission, the Trio came back onstage to get the concert rolling again and I said, "We have something really special for you tonight. A first. I think there's just something 'spiritual' about four-part harmony, even though I've sung with a trio all my life."

The crowd cheered in agreement with me, and I knew I was

on to something. I said, "Tonight we're going to premier a new singing group. See what you think."

We sang the old southern gospel classic "Your First Day in Heaven," and the audience—not really a southern gospel audience—roared in approval, calling us back for an encore. We didn't have any other songs rehearsed, so we sang "First Day in Heaven" all over again! The crowd ate it up!

If I find something that works, I'll stick with it until it doesn't. And the new vocal group was working! We did the same routine in city after city during our Trio concerts, and the response was overwhelming. People loved the old-time four-part harmonies, especially when they were done with a touch of class.

We decided to give our makeshift group a name and called ourselves the Gaither Vocal Band partially because we liked the sound of it, and partially because the name gave us the freedom to add or drop parts as we saw fit. We weren't locked into a quartet.

At first, the name was a bit confusing to audiences and promoters. Some people actually thought that the Gaither Vocal Band was an instrumental group coming in to play Gaither songs! But the name stuck, and it has worked well for us over the years.

In a sense, the Vocal Band was difficult to categorize. During the 1980s, a subtle rift had slowly developed in Christian music, causing many fine artists to part ways. Some had followed the path toward contemporary, pop, and rock sounds, while southern gospel artists had veered off on their own, literally forming their own organization separate from the Gospel Music Association. The Gaither Vocal Band didn't fit in either camp. We weren't a rock-and-roll band; we were a male quartet, but the musical arrangements we devised were not southern gospel, either.

The audiences didn't seem to mind that we didn't fit in the normal music categories. Night after night, the Vocal Band opened the concert for the Gaither Trio. Although we didn't sound much like the southern gospel quartets I had listened to as a boy, audiences responded enthusiastically to our music. As for me, I was excited because I was finally living out my dream of performing onstage with a gospel quartet.

Gloria was excited about the Vocal Band for a different reason. She had never been comfortable singing onstage. I'd had to talk her into it right from the start, so she was delighted to relinquish more and more of her singing chores to the Vocal Band.

Ironically, two-thirds of the Trio were okay-to-mediocre singers, while the Vocal Band touted the incredible voice of Steve Green, who went on to an outstanding solo career, the smooth Jake Hess style of Gary McSpadden, and later the brilliant Larnelle Harris—all great singers! But Gaither concerts have always been about communicating a message, not just the music. Like hungry teenagers at a smorgasbord, the audiences enjoyed having their more energetic material before settling in for the meat and potatoes of the Gaither Trio.

Before long, the Vocal Band became a highlight of the program. Audiences continued to clamor for more appearances and more music from the quartet. We decided to record some songs, and our first three albums were nominated for Dove Awards, the Gospel Music Association's highest honor bestowed on an album.

One Vocal Band project that was especially meaningful to me was an album titled *A Few Good Men*, which we recorded in 1990, several years before Bill McCartney called the first Promise Keepers group together in Boulder Stadium. It was clear that God was up to something, and we were just getting in on what He already wanted to do. Our daughter Suzanne and her husband, Barry Jennings wrote the title cut of the album.

Although the album didn't garner any awards or break any sales records, it made a strong statement about a man's responsibility for his actions and our accountability to one another. Everywhere we sang it, men responded positively, often standing to their feet long before the song was over.

Partially because of the song, and partly because I had just read Gordon Dalbey's excellent book, *Healing the Masculine Soul*,[1] I became fascinated by the way men function in society, especially the way we attempt to steel ourselves against vulnerability. Women seem to have far fewer problems being vulnerable. A man can be out floundering in a forty-foot-deep lake and yet when somebody yells "Do you need any help?" his first response is always "No problem. I'm fine."

Not until he gets in serious trouble will a man call out for help. Most guys won't even ask for directions when they are lost! If you don't believe me, ask any married woman!

In his book, Dalbey exposed the real male crisis in America: that guys are loners; they have many acquaintances and few close friends, even fewer with whom they will be transparently honest; they will talk to each other only on a superficial level and will do almost anything to avoid true accountability. Most men equate vulnerability with weakness, yet there is a need within every man to be able to let down his guard and to admit his own fears, insecurities, lusts, ambitions, and more, without fear that he is going to be considered less than masculine.

This concept really grabbed me! I got so excited about it, I tracked down the author and called him. I'd never before done such a thing! When I told Gordon Dalbey about the song "A Few Good Men" and how men were responding to it, he encouraged me greatly. "I applaud you," Gordon said. "Run with it!"

I called my friend James Dobson and said, "Jim, could I do a program on the importance of male responsibility and accountability? I'd like to talk about men asking for help, and having some friends who can look each other in the eye and tell the truth."

Dr. Dobson was thrilled that I had gotten so excited about the subject. I went out to Colorado and we did some programs for *Focus on the Family*, his nationwide radio show. The response was tremendously encouraging! Guys all across the nation said, "Yes! That's me!"

A few years later, the Vocal Band performed "A Few Good Men" at the Promise Keepers' second major conference in Boulder, Colorado. I was amazed at the guys' response. Men all over the stadium stood to their feet as we sang, as if to say, "Here I am, God! You can count on me!" It was a tremendously stirring moment in my life.

When I returned home I told Suzanne, "You were two or three years ahead of your time when you wrote the song 'A Few Good Men.'" The lyrics still stir me every time I read them:

> What this dying world could use is a willing man of God
> Who dares to go against the grain and work without applause,
> A man who'll raise the sword of faith, protecting what is pure,
> Whose love is tough and gentle, a man whose word is sure.
>
> God doesn't need an orator who knows just what to say.
> He doesn't need authorities to reason Him away.
> He doesn't need an army to guarantee a win;
> He just needs a few good men.
>
> Men full of compassion who laugh and love and cry,
> Men who'll face eternity and aren't afraid to die;
> Men who'll fight for freedom and honor once again,
> He just needs a few good men.[2]

Every time a fellow who has gotten in trouble asks me for help, one of my first questions is "Do you have any good friends in your life?" Invariably the answer is something like "I know a lot of guys. We can joke, goof off together, play a round of golf, but no, I don't have very many really close friends. Not the kind of guys I can be totally honest with." We all need good friends who care enough to speak the truth to us, even when it hurts.

Steve Green was certainly a man for whom the description "a good man" was applicable. I was impressed by Steve's vocal ability, but even more by his character. I've never known him to be anything but a man of integrity. When Steve decided to leave the Vocal Band and pursue a solo career, we brought in the great young singer Larnelle Harris. Larnelle had worked with a Michigan-based group known as the Spurrlows before launching out in a solo career and exciting audiences all over the country with his fantastic tenor voice. Larnelle was a tremendous addition to our group and his incredible talent transcended all racial boundaries, reminding us that before God, all believers are one family.

Larnelle sang with the Vocal Band for three years. One day he called me aside and said, "Bill, I cannot keep up this schedule, working with the Vocal Band and maintaining my solo career. I'm sorry to do it, but I'm going to have to leave." We parted ways amicably, and Larnelle remains one of my dearest friends to this day. He's appeared as a guest artist on numerous programs with us over the years and is still a crowd favorite. I was truly sorry to see Larnelle go, though. He was such an inspiration onstage and off. During the three years he was with us, never once was there a time that I saw Larnelle display anything other than a totally Christian approach to any problem that came up. Larnelle Harris was and remains a classy guy, a good friend, and a good man.

Over the years, the Gaither Vocal Band has indeed been comprised of a few good men: Lee Young, Steve Green, Gary McSpadden, Jon Mohr, Larnelle Harris, Michael English, Jim Murray, Terry Franklin, Buddy Mullins, Jonathan Pierce, Mark Lowry, and currently, Guy Penrod, David Phelps, Russ Taff . . . and me (on a good day)!

FOURTEEN

AT HOME WITH THE FAMILY

ONE OF THE MOST IMPOR-
tant qualities of a truly good man or woman is that he or she
knows how to prioritize time. Any man or woman who is trying
to balance career and family responsibilities discovers how
difficult that is. On a good day, I'm not bad at keeping my priorities in line; on a bad day, I'm terrible at it!

As I get older, though, I think I'm getting better at recognizing
and protecting what really matters. Like many grandparents, I
probably do a better job of sorting through the tough decisions
about priorities when it comes to our grandchildren than I did
with our kids. Although I'm just as busy as I was in my
younger days, I now know how to shut things down or when
to stop working better than I did when our children were
young.

It is impossible for you to understand our lives or our music
without knowing how we functioned as a family at home. After
all, Gloria and I have always written about what we experi-

enced in our own lives, whether it was raising our kids or watching them take wing.

Our kids have often said, "Dad, it doesn't take much for you to create a party!" And that's true! Coming from a small town where there wasn't a lot to do, I had to learn how to be creative about having fun.

We discovered early on that little things really do mean a lot. One of our favorite things to do when the kids were young was to go out for dinner at an Italian restaurant. It's still one of our favorite family activities, only now we have a much larger crowd. In 2001, shortly before my mom passed away, Gloria and I had the weekend off, so we met our three kids and all the grandkids at a restaurant in Marion, a small town in Indiana. I called Mom and Dad to go with us, and although Italian wasn't their favorite food, they refused to miss the fun.

With all the kids, it was pasta and spaghetti sauce everywhere! We were laughing, telling stories, and having a wonderful time. As we walked back to the car after the especially messy meal, Dad observed, "It doesn't really take that much to have a good time, does it?"

"No, it doesn't, Dad."

"Why do people allow their lives to get so busy and so complicated that they miss opportunities like this?"

I looked over at my dad, now in his nineties. He would never claim to be anything but a factory worker and a farmer, but he had a wisdom that far surpassed that of men and women who sacrificed their families on the altars of success, money, power, or prestige. And I was proud of my dad.

Dad was so right. When the family is together, we don't need high-tech entertainment. We enjoy sitting around telling stories, singing songs, laughing, crying, or praying together. Come to think of it, I'm still doing much the same thing today with our *Homecoming* videos.

When our first child, Suzanne, was just a toddler, she was terrified of having her picture taken. Of course, at concerts people often came up and took pictures of Gloria and me, sometimes snapping shots of Suzanne as well. In almost all of those photos Suzanne was sobbing. She dreaded seeing the bright flash, and it was high trauma whenever anyone took her picture.

One day Gloria told Suzanne, "Your daddy doesn't have any pictures of you that he can show his friends. Other daddies can show pictures of their children, but your daddy can't, because the only photos we have of you are from when you were just a baby."

Suzanne thought that over. Then one day she went to Gloria and said, "Mommy, maybe the best present I could give to Daddy for Christmas would be a picture. I want to get my picture taken and give it to Daddy."

"You do?" Gloria asked, amazed that Suzanne would be willing to pose for a photograph.

"Yes, I do. Please, Mom, can I?"

Gloria styled Suzanne's hair to look real cute and dressed her in a beautiful brown and cream outfit that she and Grandma Sickal had made, and they went to a photographer. Suzanne made it through a few shots before she started crying, but that was enough to get a good photo.

Suzanne's face was beaming with pride as I opened her special present to me that Christmas. When I saw the photograph, I knew what a sacrifice my little girl had made for her daddy. It was one of those special moments in my life that I will never forget.

By the time Suzanne started kindergarten, Gloria and I had

both left our jobs as schoolteachers to pursue music full-time. Nevertheless, I still had a desire to be part of public education. I decided I could best serve the community, as well as my former colleagues, by running for a position on the local school board. I was elected to the board and was proud of my unique position as a former teacher in that school system, whose administration understood the needs of the teachers as well as the management issues involved in running a school district.

Because I worked on my music at home during the weekdays and traveled on the weekends, it was usually my job to pick up Suzanne from kindergarten each day. I often ran late, though, due to incessant phone conversations or business meetings that ran too long.

Suzanne's kindergarten teacher, Ione Craig, was a seasoned veteran in the school system, a spunky woman who had a lot of experience in dealing with children and their parents. She certainly wasn't impressed with me. She didn't care how many songs I'd written, who was singing them, or how many important people or things needed my attention at work. All she knew was that Suzanne was standing outside after school, waiting for her daddy, who was constantly running late. The teacher wrote me a letter that went something like this:

Dear Mr. Gaither,

I don't know if you are aware of this fact, but school lets out at 11:25 A.M. Your daughter will be standing on the curb by 11:30 A.M. When children are left unattended on the curb for very long, they begin to feel abandoned and develop low self-esteem. From now on, for the sake of your daughter, I suggest that you be at the curb precisely at 11:25. Thank you very much.

Ione Craig

When I received the letter, I was impressed. I've always appreciated people who were not afraid to get in my face. "I like that gal!" I crowed to Gloria. I was on time from then on, and we became good friends with Ione and her family. God help me to always have people in my life who care enough to confront me and say the hard things that will help make me a better person.

I loved being a dad and I tried to balance family and work responsibilities as best I could. I especially enjoyed playing outdoors with the kids when they were young. Once when Benjy was only about five, I took the kids sledding down a large hill over in Anderson. We were having such a good time, I didn't want to quit.

"You gotta go one more time," I begged Benjy, who was standing in his snowsuit, soaked and freezing. He was ready to leave.

"Daddy, I don't want to go one more time," Benjy wailed.

"Oh, you gotta. Come on, Benj. One more time!" I encouraged him. "This is so much fun. Get on the sled and I'll give you a push."

"Okay . . ." Benjy acquiesced and plopped down onto the sled. I gave him a big push and watched him streak down the hill, skimming over the snow and bouncing merrily over the slippery slope. But then Benjy's sled veered off the beaten path. From a distance, I saw what was about to happen, but I could only look on helplessly as the course of events that I had set in motion played out. Right in front of Benjy was a big tree, and he crashed into it face first.

By the time I got to him, blood was gushing out of a gash above Benjy's eye. Benjy whirled around and cried, "You're the one! You did it!"

Benjy has found that phrase useful several times since then! And we still laugh when we recall the first time we heard it.

At the time, though, I felt horrible. "I did, Benjy, you're right. Come on, let's go get you fixed up." With a few stitches, Benjy was fine, but I'll never forget that awful feeling of having to watch helplessly as a child I loved headed for trouble.

The same factors that Gloria and I saw as the advantages of remaining in the small town of Alexandria to raise our family were often perceived as disadvantages by our kids as they were growing up. Most of the families in our area were farmers or worked at Delco-Remy, a General Motors plant. Their world revolved largely around local people and events. As much as we tried to instill within our children a sense of history and a strong connection to the family roots that ran deeply into the Indiana soil, they had never experienced farming or factory working for themselves. From the time they were toddlers, their world was a tour bus, an auditorium, or a hotel complex.

In the *Homecoming* video *Singin' in My Soul*, Tanya Goodman Sykes aptly described the dichotomy created by the lifestyle of a gospel music family and how it affected her popularity with the kids in her school. "In our school, there was this hierarchy of people. There were the popular kids, and the unpopular kids; and then there were the kids who rode around all weekend in purple buses" (the color of the Happy Goodman Family's bus).

Suzanne, Amy, and later Benjamin experienced something similar. They were constantly traveling to some new, exciting place and coming back to their local school. Suzanne says, "It was almost as though I was leading some sort of duplicitous life!" Suzanne and Benjy chose to play down their out-of-town experiences and tried to fit in the best way they could. On the other hand, our idealistic middle child, Amy—affectionately referred to as Miss Sunshine by her siblings—was extremely verbal about her travels. She'd go back to school after one of our trips, gushing, "We just had the most fabulous time! We went to Israel . . . and then we went to Europe . . ."

Meanwhile, Suzanne and Benjy were over in the corner of the hallway, saying, "Shut up, Amy! You're going to get us all killed!"

As high school teachers ourselves, Gloria and I were naturally involved in our children's education. Gloria, especially, helped the kids with their homework. Me? I couldn't resist correcting their grammar—and still do to this day! In the early days when we were on the road, Gloria would take a magazine along, and before we went out to do the concert, she'd sit down with Suzanne and find an intriguing picture in the magazine. "I want you to write me a story about what you think is happening in this picture."

Usually by the time the concert had concluded, Suzanne had spun some fanciful tale about the picture. It was great writing practice, and Suzanne loved it!

Gloria and I also encouraged Suzanne in her early attempts at songwriting. Suzanne began writing poetry as a child, then in her early teens developed a taste for songwriting. She was good, too. I was a tough critic, but she knew that whenever I complimented her work, it wasn't simply a token response. I really meant it.

By the time Suzanne was thirteen or fourteen, she was pitching her songs to all the producers who came to town. Some of them listened to Suzanne's songs out of kindness to Gloria and me; some listened because they really wanted to hear Suzanne's work. Most of them smiled condescendingly at "the little Gaither girl" who was writing music, but a few took her seriously. Today, Suzanne has written more than two hundred songs, many of which have been recorded by a wide variety of artists, and she owns her own publishing company.

Of course music was an important part of our lives and played constantly at our home. All three of our children would probably be hard-pressed to remember going to bed on a night when there wasn't music playing in the Gaither household. Gloria and I frequently hosted traveling troubadours and other music artists for dinner, and we'd often stay up late playing music for our guests, with the stereo system blaring and throbbing. We listened not only to Christian music, but to current artists of the day such as Neil Diamond and John Denver. Of course, I loved to pull out the old 33⅓-rpm quartet records, and sometimes even some of the 78 rpms I'd bought as a child. "Oh, listen to that!" I'd point out to anyone who would listen to the old songs with me.

Not surprisingly, our home got to be a favorite hangout and landing spot for many of our kids' friends, especially in their latter teen years. Kids were always at the house, listening to music, doing school art projects, creating mazes or haunted houses in the shed, watching movies, coming or going, staying overnight, or spending the weekend. The parade of young people passing through our doors never stopped. And Gloria and I welcomed them. We wanted our home to be a place where our kids felt comfortable to bring their friends.

Similarly, we hosted all sorts of visitors in our home. One night, Gloria roused Suzanne from her sleep. "Suzanne, go sleep in one of the other rooms."

"Huhh . . . wha . . . why?"

"We need your bed. We have a guest staying with us tonight."

Suzanne shuffled off to another room while Gloria hastily put clean bedding on for Senator Richard Lugar, who was visiting with us. The kids never knew whom they might meet at the breakfast table. They especially enjoyed meeting Senator Lugar, who has continued to be a good friend of our family over the years and has made us all proud of him for the way he has served our country.

Gloria and I were always on the alert for teachable moments with our children. Gloria especially took every opportunity to teach the kids a spiritual lesson from the most mundane events. She was a great role model and loved to engage the kids in long philosophical conversations. I, on the other hand, preferred to model behavior and attitudes that I wanted to teach, rather than discuss them. Gloria and I were probably a good balance for each other. Where she'd tend to see either good or evil personified in every situation, I was extremely pragmatic. Sometimes I'd say, "You know, we don't need to blame things on God or the devil. Some things just happen in life." Nevertheless, I had a few favorite sayings that our kids heard over and over. One that I think I made up myself and used frequently I mentioned in a previous chapter: "He that has no plan becomes the victim of everyone else's plan." The kids learned that line well and quoted it back to me when I occasionally let my plans fall victim to circumstances or to happenstance.

I was a pretty soft touch as a parent, especially toward the girls. It somehow seemed easier to be tougher on Benjamin. After all, he was a guy, and we Gaither guys could buck up under almost any pressure.

The one thing that would rouse my anger was when our children treated someone with disrespect or insulted another person's dignity. To this day, I still get upset when one of our kids, or someone on the road with us, belittles another person simply because he or she is in a service position, such as waitresses, hotel personnel, or sound guys on stage.

Once several members of our group and I were having a meal at a restaurant, and the waitress's service was just awful. Her attitude stank, she was downright mean, and she was slow and forgetful about serving the food. At first everyone remained patient and kind, but she continued to do terrible work. After a while, a few members of our group sniped at her about items she had forgotten.

She performed even worse.

When we left, I looked in my billfold and pulled out an exorbitant tip. "She's probably had a bad day," I told the members of our group. "I don't want to add any more to the weight she is carrying. Who knows? If I had to put up with what she does every day, I might not handle it real well either."

We developed an interesting method of evaluating potential employees when we were hiring new people for our organization. After we'd examined their resumes and looked over their basic qualifications, we often took the potential employees out to eat. We observed carefully how the candidate treated the waitresses or waiters. Regardless of how talented a person was, if he or she failed the "restaurant test," we didn't hire him or her. Why? Because a person's character is often revealed by the way they treat people in service positions.

The family fun really started heating up when the girls started dating. I tended to be suspicious of every guy who came to our house to see our daughters. I'm sure I was the typical overprotective dad.

The joys and the pains that parents feel for their children cannot adequately be described; to be truly understood, they must be experienced. The wishes, dreams, and hopes that parents have for their children are difficult to keep veiled from a child, yet good parents often have to sit back and watch as kids experience life for themselves, knowing that at some point they might get hurt.

That's how I felt as I watched Suzanne going through junior high and high school. She was always a good student, conscientious, honest, and hardworking. But she was a late bloomer, and a bit of a tomboy. She wore a baseball cap almost constantly during her early teens, and she was a pretty good softball player, too. I used to tease her, "Honey, when are you going to take off that baseball cap and dress up?"

Ironically, Suzanne seemed equally comfortable with Gloria's and my friends as she was with her own. She didn't date, and she didn't have a lot of friends, but the few she had were well-mannered, good kids. But sometimes on Friday nights after the ball games, Suzanne's friends would drop her off at the house around ten o'clock and then go out without her. Meanwhile, Gloria and I would hear Suzanne come in the house, go in the family room, and put on her sad Karen Carpenter records.

Gloria and I would lie in our bed and bawl over her. We knew she wanted to have some romance in her life, but for whatever reason, it was passing her by. Many times I told her, "You're a great kid. You have great stuff. Someday, you're going to meet a fine young man and fall in love. Just be patient."

To help maintain a strong relationship with our kids, I'd take one of them at a time out to breakfast or lunch. As they got older, I said, "Let's go walk." Our entire family loves to power walk for exercise, and I still maintain a regular walking regime. Walking was a good time for the kids and me to talk about what was going on in their lives.

During Suzanne's senior year of high school, she and I went to Jupiter Beach, Florida, together during her spring break. She'd often done things alone with Gloria, but this was a special opportunity for the two of us to spend quality time together informally, without trying to squeeze in a few rushed moments between concert schedules, business meetings, and recording sessions.

The kids were always trying to get me to spruce up my wardrobe. One night in Jupiter Beach, Suzanne and I were going out to a fancy restaurant, so she dressed up in a cute outfit. I put on my favorite pair of whitewashed slacks and a white T-shirt. When Suzanne saw me she cringed. "Dad! You're not going to wear that, are you?"

"Yeah, why?"

"We're supposed to dress up!"

"Okay. Do you think I should change?"

"Yeah, I think you should change!"

"Okay, I'll be right back." I went and changed into another T-shirt almost identical to the first. "Okay, let's go!" I said.

Suzanne just rolled her eyes. "Okay, Dad. Let's go."

The Florida spring-break trip was one of the most meaningful times I'd ever had with Suzanne. We just relaxed and had fun together, and created some indelible memories. Since then I've done similar things with Amy and Benjamin, but that first trip with Suzanne will always be a milestone for me.

Besides giving me a hard time about my moribund clothing, the kids loved to make fun of my onstage gaffs as well. Once, for instance, the Trio was singing for a large youth conference. We were doing a sing-along of Andrae' Crouch's song "Soon and Very Soon," and I was encouraging the kids to clap along with us. But the kids were clapping every which way except on the beat.

I stopped the music and said, "Okay, you're kids. You can get this! It's not that hard. Some of you are clappin' on the one and three, and some of you are clappin' on the two and four, and some of you are crappin' on the clacks."

My three wonderful children have never let me live that one down!

Suzanne enrolled at Anderson College, just ten miles down the road from home, but as far as Gloria and I were concerned, she was a thousand miles away! We missed her terribly. She moved into her dorm on Friday evening, and the first Sunday away from home, she came home to our church by herself. We saw her and called out for her to come sit with us. I asked, "Suzanne, how were your first two days of school?"

"Great!"

"Did you have fun?"

"Yeah!"

"Did you meet any new friends?"

"Yeah, I did."

"Where did you eat breakfast this morning?"

"Dunkin' Donuts."

"Who with?"

"By myself."

"Suzanne! You've gotta make some friends, okay?"

"I will, Dad. I promise I will."

It took some time for Suzanne to enter into the college social scene, and in many ways she never completely did. Instead, she went with us on the road every weekend. Eventually she started dating a young man who worked with us, and for a while she was excited. But then she discovered that the fellow was being less than honest with her.

Suzanne came to me in tears, and the Papa Bear side of me came to the fore. I was furious.

"I'll tell you what, you are done with him!" I railed. "You're not going to be treated like this! Here's what you're going to do.

You're going to get your head up and you're not going to take any garbage from anyone!"

Shocked at my outburst, Suzanne looked back at me through her tears, and her countenance began to brighten. It was almost as if she was thinking, *Well, okay! My dad is right.* My response seemed to give Suzanne the courage to do what she needed to do.

She went back to her boyfriend and told him, "We're through. This is it!"

Shortly after that, I saw Suzanne beginning to take wings and soar. She developed a new circle of friends who were positive influences in her life.

I knew it was going to happen sooner or later, but I'm not sure that any father can adequately prepare for the day his little girls fall in love. About the time Suzanne started college, Barry Jennings, a quiet, rather shy young man from Virginia, moved to Alexandria to play bass guitar with us on the road. Barry was a bright fellow, good-looking, easygoing, with a good head for business. Barry traveled with us for several years, and eventually he and Suzanne struck up a friendship at some of our concerts.

They dated for more than two years before they married. For their wedding, Suzanne and Barry asked me to sing a song Gloria and I had written, "The Things That Last Forever." Although I was thrilled that Suzanne and Barry were so happy, singing at their wedding was one of the toughest performances I've ever given. The sheer emotion of the moment threatened to overwhelm me. To keep from dissolving in a puddle of tears, I had to force myself to think of other things as I sang, *anything* but Suzanne and Barry getting married that day. I made it through the song without breaking down, but just in the nick of time.

When our CEO, Jerry Weimer, announced that he was leaving Alexandria to take a position with a Christian book publishing company, I asked him, "Whom would you recommend to do your job?"

"Your son-in-law would be excellent," Jerry said without a moment's hesitation. Jerry was right. Barry Jennings came on as CEO and has been the driving force behind the marketing of the *Homecoming* programs, getting the videos on Christian stations and mainstream television stations around the world. Nepotism has nothing to do with it. Barry is a top-quality CEO, and I have absolute confidence in him.

Our idealistic, dramatic daughter, Amy, fell in love with Andrew Hayes, a young man she met while they were students at Vanderbilt University. Andrew hailed from a wonderful family from Birmingham, Alabama, and just as Gloria and I felt about Barry and Suzanne, we could not have chosen a better match than Andrew for Amy.

At this writing, Benjamin remains single and seems quite content with that status. He is immersed in writing songs, performing music, and developing new children's products. He's a talented young man, and it's been exciting to watch him use the gifts and talents God has given him.

In high school, Amy was always interested in drama and theater and starred in several school plays, turning in outstanding performances. Amy seemed to have inherited the best of Gloria's and my artistic qualities while missing the less-complimentary aspects of many creative personality types.

Still, her siblings teased Amy mercilessly for being such a slow mover. Amy didn't believe in hurrying. She had a sign in her bedroom: "Slow Is Beautiful!"

As the middle child, Amy was our pleaser and peacemaker. No matter what, she tried to look at life through a positive lens. Once, for instance, when Gloria fixed some cinnamon rolls for breakfast, she and the kids decided to play a trick on Amy. Ordinarily, by the time Amy got down to the breakfast table, Suzanne or Benjy had already discovered which cinnamon rolls had the most delicious icing, usually the center buns, and had snatched them up for themselves. It was always a tug-of-war between Benjy and Suzanne to see who could get the cinnamon roll with the most goo on it. "I get the center roll!" "No way! You got it last time!" they'd argue.

On this morning, Gloria said to Suzanne and Benjy, "That's not fair to Amy. She never gets the center one. Let's save the center for her today."

"Okay, Mom. But don't put any icing on it to see what she says."

Gloria laughed and agreed.

When everyone gathered for breakfast, the kids said, "Amy, you get the center cinnamon roll today."

Amy said, "Fine." She daintily removed the center roll, the one with not a speck of icing on it. She started eating the roll and drinking her milk, never saying a word about the missing icing.

"How's your cinnamon roll, Amy?"

"Fine."

"My cinnamon roll is really good, Mommy. It has a lot of icing on it. How's yours, Amy?"

"Fine."

"Mmmm-mmm! Mine has lots of icing on it. It tastes so good! How's your icing, Amy?"

"I think it's okay . . . it doesn't seem to have a lot on it."

Finally Gloria couldn't take it anymore. She gave in and said, "Amy, we played a trick on you. We didn't put any icing on your cinnamon roll on purpose."

"Oh," Amy replied. "I just thought that you had run out of icing."

That peaceful, get-along personality has been a characteristic of Amy's all her life. Her unflappable character came in handy on her wedding day.

She and Andrew had planned a beautiful garden wedding in our backyard. Ever the artist, Amy had dreamed of a romantic outdoor wedding all her life. Gloria and I did our best to fulfill her dream. We had yellow tents set up where she wanted to have the reception down by the creek, complete with a great jazz band playing as guests mingled.

Unfortunately, about seven days before Amy and Andrew's wedding, it started to rain. It rained and rained. For almost a week straight, our weather was dark, dank, and dismal . . . not to mention drenching!

We were all disappointed. The day of the wedding, I walked down through the backyard to the spot where Amy had planned to have the gorgeous reception. As I looked around at the sopping ground, I angrily vented to God, "I don't usually ask for much. But, God, just this once . . . this is the one kid I have who has the greatest sense of romance and idealism. Could you not have held off the rain for a few days?"

I felt like Tevye in *Fiddler on the Roof*, as I was letting God have it. "Good grief . . . could you not? Just this once . . . Just for my daughter's wedding. . . !"

God didn't answer . . . and the rain kept falling.

Amy was disappointed but nonetheless positive. We moved the wedding inside our church, and it was a lovely ceremony, and I remembered again that God doesn't play favorites.

The day after Amy and Andrew's wedding, the sun rose against a cloudless blue sky. It was an absolutely gorgeous, perfect June day with no humidity and a temperature of about seventy-two degrees. I walked outside in the backyard, raised an eyebrow, and looked heavenward. I don't want to put in print what I said!

Andrew's father had been an attorney, as had several other members of his extended family, so Andrew grew up assuming that a career in law would be a natural for him. He earned his law degree from Vanderbilt but after a few years of practice, he decided to pursue other interests. Andrew went back to school, to the University of Nebraska, where he earned his doctorate in theater. He and Amy settled in Greencastle, Indiana, about two hours away from us, and Andrew took a position teaching theater at DePauw University. Amy, too, earned her masters degree and now teaches acting classes at DePauw, in between caring for their three children.

Sometimes I can be a rather strange guy. I don't ever mean to be rude, but sometimes I'm thinking of so many things I'm planning to do in the future, I tune out the present. When that happens, I can easily come off as though I don't care about other people's thoughts, words, or feelings.

My friend and fellow songwriter Geron Davis says my brain is like a twenty-four-track recorder . . . but I can play only one track at a time! Sometimes I'll switch tracks mentally right in the middle of a conversation. I can be talking with someone and suddenly my brain just goes to someone or something else. I don't do it intentionally or even consciously, but enough people have informed me of this quirk in my personality that I'm convinced it's real.

Once I was talking to a fellow, and I suddenly switched tracks. The man was offended and later wrote a strong letter of rebuke to me. "I know you are a busy man," he said, "but I was in the middle of telling you something that was important to me, and you just walked off!"

I didn't even remember doing it, but I felt awful about the situation. I told Gloria about what happened and she said, "Let me answer that letter."

"I know just how you feel," she wrote to the offended fellow. "I've put up with that for thirty years. If you think of a solution, please let me know!"

To help break me out of my workaholic tendencies long enough to relax, Suzanne and my brother, Danny, once planned a long cross-country bus trip for the entire family: Suzanne and Barry, Barry's mom, Amy and Andrew, Danny and his wife, Vonnie, and Gloria and me. A bus trip? Yes, despite the fact that I've spent half my life riding in buses, most of the trips have been from one concert venue to another, with precious little time spent actually enjoying the scenery or the locations where we visited. Suzanne and Danny wanted to do something about that.

Yet they were aware that they had to plan the trip carefully; they couldn't just leave such a trip to chance, or worse yet, they couldn't leave it up to me.

They meticulously drew out every stop along the way to the West Coast, with long stretches of desolate highway in between. The first few days, I nearly went bonkers with boredom. I felt like I needed to be doing something work-related. So used to being tied to a schedule, I frequently walked to the front of the bus and leaned over Danny's shoulder as he drove. "How we doin' on time?" I'd ask.

Danny smiled knowingly and replied, "You know what, Bill, we're exactly where we need to be. Right on the money."

"Okay . . ." I'd say, shaking my head and going to the back of the bus again. But as the miles slipped by and we stopped to visit several tourist spots, such as Mount Rushmore, Yellowstone National Park, the Badlands, and the Tetons, I began to slow down and relax. At night, we watched old movies, history features, and long documentaries on video. After about the third or fourth day, I was saying, "This is so much fun! Why don't we do this more often?"

Of course, everyone in the bus knew why we didn't. They looked at me, rolled their eyes, and laughed.

What can I tell you? I'm a non-recovering workaholic.

Our family relationships have been so wonderful and fulfilling, it would be easy to think that we were an "Ozzie and Harriet" type of family. But the only people who would ever think that are folks who don't really know us. While our unconditional love for each other is well known because of the public aspects of what we do, trust me, there have been plenty of times when we've lived far from Ozzie and Harriet. Every family—including the Gaithers—struggles with disagreements and other types of conflicts. It's silly to think that we have been immune from such stresses. The key is to learn how to disagree, deal with the conflicts, and still love one another.

FIFTEEN

GAITHER FAMILY FEUDS

I'M ALWAYS AMAZED THAT people think that Gloria and I and our family live in some sort of spiritual biosphere, a transparent plastic bubble where everything is perfect, life is grand all the time, we never have a problem, and we never get angry with one another. Nothing could be further from the truth.

"Do you ever argue or fight?" some people ask. Do we ever fight? We could have sold tickets for some of the Gaither family feuds! Put five opinionated, creative people together under one roof, and expect them never to rub each other the wrong way? Ha!

The Bible doesn't say that we will never get angry, disagree, or have serious conflicts with each other. It does say, "Be angry, and yet do not sin; do not let the sun go down on your anger, and do not give the devil an opportunity."[1] In other words, deal with your anger before the day is over if at all possible, so the devil does not have an opportunity to use it against you, or to cause division in the family or group.

That hasn't always been easy for me. I wish I could say that I've always lived up to that, but I can't. Sometimes it's taken a sunset—or two or three—for me to get over something. On occasion, I've spent two or three days out mowing grass, which is inexpensive therapy for me, as I've worked through my anger. But sooner or later, I've had to get the anger out of my system and behind me. At that point, I'm thankful that one of my greatest gifts is a bad memory!

In our family conflicts, no holds were barred. If someone hit below the belt, well, that was just the beginning! I sometimes had a short fuse on my temper, and Gloria and I were quite vocal during our heated discussions. Suzanne and Benjy were similar to us, while Amy was a typical peacemaker who wanted to absorb everybody's pain. We once found one of her old journals, which included an entry after a fight with her brother. Amy wrote, "Benjy and I got in trouble. I think Benjy might still be a little mad. He's kicking the wall and yelling!"

The good news was that we made up quickly. We'd have a major eruption one day, yelling at each other as though we were at war, but the next day, everything would be smoothed over and fine. All was forgiven and forgotten.

One of the most difficult parenting periods for us was when Benjamin entered his teenage years. I truly believe that there are chemicals released in a teenager's body that send signals to his brain saying, "You've got to get some distance between you and your parents!" Every generation has to find a way to be different from those who produced them. It's almost a concerted effort to show that their approach to life is radically different from Mom and Dad's.

That was true of Benjamin. When his teenage hormones kicked in gear, they hit him like a big Mack truck. He had to put some distance between him and us, and that was okay.

One of the obvious ways Benjamin displayed his departure from our patterns was in his choice of music. Whoever said that music is the universal language must have been joking! Music is extremely divisive; it can drive parents nuts! If you don't believe me, try going on vacation with three or four kids and attempting to find some agreement as to what music you'll listen to along the way. You won't be able to find a quorum.

Like many parents, I wasn't exactly thrilled when Benjamin developed a taste for certain styles of music. Beyond that, the volume concerned me. As a person who makes part of his living working with sound, doing arena concerts, I knew all too well the potential dangers of music at high decibels, especially when the equalization was not quite right, which it usually isn't for most home stereo sets.

Benjamin, of course, loved his music loud—the louder the better! During the early 1980s, the distorted guitar sounds of rock music of the day expressed the energy, attitudes, and the feelings of his generation. I tried hard to understand Benjy's music, but it was extremely difficult for me, especially since I grew up in a four-part-harmony home.

Nevertheless, when Benjy gathered some musicians and formed his own band, Gloria and I tried to be as encouraging as possible and permitted them to practice at the house. Gloria was much more open in her acceptance of new music styles and tolerant of Benjamin's music than I was. Before long, however, the noise level was more than even Gloria could handle.

Benjamin was not a bad kid; he didn't cause us any problems outside the home; he never got into alcohol or drug problems; he was just trying to find his way in an artistic family. We tried to give him as much rope as we could while still keeping him within certain family boundaries. In many Christian homes today, parents are grappling with some of those same issues.

Gloria and I disagreed strongly over how to handle some of Benjamin's rebellious streaks, creating even more tension in the family. Fortunately for all of us, Benj matured musically as well as physically and emotionally. He still enjoyed much heavier styles of music than I did, but at least we could find some common ground on which to communicate about it.

Adding to the problem, Gloria and I were on the road a lot during that time, and the kids stayed with Gloria's mom and dad. That worked fairly well as the girls proceeded through adolescence, but by the time Benjamin hit his teens, nobody was enjoying the family separations every weekend brought. Beyond that, I realized that Gloria and I were missing many of the kids' ball games, school plays, band concerts, and other events that took place on the weekends while we were away singing. In an effort to better control our travel schedule and to be home with the kids more, Gloria and I started doing short two-week "tours" rather than working concert dates every weekend. That helped for a while, but before long, that situation became untenable as well. Gloria and I seriously considered whether we should come off the road completely during our kids' teenage years. Ever the optimist, I kept trying to juggle our schedules, hoping to keep all the balls in the air, and not get hit on the head. "We can make this work," I'd say.

And for the most part, we did. But not without some serious conflicts and confrontations. Often, the toughest issue to deal with was setting and maintaining our family priorities. What is more important? As I've said before, the decisions were rarely between good and bad, right or wrong. More often, the choices were between good and better; better and best.

The hardest part for us as a family—or for any family—has been finding a good time to confront our conflicts. We don't like to argue on the road, in front of all the people who are expecting us to have a smooth life together. Besides, the other artists are looking to us for leadership; they don't need to hear us airing out our dirty laundry.

But our lives are so busy, we've had to learn to argue about the little, picayune things on the bus whether anyone is watching and listening or not. Otherwise, the tensions from the little irritations of life tend to build like pressure in a volcano, until suddenly a tiny pinprick results in a major eruption and big, ugly chunks of hot stuff fly in every direction!

Joy and Landy Gardner, directors of Christ Church Choir in Nashville, credit Gloria's and my arguing with helping their marriage. After traveling with us for a while, Joy quipped, "You two have given Landy and me so much hope! We say, 'Gloria and Bill have a lot of conflicts, and they're still married and in love after more than forty years. If they can be honest with each other, say what they need to say, and still love each other, we can learn to do that, too!'"

Many couples, especially Christians, are obsessed with being "nice," giving the appearance that they never have a problem, never disagree, and never get angry with one another. But if "nice" is just a facade or a screen, it is not more spiritual; it's hypocrisy. It is no virtue to hide things or try to sweep them under the rug when you really are upset about something.

That hasn't always been easy for me. I grew up in a family where the men didn't openly express their emotions, not even anger. If something bothered us, we'd just ignore it as long as possible. The men in my family operated under the misguided notion *If I don't talk about the issue that bothers me, it will just go away.* Most men feel that if they keep jawing about the things that bug them, they are giving in to the little boy deep within them. Somehow we need to begin acting like adults.

When Gloria and I first married, if I got upset about something, I just clammed up and didn't talk at all. Fortunately, with my poor memory, after three or four days, I couldn't remember what I was upset about anyhow!

Gloria and I haven't always been the best at getting along. Truth is, we've had more than our share of arguments. But we are irrevocably committed to each other. I know that she is a wonderful, good woman who committed herself to me long ago, and I am committed to her. That means we have to work through our disagreements, trying to find some equitable resolution to our differences of opinion. We don't have a choice.

Some of the best moments in our marriage of more than four decades have been those times when I have gone to Gloria without provocation or encouragement from her in any way and asked, "Is there something we need to talk about? I feel like there is something wrong between us."

Gloria absolutely *loves* it when I take the initiative in those situations. Simply expressing concern shows her that I care about what's bothering her, even if I can't do anything about it.

I've never understood why some people insist on carrying grudges, whether in family relationships or in business. Bitterness and resentment are like a cancer that eats at a person from the inside out.

Over my many years in the music business, I've experienced a few serious conflicts and some major differences of opinions. But I refuse to carry a grudge. Life is too short to go through it with a chip on your shoulder. At times, I've needed to get back on the lawn mower and spend some extra time mowing the yard, but eventually I do get over it. Maybe if I had a better memory, it might take me longer!

SIXTEEN

MORE NEW FACES

BY THE MID-1980S, OUR CON-
cert program had become a major production. Besides the Trio,
which was now composed of Gloria, Gary McSpadden, and me,
we had a tremendously talented troupe of young singers and musicians who traveled with us on the road, many of whom went on
to be outstanding artists on their own. We also had a comedy act
with us, Hicks and Cohagen, which may have been another first
for gospel concerts. Although humor was always a part of our program, to have two stand-up comedians do nothing but humor was
a rather novel idea at that time in Christian gatherings.

From the beginning, we've used humor in our concerts to
communicate truth. I've always felt that if we could get people
to belly laugh during the first part of our program, they could
relax and identify with us as real human beings, especially since
much of our humor pokes fun at ourselves. Later, the audience
would be more open to consider the serious things we wanted
to say through our music and message.

Then Carman came along with some wonderfully humorous approaches to biblical messages, from a streetwise Italian's point of view. Night after night, he had the audience roaring in laughter. By the time they got done holding their sides, the crowds were ready to hear some serious truth.

Carman caught on in a big way. Audiences loved his "I'm going to beat the devil out of the devil" approach to his music and his Christian life. Carman worked with us for a couple of years, and they were two of our greatest. He was more than a performer; he was a tremendous encourager. One night in Akron, Ohio, our troupe was rather down as we met for pre-concert devotions. Our stage presentation wasn't working as well as we thought it should be, and we couldn't figure out what to do to make things better.

As we got together for devotions, the discouragement had spread like a cloud over the group. Carman stood up and said, "Wait a minute! This attitude is of the devil! Satan is all about discouraging people. We need to pray about this." Carman shared some Scripture with the group, then prayed for us. By the time he finished, we were like a football team in the pregame locker room, ready to go out and take on the world!

Sandi Patty was also on our program at that time, and Larnelle Harris was still with the Vocal Band—two more showstoppers! What a stellar lineup we had onstage every night! We took that program to Radio City Music Hall in New York and sold out the house.

The Radio City Music Hall stage is enormous, plus it has several levels. At the back of the main stage is a drop-off about thirty or forty feet high. That night, when Sandi performed "We Shall Behold Him," she finished majestically and stepped back with her hands up in the air, with a fabulous artistic flair.

It was then that we noticed that Sandi was within two inches of the backstage drop-off! Fortunately she stepped sideways when making her exit, narrowly averting what could have been a real tragedy.

We finished the spring tour with Sandi and Carman, and in May 1985 Gloria decided that she wanted to expand her horizons in a way she was unable to do in our little town of Alexandria. Gloria and Suzanne took a university class together on the subject of urban ministries. Half of the four-week course involved lectures, reading, and discussion. The other two weeks they spent living and working in the hearts of two large urban centers, New York City and Washington, D.C.

Gloria and Suzanne lived for a week in each city, in the YMCA in downtown Manhattan, and in the basement of a Presbyterian church in the center of Washington. They slept dorm-style on cots and ate whatever sparse food was available at the center. Each day they worked alongside inner-city ministry staff and volunteers, feeding the hungry, helping to refurbish old burnt-out buildings to be used for urban housing, as well as serving in soup kitchens and homeless shelters.

Gloria and Suzanne returned from their inner-city experience deeply moved. Gloria said, "For the first time, I think I've begun to understand what Jesus meant when He said, 'Whatever you do for the least of these, you've done it unto me' . . . or not. I don't think I'll ever be the same."

With the inner-city experience burning in her heart and mind, Gloria penned some lyrics that expressed the heart of Jesus for the poor and downtrodden people all around us. The song was called "I Walked Today Where Jesus Walks," and Greg Nelson, a great songwriter in his own right, put it to music. Larnelle Harris performed the song with the Gaither Vocal Band and the response from crowds was overwhelming. Something about the song touched people as they recognized the truth of its message.

Gloria later said, "When I realized how much Jesus loves the poor and hurting people, and how He identified with them, I was forced out of the judgment business and into the grace and mercy business." That attitude has been a cornerstone principle for us.

Later in 1985, our bass singer, Jon Mohr, informed me that he planned to leave the Vocal Band, so we started looking for a replacement. Gary McSpadden remembered a great young lead singer with the Singing Americans, a quartet from North Carolina. His name was Michael English. "Give him a call, and see if you can work out an audition," I told Gary.

Gary called Michael and asked him to come to Nashville to audition for the Vocal Band. When Michael hung up, he excitedly told his wife, Lisa, about the opportunity. "Who is Bill Gaither?" she asked innocently.

We had been so busy doing our own programs, many people in the southern gospel community were unaware of our existence. Similarly, I hadn't stayed on top of what had been happening in the southern gospel ranks. Michael had been nominated for several *Singing News* Awards, and we were oblivious to him.

In fact, Michael first joined the Gaither Vocal Band at Praise Gathering in October as his name was being announced at the National Quartet Convention as the winner of the *Singing News* Male Vocalist of the Year Award! He also won the *Singing News* Song of the Year Award for his stirring rendition of "I Bowed on My Knees and Cried Holy." Yet only a few people at Praise Gathering even knew who Michael was! We had so developed our own audience that the Praise Gathering crowd and the southern gospel audiences overlapped very little.

Michael helped us bridge that gap and because of him, we began drawing more southern gospel fans to concerts. Many of these people didn't know the Gaithers well but enjoyed Michael's singing. At the same time, we introduced Michael to an entirely new group of people in our field who had never heard of him, but fell in love with his music.

At first, though, I had serious misgivings whether Michael was going to work with us, simply because he was so shy. For quite a while I wondered, *Is he ever going to come out of his shell?* Although Michael had an incredible voice, he was rather reluctant to interact with the audience or even those of us on-stage.

"Let's just be patient with him," I told the others in our group, "and give him a chance." To his credit, Michael learned what we wanted and needed in our stage presentation as well as the rapport we expected with our audience, and he became a remarkable performer.

About a year later, Gary McSpadden announced that he was planning to leave the Trio and Vocal Band after a twelve-year run. Gary wanted to do more solo work and television, so we started looking for a new vocalist once again. We auditioned all sorts of great singers, but none seemed to mesh just right with us.

A concert promoter, Roy Morgan, sent me a video of a fellow he thought might be a good solo performer at Praise Gathering. I watched the tape of the unusual fellow who did a little singing and a lot of corny humor. His name was Mark Lowry. I remembered the name, because Mark had recorded an album titled *He Touched Me* when he was only twelve years old. He was interesting and entertaining, but I wasn't sure Mark would fit in with us. He was an odd character, and just so . . . so obnoxiously loud!

The more I watched Mark's video, the more I thought, *Well, we are looking for a baritone, and maybe we should at least consider him because of the humor aspect.* I called Roy Morgan and invited Mark to come to Nashville to audition.

Later Mark told me that when Roy told him that I wasn't interested in booking him on the Praise Gathering program, but that I wanted him to audition for the Vocal Band, he cracked up laughing! "Well, I've always wanted to meet Bill Gaither," he told Roy. "Maybe I can make him laugh!"

Furthermore, when Mark came to Nashville to audition for the Vocal Band, we didn't know it at the time, but he'd never sung baritone. He had been a soloist for most of his life and didn't even know how to find the baritone part, much less sing it.

Nevertheless, I'd told Mark in advance that we'd be singing "Daystar," a song from a Gaither Vocal Band album, so he asked a friend to teach him the part, which he promptly memorized. When Mark showed up at the studio, he was a human dynamo of energy. Michael English, Jim Murray, and I were already there when Mark blasted into the studio, and in a matter of moments he was all over the place. He met the other members of the Vocal Band and stepped right up to the microphone, ready to audition.

We rolled an instrumental track of "Daystar" and sang along. Mark sang the baritone part relatively well, and I liked what I called "the sunshine," the positive sound I heard in his voice. More than being a good singer, he was just so quick with one-liners, offbeat expressions, and quirky humor, I was ready to hire him on the spot.

Michael English wasn't so sure. A strong vocalist, Michael was looking for another power singer for the Vocal Band. Besides, Mark drove Michael nuts with his antics. Michael got me alone in a room off the studio and cringed as he said, "Bill, you can't be serious! You're not really thinking of hiring him, are you?"

"Well, yes, Michael, I am. Just think of some of the things we could do. He's not a bad singer, and we could use him to spark up the program with a bit of humor here and there."

Michael was not amused. He wasn't looking for a singing comedian; he was hoping I'd hire a fellow singer. But I saw something in Mark that I thought might work for us, so I invited him to do a weekend of concerts along with us in Knoxville.

The next day, Mark called me and said, "Bill, I can't do that. Take me off your list. I'm not good enough. It will never work. But, hey, thanks for listening to me, though."

"Okay, Mark. I understand. Fine."

About twelve hours later, Mark called back and asked, "Have you found anyone yet?"

"No, not yet."

"Just disregard my previous call. Can I come out and at least try?"

"Sure, come on," I said. "Let's give it a try."

Michael made it clear that his opinion of Mark hadn't changed. When Mark got on the bus, Michael practically ignored him. He didn't acknowledge his presence or pay any attention to Mark when he was talking, and he refused to talk directly with him during Mark's entire first trip aboard the Gaither bus. Mark didn't mind. He chattered constantly all the way from Nashville to Knoxville. At one point Michael became so exasperated, he held a newspaper up in front of him, pretending to be reading for miles and miles just so he wouldn't have to talk to Mark!

We did several weekends of concerts with Mark traveling

with us. Mark sang a few songs with us, and then he did a few jokes. I pretended to introduce him reluctantly. "Most artists need introducing," I'd said. "This one needs explaining!"

Mark gave a couple of funny looks at the crowd, furrowing his eyebrows quizzically. He moved closer to me onstage, wearing a shirt with large, flappy sleeves.

"Do you always buy your shirts with sleeves this big?" I asked, poking at the material on his shirt.

"Yep, they remind me of my grandma's flabby fat under her arms." Mark held out his sleeve and patted the flappy material, while the audience hooted in laughter. "I used to prop that stuff up and use Grandma's flab as a pillow in church. That way I could go to sleep during the services while they were singing some of your boring songs."

The audience howled in delight.

After the concert, I said, "Mark, we could use more of those one-liners."

"Really, Bill? Who can we make fun of?"

"Well, the safest thing you could do would be to just make fun of me," I told him. "Start with my clothes, my hair, anything." Mark took me quite literally!

After three weeks, Michael's attitude toward Mark still hadn't changed. "You're not really going to go through with this, are you, Bill?" Michael asked.

"Well, the people really love him . . ."

"Yeah, but he's an idiot!"

Mark finally confronted Michael and said, "We gotta talk. What's your problem with me?" They sat down and talked and before long, I noticed Michael smiling. A few minutes later he was chuckling, and shortly after that he was laughing out loud. Michael eventually warmed up to Mark and they became tremendous friends. At Praise Gathering that year, I invited

Mark to join the Vocal Band. I couldn't have imagined that my maniacal friend would be with me on the road for fourteen years!

From the time Mark joined the Vocal Band, his humor became a mainstay in each concert. He could be funny, I could be serious, and we enjoyed playing off each other. Mark's humor was sometimes outrageous, often off-the-wall, but usually in good taste, and he had a great knack for knowing when enough was enough.

He also has a serious side, a vein in him that runs much deeper than most people suppose. To some people's amazement, Mark can be downright profound at times! His song "Mary Did You Know," written with Buddy Greene, the bluegrass-style harmonica player who travels with us, is a good example of Mark's keen insights and his ability to find truth in unexpected places.

About that same time, Gloria said, "I would love to complete my work on my master's degree."

I said, "Honey, go do it." I'd recognized Gloria's restlessness about spending so much time on the road long before she expressed it to me. I could see it in her face every time I'd announce a new concert tour or plans for a new recording project. She'd wince as her dreams and desires to write books and speak at conferences were shelved once again, but like the trouper that she is, she gulped hard and got back on the bus. She and I talked occasionally about her taking time off to pursue her graduate work, but there had never really been a good opportunity. When Mark Lowry joined the Vocal Band in 1988, Gloria and I became more comfortable with the idea of her stepping away from the stage. Besides, the university had notified her that she must complete her master's studies soon or lose the credits she had already earned.

At the same time, Suzanne wanted to finish her master's, too, so Gloria and Suzanne went back to school together, working on their degrees in literature from Ball State University in Muncie, Indiana.

The first concerts without Gloria were a bit strange for me. I was comfortable with and accustomed to Gloria's presence on the platform; she was my "security blanket." For more than twenty-five years, she had been there with me onstage night after night. I relied on her ability to create special moments during our concerts with her readings, the "talking moments" onstage that I was incapable of creating. She was much better at handling that sort of thing then, and she's still better at it than I am now.

Our crowds expected Gloria to be present. The Vocal Band was becoming more popular, but naturally, people wanted to know, "Where's Gloria? What's wrong? Is she sick? What's going on?"

I tried to answer the questions as best I could without getting bogged down every night, and before long, concertgoers realized that Gloria was still very much a part of everything we were doing, whether she was present onstage or not.

Women often put off or give up what they want to do so they can support their husbands. To me, turnabout was fair play. I genuinely encouraged Gloria to pursue her academic interests. "Have fun," I said to cheer her on. After all, as my wife she had sacrificed her dreams for more than twenty-five years so I could pursue mine. The least I could do was to support her in her academic ventures.

I have always encouraged Gloria to write songs with other, younger writers who have better or different musical ideas than

I have. And those collaborations have resulted in some incredible music! She continues to speak at women's gatherings, write books, and develop her own musical forms, and I am thrilled. The three kids and I all stand up, applaud for her, and say, "Go for it!"

SEVENTEEN

FULL CIRCLE GOSPEL

ONE OF THE FAVORITE PAS-
times on the Gaither Vocal Band tour bus was the continual
contest between Michael English, Mark Lowry, Jim Murray, and
me to see who could bring in the best rendition of southern
gospel music. Michael loved the Happy Goodman Family, having grown up listening to the Goodmans and then singing with
Rusty Goodman earlier in his career. Michael brought in a tape
of Rusty singing one of his own compositions, "Had It Not Been
(For a Hill Called Mount Calvary)" and said, "Now, that's real
music there. That's the way it should sound!"

Mark grew up loving the Singing Rambos and the many
great songs that Dottie Rambo had written. "Now, that's the
way it ought to be," he'd say as we listened to Dottie sing "If
That Isn't Love" and "He Looked Beyond My Faults and Saw
My Need." Jim loved all the old songs, having started out years
ago with the Imperials, and of course I'd bring in recordings of
Jake Hess and say, "Now, that's singing, guys." Anytime we got

233

around a piano when nobody else was paying attention, we loved to sing the old songs such as "Beulah Land," "There Is a River," and so many others that we all had tucked away in our musical repertoire.

Thanks to Michael's ability to sing either southern gospel or contemporary styles of music, in 1989 the Vocal Band had recorded a strong contemporary album called *A Piece of the Rock.* Although we performed some great music, the album didn't sell well for us. We were frustrated and wondered, *Where are we going musically with this group?*

"This is silly," I said. "We love the old southern gospel songs. Why not do some, but do them in a fresh, exciting way?" The other guys agreed wholeheartedly.

When I broached the idea of the Gaither Vocal Band doing a southern gospel album to Darrell Harris and Stan Moser at Star Song, they responded coolly. "Well, that's interesting, Bill." I could tell that they didn't want the Vocal Band going down the old gospel trails.

Nevertheless, the idea kept coming back to me. One morning, Darrell Harris and I were having breakfast at a small café in the Music Row area of Nashville. Once again, I brought up the idea of doing a southern gospel album, and possibly bringing in some special guest singers, some of the legends of gospel music, to sing on the old song "Where Could I Go but to the Lord?"

A light suddenly came on in Darrell's eyes. "Do you mean doing an album similar to the Nitty Gritty Dirt Band's *Will the Circle Be Unbroken?* Where various old-time artists participated throughout the recording along with the younger guys?"

"I've never heard that album," I replied, "so I don't really know what you're talking about." Darrell explained that the Dirt Band had included some country legends such as the

Carter Family, Roy Acuff, and others on an album, and it turned out to be a wonderful time for everyone, and quite a successful recording project. He was getting genuinely excited about the possibilities. "Why don't you call some of the old-timers in southern gospel music, Bill, and ask them to participate with you on the album? It would be like an old homecoming for them."

Darrell's suggestion piqued my interest. There was only one problem. I leaned across the table and spoke quietly, as if we were trading top-secret spy codes.

"Do you really think they'd come?"

Darrell laughed. "Of course they'd come! They wouldn't if I called them," he said, "but they'd do it if you invited them."

"Now, that sounds like something I'd really like to do. I'd just want all the old-time artists in the same room at the same time. Wouldn't that be fantastic?"

"It would be sweet," Darrell replied.

"Let me think about it." I mulled over the idea for weeks before I finally came up with what I thought was a solution. We wouldn't ask the old-timers to do an entire album with us, but if they could join the Vocal Band on one gospel classic, that might be kind of fun. I figured we could shoot some video of the old-timers singing the one song with Michael, Jim, Mark, and me, and maybe include it in a single concept video to help promote the album. But the younger marketing folks at Star Song weren't sold on that idea at all. Several of them said, "Bill, if you do this strictly southern gospel package, you're going to ruin your image."

"What image?" I deadpanned, more serious than they realized. "I don't think the music-buying public regards us as contemporary, middle of the road, or anything else. In fact, we've been trying to figure out who we are ourselves!" The marketers conceded my point but feared that by getting too close to southern gospel, the Vocal Band could easily compromise our position as a leader in the "adult contemporary" niche—whatever that was! "How's an old gospel song going to work as a promotional tool for the Vocal Band?" they wanted to know.

"I don't know," I admitted. "But let's give it a try."

One day in early September 1990, Michael English called me, and I could tell immediately by the sound of his voice that he was distraught. "Bill, our buddy Rusty Goodman is in trouble," Michael said. "He's hurtin' bad. What can we do for him?"

I was aware that Rusty had been battling cancer for some time and had been in and out of the hospital throughout the summer of 1990. He had undergone all the treatments the doctors had recommended and was no better. The chemotherapy had caused his hair to fall out and drained him physically, while the enormous medical expenses ate up his savings and drained the family financially.

Michael loved Rusty and wanted to help somehow, so he posed the idea of doing a benefit concert on Rusty's behalf. "I think it is a great idea," I said. "Let me see what we can do."

I called Rusty, ostensibly to encourage him, but also to see how he'd feel about our trying to put together a concert. Rusty was a bit uncomfortable about the idea of people giving money to him, but he admitted that the financial pressures were weighing heavily on him, making an already difficult situation all the more painful. After being self-sufficient all his life, he said the medical bills threatened to bankrupt him. "Let me make some calls and we'll see what happens," I told him.

My first call was to Amy Grant. My granddad always told me,

"Bill, there are givers and there are takers in this world. You gotta make up your mind which you're going to be."

Amy Grant is a giver. She hardly knew Rusty Goodman, but she was aware of his legacy in gospel music. As soon as I explained the need to her, Amy said, "Sure, Bill. Count me in. I'd be happy to help."

Once Amy was on board, I knew we could gather a crowd of both performers and people in the audience. We put the word out that we were planning to do a benefit concert to help pay some of Rusty's medical bills not covered by insurance, and Michael W. Smith and Gary Chapman were among the first to respond. My friends Larry Gatlin and Ricky Skaggs said, "We'll be there, and we'll be glad to help."

Steven Curtis Chapman, Russ Taff, Bebe and Cece Winans, Sandi Patty, Larnelle Harris, J.D. Sumner and the Stamps, the Imperials, the Talleys, the Gold City Quartet, and the Christ Church Choir quickly answered the call as well. More than thirty artists from across the musical spectrum volunteered to perform in a concert held at Christ Church in Nashville.

The concert was scheduled for September 18, 1990, at seven o'clock, but by six-thirty, more than forty-five hundred people had crammed into the Christ Church sanctuary that seats approximately three thousand. Another two thousand folks had to be turned away because of fire codes. Traffic near the church was backed up for miles as people tried to get near enough to park and walk to the site.

The concert itself was phenomenal! One artist after another paid tribute to Rusty's contributions and influence. Throughout the program, Rusty sat with tears trickling down his face. One of the most moving segments of the evening was a series of video clips featuring Rusty singing some of his own songs, such as "Who Am I?" "Had It Not Been," and "I've Got Leavin' on My Mind."

Then Gloria summed up the feelings of most of the people in the church that night with a dramatic reading she had prepared, artfully weaving lines from Rusty's songs throughout her prose. Tears flowed freely down Rusty's face as Gloria looked at him and concluded, "And even though we know that for a long time now, you've had leavin' on your mind, we're asking you to stay, because we need—and this sick old world needs—what you are to us: a lover, a visionary, a dreamer, a poet. We need you here to walk with us and sing your pilgrim's song."

Once again, Gloria had articulated perfectly what the rest of us in the room desired with all our hearts to say to Rusty.

At the close of the concert, Rusty sang one more song with his brothers Howard and Sam, and his sister-in-law, Vestal. The Happy Goodman Family sang for the last time a song that Rusty had written, "I Believe He's Coming Back Like He Said."

As the song concluded, it was just too good and I didn't want the music to stop, so I grabbed a microphone and led the singers on the platform in a rousing rendition of "I'll Fly Away." It was a fitting way to put a cap on Rusty's career.

Prior to the concert, Rusty's family needed $52,000 to pay medical bills not covered by insurance. Through the benefit concert, we raised $55,000. Rusty Goodman died within a few days following the concert, but at least his family was not encumbered by the medical bills that had worried our good friend during his final weeks on earth.

Something about what I experienced at Rusty's benefit concert, and then again at his funeral service shortly thereafter, increased my desire to get some of the old songs and singers on tape before it was too late. I was more committed than ever to the Vocal Band doing a southern gospel album. All the guys in the Vocal Band were excited about recording the project because after our sound check every night, we'd often gather around the piano and sing those great songs, such as "Had It Not Been," "Beulah Land," and "There Is a River." We'd look at each other, smile, and say, "Now, that's the way it should be!"

We contacted producer Ken Mansfield, who had worked with the Beatles prior to his conversion to Christianity, and Ken set up the recording sessions at the Master's Touch Studio in Nashville. Then I began contacting some of the gospel music legends who joined us for what turned out to be the first *Homecoming* video. Ironically, some of the Star Song marketing people who initially had been so skeptical of the project were in the studio that afternoon, and what they experienced blew them away. Most of them were unfamiliar with the stories behind the people in attendance, but they recognized that something special was taking place, especially after the old-timers and the Vocal Band stayed and sang around the piano for three hours! There wasn't a dry eye among the marketing folks. "We didn't even know these people," they said. "This is sweet! The world will love this!"

And they were right.

When the first *Homecoming* video came out, the sales shot through the roof. We could not have imagined then that the original tape would lead to another, and another, and to the eventual distribution of millions of *Homecoming* videos around the world.

I was thrilled at our success, but beyond that I began to wonder if there wasn't some better way we could help other artists, some of whom had gathered at the Masters Touch to sing with us that day; artists similar to Rusty Goodman who had given their entire lives to spreading the Word through music, but who had more recently fallen on hard times.

There had to be something more that we could do . . . but what?

During the summer of 1991, following the enormous success of the first *Homecoming* video, I felt as if one of my dreams had come true: I had enjoyed the opportunity to sing with some of my lifelong heroes. When Gloria and I took a trip out to California, we decided to fulfill one of her lifelong dreams. Gloria is a John Steinbeck scholar and had always wanted to trace the famous author's steps in and around Monterey and Carmel, along the gorgeous Pacific coastline.

The author of such classics as *Of Mice and Men, East of Eden, Cannery Row, The Pearl,* and *The Grapes of Wrath,* for which he won a Pulitzer Prize, Steinbeck lived in the Monterey area and gleaned much of his material for characters and story lines from the people with whom he lived and labored. Gloria could hardly wait to see the places that had inspired the prolific author, who had received the Nobel Prize for Literature in 1962.

We trekked around Carmel, up through the gorgeous Seven Mile Drive past Pebble Beach golf resort and down to Monterey's waterfront, where Steinbeck conceived *Cannery Row.* Some friends even arranged for us to dine at the former home of John Steinbeck.

Gloria was ecstatic! She talked nonstop about the intricacies of Steinbeck's plots, and the variations of his prose in various books. She began to dream seriously about one day writing a Broadway show based on Steinbeck's life and writings, and I encouraged her to pursue her dreams.

By late summer of that year, I was already calling together the artists who had been a part of the original *Homecoming* video to attempt another, better-organized and planned-out video that we intended to title *Reunion*. Everyone I called was excited about coming.

The *Reunion* video had much the same feel as the initial *Homecoming* tape, although this time we were much better prepared. Many of the same artists who had been a part of the first video returned for the second. In addition, a number of other artists joined us, including Joy Gardner, Russ Taff, Kenny Hinson, Mylon LeFevre, and my brother, Danny, as well as some gospel greats such as Rex Nelon, Earl and Lily Weatherford, Dottie Rambo, and others.

As in the original *Homecoming* video, the day was fraught with emotion. James Blackwood stirred our hearts as he tearfully thanked the group for our prayers; he had suffered a stroke since he had been with us in February. Although he said that he felt only about 75 percent recovered, when he sang the Dottie Rambo song, "Sheltered in the Arms of God," he sounded 100 percent convinced that God would take care of him in this life and the next.

Another highlight came when Glen Payne and George Younce of the Cathedrals sang with Earl and Lily Weatherford. Years before, Glen and George had sung with the Weatherfords when they were partners in ministry at the Cathedral of Tomorrow, which Rex Humbard pastored in Akron, Ohio. It was great to hear them sing together again. Little did we know that this would be the last time they'd ever be together. Earl Weatherford passed away within months of the *Reunion* taping, making his last song that much more precious to Lily and to all of us who witnessed it.

Paul Downing, another fine bass singer, also passed away within weeks of the taping. The deaths of our friends was both a sad loss and a motivation to me. I felt compelled to get more of these people on tape before it was too late.

Not surprisingly, the highly charged spiritual atmosphere during the taping lent itself to a time of honest confession, repentance, and restoration. One beautiful picture of restoration was Mylon LeFevre. Mylon had grown up in a gospel-music-singing family. At seventeen years of age, Mylon wrote "Without Him," a song destined to be a gospel classic, but then he strayed far away from the Lord, his family, and anything to do with the gospel. He pursued a career in rock music, and along the way, Mylon got messed up in drugs and other destructive habits.

But God never gave up on Mylon, and in his late forties, he came back home to the Lord. He toured the country with a Christian rock band, Mylon LeFevre and Broken Heart, and won thousands of young people to Christ. Now in his fifties, with his mom at the piano, Mylon stood up to sing a powerful rendition of "Without Him." Just seeing the two of them, mother and son, reunited by the love of Jesus, was enough to reduce most of us in the room to tears.

By far the most poignant moment of the *Reunion* video to me—and one of the most poignant moments of all the videos we have done over the years—took place when Gloria presented a special piece she had written. Since Gloria had not been a part of the first *Homecoming* video, the night before the *Reunion* taping I had asked her to write something special that she could do on the video. "I know you are capable of writing something that will be just smashing!"

"Oh, Bill, those people don't want to hear me do anything," she said.

"Yes, they do, Gloria. Just be honest with it. Tell them about how you first heard this kind of music and your reluctance to embrace it."

But I have to admit that even I was not prepared for the reading that Gloria presented during the *Reunion* taping. She stepped over near the piano, pulled out some papers, and began to read while I played softly.

"I first heard about you from a college friend who loved gospel quartets and had heard you and your brother and sister sing at an all-night singing in Detroit," she began.

"When she found out I was going to fill in for a teacher at the high school where you taught, she couldn't wait for me to meet you . . . and then for me to get her a date with your brother." The room erupted in laughter.

Gloria smiled slightly and continued, "I never did get her a date with your brother, but I did fall in love with you.

"Little did I know that this English teacher with the crew cut and weird sense of humor, who talked about politics and literature, had another love. But I was soon to find out.

"After we had dated long enough to know that this was more than just another social relationship, you took me to your parents' farm, where you lived, and played a couple of songs by a group called the Speer Family.

"When the songs were through you asked what I thought. I said I liked the songs, and you said you wrote them. The songs were 'I've Been to Calvary' and 'The Joy of Serving the Lord.'

"Then you played me recordings by the Statesmen, the Blackwoods, and finally Jim Hill singing 'Lovest Thou Me?' and 'The Old-Fashioned Meeting.' I asked if you wrote those songs, and you said you did. I've often wondered what might have become of us had I not been impressed by those songs.

"After I passed my 'initiation,' we would often end our Saturday night dates driving through the Indiana countryside listening through the come-and-go reception to see if J. Bazzel Mull would play any of your songs on his gospel radio show." The singers in the room cracked up laughing at that. They knew how significant radio airplay was to the success of a song, and everyone in the room could identify. More than that, no doubt they could imagine me anxiously hoping to hear one of my songs on the radio!

"Since southern gospel music was not a part of my heritage," Gloria went on, with a slice of understatement, "I had a lot to learn. You were a walking encyclopedia of strange names, song titles, group personnel, and all-night-singing tour schedules. You knew who played piano for the Rangers in 1952, what bass singer sang when for the Foggy River Boys, and which tenors had ever sung with the Homeland Harmony Boys. The names you rattled off I was certain you made up, but I was soon to learn that there really were people named Burl Streval and Denver Crumpler."

Laughter rippled through the room again.

"Though we began to write songs together and were soon to tell, with one family combination or another, the story of what God was doing in our own lives, still you couldn't resist stopping by a gospel sing somewhere now and then to hear the Weatherfords or Wendy Bagwell and the Sunlighters, the Statesmen, or the Speer Family, and of course the Blackwood Brothers and the Happy Goodman Family.

"You even did some promoting in our area and made me go with you to tack up posters and flyers all over central Indiana, announcing a new group called the Imperials with Jake Hess and Henry Slaughter.

"I'll never forget the night our son was to be born. I was in the first stages of labor, but I had to hold off till you got home from an all-night sing in Indianapolis. You had gone to hear just a few groups, you'd said, and deliver some sheet music. That night, I'll have to admit, was not the night I loved gospel music the best.

"Over the years, these [names] I thought you made up first became real people to me, then precious friends. Vestal and Howard Goodman, Brock and Faye Speer, Hovie and Jake, Buck and Dottie Rambo, Henry Slaughter and Hazel, and so many more have become dear to us both.

"I remember holding our little Suzanne by the seat of the pants while her little legs danced up and down on the back of our couch to 'I Wouldn't Take Nothin' for My Journey Now.' And I couldn't count the summer nights when we piled all three of our kids, wrapped in blankets in the old red convertible, and drove out under the starry Indiana sky singing in family harmony 'Jesus Is Coming Soon,' while the crickets and cicadas sang their counterparts.

"Now our kids are writing songs of their own, singing harmonies with their kids, and making demos better than we ever learned to make."

Gloria paused briefly and looked over at me, her eyes filled with emotion. "Once again, it's just you and me, Babe. And more and more I notice you getting out the old records that started you on this journey, or sitting down after supper to play again a few measures of some song you used to pretend to broadcast out the window of that old farmhouse in Scotts Addition when you came home from Cunningham School.

"For these are the songs that got your attention, captured your imagination, and showed you the way to Jesus. And the harmonies you loved became the seed of your dream, dreams we have together realized more than you . . . even you, could have ever imagined."[1]

I am supposed to be the person who knows what to do after a special moment has occurred. But to be honest, this was too overwhelming even for me. I didn't know what to do, what to say, or how to respond. Gloria had once again astounded all of us, including me, with her ability to sum up the inner thoughts and feelings most of us were reluctant to express. All I knew to do was to begin singing softly Andrae' Crouch's song "Through It All," because that song so aptly described what Gloria's and my lives had been about. "Through it all, through it all . . . I've learned to trust. . . ."[2]

Two kids coming from two widely diverse cultural worlds had finally collided emotionally in a recording studio in Nashville, in front of some people who were extremely suspect to Gloria. But I could tell that something special was happening, and some long-standing walls were coming down.

"Through it all . . . I've learned to trust."

Shortly after the *Reunion* video was recorded, we received word that Kenny Hinson had beed diagnosed with terminal cancer. Kenny had sung for years as a soloist and in a group with his brother, Ronny Hinson, who had written the well-known song "The Lighthouse,"which the great Rusty Goodman had popularized. Similar to Rusty, Kenny fought the cancer with all his physical and financial strength, but it soon became obvious that he was losing on both fronts.

Once again, the gospel music community came together to raise money for one of its own who had fallen on hard times. We had hoped to raise $35,000 through the benefit concert for Kenny Hinson, and we raised more than $33,000.

Nevertheless, I realized that we couldn't keep blowing the sirens every time there was another emergency and asking people to pitch in to help. We needed to do something in advance to prepare for the challenges that were sure to come.

Herman Harper, the president of the Harper Talent Agency in Nashville, had begun a Gospel Music Trust Fund in 1983, starting with an initial donation of $10,000, raised from the Marvin Norcross Golf Classic, a tournament Herman had organized at the 1982 National Quartet Convention. The purpose of the fund was to help provide financial assistance to individuals who had derived their income from Christian music when large medical expenses were incurred, or when insurance coverage was insufficient. Herman's son, Ed Harper, now managed the fund, and the organization's primary fund-raising method was still an annual golf tournament. Folks enthusiastically supported this event, but the proceeds were barely enough to help more than the occasional hardship case. I began to see a way that my desire to help some of our aging artists could play out.

By now the first *Homecoming* video was selling extremely well, so the Gaither organization decided to devote a portion of the proceeds from the *Homecoming* videos to help care for the artists. Beyond that, Star Song Communications, our record company, offered a challenge, promising to match any royalties the Vocal Band donated from the sales of our new southern gospel album. Soon the trust fund's bank account topped $40,000. When the *Reunion* tape came out, we did something similar, boosting the trust fund's holdings to around $100,000. "If we get serious about this," I told the fund's board of directors, "we might really be able to help a lot of people."

Like many artists, I suppose, I can't even count how many times I have been "hit on" to support some cause I've never even heard of. Fortunately, Gloria and I sat down with Dr. Robert Reardon early in our career, not simply to plan our charitable giving, but also to set some guidelines regarding to whom we should give. Just because somebody has a pet cause does not necessarily mean that Gloria and I should help support him or her.

But I knew in my heart from the beginning that the Gospel Music Trust Fund was a good cause. If country artists and artists from other genres of music could take care of their own senior statesmen, how much more should we in Christian music respectfully, and sacrificially if necessary, help those who have paved the way for us?

Ed Harper invited me to serve as a trustee of the fund, and when I saw the trust fund's mission statement, I was even more convinced to actively support the cause. At the heart of the organization's mission statement was a quote from Israel's second king, David: "I have been young, and now I am old; / yet I have not seen the righteous forsaken, / or his descendants begging bread."[3] When I saw that statement, I said, "Yes, that's what we're about! Our people should not have to go out grubbing after having given their whole lives to serving other people through music."

We planned a benefit concert at the arena in Nashville, specifically to raise money for the trust fund, rather than an individual artist or artist's family. The Gaither organization and Premier Production Company partnered and agreed to split the costs of the arena rental if the artists would donate their time to do the program. Furthermore, we provided all the sound equipment and lighting for the program. Our goal was to have a benefit in which ticket sale revenues went solely to support the cause. Personally, I'm weary of participating in "benefits" that don't really benefit the people for whom the money is being raised. I was glad to be able to tell the audience that night, "Every penny from ticket sales will go toward helping to care for hurting gospel artists."

The concert that night looked like a who's who of Christian music. Just about everybody who was anybody in the Christian music industry was on the long program, and we had a ball!

More importantly, we raised $250,000, a feat that had never before been accomplished in our industry.

The trust fund then had half a million dollars in its coffers. In the meantime, we continued to donate a portion of the *Homecoming* video sales, and the fund soon topped three-quarters of a million dollars!

Ed Harper and I talked over some ideas for expanding our horizons again and we said, "Let's enlarge this board." I'd learned from my service on the Anderson University board that one way of drawing in more funds is to bring new people onto the board. They may not always be able to donate heavily themselves, but they can often lead to other resources.

We invited several heads of Christian music companies to join us: Bill Hearn from Sparrow, Darrell Harris of Star Song, and Kenny Harding from Canaan Records. The company heads came up with a challenge: their companies would donate $100,000 each for three years if the Gaither videos would match it for three years; and we encouraged the gospel artists to contribute another $100,000 for three years, for a total of $900,000. We appealed to the entire gospel music community, southern gospel, traditional, black gospel, and contemporary. We stressed to the young artists, "You are contemporary only today; you're going to be old, or at least traditional, in a few years, so this fund may be important to you as well."

To their credit, even most of the younger artists recognized the value of having a safety net for medical and other financial crises. At present, we have more than $1.5 million available to help artists in need, and the Gospel Music Trust Fund receives donations from individuals, music companies, and other music agencies, as well as the annual donation of royalties from the *Homecoming* videos and the Marvin Norcross Golf Classic.

While the trust fund is available to all segments of the Christian music industry, the dispensation of the funds is strictly governed and is not an automatic dole. Those who receive assistance must prove their need, and the board of trustees, comprised of eleven directors, votes on every request for financial help. We attempt to be frugal managers of the resources. We know that we can be of help to all only if we are fair and stringent with the money that comes in to the organization.

I refuse to waste time, energy, or money, so I try to manage those resources well, but I thoroughly enjoy giving all three generously to a good, worthy cause. Mark Lowry has laughed at me for years, saying, "Bill, you are the tightest guy I've ever seen in my life!"

"I'm not tight, I'm frugal," I say. "And Mark, let me teach you something: you will never be generous—or at least not for long—until you learn how to be frugal." I just refuse to be wasteful. For instance, when we leave a hotel room, occasionally I'll notice that there is a small bottle or two of some unopened shampoo supplied by the hotel. I *cannot* walk out the door and leave that shampoo! In my mind, I know that somewhere down the road, we will be arriving at a concert venue in a rush and have to shower at the arena, and one of us will be looking for some shampoo. Besides that, I paid for that shampoo!

I tease Mark, "I never leave the shampoo or the soap behind, but it's a little more difficult getting those hotel hair dryers off the wall these days!"

EIGHTEEN

OLD FRIENDS AND NEW ONES

ONE OF THE MOST POPULAR baseball movies released in recent years was *Field of Dreams*. It's an intriguing story about a thirty-six-year-old Iowa corn farmer, Ray Kinsella, played by Kevin Costner, who hears a voice while working in his cornfield. The voice promises, "If you build it, he will come."

The "it" that Ray is to build turns out to be a baseball diamond in the middle of his cornfield! And initially, the "he" is "Shoeless" Joe Jackson and seven of his buddies, who were tossed out of baseball for allegedly throwing a championship game. Joe and his cronies show up at Ray's cornfield ready to play, although they have the distinct disadvantage of being dead. The movie pulsates with spiritual overtones, but its main theme is that of another chance to see unfulfilled dreams come true—especially when it climaxes with the apparent reconciliation between Ray and his father.

In a very real sense, that's what the *Homecoming* videos have always been about: seeing unfulfilled dreams come true, and reconciliation with our heavenly Father and with one another. And as artists began to arrive in our little town of Alexandria from all over the country for the taping of the *Old Friends* video, I looked out on the cornfields that my granddad and father once cared for. A large tent now stood in the fields behind our property, so we could all eat our meals together during the three-day taping sessions. I couldn't help thinking of the famous line from *Field of Dreams*: "If you build it, they will come."

Indeed, for the eighteen months since we recorded the first video, we had been building the *Homecoming* phenomenon and people were coming to the old-time southern gospel music like never before. Now, as I looked across the cornfields, the music artists' tour buses lined our studio parking lots and the roads running up and down and all around Pinebrook Studios. More than one hundred artists were coming to Alexandria, Indiana, to sing on the next video.

I understood a little of what Ray Kinsella might have felt. All my childhood heroes were coming—Hovie, Jake, Eva Mae, Vestal, James, George, and so many more! They were all there—on my ball diamond! I built it, and they came!

It's difficult to describe a few special moments during the Old Friends taping because there were so many of them! One of the highlights for me was when Doris Akers, who had written the song "Sweet, Sweet Spirit," stood up to sing one of her own compositions. I sat down at the piano to accompany the energetic elderly woman, but apparently Doris didn't like the way I was playing her song. She came right over to the piano, motioned me off the bench, and slid in behind the keyboard herself, to the enthusiastic applause and whistles of the other singers in the studio! She sang and accompanied herself, finishing to a rousing standing ovation from the rest of the *Home-coming* singers.

It was a special treat for me to have Doug Oldham with us for the *Old Friends* video. Doug had been one of the first friends to sing some of our songs, such as "He Touched Me," "Have You had a Gethsemane?" "The King Is Coming," "Something Beautiful," and, of course, "Thanks to Calvary." The studio was hushed as Doug sang, "Thanks to Calvary, I am not the man I used to be. Thanks to Calvary, things are different than before; while the tears ran down my face, I tried to tell her, 'Thanks to Calvary I don't live here anymore.'"[1]

There was indeed a sweet, sweet spirit among the old friends gathered in the studio that day. We all felt as though we were standing on hallowed ground. And in a sense, we were.

I mentioned earlier that Michael English eventually learned to tolerate Mark Lowry; he even taught him how to belt out a song. They were a great team. They also had good ears for new talent.

When we were taping *Landmark* and *Precious Memories*, two new videos, in Alexandria, Mark and Michael invited a new family group to attend the taping. Judy, Joyce, and Jonathan Martin had recorded a few custom albums and they were growing in popularity in Arkansas and other southern states. Michael and Mark recognized that the Martins were something special, especially when they sang a capella, without instrumental accompaniment.

The Martins were singing in a church in Indianapolis, so Michael and Mark encouraged them, "Come on over to Alexandria, and we'll try to introduce you to Bill and Gloria."

The Martins came to the taping, but it was so busy, and there were so many artists involved, I never really got a chance to listen to them. Finally, while I was working in the studio, Michael and Mark nudged Gloria toward the hallway. "Gloria, you have to hear these guys sing!" Michael said. Mark nodded emphatically. Gloria was glad for a break, so they stepped outside the studio, and Mark pulled them toward the rest-room door. "The acoustics will be better in here," he said.

The three Martins, Gloria, Mark, and Michael all crowded into the tiny rest room off the main studio. The moment the Martins began singing, Gloria fell in love with them. Their voices were impeccable and their harmonies were breathtaking! Gloria and Mark brought the Martins into the main studio and caught my attention. "Bill, you gotta hear these kids!" Mark insisted.

It was near the end of the two-tape session and everyone was tired, but I recognized that look in Gloria's and Mark's eyes: they had found something extremely special. "Okay," I said to the group. "We've run out of time, but real quick, I want these three kids that Gloria and Mark have told me about to come and sing for us."

Judy, Joyce, and Jonathan stepped up in front of the entire *Homecoming* group and sang the Doxology and then "It Is Well with My Soul" a capella. As tired as we were, the Martins knocked our socks off with their incredible talent. They've been singing with us at *Homecoming* events and concert venues around the country ever since!

After the first few videos, I got in the habit of preparing for each taping by assembling a repertoire of about fifty or sixty songs that seemed to fit with the theme I had in mind. Then I went into the studio and recorded basic music tracks and some guide vocals. But the formula for the *Homecoming* videos remained much the same: we'd get everyone together for a two-

or three-day "retreat," with a loose agenda and song order, but what happened between the songs, and sometimes *during* the songs, was totally unscripted. Sometimes I'd ask certain people to prepare to sing a specific song or tell a story, but most of what occurred once the tape started rolling was spontaneous.

All of the people who gathered for the tapings were comfortable singing in front of a camera, but not all of them were at ease in sharing from their hearts in their own words. Inevitably, though, after a day or so reminiscing and enjoying the time with old friends, even the bashful types began to open up. Many times, we'd simply stop what we were doing to pray for someone who expressed a need. At other times, a particular song might send us in an entirely different direction from what I had anticipated. I tried to maintain a light hand when it came to directing the *Homecoming* singers, fostering a sense of freedom and encouraging people to respond to God, not just the words on our TelePrompTers. Sometimes I felt as though I were hanging on to Ben-Hur's chariot racing around the Colosseum, and at other times it was as though I was the guide sitting on a river raft, easing downriver.

We did on-location videos in many areas where the history of gospel music was well known. We taped in Birmingham, Atlanta, Nashville, Memphis, and Dallas and created theme-driven videos about various aspects of Christianity. We did entire video projects comparing our journey with God to a river; we did other projects in which we talked about mountaintop experiences as opposed to walking through the valley. For these programs, we incorporated many of the great songs using those metaphors to describe the Christian pilgrim's progress through life experiences. Often we'd try to film in locations that would help the viewers draw the comparisons for themselves as they heard the music.

Sometimes Gloria added "B-roll" material, insights drawn from the location where we were shooting, or we might insert interviews with selected artists for each video. Usually, however, I wouldn't even try to weave the events of the taping together until everyone had gone home and I'd had a chance to review the tapes.

One of the most popular videos we produced we titled *Down by the Tabernacle*, and we filmed it on location in September 1997 at Bethel Tabernacle, an old Wesleyan camp meeting site in Fairmount, Indiana. It was a warm, balmy evening, so we opened all the windows and doors of the tabernacle. That way, people could sit outside on benches and lawn chairs as well as in the building, just as folks may have done more than a hundred years ago as they listened to evangelists preach about getting right with God and getting ready for heaven. We had more than seventy members of our *Homecoming* singers on the platform, and the "live" program had the feel of an old-time revival meeting.

At the other extreme, we've done video projects at the Kennedy Center in Washington, D.C., and Carnegie Hall in New York. Wherever we have gone, we've discovered audience members with a great appreciation for the old gospel songs as well as a longing to reaffirm their faith in God.

The demand for the videos soon became so great, we decided to set up our own "call center" in our office building to handle the requests. Each day, our operators receive more than four hundred requests for videos and other Gaither products. We ship out more than half a million pieces of product every year!

After the first three or four videos began to circulate, people developed an almost familial attitude toward the *Homecoming* friends. After all, we were in their homes—on their TV screens, so they felt as though we were family. We noticed more and more people dropping by Alexandria just to stop in and see us, or to visit our offices to see where the videos were born.

One day I said to Barry Jennings, "We don't have enough room here to entertain guests when they stop by. All they get to see is people working in offices. It would be nice to have a retail outlet where they could stop and find some of our products."

Gloria picked up on my comment to Barry and took my idea literally. She developed "Gaither Family Resources, and the Latte Gourmet Coffee & Lunch Bar," a place where people could find all our music, songbooks, and videos, as well as materials that we considered valuable in raising our children, handling money, writing, and caring for nature, gardening, or other areas of life. Gloria created a lovely coffee shop and store where people could have breakfast or lunch, visit, and in a comfortable, leisurely atmosphere, sit down and talk about ideas, problems, or opportunities they were encountering in their own lives.

Unlike most stores that are stocked according to subject or products, Gloria divided the center according to life-needs. Her concept grew from the idea that we all have basically the same concerns: we want a comfortable home; we need to care for our bodies; we have children or grandchildren for whom we want to provide positive, encouraging stimulation; and most of us have stresses in our lives that need to be eliminated, conquered, or managed.

Every time I walk into the shop I am amazed. It's such a warm, cozy, inviting atmosphere. Gloria has done with the shop the same thing that she has done with our song lyrics all these years: expanded on a kernel of an idea and made it something special. All I wanted was a place where people could stop to buy some of our videos, but Gloria took it to a whole other level!

We invited some of our *Homecoming* friends to stop in every so often so the people visiting could interact with them and get to know them on a personal basis. Some of the first to visit were Guy Penrod and Janet Paschal, and many others have come by since just to sit and share with the friends who know them from the videos.

One of the funniest evenings we ever had during these "fireside chats" was with J.D. Sumner and Mark Lowry. J.D. had been the bass singer for the Blackwood Brothers Quartet and the Stamps Quartet, and was a strong leader in the National Quartet Convention. He was also one of the characters in southern gospel music that Gloria liked the least, and the feelings were mutual.

During the last years of J.D.'s life, however, especially after the death of his dear wife, Mary Agnes, Mark Lowry became a close friend. Mark had read J.D.'s articles in the *Singing News* for years, and he appreciated J.D.'s honesty, which at times could be brutal. Mark said, "I've watched J.D. sing all my life, and I'd really like to get to know him." He made special efforts to visit with J.D. whenever possible, and they became an odd couple of inseparable friends.

Meanwhile, Mark and Gloria were breakfast buddies, and Mark constantly spoke up for J.D. "Gloria, J.D. is not well educated, but he is smart. He comes up with the greatest ideas. I think you'd really like him if you'd ever get to know him." He told J.D. something similar about Gloria.

Mark eventually talked Gloria into having a night at the Gaither Resource Center featuring J.D. and him just ad-libbing. We had such a large crowd attend the event, we had to move the program inside to the studio. The studio holds about three hundred people, and it was packed. With nothing scripted or prepared ahead of time, J.D. and Mark kept the hometown folks and visitors in stitches. It was a crazy, wild night as both guys spouted off anything they thought.

At the time, Suzanne and Barry's little boy, Jesse, was about two or three years old, but already he had the run of the studio—literally! He was running every which way, all over the room, laughing and having a ball. Before long, Jesse's romping started to bug J.D. Finally, in a voice three octaves lower than most human beings' voices, J.D. snarled, "Would somebody please grab that kid and sit him down in a chair!"

Mark said, "You better be careful. That's Gloria's grandson."

"Oh, he is? What a brilliant, beautiful child!" J.D. quipped.

Mark and J.D. stayed overnight at Grover's Corners, the Gaither family guest house that was the home where my grandma and grandpa had lived. The house is filled with old family photos, old books, and plenty of music. The one thing it does not have is a television. Poor J.D. and Mark nearly suffered severe withdrawal pains!

But the following day, Gloria and J.D. had a long talk. In the process, they really started to like each other, and it was the beginning of an entirely new relationship for them. Long-standing walls that had separated Gloria's and J.D.'s worlds began to crumble as the two of them reconciled. Mark and J.D.'s trip to Alexandria will always be especially meaningful to us, since J.D. passed away not many months after that, but not before he and Gloria had one more special moment that touched our hearts. I'll tell you about it in the pages ahead.

NINETEEN

SPECIAL MOMENTS

From the beginning of the *Homecoming* video series we have experienced special moments, times during the taping when we sensed God's presence in unusual, powerful ways.

One such moment took place during the taping of the *Singin' in My Soul* video. The *Homecoming* group had been together for nearly two full days, singing in our Pinebrook studio in Alexandria and having a great time. On the last evening, our daughter Suzanne presented a poignant piece of prose she had written titled "Red Wing." Alluding to the many times Gloria and I had entertained guests during her childhood, Suzanne led off by saying, "In this little town, I would dare say the vast majority of people in my school didn't sit up half the night listening to southern gospel music and fall asleep in a sheet music box, but you don't get it out of your system. So I wrote this for my son, Will."

We all sat in rapt attention as Suzanne began to read.

The minute we get into the car and you get all buckled up, the first words out of your mouth are, "Let's listen to 'Red Wing'!"

"Red Wing" is the first song on the first side of a collection of dulcimer mountain music that we bought at Grandma's store. I always think it's funny that you became fixed on that one particular tune on that particular tape when there are so many high-tech Mickey Mouse marketers vying for your attention. . . .

I look over at you bobbing right and left in your car seat, and you look almost as if you could jump down and dance an Irish jig without ever having to be taught. Watching you makes me wonder about the substances that run through our veins, and I can't but think that somewhere down the road, you may develop a distaste for all of us.

You may load up a car and move away to some distant city. You may leave this little town and never look back. You may vow never to do certain things you grew up watching all of us do. You may wash the Indiana dirt from your face, put on new clothes, eat exotic food, and drink the sweet nectar from a thousand unfamiliar ports of call. You may fine-tune your ears to appreciate the music of a cultured and refined society.

But do not be surprised, my son, if every now and then you get hungry for deep-dish macaroni and cheese, or fried green tomatoes, or homemade chocolate pie. Don't be alarmed when your hands have a yearning to feel the smoothness of a good piece of pine. Don't get upset if on some sunny spring day you get the urge to plant some beans and cucumber plants. Never fear when your pale blue eyes wander happily over a patch of zinnias or marigolds. Don't be afraid of a strain of southern gospel music, or [when] the faint hammering of a dulcimer catches your ear and deep inside you somewhere begins a fluttering you never knew existed, and it rises up in your throat with a pulse so strong it brings you to tears.

My sweet boy, with your Boster blond hair, and blue Sickal eyes; you with your Hartwell sense of justice, and your Gaither sense of humor; you with your slender Jennings body and your Smith reserve; you, my son, are but a cell in this connective tissue of life. Like it or not, we all dance to the tunes we know.[1]

Suzanne's reading reminded us of what we all recognized but rarely vocalized: that this music was in our blood, a part of us from which we could never flee, even if we wanted to. Her words weren't just for Will; they were for every one of us. Following Suzanne's reading, Tanya Goodman Sykes presented a moving rendition of "Look for Me," a song about heaven that her daddy, Rusty Goodman, had written. Rusty had been a mainstay in the Happy Goodman Family for years, and his songwriting and his deep, strong singing voice had given the Goodmans a unique sound. As I mentioned earlier, Rusty passed away in 1991 after a long, difficult battle with cancer.

As Tanya sang we were all deeply moved, but Howard Goodman, Rusty's brother, was nearly overwhelmed as his niece voiced Rusty's words. Tears flowed freely down Howard's face. It was easy to imagine that Rusty was finally home.

After we sang the chorus again, Howard, seventy-nine years old himself at the time, said, "Bill, let me say something." I handed Howard the microphone. Howard breathed heavily as he spoke. "You know, time moves on; everybody has to go the way of growing old. Now, I don't think too much about that. It doesn't bother me to know that I'm getting old, and sometimes I can't get around too well. But for the last few weeks or month or so . . . and I haven't told Vestal this . . . the devil has come to me in the night a time or two, and said, 'Do you really think that there is a heaven, and you will see your folks again, that you'll see Rusty and Sam, and [your] mom and dad, and all?"

"I'd have to really pray and run that devil out of my room. But let me tell you something. Moments like this with this song, and this Spirit, reaffirm again that what I have believed is true."

Tanya slipped across the room, leaned down to the chair where Howard was sitting, and hugged his neck. What a beautiful sight.

Doubt is a word that believers are not supposed to say aloud. I often wonder how the disciple Thomas would have made it in our modern Christian circles.

As Howard and Tanya hugged, I looked at Howard and said, "You give us all hope. Thanks for being honest enough to admit that you have to deal with doubt, too. I'd like to sing a song that Gloria and I wrote several years ago."

> I believe, help Thou my unbelief.
> I take the finite risk of trusting,
> Like a child.
> I believe, help Thou my unbelief.
> I walk into the unknown trusting
> All the while.
> I long so much to feel the warmth
> That others seem to know,
> But should I never feel a thing,
> I claim Him even so.
> I believe, help Thou my unbelief.
> I walk into the unknown
> Trusting like a child.
> I walk into the unknown,
> Trusting. . . .[2]

Following the song, I noticed Roger Bennett motioning to me from the top row of seats where he was sitting. Once the pianist with the Cathedrals, Roger had recently been diagnosed with cancer. "Bill, I want to say something."

Roger stood up straight and in a soft, wavering voice said, "I think Satan knows a lot of things. I know he's not all-knowing, but somehow he knows my weaknesses. For the last five minutes, I've been thinking about my doubts. And the day I was diagnosed with leukemia . . . I don't remember a lot about that day, but I remember the words 'You've got cancer.' I remember talking to Glen [Payne] and George [Younce] . . . and I remember distinctly Satan coming to me immediately.

"The very first mental picture I had after the doctor said, 'You have cancer'—I'm a little ashamed to admit this to you—but the first mental picture I had was of me in the future, on my deathbed, seconds away from closing my eyes, wondering if all of this is true. Wondering if the second after I closed my eyes if it would be oblivion, or would it be the new Jerusalem? And of all the things that happened to me that afternoon, the worst thing wasn't getting cancer . . . but the worst thing was coming face-to-face with my own doubt in my heart . . . but 'I walk into the unknown, / trusting like a child.' "

Roger had voiced what many sincere Christians sometimes wonder but rarely have the courage to admit: Is this gospel message true? Will it hold up in the end? He had faced his doubts honestly and come out on the other side of them, believing, trusting. To me, this is where the rubber hits the road. Does your faith work when you are facing life-threatening situations? That day in the studio, we knew that our faith was real. It was a poignant moment that none of us will ever forget.

A truly significant moment took place in 1998 during our *Rivers of Joy* video, when J.D. Sumner took the microphone and began speaking from his heart. He said, "A lot of people tell us what these [*Homecoming*] tapes have done for them. Every night at our concerts people tell us how much they've been blessed. But you don't know the half of it . . . how much J.D. Sumner has been blessed." J.D.'s voice dropped to a whisper as he said, "How much these tapes have changed me." J.D. paused to regain his composure before going on, "I used to have an old, hard crust on me for a lot of years, but the Holy Spirit has melted that."

"Amen! Praise God!" shouted several people in the room. Several others exchanged knowing looks as if they were recalling the old J.D. compared to the fellow who was now speaking.

"And in these tapings, there have been people that I have grown to love that I used to dislike." J.D. looked at bass singer George Younce and quipped, "I even love George now!" The singers sitting in the studio convulsed in laughter.

"But two people—one was Mark [Lowry] my little buddy sitting behind me. Mark's spiritual life is so deep. That stupid comedy stuff he does just opens the door. I used to hate his guts!"

The people in the studio were almost in tears from their laughter.

"He'd come into a room and completely destroy anything that you had going on. But through these tapings I got to know Mark, and we became buddies. Mark and I would spend many hours at my condominium, just he and I, talking. He tries out all his stupidity on me. I have to go through it first.

"But I learned to love, love, *love* a man that I used to not like. You know, it's no fun to eat by yourself." J.D. was close to tears, and for a moment it seemed as though he might lose his composure completely. He struggled on: "If you ever lose your

wife . . . I lost about forty pounds. I didn't know it, but I wanted
to die.

"Then I met Mark [Lowry]. About three or four times a week,
we'd go out and have supper together. And of course, Mark's
cheap, so I'd have to pay for it." Everyone cracked up again.

"And then, somebody else I didn't like—I just absolutely despised Gloria Gaither."

The room exploded in laughter at J.D.'s audacity.

"No, I'm serious, though," J.D. said. The group was in tears.
"She'd start reading one of those poems, and I'd say, 'Here we
go again!'

"Then one day, Bill asked Gloria to pray, and I thought, *J.D.*,
you better listen to this prayer. It was the sweetest prayer I'd ever
heard in my life." He reached over and put his hand on Gloria's
shoulder and said, "This lady right here is profound." Gloria
smiled at him and he said, "If you want to know why there's a
Bill Gaither, it's this woman right here." Gloria winked at J.D.
as the room full of gospel singers applauded.

"I don't know a woman I love more than Gloria Gaither . . .
now. We had breakfast in Lakeland, Florida, one morning.
Mark wanted the two of us to have breakfast with Gloria. Of
course, I knew that I'd have to pay for that, too.

"But we had a beautiful talk and Gloria asked me some profound questions. She said, 'J.D., what's the first thing you're
going to ask Jesus?'

"My mind thought of a thousand things." J.D.'s voice
dropped to a hoarse whisper. "Where's my wife? Where's Mama?
Where's Daddy? But the first thing I'm going to ask Jesus is 'Is
this for real? You mean that *I'm* in heaven? Do you mean that
you died for *me*? That God gave His only Son to die for someone like *me*? I wouldn't give up my child for anybody. The most
important thing in our lives is to just give your heart to Jesus.

"I love everybody in this room. I thank God for the privilege of being able to sit in this little chair. Jake, George, James, Hovie, Glen, Rex, my nephew Donnie, I could name every one of you, and I love you. And Gloria, I love you, Baby."

J.D. leaned over and he and Gloria embraced warmly.

More than thirty years' worth of suspicion, misunderstanding, and mutual disdain melted away with that hug as J.D. and Gloria publicly embraced.

It was more than a special moment; it was monumental for all of us.

The moment was made even better by the miracle that took place when the group began singing "We'll Talk It Over (In the By and By)" with my brother, Danny, singing the solo.

Nearly everyone in the room knew that Danny was fighting hard against the lymphoma that was sapping his body's strength. He had been to the hospital that very morning for a radiation treatment. He wasn't sure if he'd be able to sing at all when he returned, but he hit every note as he sang:

> I'll hide my heartache behind a smile
> And wait for reason till after while.
> And though He tries me,
> I know I'll find,
> That all my burdens are silver lined.
> We'll talk it over in the by and by.[3]

None of us wanted to think that within three years both J.D. and Danny might be gone. It was a once-in-a-lifetime moment, captured on tape forever.

One of the most interesting aspects of the videos has been the way viewers have picked up on the love of God that is so evident in the lives of the performers, and especially the unspoken gestures of love and respect between the *Homecoming* artists. Once, for example, James Blackwood was performing a song on camera. Glen Payne, former lead singer for the Cathedrals, was sitting next to James and noticed that the great singer's jacket pocket flap was stuck inside the pocket. Without making a scene, Glen reached over while James sang and unobtrusively straightened the flap.

A psychologist saw the tape of that moment and it touched her heart. She was impressed that one man would do such a thing simply to keep another from being embarrassed. She wrote to us, saying, "It is so obvious that these people love each other," and she said that as a result, she renewed her own commitment to God.

To me, that is true Christianity. I've always felt that there is a profound difference between piety and true spirituality. I've never considered myself to be a pious person, but I hope that in some measure each day, I can live out genuine spirituality in the most honest sense.

Another special moment occurred when a former member of the Gaither Vocal Band, Michael English, returned to be with us on the *Good News* video. Michael had been drummed out of gospel music after winning seven Dove Awards in 1994, only to be found in a moral failure that toppled him from the pinnacle of success. Gloria and I refused to give up on Michael, so several years later I invited him to join us in Alexandria for a *Homecoming* taping. Everyone in the room loved Michael and although no one condoned the misconduct that had led to his demise, everyone was rooting for him to rebuild his life.

A special guest during that taping was Meadowlark Lemon, the incredible basketball legend who mesmerized crowds for years with the Harlem Globetrotters. As the *Homecoming* singers extended wonderful grace, received Michael back into the fold, and so warmly assured him of unconditional love, Meadowlark leaned over to me and whispered, "This is a beautiful thing that is happening here. This is what I thought the church was going to be like."

Not surprisingly, one of the most special moments of all was when we taped a tribute *Homecoming* video at Montreat, North Carolina, the home of Dr. Billy Graham and his wife, Ruth. Like so many Americans, Gloria and I had admired the Grahams all of our lives. What a thrill it was for us when the Gaither Trio first sang at a Billy Graham crusade in Toronto in 1976. In addition to the Trio, our daughter Amy sang the kids' song Gloria and I had written, "I Am a Promise." My little nephew watched us on television and heard someone say there were sixty thousand people there. My nephew was amazed. "My goodness," he said to his mom. "Uncle Bill is drawing big crowds, isn't he?"

In typical Gaither humor, Mary Ann cracked, "Yes, and Billy Graham is drawing some pretty big crowds, too!"

One of the most humbling yet awesome sounds I've ever heard has been a Billy Graham Crusade choir singing "He Touched Me," "Because He Lives," or some other song that Gloria and I have written. I recall seeing one crusade in which Billy and his team were broadcasting in China, and choir leader Cliff Barrows had the song "Because He Lives" translated into Chinese so the choir could sing it. When I saw it on the broadcast in America, I got so excited, I called to Gloria, "Honey, come quickly! You've got to hear this! They're singing our song!"

One time when the Trio was invited to participate in a Billy Graham crusade, we were sitting on the platform as Cliff introduced us to the audience. "'Because He Lives' is Dr. Graham's favorite song," he told the crowd. Unobtrusively, Billy Graham got up from his seat and slipped over to where we were sitting. "He's not kidding," Dr. Graham said. "That really is my favorite song!"

It would be difficult to receive a higher compliment in this life.

The Vocal Band sang at a Billy Graham crusade in Indianapolis on June 3, 1999. By this time in their careers, soloist George Beverly Shea was in his late eighties and Dr. Graham was in his late seventies, as was Dr. Graham's longtime song leader, Cliff Barrows. As I watched the three elderly gentlemen still going about their ministry as though they were in their twenties, I began to toy with the idea of doing a special *Homecoming* video to honor them. We had learned that Mrs. Graham in particular loved to watch our videos. She watched and listened to the old songs for hours on end, and she especially loved the offbeat humor of Mark Lowry.

Mrs. Graham took part in the filming, but Dr. Graham was suffering from a severe case of shingles and was unable to attend. Gloria and I visited with Billy and Ruth in their home during our stay, and they were so apologetic for not feeling well enough to greet all the *Homecoming* singers. Their self-effacing humility stood in stark contrast to so much of the egotism sometimes associated with celebrities and famous ministers.

One special moment during the filming of the Billy Graham video took place when country and bluegrass artist Ricky Skaggs sang the song "Somebody's Praying." As Ricky sang, it was almost as though everyone in the room could recall someone's prayers making the difference in his or her life. Another special moment occurred as we sang Ray Boltz's song, "Thank You." Many of the *Homecoming* artists sang the song while looking at George Beverly Shea and Cliff Barrows, two men who had impacted all of our lives through their longevity, but more importantly through their consistency and integrity throughout their ministry.

Perhaps one of the most unusual special moments related to the *Homecoming* videos was not really part of a taping. On April 17, 2000, the American Society of Composers, Authors, and Publishers honored Gloria and me as their Gospel Songwriters of the Century! U.S. Attorney General (then U.S. Senator) John Ashcroft of Missouri presented the first-ever award to us at a special dinner.

When I was informed that ASCAP wanted to present the award to us, my first thought was, *You're kidding! So many other songwriters are more deserving than we are. Why should we be so honored?* It was indeed an honor. ASCAP licenses songs for thousands of writers and publishers, and just to be considered in the company of such great writers is more than I could have imagined when I scrawled the notes and lyrics to "Have You Had a Gethsemane?" nearly forty years earlier.

Amy Grant, Michael W. Smith, and Vince Gill performed a moving musical tribute that incorporated many of the songs that Gloria and I had written. In her kind introduction of Gloria and me, Donna Hilley, the president and CEO of Sony-ATV Tree Music Publishing Company said, "The Gaithers are to Christian music what the Beatles are to pop music."

I had to smile when I heard that. I guess I had never thought of us in that way. In my mind, we were still a couple of school-teachers trying to communicate through music some truths we believed in passionately. It was announced at the ASCAP ceremony that thanks to the *Homecoming* videos, Christian video sales were up 68 percent. Apparently, a lot of people still want to hear the great old gospel songs.

We often tell our kids, "We don't sing old songs because

they're old. We sing them because they are great and they deserve to live."

Music styles come and go, but the message of the song goes on. My vision for the *Homecoming* videos was more about honor than anything else. Some of the older artists were being left out of Christian music. They didn't have a place to give voice to the message that still burned brightly in their hearts. I wanted to show respect to those early gospel songs, their writers, and the people who sang them.

Something about what we do on those videos has struck a chord of reality with people. I continually get letters similar to one I received from a dear Christian woman who wrote:

> I could not get my husband interested in anything spiritual at all. But he'd come home, go to the fridge, grab a can of beer, and sit down and watch your videos. Sometimes he'd laugh, sometimes he'd cry, but he was often moved.
>
> When I asked him why he liked to watch them, he replied, "These people aren't too religious." Eventually, though, the videos were instrumental in his coming to the Lord and beginning a relationship with Him.

Now, when that sort of thing happens, you know that it is more than just the music.

TWENTY

DEALING WITH DEATH

ALMOST FROM THE BEGIN-
ning, the success of the *Homecoming* videos spawned an ava-
lanche of mail pouring into our office from viewers, but also
from other artists who wanted invitations to the party. We were
always glad to have old friends, even a few that I knew were not
living spiritually where they once were in their relationship
with the Lord. It was risky, but I felt that perhaps just being in
the environment of the *Homecoming* family might help them to
reconnect with their friends and, more importantly, with their
faith in God. In most cases, however, we were slow to bring in
outside people we didn't know.

One day Jake Hess asked, "Bill, could I bring a friend along
to the next *Homecoming* taping? He's a really great guy who used
to own a famous nightclub in Birmingham. He's an amazing
trumpet player. I've always loved his music, and not long ago he
became a Christian. Because of that, he felt that he should sell
his nightclub. I just think it would a great encouragement to

him if I could bring him to a taping . . . if you wouldn't mind, that is."

Jake Hess is one of the most humble, unassuming men I've ever known. He was a mainstay in our *Homecoming* family right from the beginning, yet I can't recall him ever making any demands or asking for any favors. So when Jake voiced this request, there was no doubt in my mind about my response.

"Sure, of course, Jake," I said. "Tell him to bring his trumpet."

When we arrived at the taping, Jake introduced his friend Bob Cain. At some point in the taping, I asked Bob, "Would you like to play something for us?"

"I'd be glad to," Bob replied.

When Bob began to play and sing, he literally blew us away. The guy was an incredible jazz musician. He had a Louis Armstrong type of voice and played the trumpet similarly to the great Satchmo as well. But more importantly, God's presence was so evident in his life that everyone in the room just fell in love with him. Later, when we released another video, *When All God's Singers Get Home*, the audience was wondrously impressed with Bob's musicianship and attracted to his obviously vibrant relationship with God.

Bob and his wife, Penny, became dear friends of Gloria's and mine, and Bob performed in numerous *Homecoming* concerts. His trumpet playing added a phenomenal dimension to our Christmas shows especially.

Beyond his excellence as a performer, Bob had an amazing spiritual depth, especially for a relatively new believer. He often caught the subtleties in Gloria's messages during our concerts; he quickly perceived the concepts that we wanted to express in our songs and in our public statements, and he was quick to acknowledge someone for contributing to his spiritual growth and understanding. He'd often say something like, "I never heard that concept before in the Bible, but now I see it."

Then as suddenly as this incredible human being had been dropped into our lives, he was gone. Bob Cain was diagnosed with cancer and died within months. Certainly we grieved for Penny and the Cain family, and we grieved for ourselves, too. We felt as though we had been robbed. To this day, every once in a while I'll look at Gloria and say, "Do you know who I really miss? I miss Bob Cain." Bob's life and sudden death caused us to appreciate more fully the great gifts God has given us in each of our friends and family members. We know others will be snatched from our presence without warning, and we don't want to miss a single day of the joy of knowing them, working with them, and living together in community with them.

Although the death of a loved one is always difficult, for a Christian, death is not the final word. We believe that we will live forever with God in heaven, so when a saint passes away, it is more of a celebration than a pity party. Certainly we miss our friends and family who have gone on before us, but I'm convinced that a healthy attitude toward dying makes it possible to have a better attitude toward living.

Unfortunately, due to the ages of many of the early *Homecoming* performers, dealing with death has been a regular part of our interaction. One of the elder statesmen of gospel music, Rex Nelon, had been married to Judy Spencer for less than a year when we took our *Homecoming* touring group to Ireland and England for a series of concerts.

The night before the London taping, Rex and Judy retired to their hotel room and suddenly Rex complained that he was having pains in his chest. Judy immediately called the paramedics, then their friends Amos and Sue Dodge and Claude and Connie Hopper, who were in rooms nearby.

Paramedics attempted to revive Rex in the hotel, to no avail. They rushed Rex to a hospital, but there was little the doctors could do. Shortly after they got Rex in the emergency room, he passed away.

Mark Lowry arrived along with Rick Goodman, Joy Gardner, and others. Mark and Judy entered the room where Rex's body was lying. Mark put his arm around Judy.

"Are you sure he's gone?" she asked.

"Yes, Judy," Mark responded softly, "he's gone."

Judy immediately turned to God. She prayed, "Father, I trust you. I praise you for the life of my wonderful husband. I thank you for the time of happiness that we've had together, and that Rex is now with you. My heart is broken, but I'm going to believe that everything is going to be all right."

Some of the *Homecoming* singers began singing softly in the hospital room. They cried together and they laughed together as they told stories about Rex.

We'd lost a number of our *Homecoming* friends since that first video back in 1991, but Rex was the first (and only) one of our group to die while on the road. As difficult as it was, the *Homecoming* team went onstage in London later that night and performed with excellence. It was what Rex would have wanted.

For a while, it seemed we were losing our friends in rapid-fire succession. For each funeral, the *Homecoming* singers gathered to pay their final respects, to sing, and to celebrate the going home of one of their own. The funeral services were profound evidence that as Christians we mourn, but we do not mourn as those who have no hope.

J.D. Sumner's funeral was particularly a hoot. The congregation gathered for that funeral was one of the most eclectic I've ever seen. The high and the low in society were there, which no doubt was one of the best commentaries on J.D.'s life. Everyone from high-ranking political figures and religious leaders to a number of Elvis impersonators joined at Christ Church in Nashville to say a final good-bye to J.D.

Mark Lowry eulogized J.D. eloquently, then said, "During the last five years of his life, J.D. and I became good friends and would eat out together quite often. I told him one night, 'J.D., how am I going to make it after you are dead and gone? Who am I going to eat with?' And he said to me, 'Mark, ten years after you are dead and gone, I'll be dancing on your grave.'" The congregation chuckled quietly.

Mark paused for about five seconds before admitting, "Well, that's not exactly what he said, but we are in church!" The crowd laughed hilariously. That was the J.D. we knew and loved.

TWENTY-ONE

KEEP ON PUMPING!

FOR SIXTY CONSECUTIVE Christmas Eves, the Gaither family gathered at Mom and Dad's house to celebrate. On Christmas Eve, 2001, we all knew that Mom's health was deteriorating rapidly. The previous few years had been extremely tough on her. She'd endured two or three operations, she had already suffered several strokes, and dementia was setting in. It was difficult to watch the disease take its toll on such a strong, active woman as Mom.

Since Mom could no longer get around by herself, Dad did most of the daily chores, including the cooking, laundry, and housecleaning. Dad was wonderful; his patience with Mom seemed inexhaustible as Mom's mind faded further from reality.

The situation, sad as it was, provided us with some unexpected but much-needed moments of comic relief. For instance, we hired a nurse to stay with Mom during the daytime, and our family members took turns giving Dad a break after work. One day, however, the nurse couldn't make it, and Mom was experiencing a severe lapse as Dad was struggling to bathe her. He apparently wasn't doing things to suit her, so Mom looked at him and said, "Have you ever bathed a woman before?"

"Oh, yeah," Dad answered facetiously. "Hundreds of 'em."

"Well, you sure didn't learn much!" Mom cracked.

Over Memorial weekend 2001, she had another bout with a stroke and we thought for sure that we had lost her. When we got the call that Mom had been hospitalized, my dad, Gloria, and I were at Family Fest, a weekend of concerts and special family events we hold annually in Gatlinburg, Tennessee. Dad and Gloria immediately raced back to Indiana, while I stayed to close out the last concert.

My brother, Danny, had died just a few weeks earlier, and our family was still reeling from the loss and the emotional drain due to Danny's long, drawn-out battle with lymphoma. By the time I arrived at the hospital, Mom was in bad shape. Her vital signs were extremely poor, and it seemed she was hanging on to life by a thin thread. Dad, Gloria, and my sister, Mary Ann, had been by her side, staying there in the hospital with her throughout the weekend. After I had been at the hospital awhile, Dad said, "I think I'll go home and take care of a few things out at the house."

"Good idea, Dad," I said. "If anything changes, I'll call you right away."

"Oh, I won't be long," Dad promised.

When he hadn't returned in more than an hour, I began to worry. I said to Gloria, "I think I'll go check on Dad. It's his first time to be in the house alone since Mom's been in the hospital."

I went over to the house and found that Dad had just returned from the grocery store. My mom had always been a fabulous cook, but since the dementia had set in, she could no longer remember the ingredients to most of the meals she had once prepared with hardly a thought. Consequently, Dad did the grocery shopping.

When he came in, we exchanged a bit of small talk. In the Gaither family, the men were always rather stoic, never expressing deep, intimate emotions to one another, so our conversation was a bit stilted. It didn't matter to Dad or to me. The important thing was that we were there, hurting together. We didn't need words to communicate the pain we felt.

After a few minutes, I said, "Let's go outside."

We went out and looked at Dad's garden behind the white frame house. Dad and Mom always had a fabulous garden filled with bright red tomatoes, green zucchini, lettuce, peppers, and more. "At least your garden's coming in pretty well and looking good," I said, making more small talk.

"Yeah," Dad answered quietly. He walked over behind the shed to the side of the garden and stood there for a minute or so, his back to me. It was then that I noticed his shoulders shaking. Dad rarely showed much emotion because he was such a strong man. I could count on one hand the number of times I'd seen him cry in my lifetime. But he was shaking now, and I knew he was crying.

I went over and put my arms around him and said, "Dad, it's okay. You just lost a son a month ago in April, and now it looks like you're going to lose your wife, too. It's okay."

Dad was part of the generation in which tough men didn't cry or express their emotions in any way that showed weakness or vulnerability. I wasn't surprised when he didn't say anything. Instead, for the longest time, Dad just stood there with the tears dripping down his rugged face.

After what seemed to be a long while but was probably just a few minutes, I managed to form the words, "Have you . . . have you pumped water for the cows?"

"No, not for a day or two."

"Okay, let's go down back and fill up the tank," I said, pulling him gently away from that spot.

We walked to the back of the field, primed the old pump, and began filling the cows' water tank. While we pumped the water, we talked about the old days and the work seemed to relieve a bit of the awkward tension. We both knew that Mom wouldn't be with us much longer, and it was okay.

But like her dad before her, my mom had a strong heart and an intense desire to live. The family gathered in the hospital to say good-bye, but Mom surprised us by rallying and getting better!

In a way, Mom's hospitalization was a blessing. It gave us all an opportunity to say the important things that sometimes go unsaid when an aging relative departs unexpectedly. In the months that followed, we told and retold all the old family stories—especially the ones about Mom—and enjoyed reliving some of the wonderful times we had shared together over the years.

For her part, even when she had no idea that she was doing so, Mom kept adding to the repertoire of Gaither family stories that our kids will tell for years to come. For instance, one morning I went out to the house, and Dad had gotten up early and was already out working on something. Mom was discouraged and disgruntled about being alone. "I don't know why I even bother to get up in the morning and put my clothes on," she groused to me. "There's nowhere to go, nothing to do, and besides, George isn't here anyway."

Trying to cheer her up, I said, "Well, you've got me, Mom."

Mom looked over at me and deadpanned, "Well, I guess you're better than nothing at all!"

Mom usually functioned fine through the day, but in the

evenings she'd get restless and couldn't sleep. Mary Ann, Gloria, Dad, and I took turns staying with her until she'd nod off. My vigil was normally between 7:00 and 9:30 P.M., and the family soon discovered that I was the best sedative Mom could have. They were astonished that Mom was able to sleep so well during my watch.

My secret? I'd sing to her.

Throughout my music career, I've been up-front about the truth that Danny was the singer in our family, not me. It didn't matter to Mom. To her, I was the best of singers. My singing calmed her better than anything else we tried.

Each evening as she rested in her bed, I'd sing her songs that she used to sing to us as children—classics such as "Old Shep," and love songs, and hymns. Then, without Mom knowing it, I'd slip in a tape of Danny singing. Even in Mom's dementia-induced, semiconscious state, when she heard Danny's voice she'd say, "That's Danny, isn't it?"

"Yes, Mom," I'd whisper. "That's Danny."

A slight smile creased her mouth. "He could sing, couldn't he?"

"He could sing, Mom," I answered quietly.

How precious it was to sit with my mom as we listened to my brother sing "Does Jesus Care?" While Mom drifted toward sleep, tears wet the corners of my eyes, especially when Danny got to the chorus in the song that said,

"Oh, yes, He cares! I know He cares. His heart is touched with my grief. When the days are weary, the long nights dreary, I know my Savior cares."[1]

I'd pull the covers around my mom and turn down the lights. "Good night, Bill," she'd say softly.

"Good night, Mom."

One night as I sang to her, Mom perked up, lifted her head slightly off her pillow, looked at me, and said, "Bill, you're good. You ought to make a record!"

She lay back down and went fast to sleep.

Caring for an incapacitated, aging loved one can be draining on any family, and it takes a lot of cooperation and teamwork to do it. But what a gift! What a privilege to care for someone who once cared for you so unselfishly. No parent and child should be robbed of those special moments at the close of an aging loved one's life.

I'm glad that Gloria's and my children and grandchildren had the privilege of discovering firsthand who they are as a family, and to know that they have inherited a history handed down by some strong grandparents who faced life with dignity, grace, and humor. That's an important legacy to pass along, and we encourage our kids and grandkids, "Keep telling those stories, because those stories tell who we are."

Mom's hospitalization and weakened condition also prepared us for the inevitable. On Christmas Eve 2001, it was obvious that Mom was not doing well. Nevertheless, Benjy brought his guitar over and the entire family—adults, kids, grandkids, and great-grandkids—gathered around and sang Christmas carols and other songs that Mom knew. Several times that night, Mom's dementia caused her to be confused. "George, it's time for us to go home," she said as she got up from her chair.

"Honey, you're at home already," Dad told her kindly, and helped her sit back down.

"Oh, okay," she said. The old songs brought a smile to her face, and we laughed and sang just as we had in years gone by. Mom even mustered a bit of a smile for a photograph of her and Dad.

Gloria, Mary Ann, Mary Ann's daughter, Becky, and Vonnie, Danny's wife, stayed with Mom constantly. We knew it was only a matter of time, and Mom died in her own bed two days after Christmas.

A week later, Mary Ann, Becky, and I went over and helped my dad clean out Mom's clothes. It was tough, because each item represented some special memory to Dad. But we knew that we had to help him move on, or Dad, too, could easily wither and die. Since my dad's retirement from Delco-Remy at fifty-nine years of age, he has traveled with us on the road, handling the product sales at our concerts. To almost no one's surprise, the following weekend I had him back on the bus with the *Homecoming* tour.

Sometimes the best thing you can do in the midst of tough times is to just keep on pumping . . . even though you may be pumping through your tears.

TWENTY-TWO

THE END OF AN ERA

THE DAY AFTER MOM DIED on Thursday, December 27, 2001, one of my greatest heroes and dearest friends passed away. That Friday, Hovie Lister lost his battle with cancer and went home.

When Hovie Lister died, it was the end of an era. Hovie had battled lymphoma for eight years. I knew what kind of living hell that could be, having watched my brother make that same valiant effort. But no matter how sick Hovie got, his attitude was irrepressible. He showed up at a number of *Homecoming* concerts following his chemotherapy, wearing a fashionable suit and a multicolored tassle hat. After his hair came back, Hovie wore a type of sailor's cap, even when he was indoors in the recording studio or at concerts.

The audiences loved to see him, too. One night in Indianapolis, as Hovie was coming out toward the stage, Russ Taff began shouting Hovie's name as though he were at a ball game rooting for his favorite player. "Hovie! Hovie!" Russ called. The crowd picked up on Russ's call and before long, the entire arena was echoing with a massive chant, "Hovie! Hovie!"

Hovie sat down at the piano and began to sing an old hymn. Just then, I glanced over at Duane Allen, lead singer for the Oak Ridge Boys, and it was plain to see that Duane had lost it. Duane later said, "When Hovie started singing and playing that piano. . . . I didn't know whether to shout or cry." Hovie's voice was raspy, ragged, and husky, but did he ever have soul!

Hovie represented in a wonderful way that gospel music was part of life. It wasn't something spooky or mystical, it was natural and normal. Hovie brought an exuberance and joy to his performance, and he made no apologies for the entertainment quality of his music. When interviewers asked him, "Are you an entertainer or a minister?" Hovie would wave them off, saying, "Yes, yes. Next question."

Yet Hovie had great faith, and he taught me as much about faith as anyone I've ever known. Whenever I saw him, I asked, "How are you doing, Hovie?"

"Well, I'm kind of encouraged. I got a good report from the doctors last week."

One night at a concert in Fort Worth, when Hovie sat down at the piano I said onstage, "Hovie, a lot of people here have been asking about your health."

In a husky voice, Hovie replied, "My last report . . . when I went to the doctor . . . was good."

The audience applauded wildly, but Hovie held up his hand to quiet them. "Now, wait a second. I'm not naïve," Hovie said from the piano. "I'm only as good as my last report." He paused to look around the arena as though he were speaking to each person individually. "And so are you," Hovie added.

The audience seemed to catch its breath collectively.

"But let me tell you something," Hovie continued. "Bill's

asked me to come back to Fort Worth next year, and I've written it down in my date book. I'm planning on seeing you folks. But if I don't see you here, I'll see you there!" Hovie pointed heavenward.

The audience applauded again.

"Now, in the meantime, I'm tired of talking about my health. Let's sing about Jesus!"

The crowd appreciated Hovie's honesty and his tremendous faith all the way to the end of his life.

Developing the *Homecoming* videos and concert tours has been such a marvelous experience for me, yet there is always the nagging knowledge that *this isn't going to last*. Many of the dear friends in the videos were old when we started making them, and they are getting older more quickly these days. It seems that every few months we are attending a funeral of another dear friend.

Gloria has repeatedly encouraged me, "Bill, you need to bring in younger artists such as Jeff and Sheri Easter and the Martins, and introduce them to the audience. Let the audience fall in love with the new generation of singers."

"But I don't want to lose these people who brought us to the party," I'd object, thinking of all the old-timers in some of the first videos.

"Bill," Gloria would say lovingly but firmly, "you *are* going to lose them whether you want to or not, so you need to cultivate the younger kids and allow the elderly people at the party to say, 'Aren't those kids great? I'm so glad another generation is coming up that will love and appreciate the old songs, as well as write wonderful new expressions of their faith in God.'"

———— ✥ ————

Maybe because I knew it was only a matter of time before we'd lose more of our good *Homecoming* friends, I unconsciously became obsessed with getting them on tape while we could.

I've always loved a good party. It's especially nice to get to be able to throw another party every week someplace around the country. That's what I get to do with the *Homecoming* Concert Tour. It feels wonderful when I see the number of gospel music artists and the large number of people in the audience who want to attend our "party." Consequently, I've developed some great bashes over the years: Jubilate, Praise Gathering, and Family Fest, to name a few.

"Let's have a party in Charlotte, let's have a party in Atlanta." It sounds great, but after a while, it can become draining. We love doing the concerts, but I tend to think that I am responsible for everyone's joy, even though I know that is impossible. Years ago we wrote a song, "Jesus Is the Center of My Joy." Anytime a person loses that focus, the work can become compulsive or even addictive, especially for someone like me, who has been raised with such a strong work ethic.

My work is a major part of who I am. I know that God values me regardless of what I accomplish on earth, but I also know that I find immense satisfaction in doing a job well. Indeed, my work is entwined with my spiritual life. I try to do as the Bible says: "Whatever you do, do your work heartily, as for the Lord rather than for men."[1] The trick, of course, is to do what we do for God's pleasure, rather than to earn the acceptance of the public or even our peers.

My good friend Dr. Archibald Hart told me about a "pleasure center" in my brain and said that I should widen it to include, for instance, our family's needs more than just my wants. It sounds simplistic but it worked; like most guys, give me a road map and I'll follow it.

When you narrow your pleasure base—those things that bring joy, acceptance, and satisfaction for you—to the point that everything in your life has to enter your sphere through a narrow gate of only one area of interest, you are asking for trouble.

You also have to recognize the danger signals. I could work all night long every night, but I don't allow myself to do that for my family's sake, and for my own. I've learned the hard way.

For a while, I became so obsessed with getting my heroes on tape before it was too late, the *Homecoming* video phenomena took over our lives and threatened to destroy our family. I was gone so much, then when I got home, I immediately ran off to Nashville for a few days to work on another project. I was working all the time, and our lives were out of balance. Our entire family became aware that after all the years of ministry, it seemed we, too, might implode, as we had seen happen to far too many other families in the music business. We had thought that we were above such concerns after all those years of wonderful marriage, music, and ministry. But I discovered it doesn't matter who you are or how long you've been living for God; if you don't regularly maintain your primary relationships in life—with God, your family, and your friends—the law of entropy comes into play: all things tend to disintegrate. Before long, even the best of relationships can fall apart if not properly nurtured.

Jake Hess once said, "If the lights are shining brighter on the stage than they are at home, you're in bad trouble." Jake and his wife, Joyce, were married for more than fifty years and raised three fine Christian children before Joyce passed away. I appreciated Jake's down-to-earth insights and took his advice to heart.

Slowly but surely, I came to realize that anytime that you

want something more than your relationship with God—even if it is God's work—you are in danger of losing both! If you read the Bible only to teach, preach, or write songs for others, you are missing the point. Doing spiritual things will not maintain your relationship with God; your relationship with God will stimulate you to do spiritual things. Many pastors and Christian musicians fall into the trap of running on empty, trying to protect their ministries or businesses, while their personal lives are going down the drain. But without a good, unobstructed relationship with God, there is no ministry. Moreover, even if you hold on to your "ministry" but lose out in your relationship with God, your marriage, your family, and your friends, what do you have? Jesus put it this way, "For what does it profit a man to gain the whole world, and forfeit his soul?"[2]

Today, Gloria and I are busier than ever. With the help of some wise counselors, we've learned to keep a better balance in our lives. She is pursuing her goal of producing a Broadway musical, and I have been developing new *Homecoming* videos as fast as we can produce them. In addition, we've recently begun creating concept videos such as *Heaven,* in which we've combined some of the old songs about heaven with colorful insights on the subject from writers and speakers across the spectrum of Christianity.

People often ask, "How long are you going to do this, Bill?"

I don't know, so I always answer, "As long as we can!" As long as God allows us to make music with a message, we'll keep doing it.

TWENTY-THREE

REAL PEOPLE

IT'S ALWAYS FUN FOR GLORIA and me to have people to our home who don't really know us except professionally or by reputation or what they've seen or read in the media. Most of our guests seem somewhat surprised that our family is so ordinary and down-to-earth. I'm not quite sure what they expected, but apparently, we aren't it! At the end of such an evening recently, a couple said to us, "It has been so refreshing spending time with you. You are just such real people!"

I thought that was one of the nicest compliments anyone could pay us. Because that's who we are—just real people trying to live for God and love each other and the people God allows us to know. Along the way, we sure have had some fun!

One of the least known of Gloria's many attributes is her marvelous sense of humor. She's always quick to laugh and is the perfect straight person for comics such as Mark Lowry. But away from the stage, she has her own sardonic sense of humor that comes out in various ways. For instance, she and the kids are always chiding me because I'm so serious, that I never seem to have any fun apart from work. It's true; the most fun I can have is not out on the golf course or going to an Indiana Pacers' game—although I enjoy those things. For me, a great day of work in which I have accomplished something worthwhile is fabulous fun.

As I've mentioned, even on vacations, I have a hard time relaxing. For Christmas one year, Gloria compiled a large scrapbook with the title *Bill Having Fun in* . . . boldly printed on the front. Inside, she had pictures of her and the kids having fun in various places around the world, and a picture of me in each location, looking bored, tired, and ready to get home and get back to work. On one page, she had a picture of herself climbing a mountain while I looked on with the same doleful expression, as though I were watching the rocks erode. She had pages filled with photos from exotic locations: "Bill having fun in Dublin . . ." "Bill having fun in Lake Barkley . . ." "Bill having fun in New York . . ." and in Nantucket, Ireland, Scotland, England. In each photo, my countenance and expression were pretty much the same: bored stiff.

On the last page of the scrapbook Gloria placed a photo she'd taken of me in Russia, standing below a huge, white marble statue that resembled the *Venus de Milo*. The sculptor had clothed the woman with a toga type of garment draped over her shoulder and exposing one of her breasts. Gloria had caught me on camera with a twinkle in my eye and an impish look on my face, gazing up at the statue's bare breast. The caption on that page in the scrapbook said, "Bill *finally* having fun!" Who could have imagined such a prank from my sweet, shy wife . . . ?

Anyone who knows her well!

Gloria loves life, and she loves to laugh and have a good time. She's learned how to do that without compromising her integrity.

Part of what we do causes people to think that Gloria and I are something special, that we have some sort of unique "in" with God. Nothing could be further from the truth. I don't take it too seriously when people put me on a pedestal, because I know who I am, a sinner saved by grace. That's why I can write and sing with such conviction the song we wrote by that title, "I'm Just a Sinner Saved by Grace."

One of my favorite songs that I didn't write is Kris Kristofferson's "Why Me, Lord?" I can relate to the plaintive cry of Kris's heart. As much as a person can honestly say it, I believe I know who I am and what my life has been about. I'm painfully aware of my own "earthiness," my own shortcomings. And I know that I've been blessed beyond anything I deserve. Yet over the years, I've tried to be honest about my strengths and weaknesses, and somehow God has been able to use that.

Gloria and I have had a wonderfully blessed life together. We have shared a deep, glorious love for each other; we've been privileged to be mom and dad to three great kids who love God and are serving Him. We are enjoying being grandparents more than anything we've ever done.

Our lives can be summed up by a song Gloria and I wrote in 1997. When people ask, "What do you mean, 'It's more than the music'? What is it that motivates you? What really is the key to your success?" I tell them:

It's loving God, loving each other;
Making music with my friends;
Loving God, loving each other
And the story never ends.[1]

We've shared some incredible experiences together, traveling the world over and seeing the wonders of the earth. But the greatest treasure of our lives has been our relationships with some long-lasting friends, and the joy of walking through life hand in hand with the One who chooses to call Gloria and me His friends. To us, those relationships far surpass the momentary thrill of a standing ovation, a number-one song, or an award. Those relationships are really all that matter . . . and in many ways the music of our lives flows from the relationships in our lives. And that's why what we do—and who we are—is much more than the music.

NOTES

Chapter 2

[1] All but one of the original members of the Dixie Four are now deceased. Dr. Frank Collins, a retired pastor, now lives in Florida. I have maintained contact with Dr. Collins and he is still a dear friend to this day.

[2] William J. and Gloria Gaither, "I Heard It First on the Radio." Lyrics by Gloria Gaither, music by William J. Gaither. Copyright © 1999 by Gaither Music Company. All rights reserved. Used by permission.

[3] Samuel T. Scott, and Robert L. Sands, "Prayer Is the Key to Heaven." Copyright © 1955 by Duchess Music Corporation. Rights administered by MCA Music Publishing, Nashville, TN. All rights reserved. Used by permission.

Chapter 3

[1] See Genesis 1:10, 12, 18, 21, 31.

Chapter 4

[1] Gloria and William J. Gaither, "I Am Loved." Lyrics by Gloria and William J. Gaither, music by William J. Gaither. Copyright © 1978 by William J. Gaither. All rights reserved. Used by permission.

Chapter 5

[1] Luke 22:42.

[2] William J. Gaither, "He Touched Me," words and music by William J. Gaither, copyright © 1963, William J. Gaither. All rights reserved. Used by permission.

Chapter 6

[1] "Don't Cry, Suzanne" by T. Wadsworth. Copyright © 1962, 1990 Columbia/Sony Music Publishing.

[2] William J. Gaither, "The Longer I Serve Him (The Sweeter He Grows)." Lyrics and music by William J. Gaither. Copyright © 1965 by William J. Gaither. All rights reserved. Used by permission.

Chapter 7

[1] Lyrics and reading by Gloria Gaither and William J. Gaither; music by William J. Gaither. Copyright © 1970 by William J. Gaither. All rights reserved. Used by permission.

[2] See John 12:32.

Chapter 8

[1] Gloria and William J. Gaither and Charles Millhuff, "The King Is Coming." Copyright © 1970 by William J. Gaither. All rights reserved. Used by permission.

[2] Matthew 10:10.

[3] Tracy Dartt, "God on the Mountain." Copyright © 1975 by Gaviota Music, 35255 Brooten Rd., Pacific City, OR 97135. All rights reserved. Used by permission. (BMI)

Chapter 9

[1] See Luke 6:38.

[2] See Psalm 30:5.

Chapter 10

[1] A. H. Ackley, "He Lives." Copyright © 1933, renewal 1961 by the Rodeheaver Co., owner. International copyright secured. Used by permission.

[2] William J. and Gloria Gaither, "Because He Lives." Lyrics by William J. and Gloria Gaither, music by William J. Gaither. Copyright © 1971 by William J. Gaither. All rights reserved. Used by permission.

[3] William J. and Gloria Gaither, "Let's Just Praise the Lord." Lyrics by

William J. and Gloria Gaither, music by William J. Gaither. Copyright ©
1972 by William J. Gaither. All rights reserved. Used by permission.

4 Wordaction Publishing Company. *Adult Bible Fellowship Study Book.*
Kansas City, MO: Wordaction Publishing Co., 8 Dec. 2002.

Chapter 11

1 See 1 John 4:4.

2 See Romans 8:28.

3 William J. and Gloria Gaither, "I Believe, Help Thou My Unbelief."
Lyrics by William J. and Gloria Gaither, music by William J. Gaither.
Copyright © 1975 by the Gaither Music Company. All rights reserved.
Used by permission.

Chapter 12

1 See Romans 8:28.

2 "He's Alive." Written by Don Francisco. Copyright © 1977 by New Pax
Music Press. All rights reserved. Used by permission.

Chapter 13

1 Gordon Dalbey, *Healing the Masculine Soul* (Waco, Texas: Word
Publishing, 1988).

2 Suzanne Gaither Jennings and Barry Jennings, "A Few Good Men."
Copyright ©1990 by Townsend and Warbucks Music. All rights reserved.
Used by permission.

Chapter 15

1 Ephesians 4:26-27.

Chapter 17

1 "About Bill." Written by Gloria Gaither. Copyright © 1992 Gaither
Music Company. All rights controlled by Gaither Copyright
Management. Used by permission.

2 Andrae' Crouch, "Through It All." Copyright © 1971, 1999 by Manna
Music. All rights reserved. Used by permission. (ASCAP)

3 Psalm 37:25.

Chapter 18

1 William J. and Gloria Gaither, "Thanks to Calvary." Lyrics by William J.

and Gloria Gaither, music by William J. Gaither. Copyright © 1969 by Gaither Music Company. All rights reserved. Used by permission.

Chapter 19

[1] Suzanne Jennings, "Red Wing." Copyright © 1999 by Townsend and Warbucks Music. All rights controlled by Gaither Copyright Management. All rights reserved. Used by permission.

[2] William J. and Gloria Gaither, "I Believe, Help Thou My Unbelief." Copyright © 1975 by Gaither Music Company. All rights reserved. Used by permission.

[3] Written by Ira F. Stanphill, "We'll Talk It Over (In the By and By)." Copyright © 1949 by Singspiration Music. Administered by Brentwood-Benson Music Publishing, Inc. All rights reserved. Used by permission.

Chapter 21

[1] Frank E. Graeff and J. Lincoln Hall, "Does Jesus Care?" Public Domain.

Chapter 22

[1] Colossians 3:23.

[2] Mark 8:36.

Chapter 23

[1] William J. and Gloria Gaither, "Loving God, Loving Each Other." Lyrics by William J. and Gloria Gaither, music by William J. Gaither. Copyright © 1997 by Gaither Music Company. All rights reserved. Used by permission.

BILL AND GLORIA GAITHER:
FIVE DECADES OF AWARDS

1968 ASCAP, Gospel Songwriter of the Year—Bill Gaither

1969 DOVE AWARD, Gospel Songwriter of the Year
—Bill Gaither

1970 DOVE AWARD, Gospel Songwriter of the Year
—Bill Gaither

1972 SESAC, awarded the International Award for American
Composer with the Greatest International Exposure for the song
"He Touched Me"

1972 DOVE AWARD, Gospel Songwriter of the Year
—Bill Gaither

1973 Honorary Doctor of Music degree conferred on Bill Gaither by
Anderson College

1973 DOVE AWARD, Gospel Songwriter of the Year
—Bill Gaither

1973 GRAMMY AWARD, Best Inspirational Performance, for "Let's
Just Praise the Lord"
—The Bill Gaither Trio

1974 ASCAP, Gospel Song of the Year, for "Because He Lives"
      —Bill Gaither

1974 DOVE AWARD, Gospel Songwriter of the Year
      —Bill Gaither

1974 DOVE AWARD, Gospel Song of the Year, for "Because He Lives"
      —Bill Gaither/Gaither Music (ASCAP)

1975 DOVE AWARD, Gospel Songwriter of the Year
      —Bill Gaither

1975 GRAMMY AWARD, Best Inspirational Performance, for "Jesus,
      We Just Want to Thank You"
      —The Bill Gaither Trio

1976 Bill Gaither received the highest honor given by the American
      Indians: God's Songbird

1976 DOVE AWARD, Gospel Songwriter of the Year
      —Bill Gaither

1976 DOVE AWARD, Inspirational Album of the Year, for *Jesus, We
      Just Want to Thank You*
      —The Bill Gaither Trio/Bob MacKenzie, producer/Heartwarming

1976 Awarded HONORARY CITIZEN OF TENNESSEE
      —Bill Gaither

1977 DOVE AWARD, Gospel Songwriter of the Year
      —Bill Gaither

1977 Album *Alleluia—A Praise Gathering for Believers* certified Gold by
      the Recording Industry Association of America (RIAA)

1977 DOVE AWARD of Merit in recognition of Bill Gaither's
      contribution to the world of gospel music

1978 DOVE AWARD, Record Album of the Year, Inspirational, for
      Pilgrim's Progress
      —The Bill GaitherTrio/Bob MacKenzie, John W.
         Thompson, producers/Impact Records

1980 ASCAP AWARD of Merit to Bill Gaither and Gloria Gaither for "I Am Loved," Song of the Year Nominee

1980 DOVE AWARD, Mixed Group of the Year
—The Bill Gaither Trio

1981 DOVE AWARD, Gospel Album of the Year, Children's Music, *The Very Best of the Very Best, for Kids*

1982 DOVE AWARD, Children's Music Album of the Year, for *Kids Under Construction*
—Bill and Gloria Gaither, Ronn Huff, and Joy MacKenzie

1983 Bill Gaither inducted into the Gospel Music Hall of Fame, Gospel Music Association

1985 DOVE AWARD, Song of the Year, for "Upon this Rock"
—Gloria Gaither and Dony McGuire/Gaither Music/
  It's-N-Me Music/Lexicon Music (ASCAP)

1986 DOVE AWARD, Gospel Music Album of the Year, Worship and Praise, for *I've Just Seen Jesus*
—Bill Gaither and Randy Vader, producers/Gaither Music
  Company

1986 DOVE AWARD, Gospel Songwriter of the Year
—Gloria Gaither

1986 The Anderson, Indiana, Chamber of Commerce awarded the mayor's CHIEF ANDERSON AWARD "for enhancing nationwide community recognition" to Bill and Gloria Gaither (May, 1986)

1987 DOVE AWARD, Southern Gospel Album of the Year, for *The Master Builder*
—The Cathedrals, Bill Gaither, Gary McSpadden/
  Riversong

1988 DOVE AWARD, Song of the Year, for "In the Name of the Lord"
—Gloria Gaither, Phil McHugh, Sandi Patty/River Oaks
  Music, Gaither Music, Sandi's Songs

1988 HOOSIER PRIDE AWARD (July 6, 1988)
—Bill and Gloria Gaither

1989 Inducted into Madison County Business Leaders Hall of Fame
(February 15, 1989)

1989 The state of Indiana's SAGAMORE OF THE WABASH
AWARD, presented to Bill Gaither by Governor Robert D. Orr

1990 DOVE AWARD, Song of the Year, for "Thank You"
—Ray Boltz/Gaither Music/Shepherd Boy Music (ASCAP)

1990 CHRISTIAN ARTIST MUSIC ACHIEVEMENT AWARD
—Bill and Gloria Gaither

1991 GRAMMY AWARD, Best Southern Gospel/Country Gospel
Album for *Homecoming*
—The Gaither Vocal Band (Bill Gaither, Michael English,
    Mark Lowry, Jim Murray)

1991 DOVE AWARD, Best Southern Gospel Record, for *Climbing
Higher and Higher*
—The Cathedrals/Bill Gaither, producer

1992 National Association of Evangelicals LAYPERSONS OF THE
YEAR AWARD
—Bill and Gloria Gaither (Chicago, March 3, 1992)

1992 DOVE AWARD, Southern Gospel Album, for *Homecoming*
—The Gaither Vocal Band (Bill Gaither, Michael English,
    Mark Lowry, Jim Murray), Ken Mansfield/Star Song

1992 LIVING LEGEND AWARD, by *The Gospel Voice* magazine

1992 FAN AWARD, Favorite Southern Gospel Video, for *Homecoming*
—Bill Gaither and Friends

1993 DOVE AWARD, Southern Gospel Album of the Year, for
Reunion: A Gospel Homecoming Celebration
—Bill and Gloria Gaither/Bill Gaither, producer/Star Song

1993 GOLD VIDEO AWARD, for *Reunion*
—City Music USA

1993 GOLD VIDEO AWARD, for *Homecoming*
—City Music USA

1993 #1 Single on CCM's Inspirational Chart of the Week (August 16, 1993) for "I Can't Believe My Eyes"
—Star Song

1993 ANDERSON UNIVERSITY AWARD, presented to Bill and Gloria Gaither "in recognition of the creative gifts given to the church and devoted commitment to Anderson University"

1994 GOLD VIDEO AWARD, for *Homecoming*
—Bill and Gloria Gaither/Star Song

1994 THE RAY DE VRIES LIFETIME SERVICE AWARD
—Bill and Gloria Gaither (April, 1994)

1994 THE GOSPEL MUSIC ASSOCIATION LIFETIME ACHIEVEMENT AWARD
—The Gaither companies

1994 DOVE AWARD, Southern Gospel Album, for *Southern Classics*
—The Gaither Vocal Band (Bill Gaither, Michael Sykes, Michael English)/Benson Records

1994 DOVE AWARD, Southern Gospel Recorded Song, for "Satisfied"
—The Gaither Vocal Band/Benson Records

1994 TELLY AWARD, second place, Television Production and Commercials, for the "Opening Night" infomercial

1994 NAIRD 1993 AWARD, Honorable Mention to Benson Records in the category of Gospel/Religious Music for *Southern Classics* by the Gaither Vocal Band

1994 *Singing News* magazine's FAN AWARDS, Favorite Southern Gospel Video, for *Turn Your Radio On*
—Bill and Gloria Gaither and Their *Homecoming* Friends

1994 FAN AWARD, from readers of *The Gospel Voice*, a Music City News Publication, for the video *Old Friends*
—Bill and Gloria Gaither and Friends/Gaither Music Company

1994 MUSICCALIFORNIA RAY DE VRIES MUSIC MINISTRY AWARD
—Bill and Gloria Gaither

1995 DOVE AWARD, Southern Gospel Recording Song of the Year, for "I Bowed on My Knees"
—The Gaither Vocal Band/Benson Records

1995 THE *GOSPEL VOICE* AWARD, Video of the Year, for *All Day Singing and Dinner on the Grounds*
—Bill and Gloria Gaither/Gaither Music Company, Inc.

1996 Christian Booksellers Association (CBA) IMPACT AWARD, Hall of Honors
—Bill and Gloria Gaither (July 4, 1996)

1996 *Singing News* magazine's FAN AWARDS, Favorite Southern Gospel Video, for *Ryman Gospel Reunion*
—Bill and Gloria Gaither and Their *Homecoming* Friends

1997 Southern Gospel Music Association, (SGMA) Hall of Fame, 1997 inductee
—Bill Gaither

1997 NASHVILLE MUSIC AWARD, Traditional Gospel Album, for *Southern Classics Volume II*
—The Gaither Vocal Band

1997 CHIEF ANDERSON AWARD, for outstanding community service
—Bill and Gloria Gaither

1999 The Bill Gaither Trio was inducted into the Gospel Music Hall of Fame

1999 GRAMMY AWARD, Southern, Country, or Bluegrass Gospel Album—for *Kennedy Center Homecoming*
—Bill and Gloria Gaither and their *Homecoming* Friends

1999 DOVE AWARD, Southern Gospel Album, for *Still the Greatest Story Ever Told*
—The Gaither Vocal Band (Bill Gaither, Michael Sykes, Guy Penrod)/Spring Hill Music Group

1999 DOVE AWARD, Southern Gospel Recorded Song, for "I Believe in a Hill Called Mt. Calvary" from *Lovin' God, and Lovin' Each Other*
—The Gaither Vocal Band/Bill and Gloria Gaither/Spring Hill Music Group

2000 ASCAP Gospel Songwriters of the Century—Bill and Gloria Gaither. The award was presented by Senator John Ashcroft of Missouri to Bill and Gloria on April 18, 2000. It recognized that their collective works of religious music are the most performed, as discovered in a survey conducted by ASCAP. The award was the first of its kind in the eighty-six-year history of ASCAP.

2000 DOVE AWARD, Southern Gospel Album, for *God is Good*
—The Gaither Vocal Band (Bill Gaither, Guy Penrod, Mark Lowry, David Phelps)/Bill Gaither, Michael Sykes, Guy Penrod, producers/Spring Hill Music Group

2001 Pewter tray presented to Bill and Gloria at the April 6, 2001 concert in Mobile, Alabama, in Commemoration of five straight sold-out concerts at the Mobile Civic Center from 1997 to 2001.

2001 Best of Madison County—Bill and Gloria Gaither were chosen as the most creative couple of the county. The *Herald Bulletin* asked its readers to identify the best of Madison County from pie to politicians. (Article and picture: the *Herald Bulletin*, April 13, 2001)

2001 SGMA Video of the Year 2001 for *A Farewell Celebration*
—The Cathedrals/Bill Gaither, producer

2001 DOVE AWARD, Southern Gospel Album of the Year, for *I Do Believe*
—The Gaither Vocal Band (Bill Gaither, Guy Penrod Michael Sykes)/Spring Hill Music Group

2001 DOVE AWARD, Long Form Music Video, for *A Farewell Celebration—The Cathedrals*
—Bryan Bateman, Bill Gaither, Dennis Glore/Spring House Music Group

2001 DOVE AWARD, Southern Gospel Recorded Song, for "God Is Good All the Time"
—The Gaither Vocal Band (Bill Gaither, Michael Sykes, Guy Penrod)/Spring Hill Music Group

2001 GAITHER HOMECOMING MUSIC DAY—Proclamation by the governor of the state of Arkansas, Governor Mike Huckabee (December 6, 2001)

2002 GRAMMY AWARD, Southern, Country, or Bluegrass Gospel Album—for *A Billy Graham Music Homecoming*
—Bill and Gloria Gaither and Their *Homecoming* Friends

2002 The Indiana General Assembly presented a concurrent resolution to honor Bill and Gloria Gaither and the *Homecoming* Friends upon receiving a Grammy Award (March 5, 2002)

2002 Gloria Gaither received the Mark O. Hatfield Leadership Award from CCCU (Coalition of Christian Colleges and Universities) in Washington, DC (February, 2002)

2002 DOVE AWARD, Southern Gospel Recorded Song of the Year, for "He's Watching Me"
—The Gaither Vocal Band/Tim Sadler/Spring Hill Music Group

2002 DOVE AWARD, Southern Gospel Album of the Year, for *Encore: Old Friends Quartet*
—Bill Gaither, Wesley Pritchard, Ben Speer/Spring House

2002 Doctor of Humane Letters awarded to Gloria Gaither by Indiana Wesleyan University (April 27, 2002)

2002 International Worship Institute's CHERUB AWARD "to honor those who have made outstanding contributions within the area of worship"
—Bill and Gloria Gaither

2002 GOSPEL MUSIC HALL OF FAME AND MUSEUM, for appreciation of their past and continuing efforts to promote the furtherance of quality gospel music in our world today
—Bill and Gloria Gaither (Detroit, Michigan, October, 2002)

2002 RIAA plaque presented to Bill and Gloria Gaither to commemorate RIAA's platinum certification of Michael W. Smith's CD *Worship* (program shown as part of *Precious Memories Hour*)

2002 SOGOSPELNEWS.COM MUSIC AWARD, Male Group of the Year
—The Gaither Vocal Band

2002 SOGOSPELNEWS.COM MUSIC AWARDS, Special Event of the Year
—Gloria Gaither and The *Homecoming* Friends

2002 SOGOSPELNEWS.COM MUSIC AWARDS, Web Site of the Year
—Gaithernet.com

2002 SOGOSPELNEWS.COM MUSIC AWARDS, Male Vocalist of the Year
—David Phelps, member, the Gaither Vocal Band

2003 DOVE AWARD nomination, Southern Gospel Recorded Song of the Year: "More Than Ever," from *I Do Believe*
—The Gaither Vocal Band/Gloria Gaither, Bill Gaither, Woody Wright/Spring Hill Music Group

2003 DOVE AWARD nomination, Country Album of the Year, for *Everything Good*
—The Gaither Vocal Band (Bill Gaither, Michael Sykes, Guy Penrod)/Spring House

2003 SOGOSPELNEWS.COM MUSIC AWARDS, Album of the Year, for *Everything Good*
—The Gaither Vocal Band (March 15, 2003)

2003 SOGOSPELNEWS.COM MUSIC AWARDS, Male Group of the
Year, for the Gaither Vocal Band (March 15, 2003)

2003 SOGOSPELNEWS.COM MUSIC AWARDS, Country Gospel
Song, for "I'm Gonna Sing"
—The Gaither Vocal Band/written by William J. and
Gloria Gaither and Woody Wright (March 15, 2003)

2003 SOGOSPELNEWS.COM MUSIC AWARDS, Special Event
Project, for *Let Freedom Ring*
—Bill and Gloria Gaither and Their *Homecoming* Friends/
Bill Gaither, Barry Jennings, Bill Carter—executive
producers; Bill Gaither—producer; Jim Hammond—
associate producer/Spring House Music Group (March 15,
2003)

2003 SOGOSPELNEWS.COM MUSIC AWARDS, Male Vocalist of
the Year—David Phelps, member, the Gaither Vocal Band
(March 15, 2003)